BLOOD™

ALL TOGETHER NOW

FLASHBACK SEQUENCES BY **ELENA** CASAGRANDE,
DAVID MESSINA, SERENA **FICCA,**
VANESSA GARDINALI, FREDERICA **MANFREDI,**
ELENA OLIMIERI, & **TINA** VALENTINO

LETTERING BY **NEIL** UYETAKE

ORIGINAL SERIES EDITS BY **SCOTT** DUNBIER

COLLECTION SERIES EDITS BY **JUSTIN** EISINER

COLLECTION DESIGN BY **NEIL** UYETAKE

Special thanks to HBO for their invaluable assistance.

www.**IDWPUBLISHING**.com   ISBN: 978-1-60010-868-6   14 13 12 11   1 2 3 4

IDW Publishing is: Operations: Ted Adams, CEO & Publisher • Greg Goldstein, Chief Operating Officer • Matthew Ruzicka, CPA, Chief Financial Officer • Alan Payne, VP of Sales • Lorelei Bunjes, Director of Digital Services • Jeff Webber, Director of ePublishing • AnnaMaria White, Dir., Marketing and Public Relations • Dirk Wood, Dir., Retail Marketing • Marci Hubbard, Executive Assistant • Alonzo Simon, Shipping Manager • Angela Loggins, Staff Accountant • Cherrie Go, Assistant Web Designer • Editorial: Chris Ryall, Chief Creative Officer, Editor-In-Chief • Scott Dunbier, Senior Editor, Special Projects • Andy Schmidt, Senior Editor • Justin Eisinger, Senior Editor, Books • Kris Oprisko, Editor/Foreign Lic. • Denton J. Tipton, Editor • Tom Waltz, Editor • Mariah Huehner, Editor • Carlos Guzman, Assistant Editor • Bobby Curnow, Assistant Editor • Design: Robbie Robbins, EVP/Sr. Graphic Artist • Neil Uyetake, Senior Art Director • Chris Mowry, Senior Graphic Artist • Amauri Osorio, Graphic Artist • Gilberto Lazcano, Production Assistant • Shawn Lee, Graphic Artist

INTRODUCTION

A little over 100 years ago, the first comic strips were born. In the time since those initial newspaper cartoons appeared, the boundaries of comics, more recently known as graphic novels, have continually stretched and grown to encompass nearly every subject matter that can appeal to a myriad of readers. From the Pulitzer prize-winning *Maus* to the cult-favorite *Hellboy*, there is something for everyone.

While I am myself a neophyte to the comic world, I am learning fast and enjoying what I am seeing. The graphic novel we've put together in this collection is fun and entertaining, and features all the main characters from the show, as well as some very revealing bits of back story. I am quite pleased with both the experience and the final results of this project.

Many writers are only bound by the limits of their imaginations, but television and film writers are bound by the limits of production. Logistics, money, time, and technology all need to be taken into account when breaking story. But the world of *True Blood*, I am happy to say, has a brand-new medium to play in. One that is both exciting and liberating. It is a road that leads to unknown possibilities and endless potential—and I, for one, cannot wait to see where it takes us.

Alan Ball
creator of *True Blood*

art by DAVID MESSINA
colors by GIOVANNA NIRO

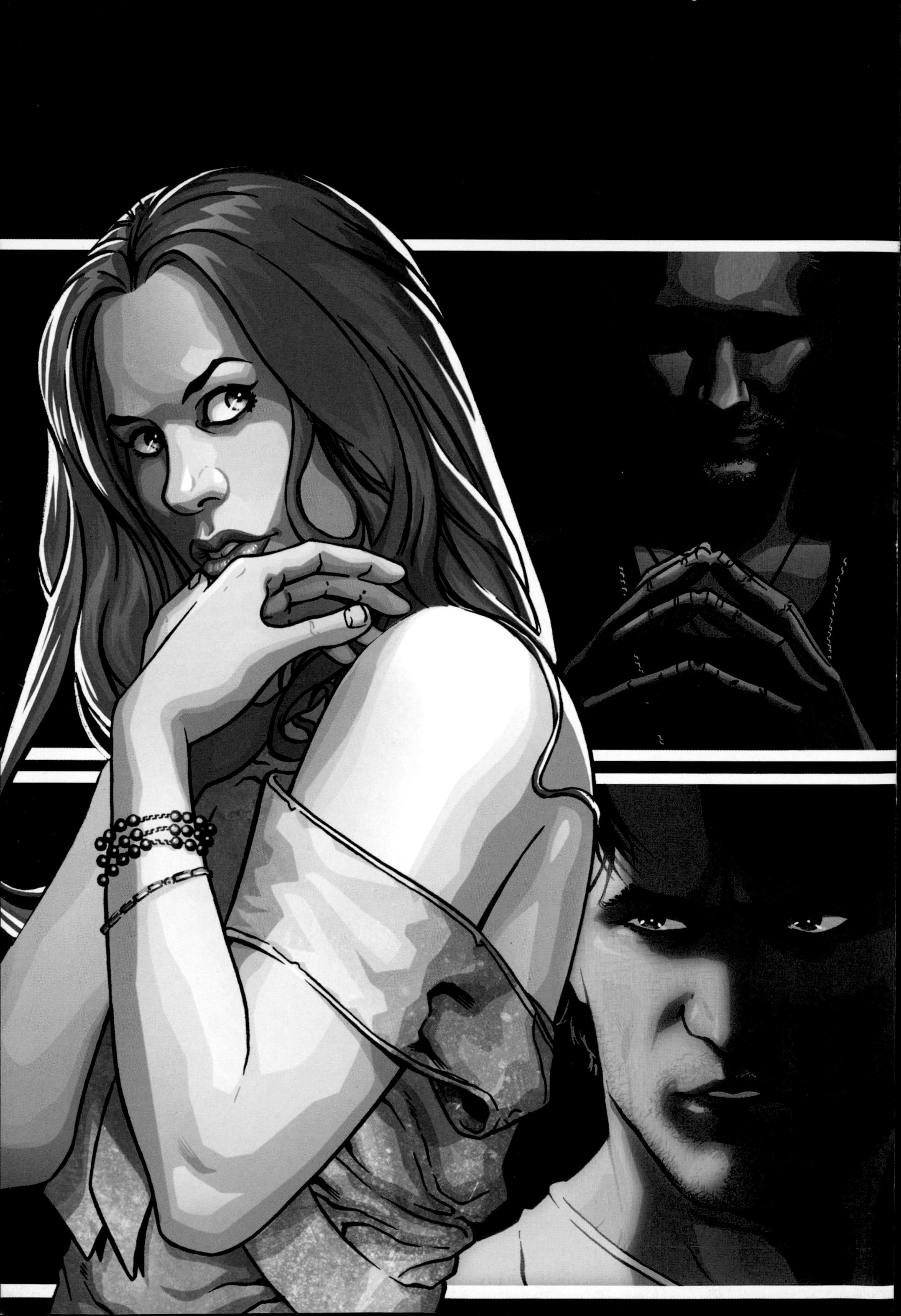

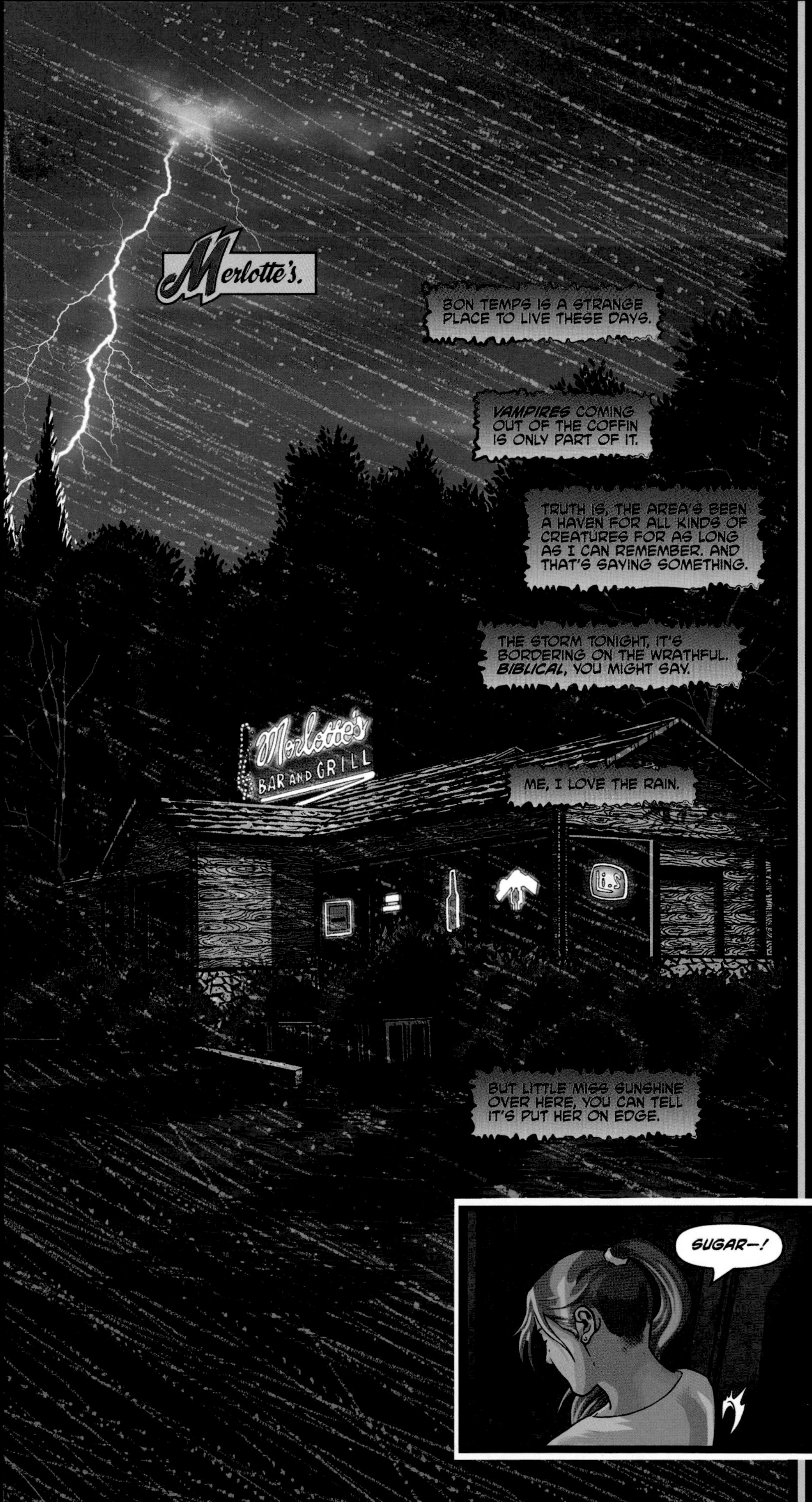
Merlotte's.
BON TEMPS IS A STRANGE PLACE TO LIVE THESE DAYS.
VAMPIRES COMING OUT OF THE COFFIN IS ONLY PART OF IT.
TRUTH IS, THE AREA'S BEEN A HAVEN FOR ALL KINDS OF CREATURES FOR AS LONG AS I CAN REMEMBER. AND THAT'S SAYING SOMETHING.
THE STORM TONIGHT, IT'S BORDERING ON THE WRATHFUL. BIBLICAL, YOU MIGHT SAY.
Merlotte's BAR AND GRILL
ME, I LOVE THE RAIN.
BUT LITTLE MISS SUNSHINE OVER HERE, YOU CAN TELL IT'S PUT HER ON EDGE.
SUGAR—!

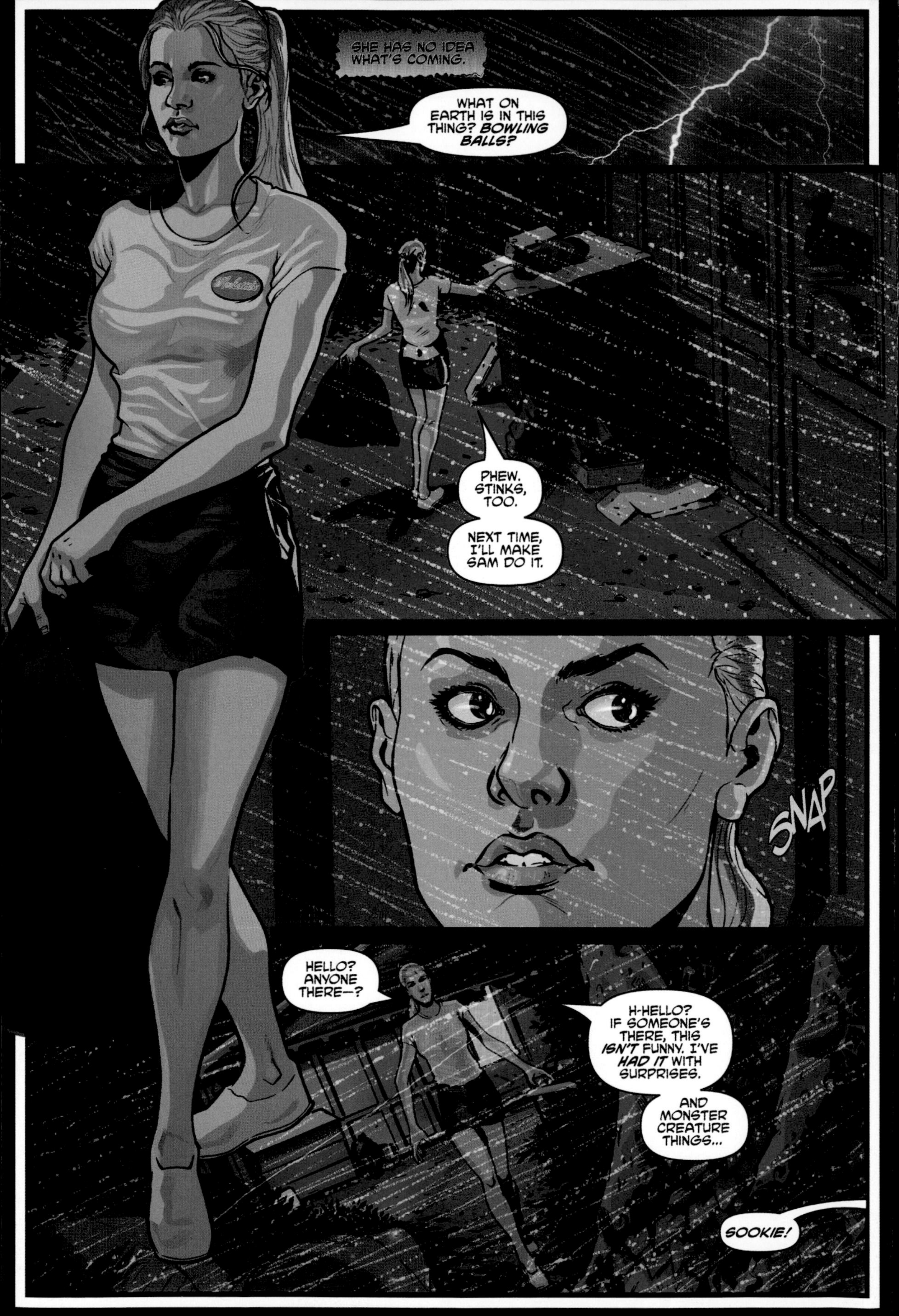
SHE HAS NO IDEA WHAT'S COMING.
WHAT ON EARTH IS IN THIS THING? *BOWLING BALLS?*
PHEW. STINKS, TOO.
NEXT TIME, I'LL MAKE SAM DO IT.
SNAP
HELLO? ANYONE THERE--?
H-HELLO? IF SOMEONE'S THERE, THIS *ISN'T* FUNNY. I'VE *HAD IT* WITH SURPRISES.
AND MONSTER CREATURE THINGS...
SOOKIE!

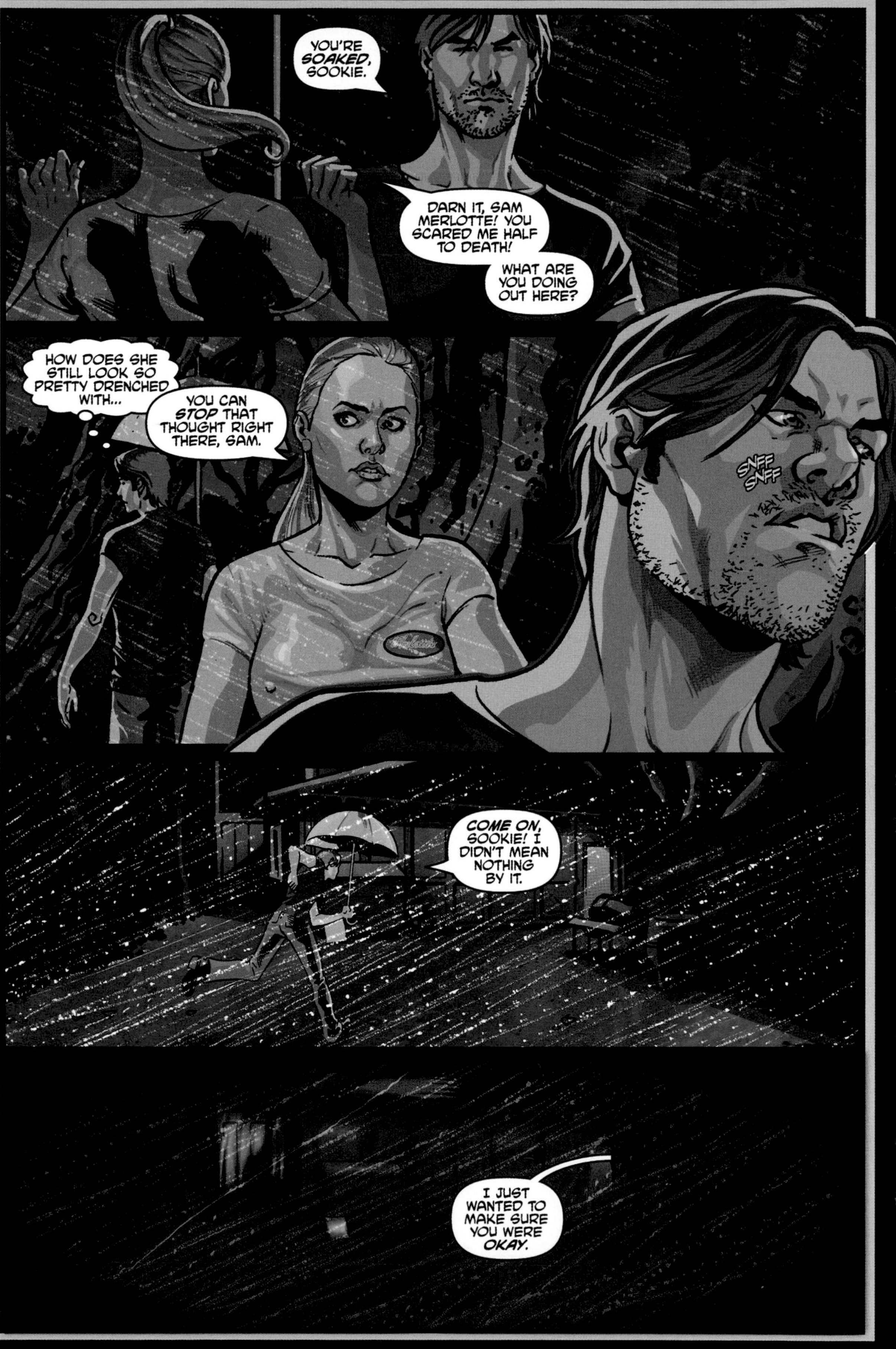
YOU'RE *SOAKED*, SOOKIE.
DARN IT, SAM MERLOTTE! YOU SCARED ME HALF TO DEATH!
WHAT ARE YOU DOING OUT HERE?
HOW DOES SHE STILL LOOK SO PRETTY DRENCHED WITH...
YOU CAN *STOP* THAT THOUGHT RIGHT THERE, SAM.
SNFF SNFF
COME ON, SOOKIE! I DIDN'T MEAN NOTHING BY IT.
I JUST WANTED TO MAKE SURE YOU WERE *OKAY*.

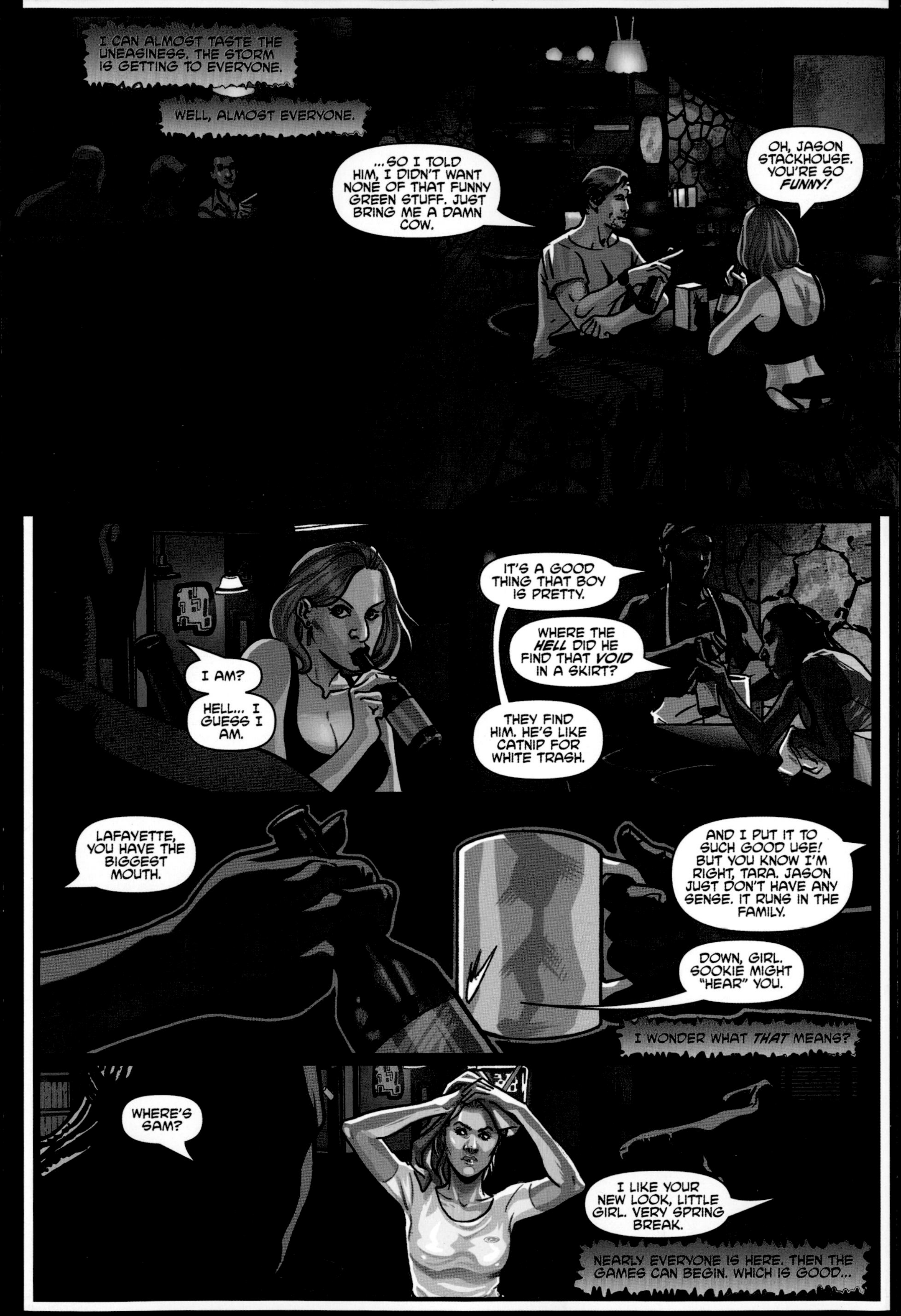

I CAN ALMOST TASTE THE UNEASINESS. THE STORM IS GETTING TO EVERYONE.
WELL, ALMOST EVERYONE.
...SO I TOLD HIM, I DIDN'T WANT NONE OF THAT FUNNY GREEN STUFF. JUST BRING ME A DAMN COW.
OH, JASON STACKHOUSE. YOU'RE SO *FUNNY!*
IT'S A GOOD THING THAT BOY IS PRETTY.
WHERE THE *HELL* DID HE FIND THAT *VOID* IN A SKIRT?
I AM?
HELL... I GUESS I AM.
THEY FIND HIM. HE'S LIKE CATNIP FOR WHITE TRASH.
LAFAYETTE, YOU HAVE THE BIGGEST MOUTH.
AND I PUT IT TO SUCH GOOD USE! BUT YOU KNOW I'M RIGHT, TARA. JASON JUST DON'T HAVE ANY SENSE. IT RUNS IN THE FAMILY.
DOWN, GIRL. SOOKIE MIGHT "HEAR" YOU.
I WONDER WHAT *THAT* MEANS?
WHERE'S SAM?
I LIKE YOUR NEW LOOK, LITTLE GIRL. VERY SPRING BREAK.
NEARLY EVERYONE IS HERE. THEN THE GAMES CAN BEGIN. WHICH IS GOOD...

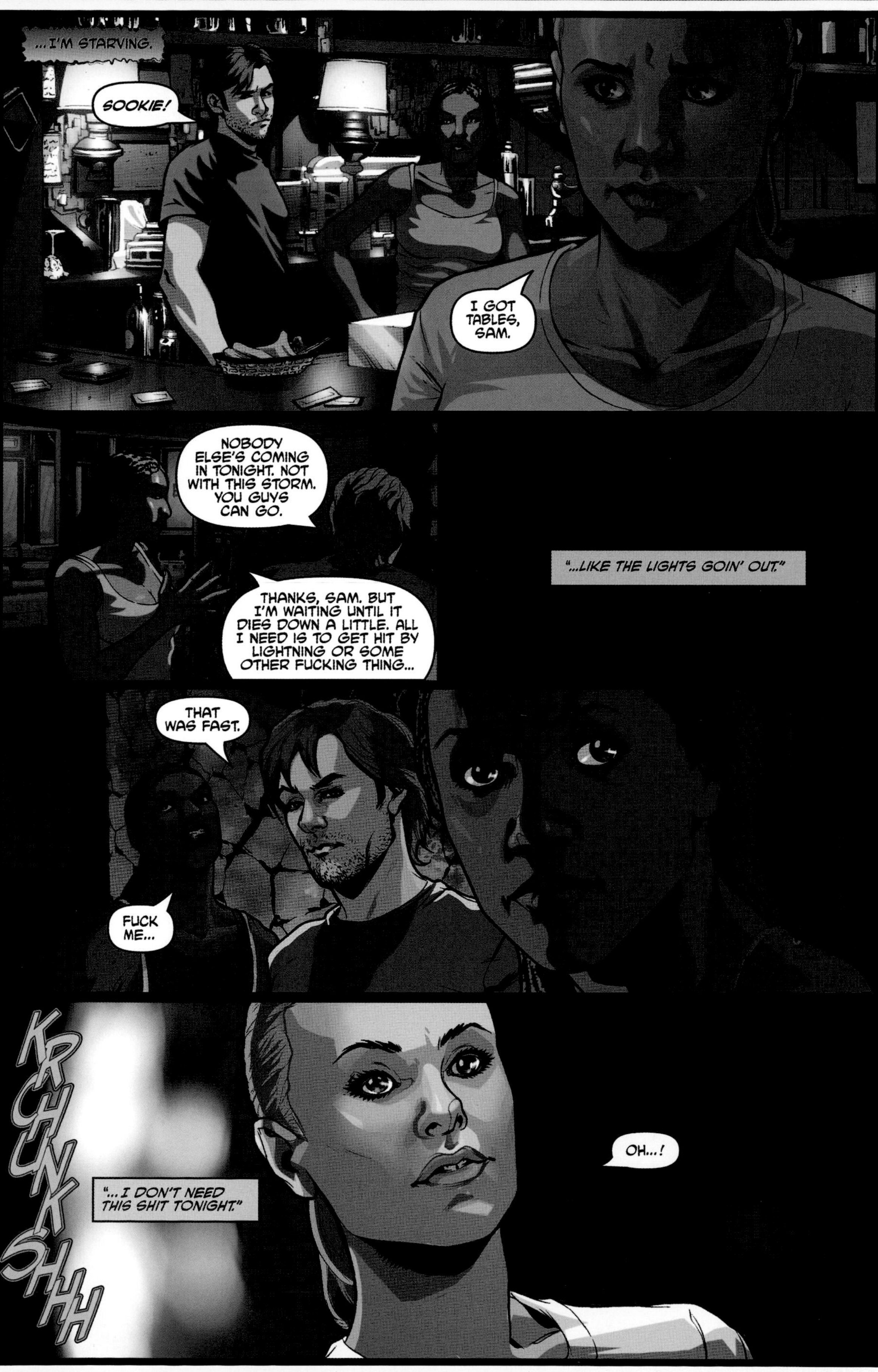
...I'M STARVING.
SOOKIE!
I GOT TABLES, SAM.
NOBODY ELSE'S COMING IN TONIGHT. NOT WITH THIS STORM. YOU GUYS CAN GO.
THANKS, SAM. BUT I'M WAITING UNTIL IT DIES DOWN A LITTLE. ALL I NEED IS TO GET HIT BY LIGHTNING OR SOME OTHER FUCKING THING...
"...LIKE THE LIGHTS GOIN' OUT."
THAT WAS FAST.
FUCK ME...
KRCHUNKSHHH
"...I DON'T NEED THIS SHIT TONIGHT."
OH...!

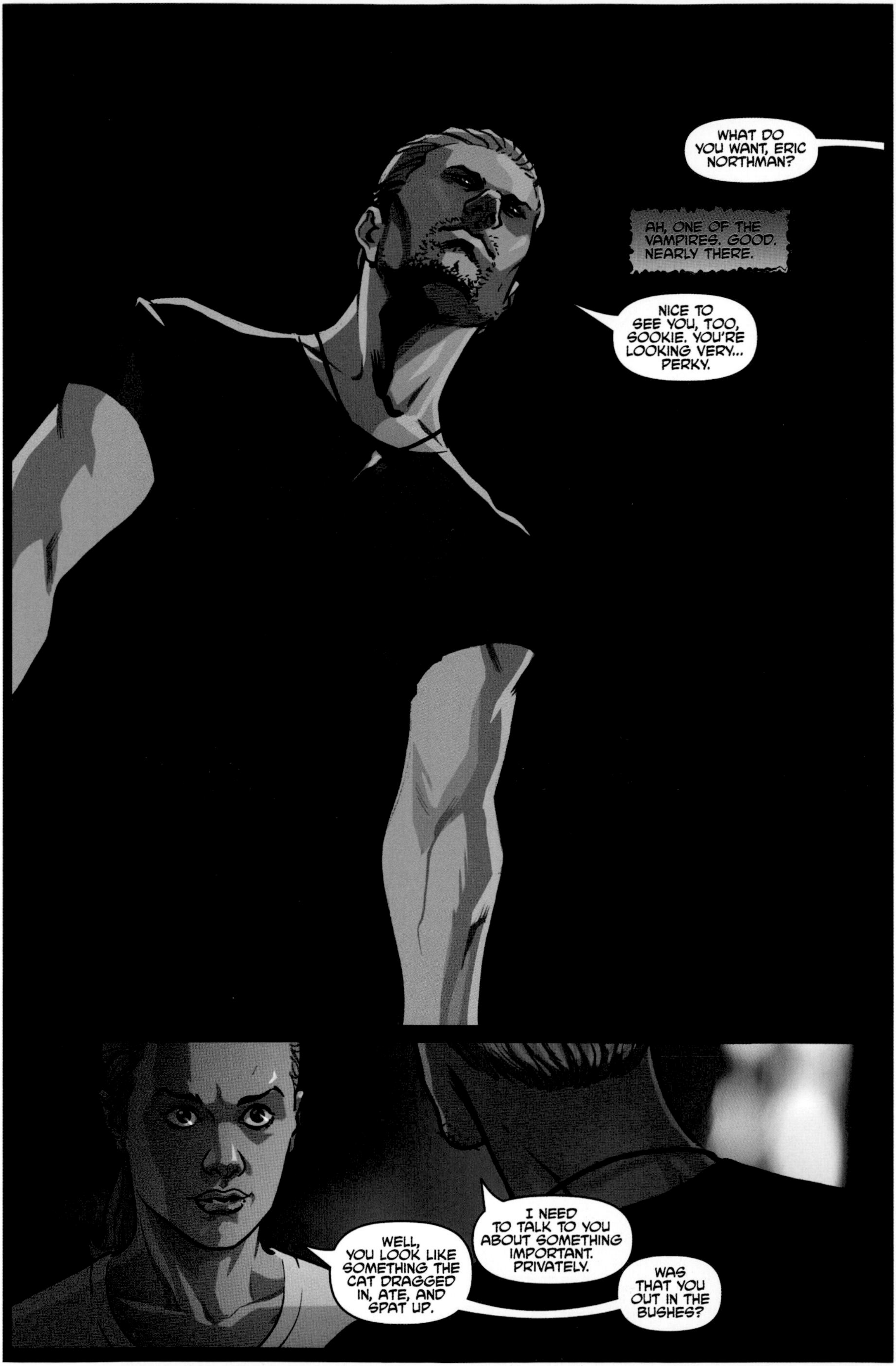
WHAT DO YOU WANT, ERIC NORTHMAN?
AH, ONE OF THE VAMPIRES. GOOD. NEARLY THERE.
NICE TO SEE YOU, TOO, SOOKIE. YOU'RE LOOKING VERY... PERKY.
WELL, YOU LOOK LIKE SOMETHING THE CAT DRAGGED IN, ATE, AND SPAT UP.
I NEED TO TALK TO YOU ABOUT SOMETHING IMPORTANT. PRIVATELY.
WAS THAT YOU OUT IN THE BUSHES?

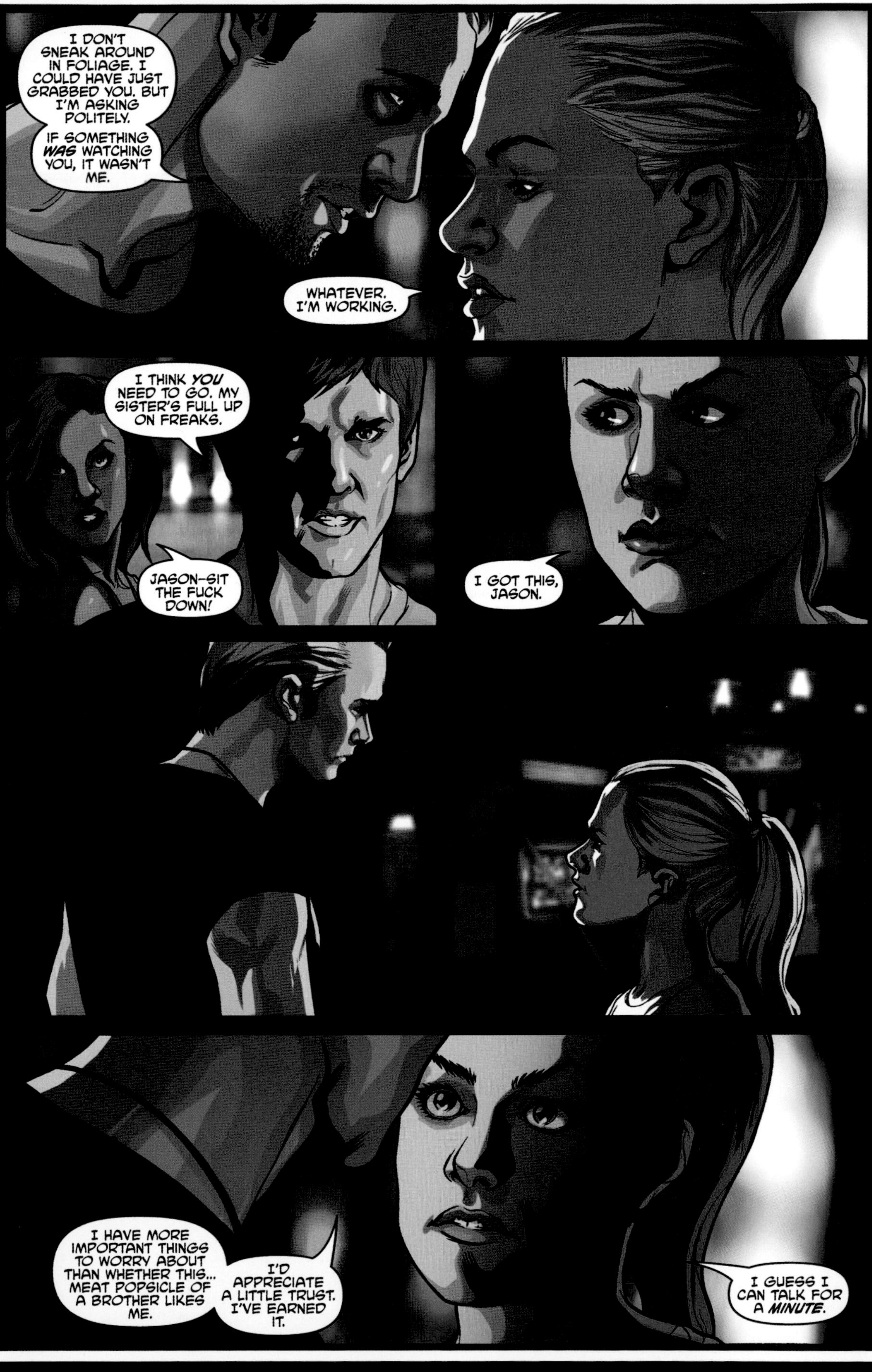
I DON'T SNEAK AROUND IN FOLIAGE. I COULD HAVE JUST GRABBED YOU. BUT I'M ASKING POLITELY.
IF SOMETHING *WAS* WATCHING YOU, IT WASN'T ME.
WHATEVER. I'M WORKING.
I THINK *YOU* NEED TO GO. MY SISTER'S FULL UP ON FREAKS.
JASON--SIT THE FUCK DOWN!
I GOT THIS, JASON.
I HAVE MORE IMPORTANT THINGS TO WORRY ABOUT THAN WHETHER THIS... MEAT POPSICLE OF A BROTHER LIKES ME.
I'D APPRECIATE A LITTLE TRUST. I'VE EARNED IT.
I GUESS I CAN TALK FOR A *MINUTE*.

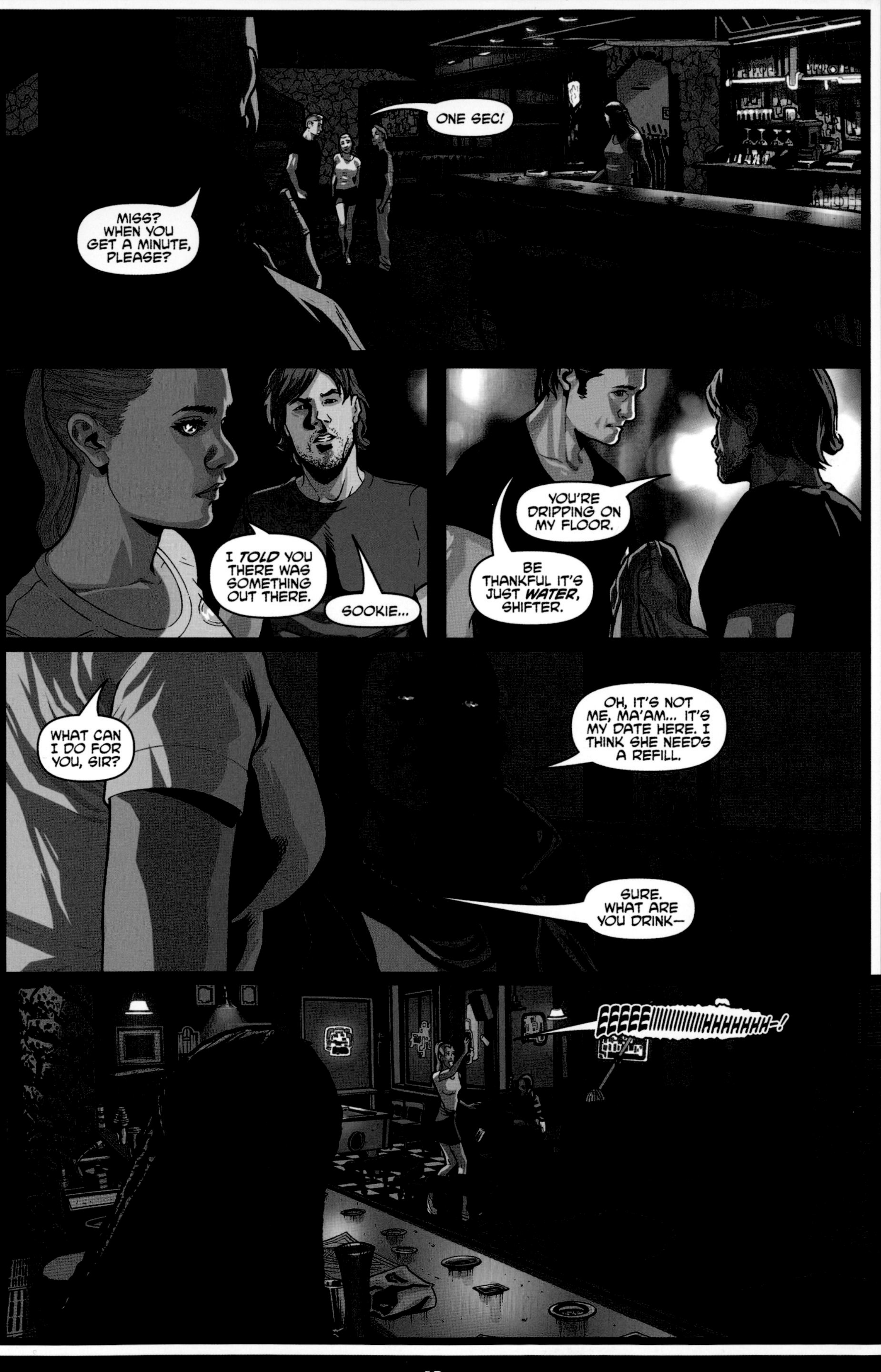
ONE SEC!
MISS? WHEN YOU GET A MINUTE, PLEASE?
I *TOLD* YOU THERE WAS SOMETHING OUT THERE.
SOOKIE...
YOU'RE DRIPPING ON MY FLOOR.
BE THANKFUL IT'S JUST *WATER*, SHIFTER.
WHAT CAN I DO FOR YOU, SIR?
OH, IT'S NOT ME, MA'AM... IT'S MY DATE HERE. I THINK SHE NEEDS A REFILL.
SURE. WHAT ARE YOU DRINK—
EEEEEIIIIIIIIIIIIIIIHHHHHHH-!

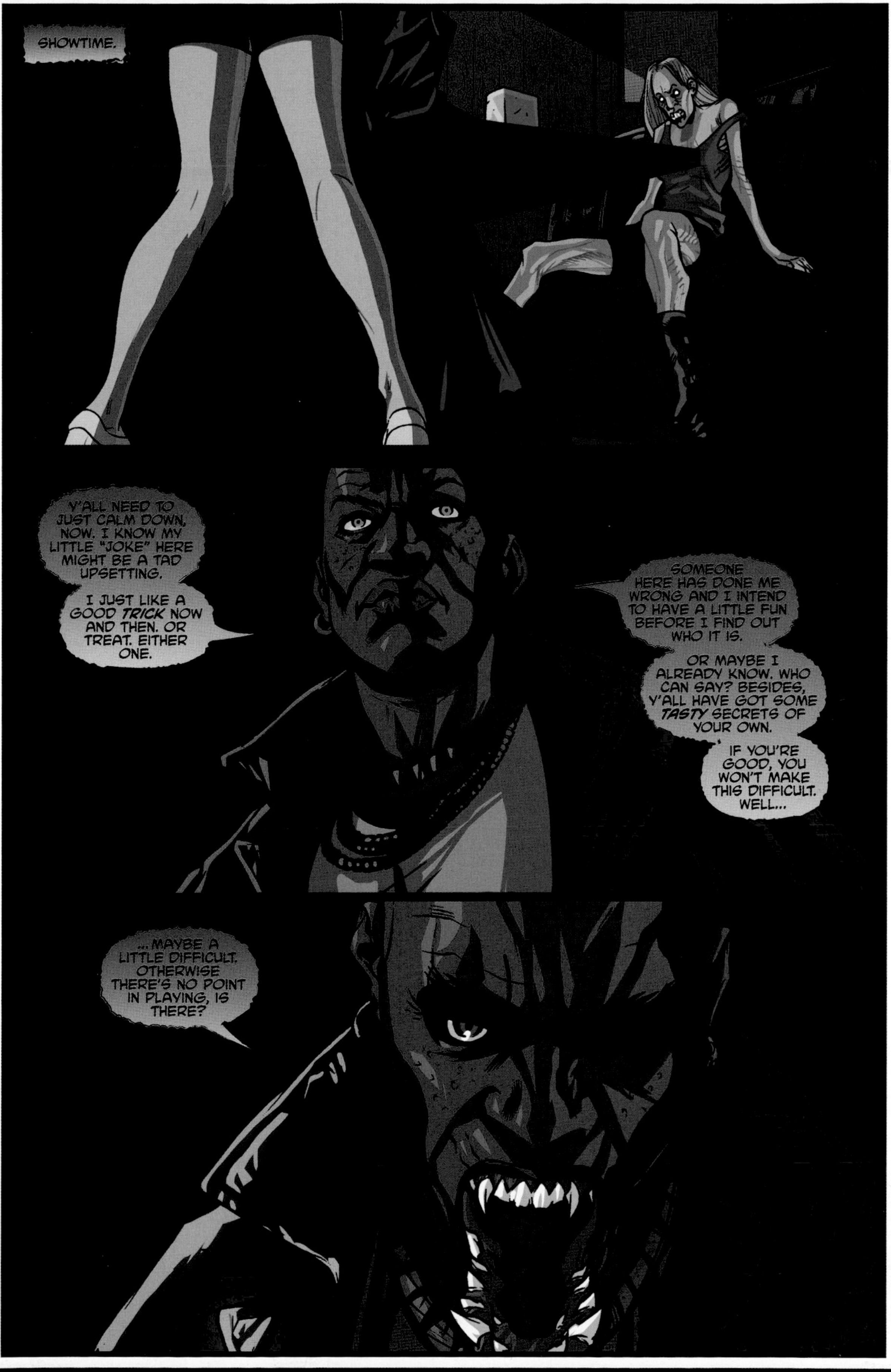
SHOWTIME.
Y'ALL NEED TO JUST CALM DOWN, NOW. I KNOW MY LITTLE "JOKE" HERE MIGHT BE A TAD UPSETTING.
I JUST LIKE A GOOD *TRICK* NOW AND THEN. OR TREAT. EITHER ONE.
SOMEONE HERE HAS DONE ME WRONG AND I INTEND TO HAVE A LITTLE FUN BEFORE I FIND OUT WHO IT IS.
OR MAYBE I ALREADY KNOW. WHO CAN SAY? BESIDES, Y'ALL HAVE GOT SOME *TASTY* SECRETS OF YOUR OWN.
IF YOU'RE GOOD, YOU WON'T MAKE THIS DIFFICULT. WELL...
...MAYBE A LITTLE DIFFICULT. OTHERWISE THERE'S NO POINT IN PLAYING, IS THERE?

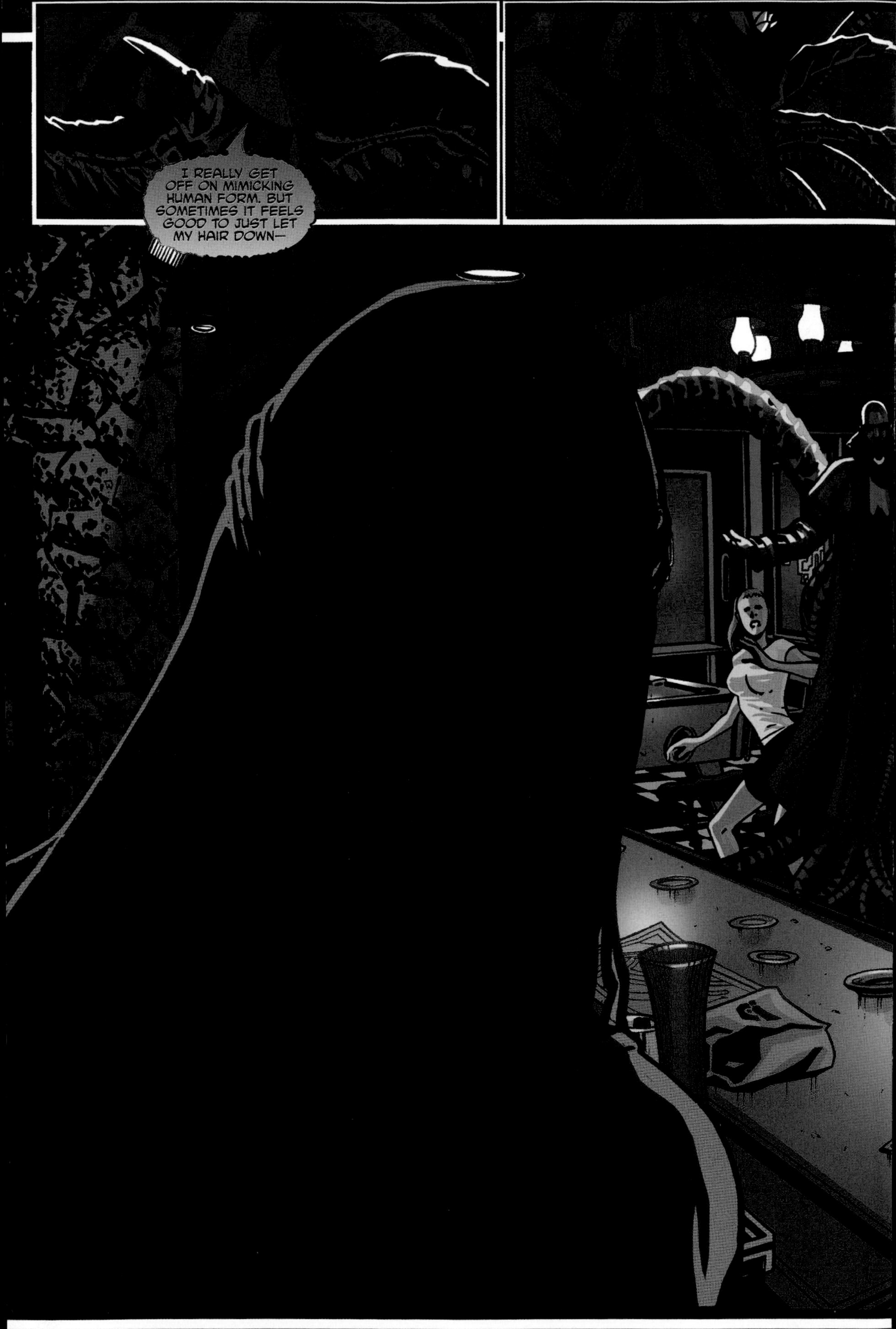
I REALLY GET OFF ON MIMICKING HUMAN FORM. BUT SOMETIMES IT FEELS GOOD TO JUST LET MY HAIR DOWN—

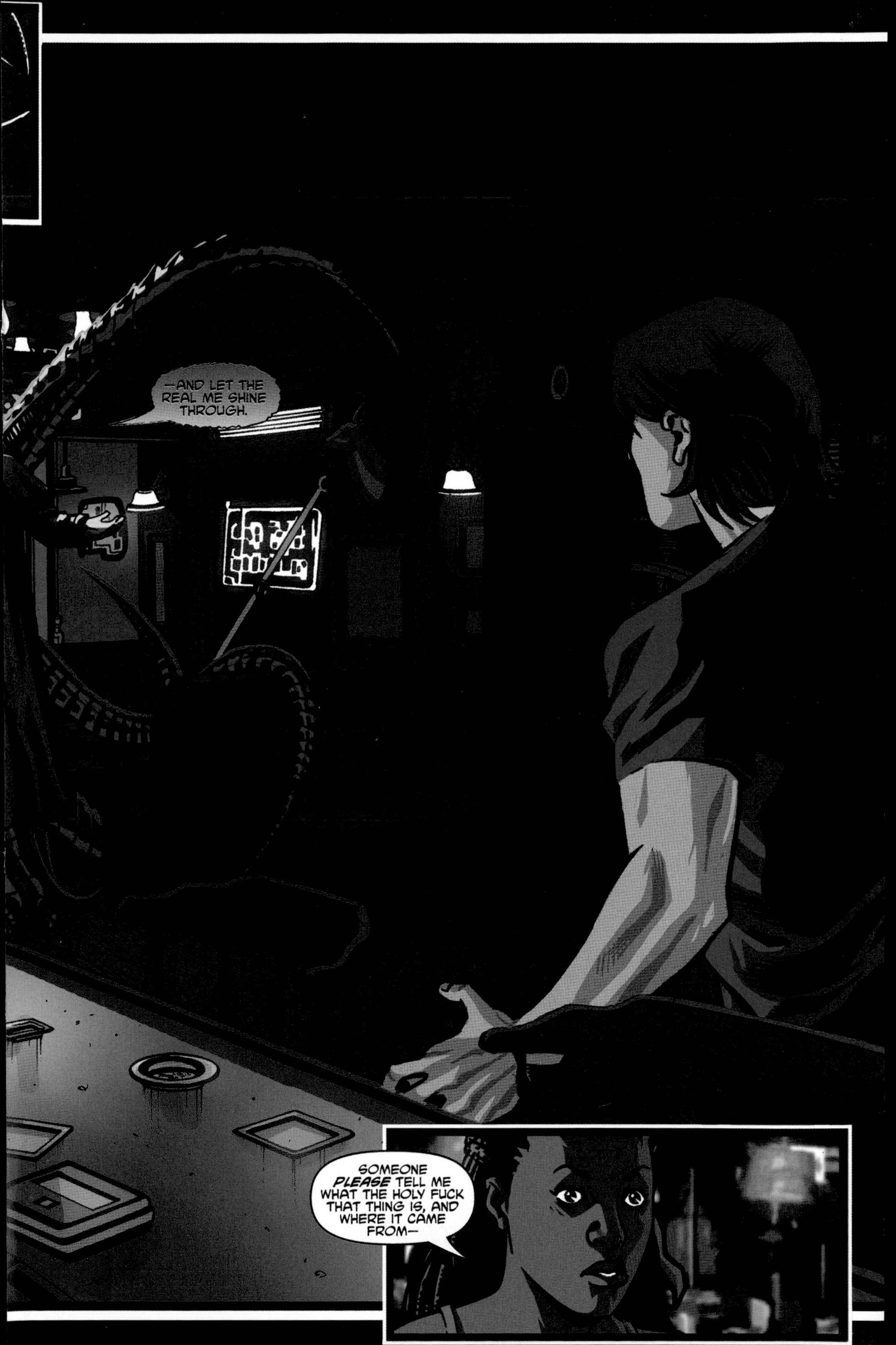
—AND LET THE REAL ME SHINE THROUGH.
SOMEONE *PLEASE* TELL ME WHAT THE HOLY FUCK THAT THING IS, AND WHERE IT CAME FROM—

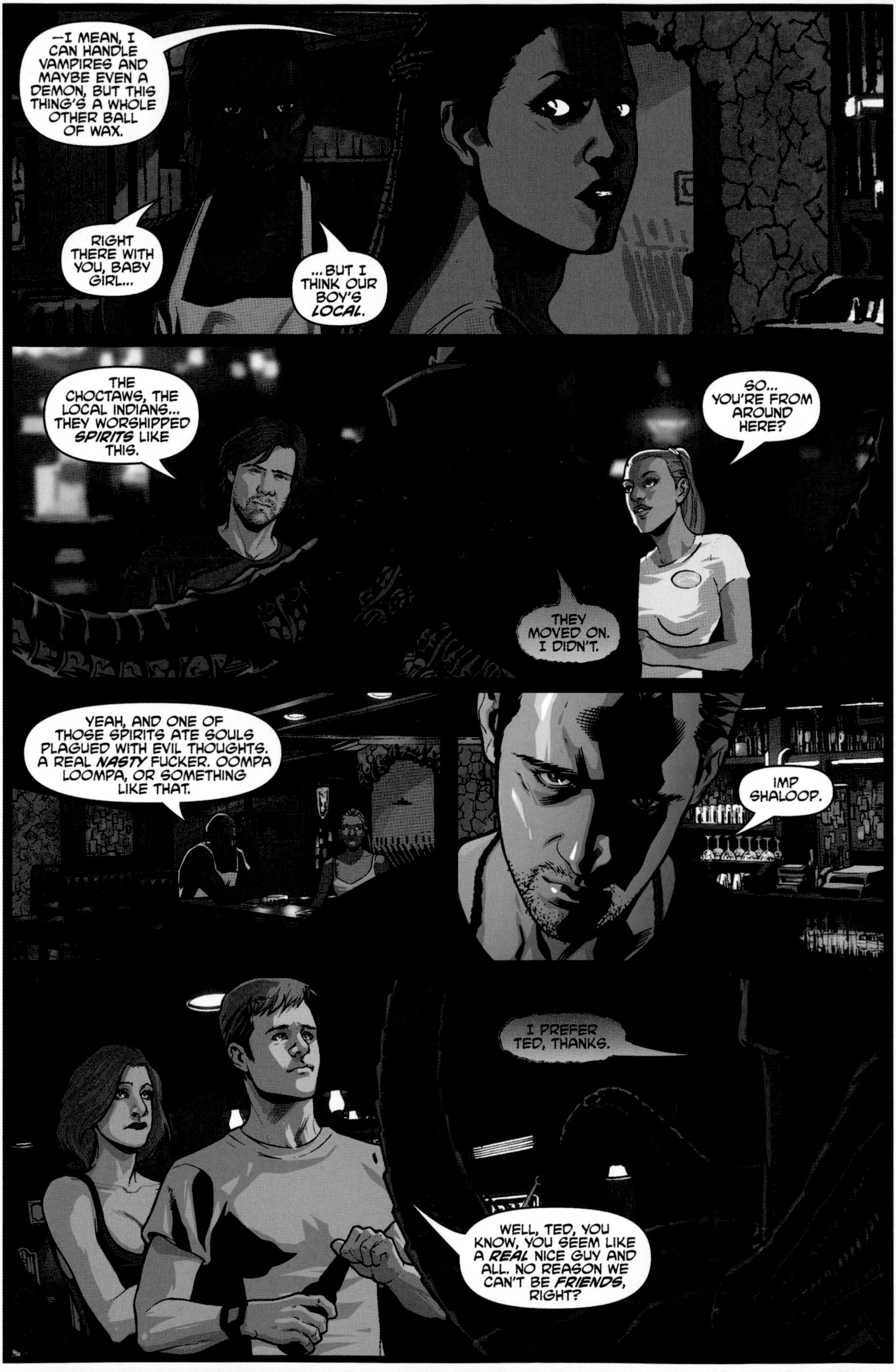
—I MEAN, I CAN HANDLE VAMPIRES AND MAYBE EVEN A DEMON, BUT THIS THING'S A WHOLE OTHER BALL OF WAX.
RIGHT THERE WITH YOU, BABY GIRL...
...BUT I THINK OUR BOY'S *LOCAL*.
THE CHOCTAWS, THE LOCAL INDIANS... THEY WORSHIPPED *SPIRITS* LIKE THIS.
SO... YOU'RE FROM AROUND HERE?
THEY MOVED ON. I DIDN'T.
YEAH, AND ONE OF THOSE SPIRITS ATE SOULS PLAGUED WITH EVIL THOUGHTS. A REAL *NASTY* FUCKER. OOMPA LOOMPA, OR SOMETHING LIKE THAT.
IMP SHALOOP.
I PREFER TED, THANKS.
WELL, TED, YOU KNOW, YOU SEEM LIKE A *REAL* NICE GUY AND ALL. NO REASON WE CAN'T BE *FRIENDS*, RIGHT?

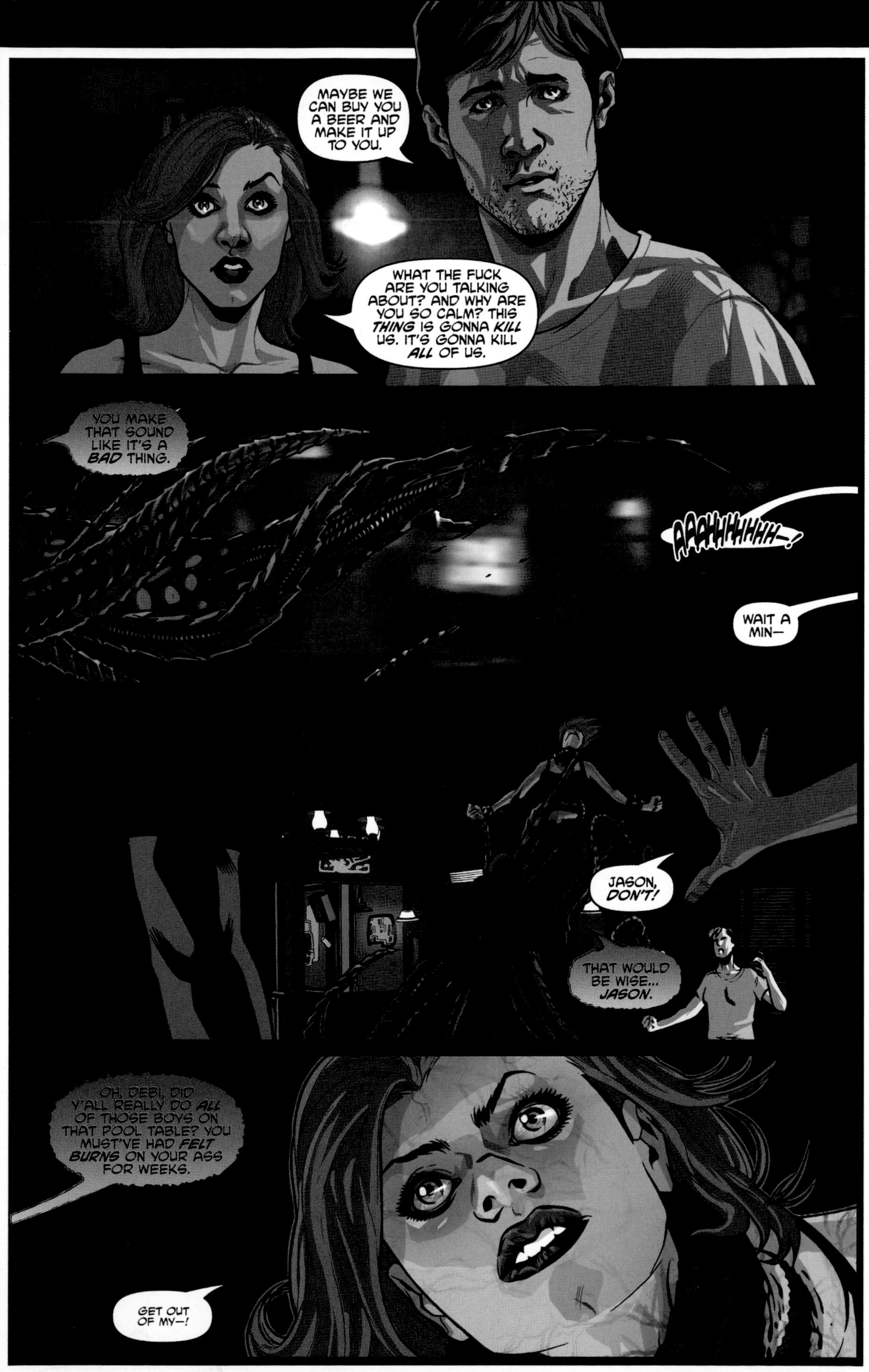
MAYBE WE CAN BUY YOU A BEER AND MAKE IT UP TO YOU.
WHAT THE FUCK ARE YOU TALKING ABOUT? AND WHY ARE YOU SO CALM? THIS *THING* IS GONNA *KILL* US. IT'S GONNA KILL *ALL* OF US.
YOU MAKE THAT SOUND LIKE IT'S A *BAD* THING.
AAAHHHHHH—!
WAIT A MIN—
JASON, *DON'T!*
THAT WOULD BE WISE... *JASON.*
OH, DEBI, DID Y'ALL REALLY DO *ALL* OF THOSE BOYS ON THAT POOL TABLE? YOU MUST'VE HAD *FELT BURNS* ON YOUR ASS FOR WEEKS.
GET OUT OF MY—!

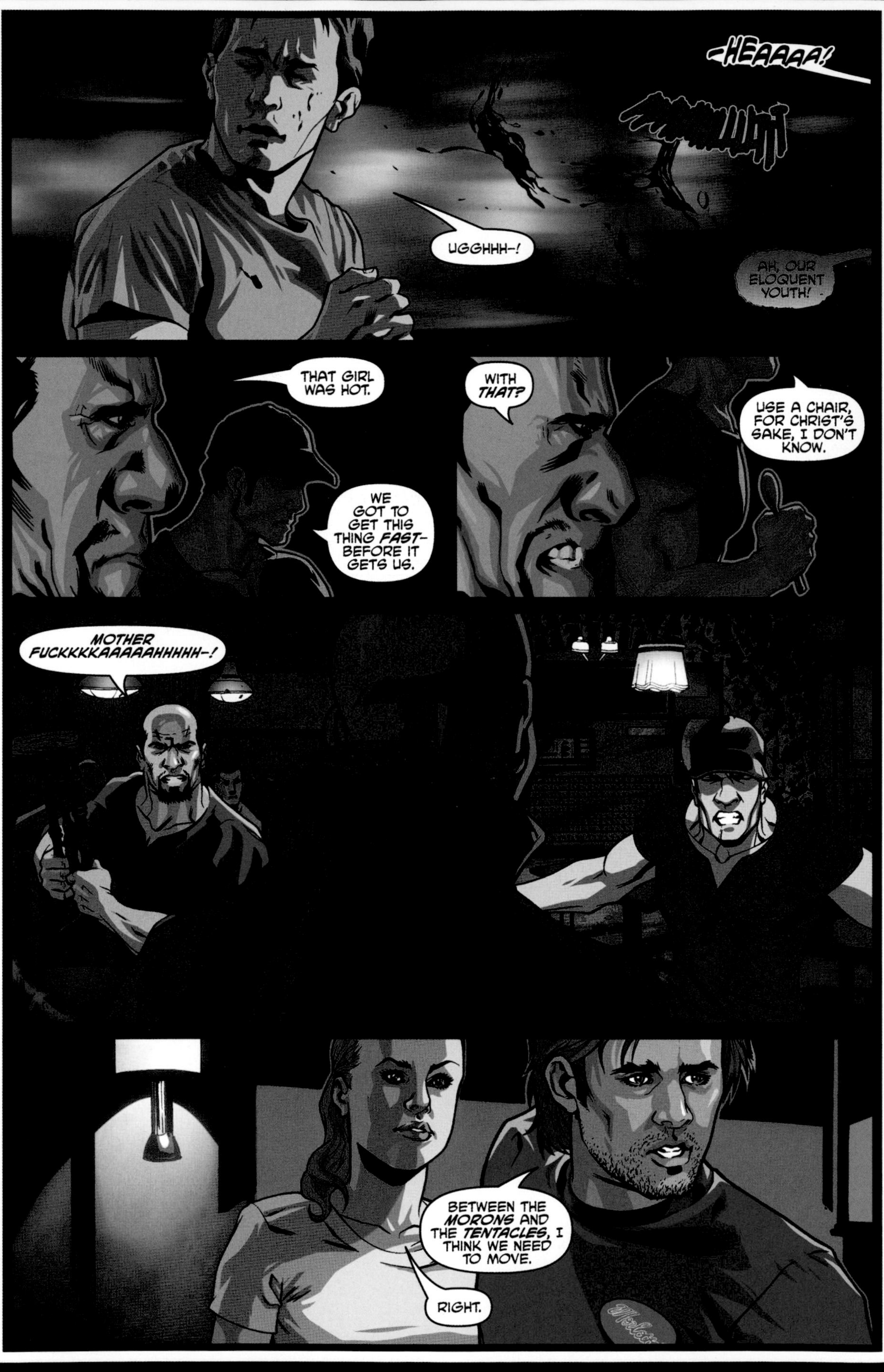
-HEAAAA!
UGGHHH-!
AH, OUR ELOQUENT YOUTH!
THAT GIRL WAS HOT.
WE GOT TO GET THIS THING FAST- BEFORE IT GETS US.
WITH THAT?
USE A CHAIR, FOR CHRIST'S SAKE, I DON'T KNOW.
MOTHER FUCKKKKAAAAAHHHHH-!
BETWEEN THE MORONS AND THE TENTACLES, I THINK WE NEED TO MOVE.
RIGHT.

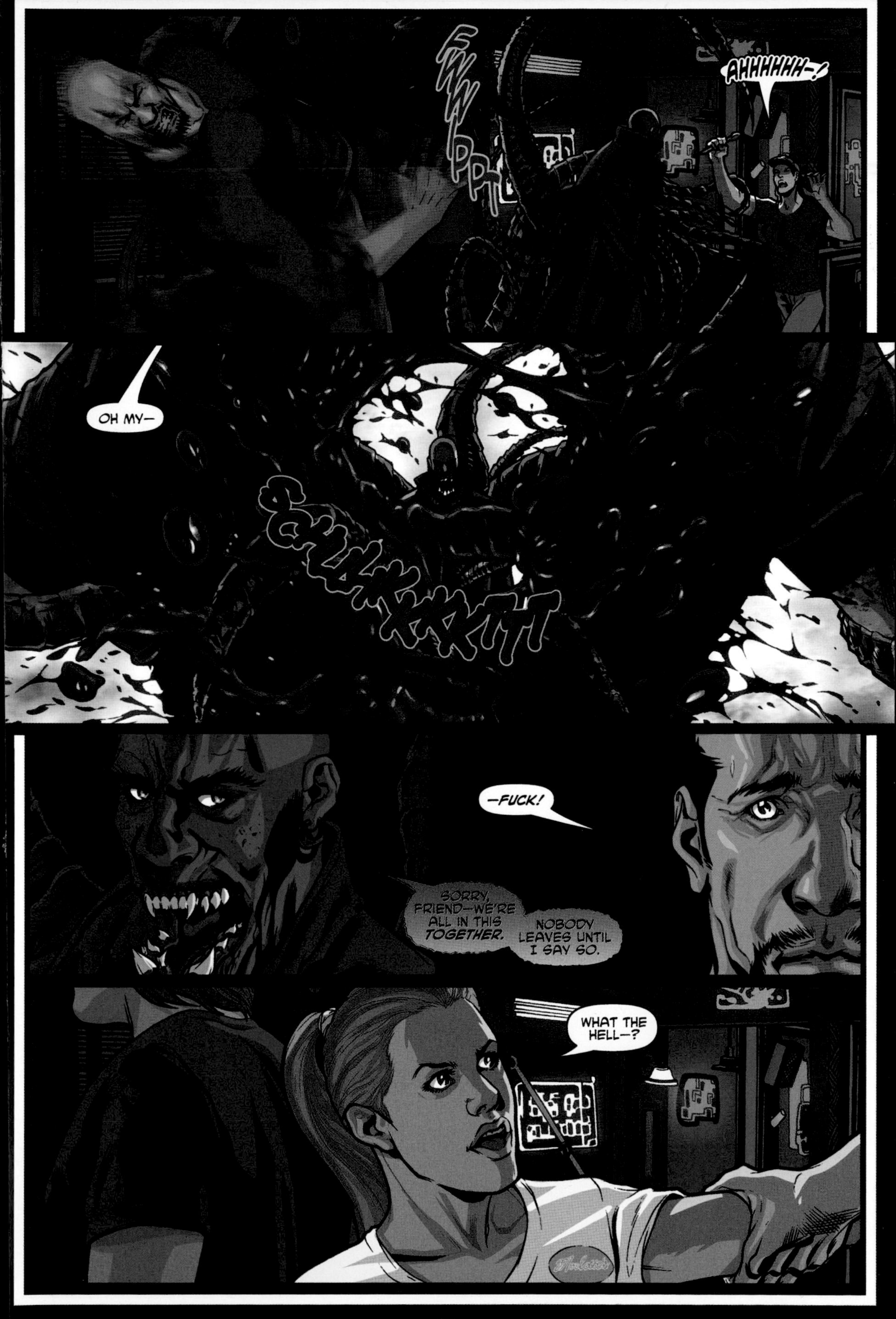
FWWIPPT
AHHHHHH-!
OH MY—
SCHLUKKRTT
—FUCK!
SORRY, FRIEND—WE'RE ALL IN THIS TOGETHER.
NOBODY LEAVES UNTIL I SAY SO.
WHAT THE HELL—?

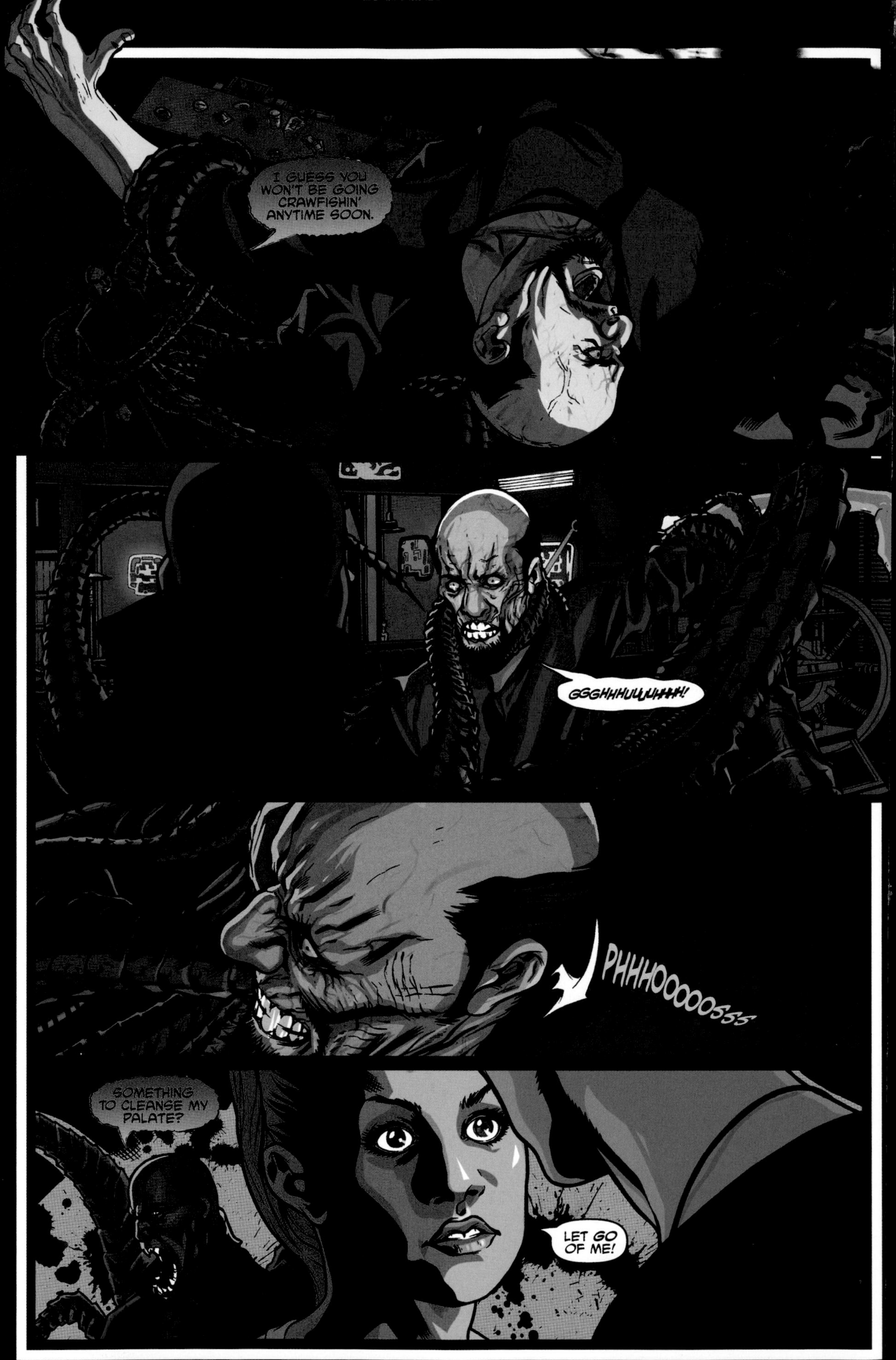
I GUESS YOU WON'T BE GOING CRAWFISHIN' ANYTIME SOON.
GGGHHHUUUUHHH!
PHHHOOOOOOSSS
SOMETHING TO CLEANSE MY PALATE?
LET GO OF ME!

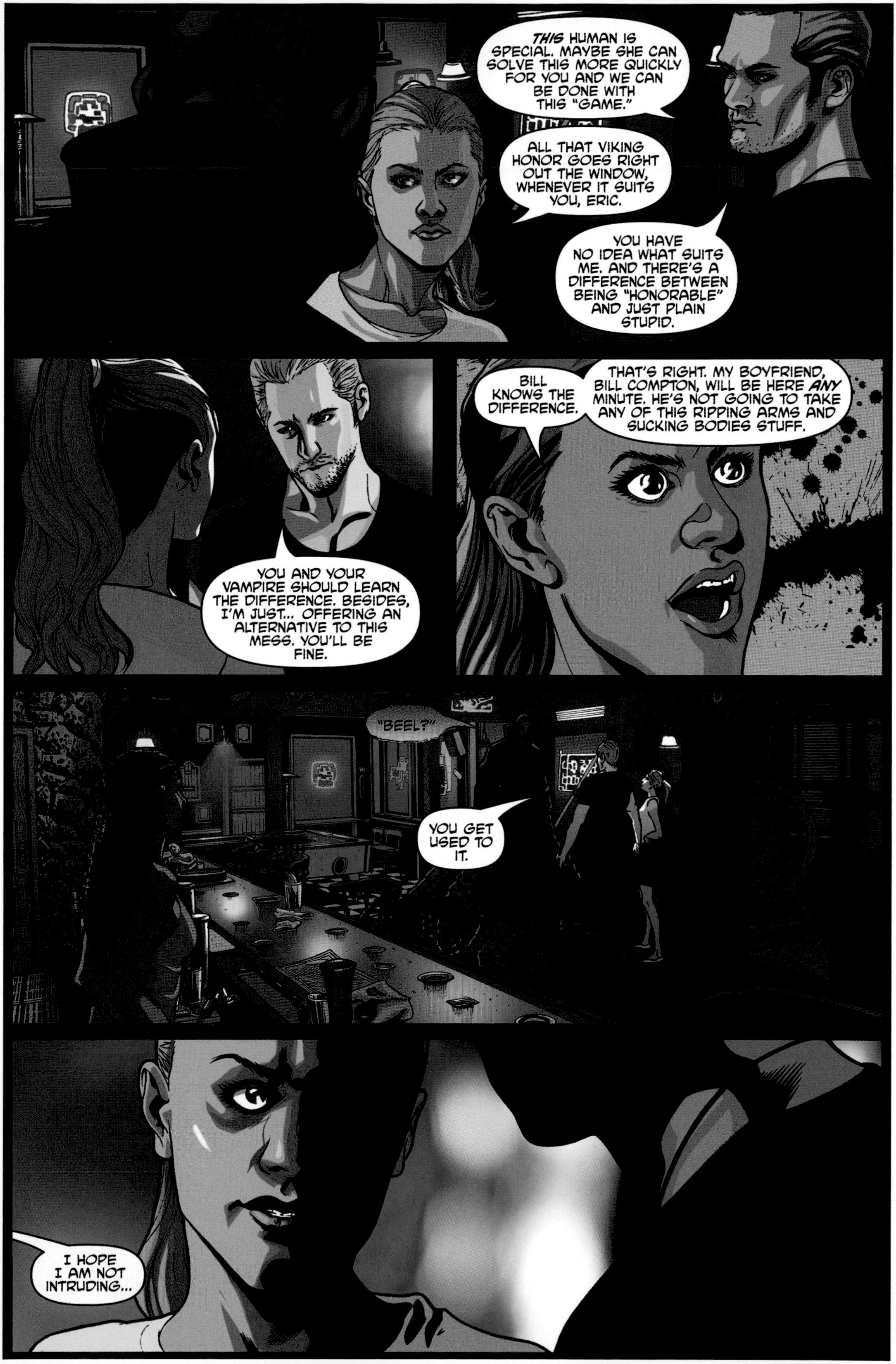
THIS HUMAN IS SPECIAL. MAYBE SHE CAN SOLVE THIS MORE QUICKLY FOR YOU AND WE CAN BE DONE WITH THIS "GAME."
ALL THAT VIKING HONOR GOES RIGHT OUT THE WINDOW, WHENEVER IT SUITS YOU, ERIC.
YOU HAVE NO IDEA WHAT SUITS ME. AND THERE'S A DIFFERENCE BETWEEN BEING "HONORABLE" AND JUST PLAIN STUPID.
YOU AND YOUR VAMPIRE SHOULD LEARN THE DIFFERENCE. BESIDES, I'M JUST... OFFERING AN ALTERNATIVE TO THIS MESS. YOU'LL BE FINE.
BILL KNOWS THE DIFFERENCE.
THAT'S RIGHT. MY BOYFRIEND, BILL COMPTON, WILL BE HERE ANY MINUTE. HE'S NOT GOING TO TAKE ANY OF THIS RIPPING ARMS AND SUCKING BODIES STUFF.
"BEEL?"
YOU GET USED TO IT.
I HOPE I AM NOT INTRUDING...

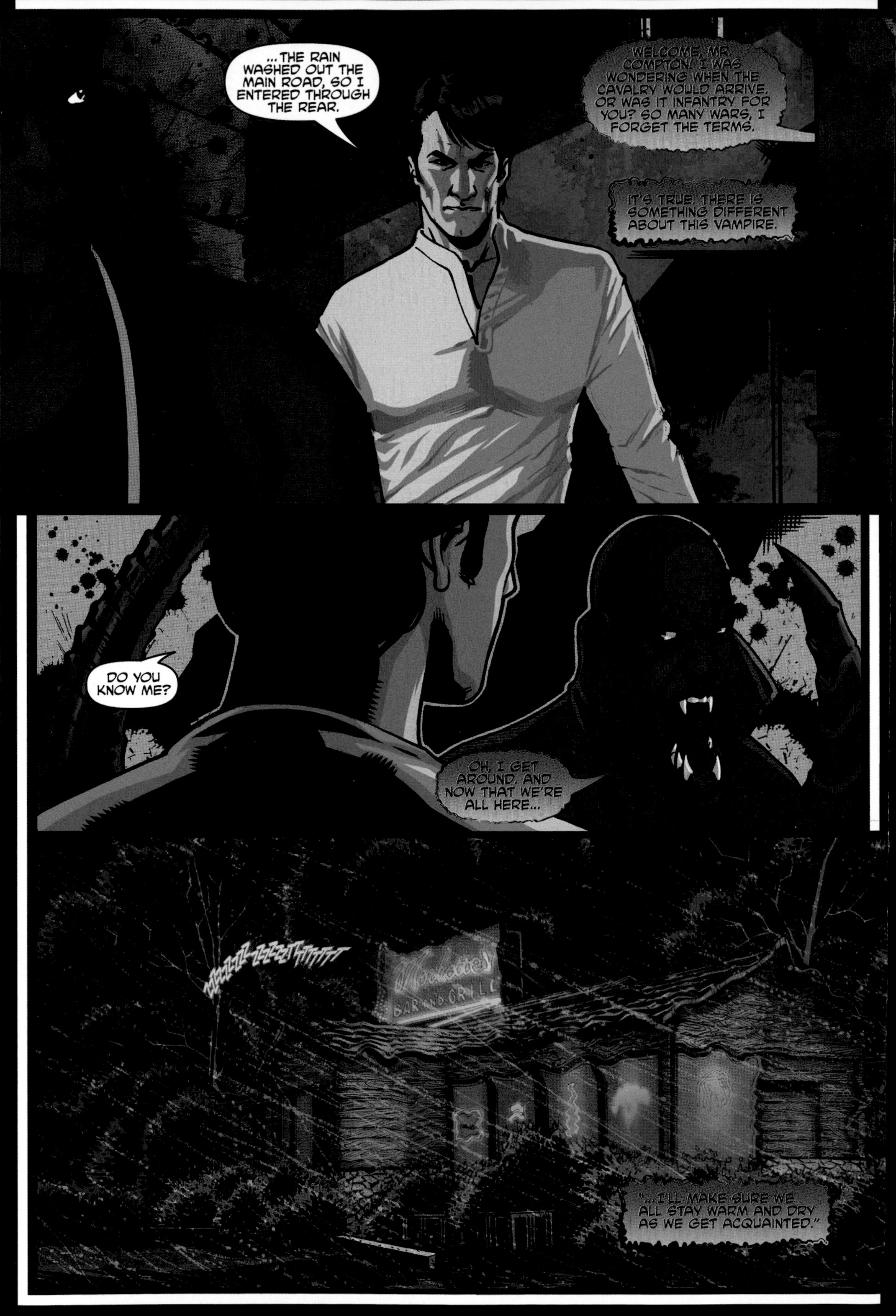
...THE RAIN WASHED OUT THE MAIN ROAD, SO I ENTERED THROUGH THE REAR.
WELCOME, MR. COMPTON! I WAS WONDERING WHEN THE CAVALRY WOULD ARRIVE. OR WAS IT INFANTRY FOR YOU? SO MANY WARS, I FORGET THE TERMS.
IT'S TRUE. THERE IS SOMETHING DIFFERENT ABOUT THIS VAMPIRE.
DO YOU KNOW ME?
OH, I GET AROUND. AND NOW THAT WE'RE ALL HERE...
ZZZZZ-ZZZZZZTTTTTTT
BAR AND GRILL
"...I'LL MAKE SURE WE ALL STAY WARM AND DRY AS WE GET ACQUAINTED."

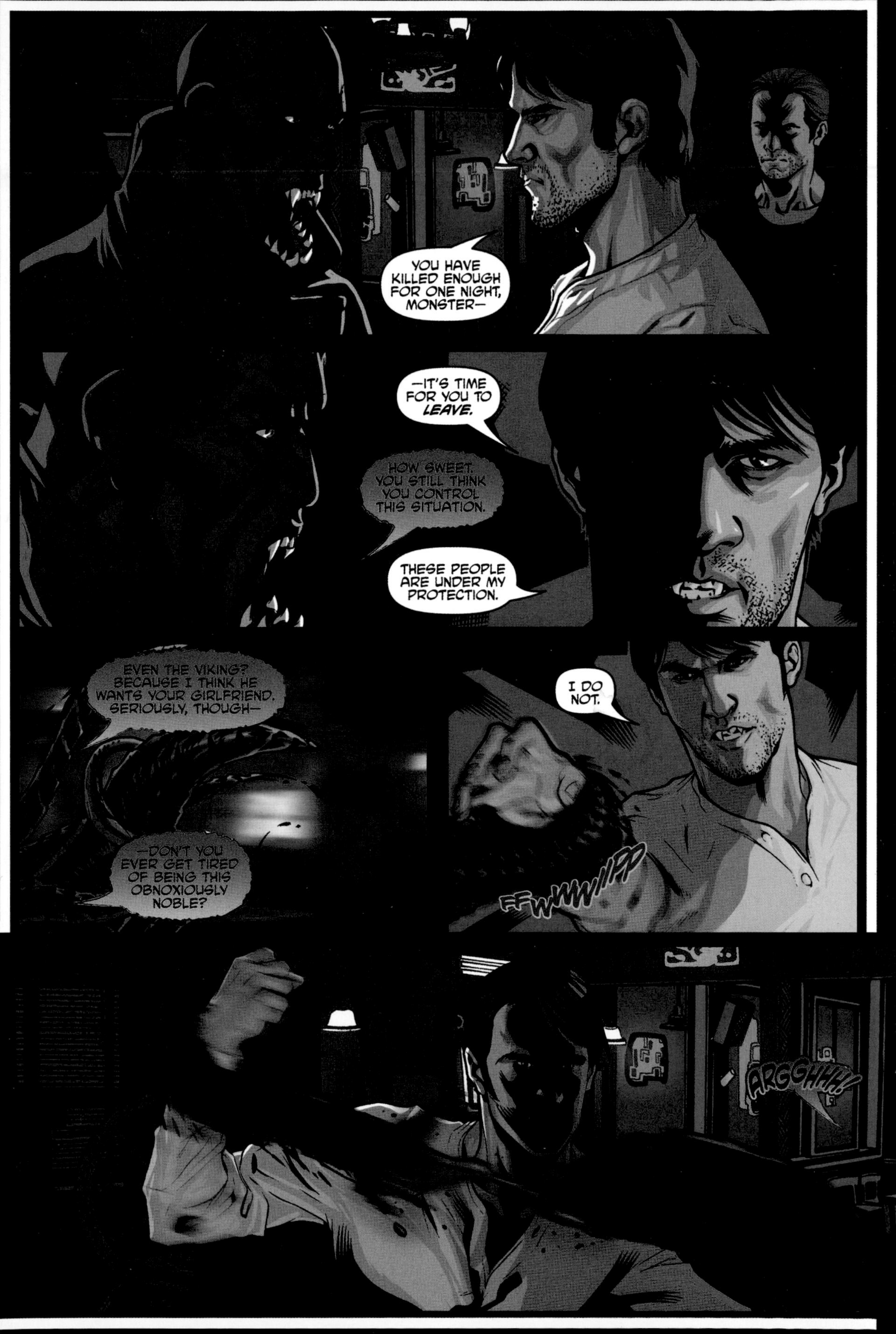
YOU HAVE KILLED ENOUGH FOR ONE NIGHT, MONSTER—
—IT'S TIME FOR YOU TO *LEAVE.*
HOW SWEET. YOU STILL THINK YOU CONTROL THIS SITUATION.
THESE PEOPLE ARE UNDER MY PROTECTION.
EVEN THE VIKING? BECAUSE I THINK HE WANTS YOUR GIRLFRIEND. SERIOUSLY, THOUGH—
—DON'T YOU EVER GET TIRED OF BEING THIS OBNOXIOUSLY NOBLE?
I DO NOT.
FFWWWIIPP
ARGGHHH!

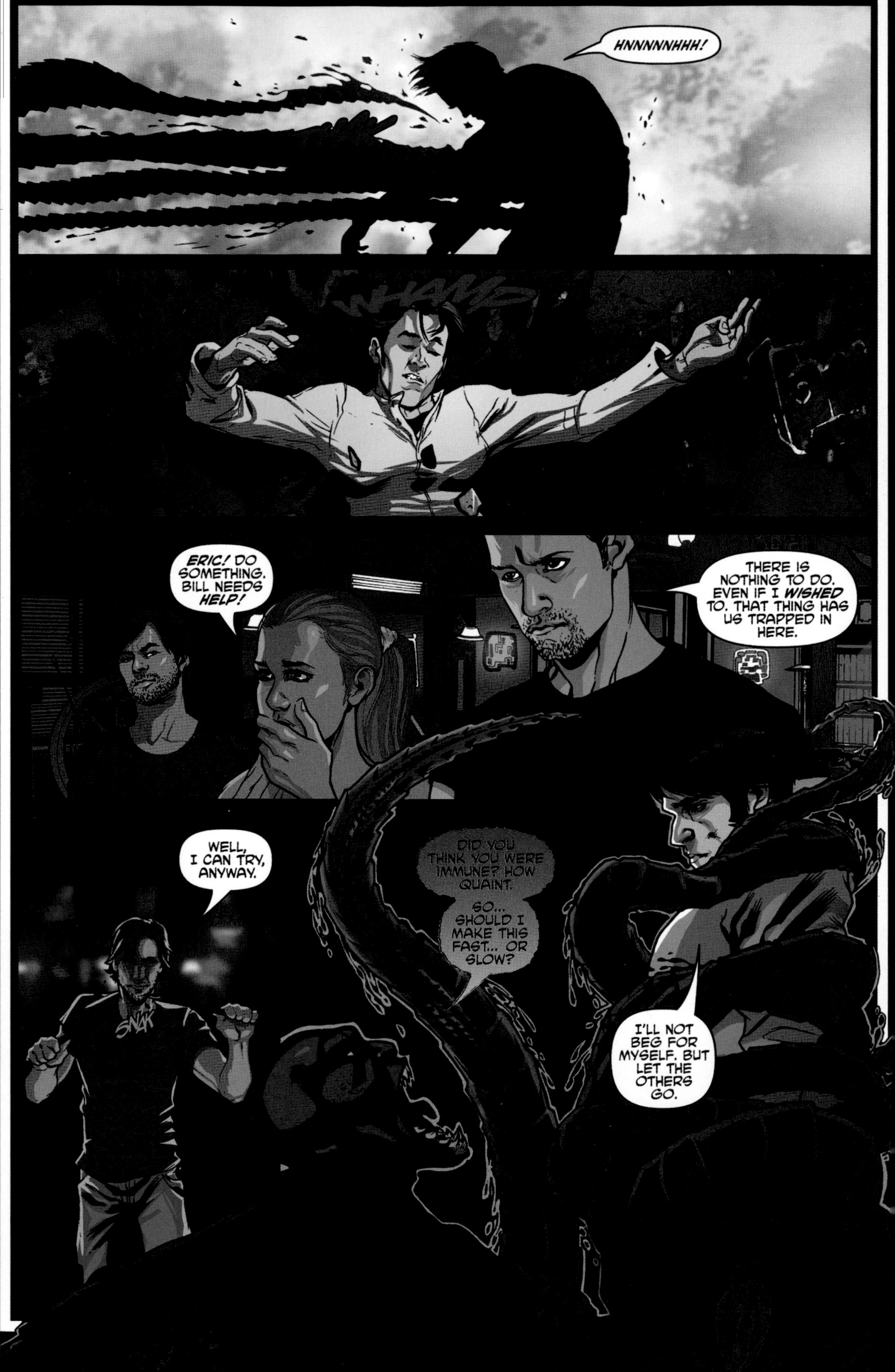
HNNNNNHHH!
ERIC! DO SOMETHING. BILL NEEDS HELP!
THERE IS NOTHING TO DO. EVEN IF I WISHED TO. THAT THING HAS US TRAPPED IN HERE.
WELL, I CAN TRY, ANYWAY.
DID YOU THINK YOU WERE IMMUNE? HOW QUAINT.
SO... SHOULD I MAKE THIS FAST... OR SLOW?
I'LL NOT BEG FOR MYSELF. BUT LET THE OTHERS GO.

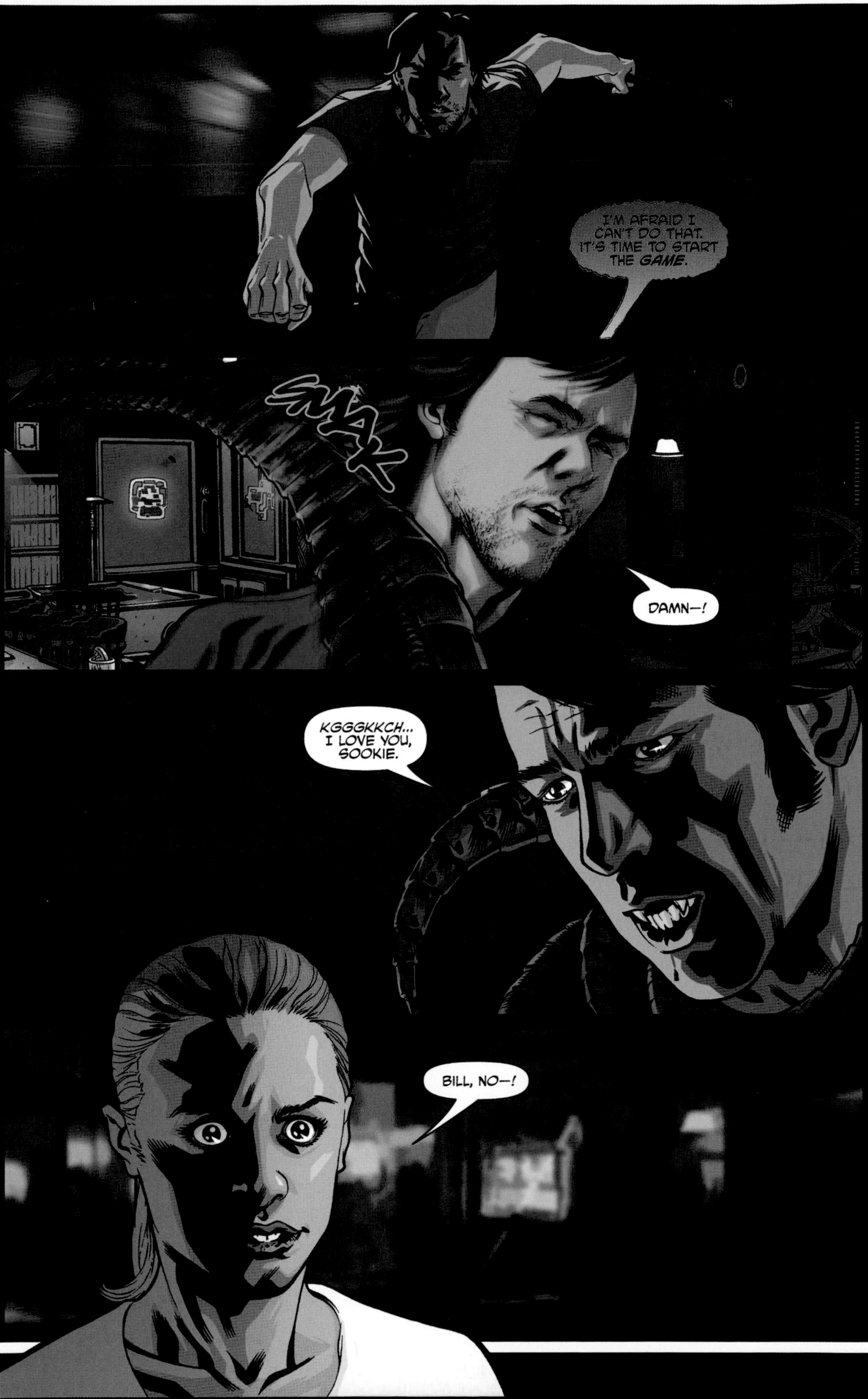
I'M AFRAID I CAN'T DO THAT. IT'S TIME TO START THE *GAME*.
SMAK
DAMN--!
KGGGKKCH... I LOVE YOU, SOOKIE.
BILL, NO--!

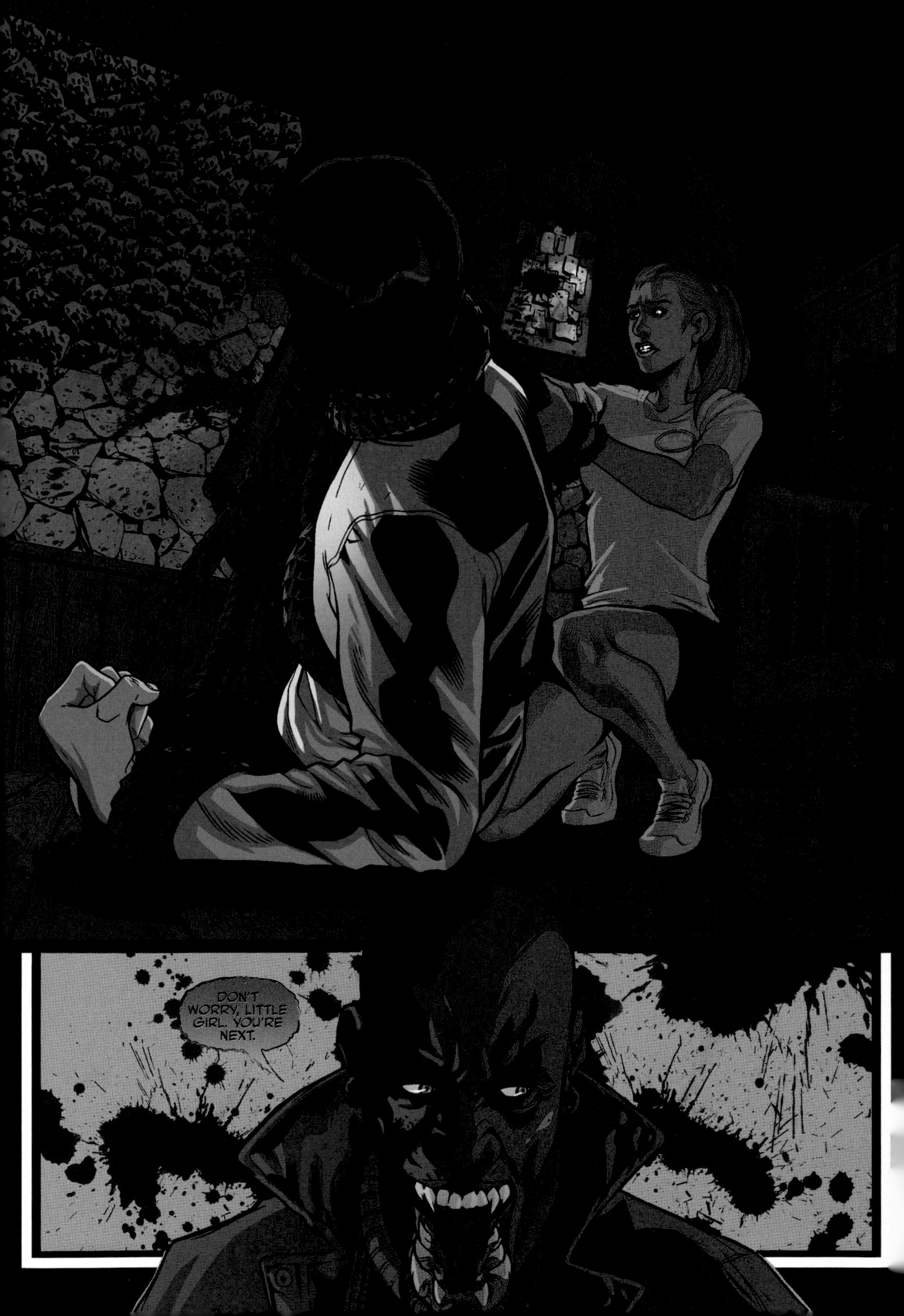
DON'T WORRY, LITTLE GIRL. YOU'RE NEXT.

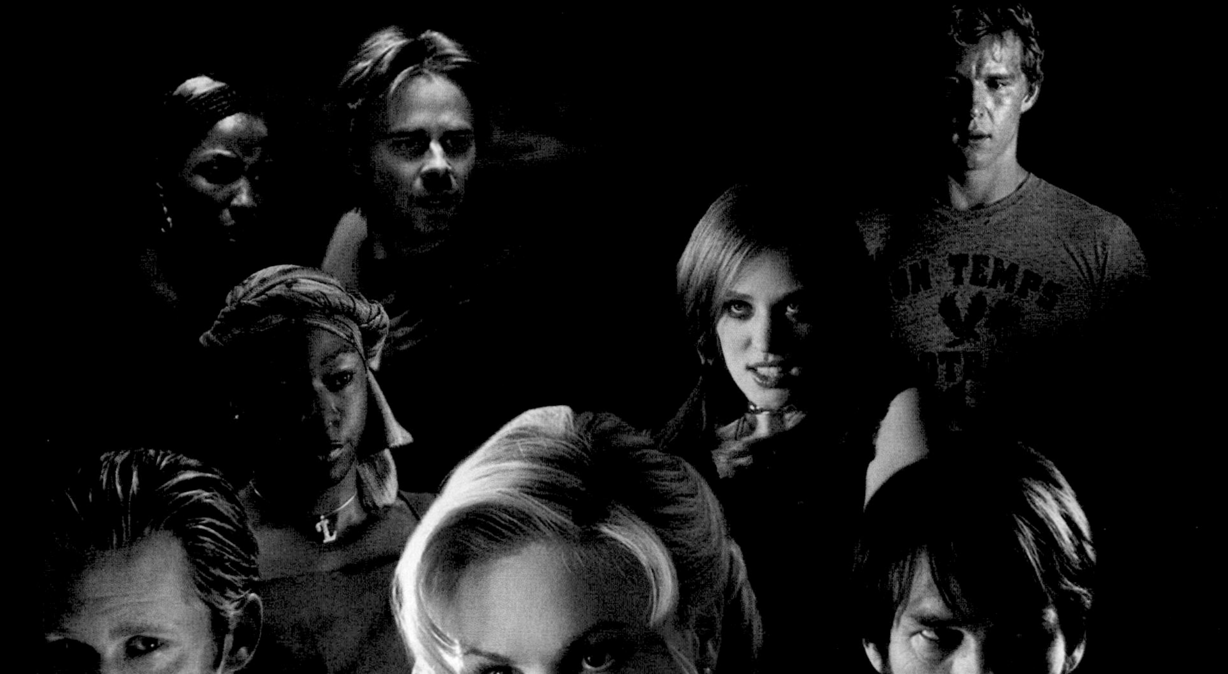
TEMPS

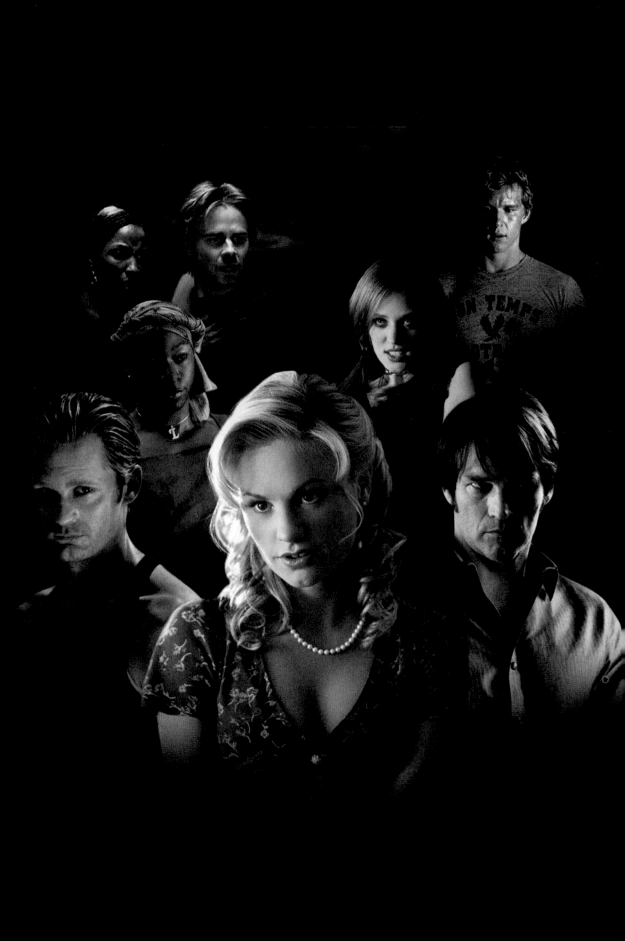

art by DAVID MESSINA
colors by GIOVANNA NIRO

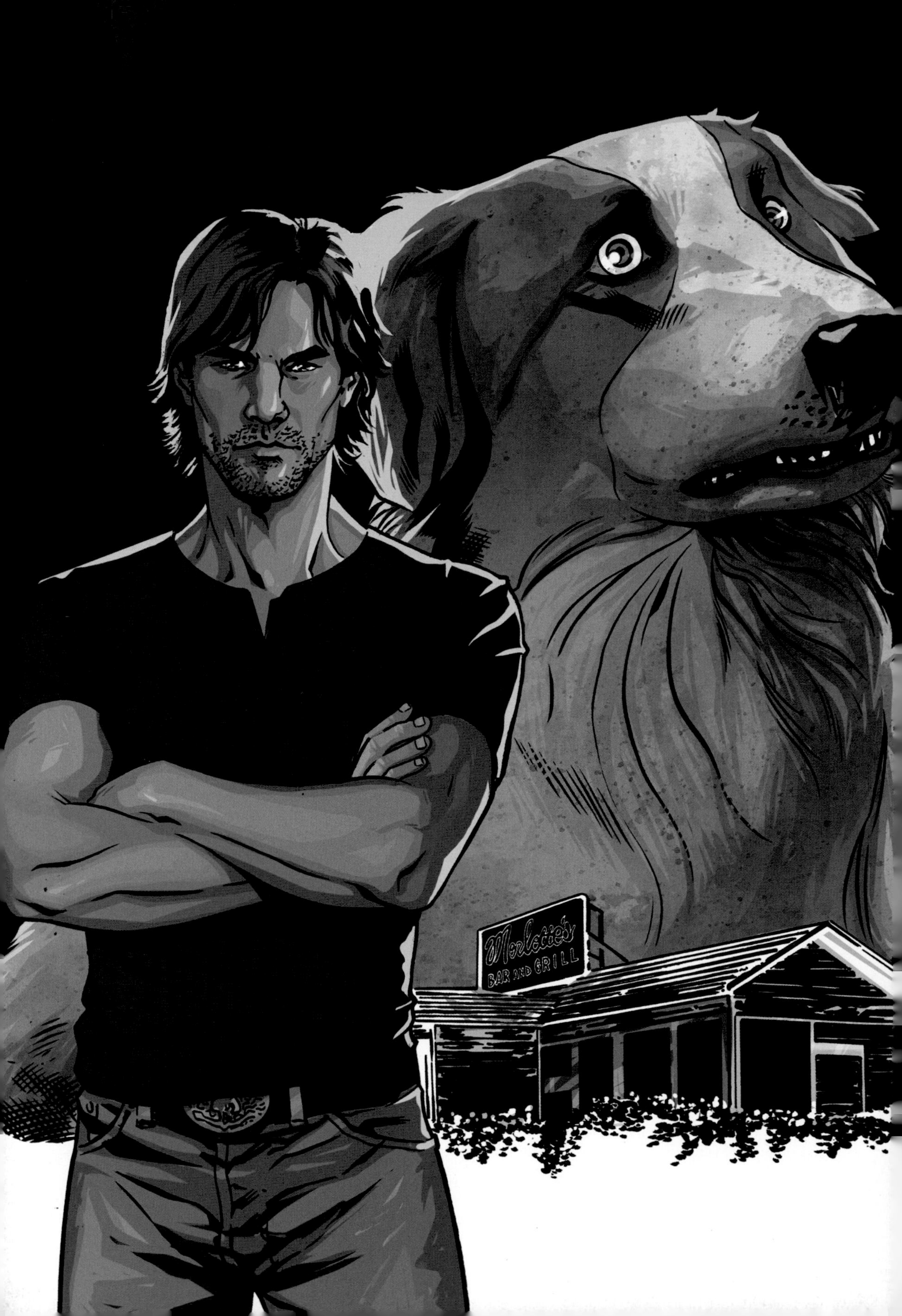
Merlotte's
BAR AND GRILL

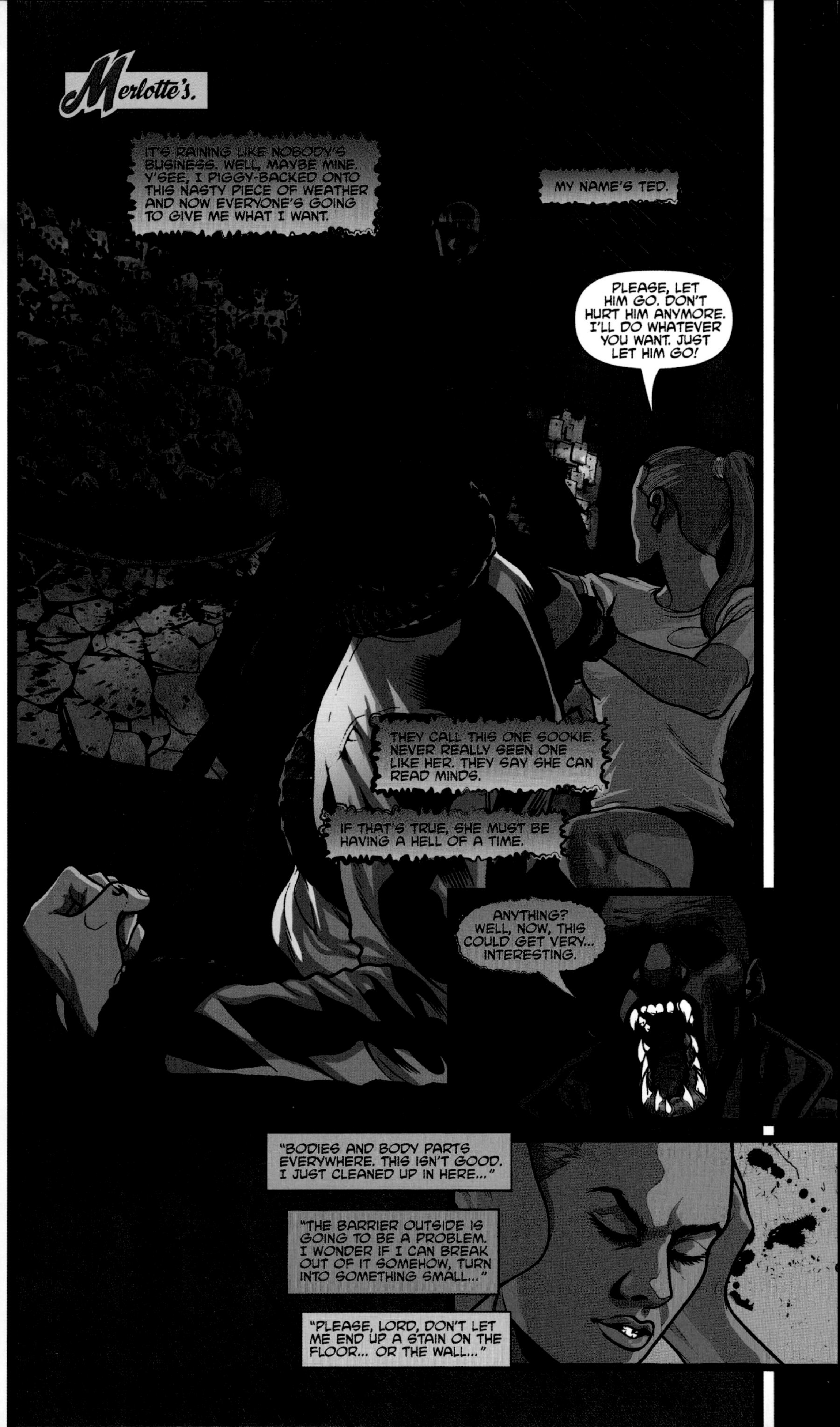
Merlotte's.
IT'S RAINING LIKE NOBODY'S BUSINESS. WELL, MAYBE MINE. Y'SEE, I PIGGY-BACKED ONTO THIS NASTY PIECE OF WEATHER AND NOW EVERYONE'S GOING TO GIVE ME WHAT I WANT.
MY NAME'S TED.
PLEASE, LET HIM GO. DON'T HURT HIM ANYMORE. I'LL DO WHATEVER YOU WANT. JUST LET HIM GO!
THEY CALL THIS ONE SOOKIE. NEVER REALLY SEEN ONE LIKE HER. THEY SAY SHE CAN READ MINDS.
IF THAT'S TRUE, SHE MUST BE HAVING A HELL OF A TIME.
ANYTHING? WELL, NOW, THIS COULD GET VERY... INTERESTING.
"BODIES AND BODY PARTS EVERYWHERE. THIS ISN'T GOOD. I JUST CLEANED UP IN HERE..."
"THE BARRIER OUTSIDE IS GOING TO BE A PROBLEM. I WONDER IF I CAN BREAK OUT OF IT SOMEHOW, TURN INTO SOMETHING SMALL..."
"PLEASE, LORD, DON'T LET ME END UP A STAIN ON THE FLOOR... OR THE WALL..."

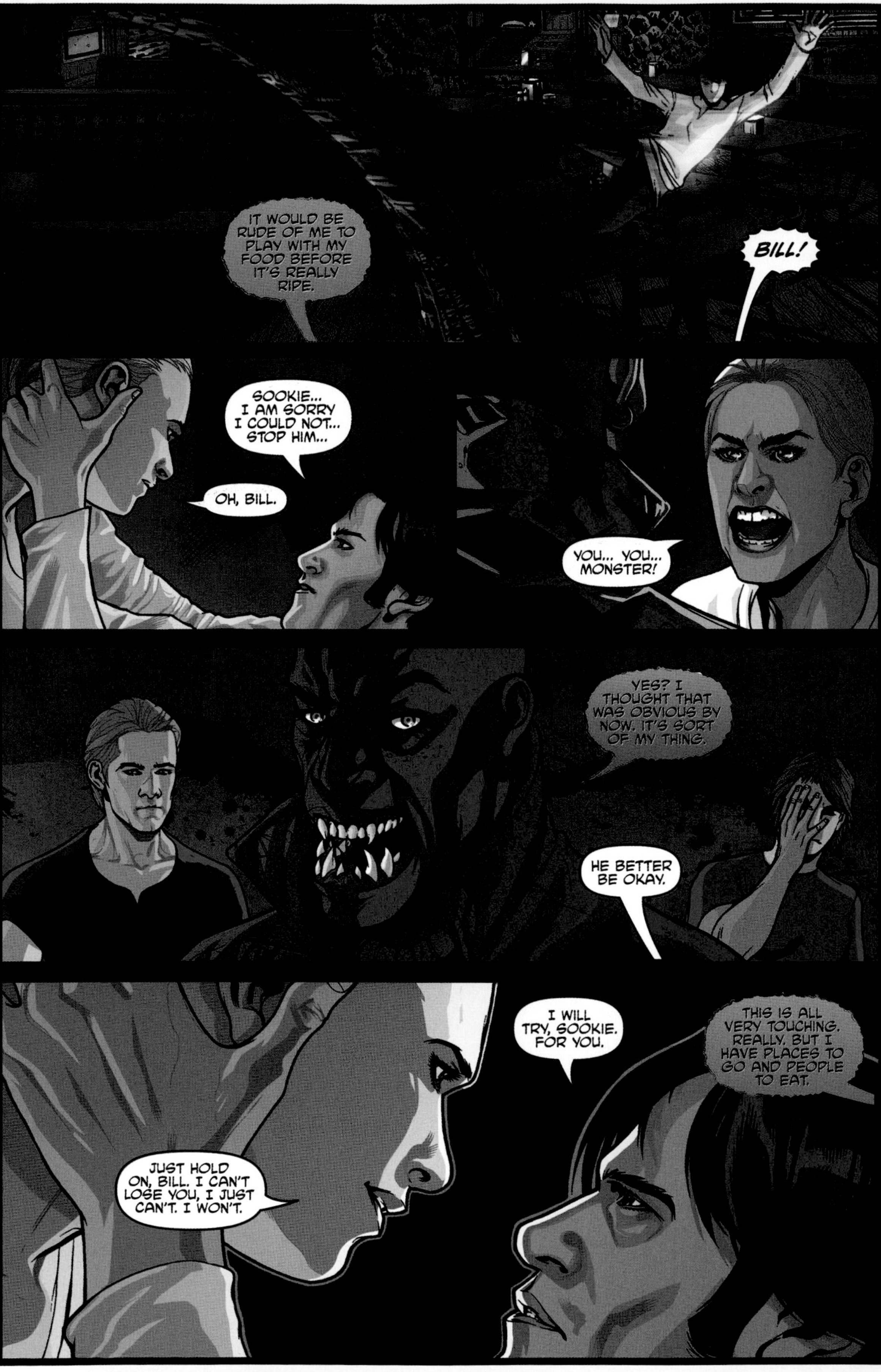
IT WOULD BE RUDE OF ME TO PLAY WITH MY FOOD BEFORE IT'S REALLY RIPE.
BILL!
SOOKIE... I AM SORRY I COULD NOT... STOP HIM...
OH, BILL.
YOU... YOU... MONSTER!
YES? I THOUGHT THAT WAS OBVIOUS BY NOW. IT'S SORT OF MY THING.
HE BETTER BE OKAY.
I WILL TRY, SOOKIE. FOR YOU.
THIS IS ALL VERY TOUCHING. REALLY. BUT I HAVE PLACES TO GO AND PEOPLE TO EAT.
JUST HOLD ON, BILL. I CAN'T LOSE YOU, I JUST CAN'T. I WON'T.

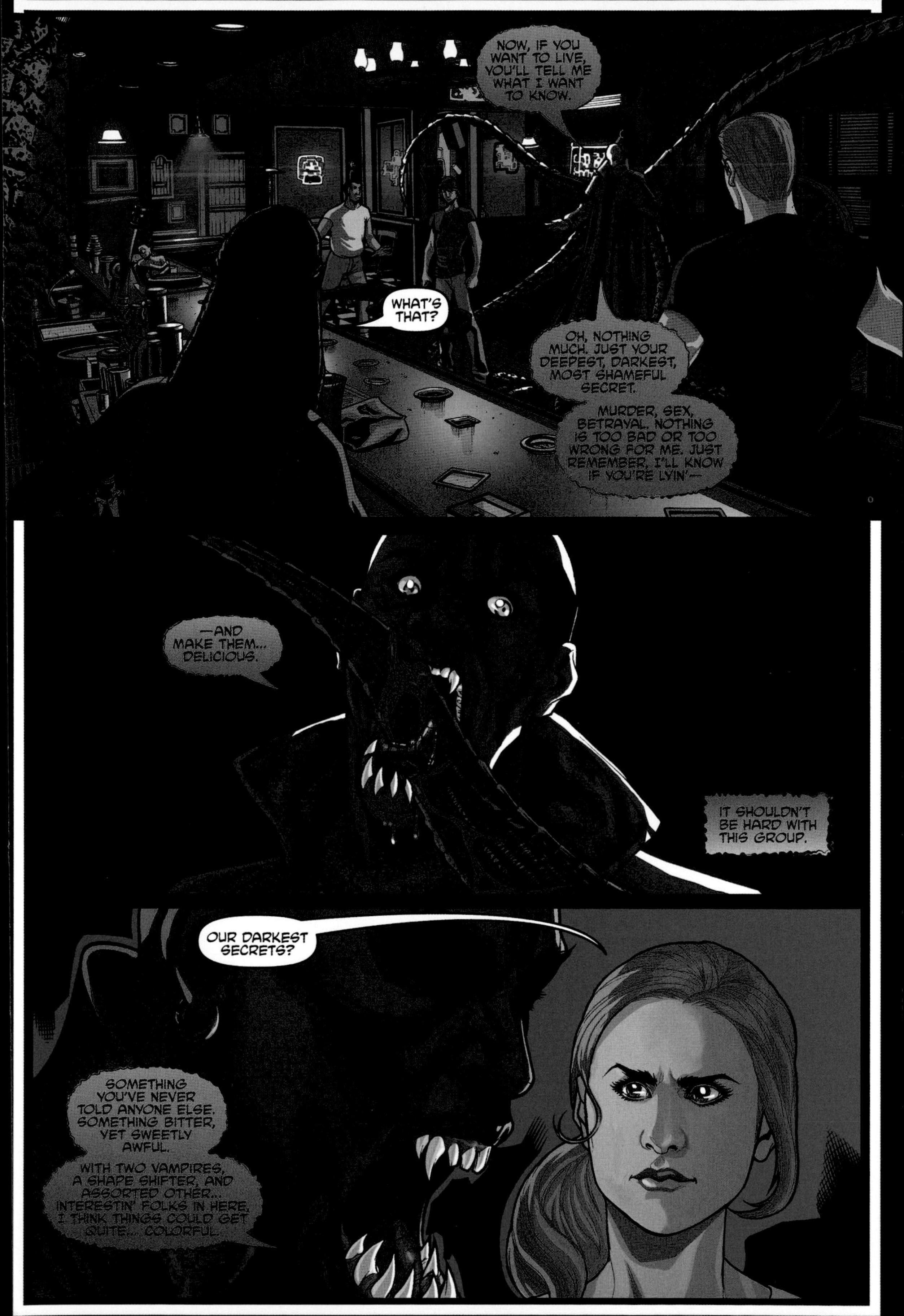
NOW, IF YOU WANT TO LIVE, YOU'LL TELL ME WHAT I WANT TO KNOW.
WHAT'S THAT?
OH, NOTHING MUCH. JUST YOUR DEEPEST, DARKEST, MOST SHAMEFUL SECRET.
MURDER, SEX, BETRAYAL. NOTHING IS TOO BAD OR TOO WRONG FOR ME. JUST REMEMBER, I'LL KNOW IF YOU'RE LYIN'—
—AND MAKE THEM... DELICIOUS.
IT SHOULDN'T BE HARD WITH THIS GROUP.
OUR DARKEST SECRETS?
SOMETHING YOU'VE NEVER TOLD ANYONE ELSE. SOMETHING BITTER, YET SWEETLY AWFUL.
WITH TWO VAMPIRES, A SHAPE SHIFTER, AND ASSORTED OTHER... INTERESTIN' FOLKS IN HERE, I THINK THINGS COULD GET QUITE... COLORFUL.

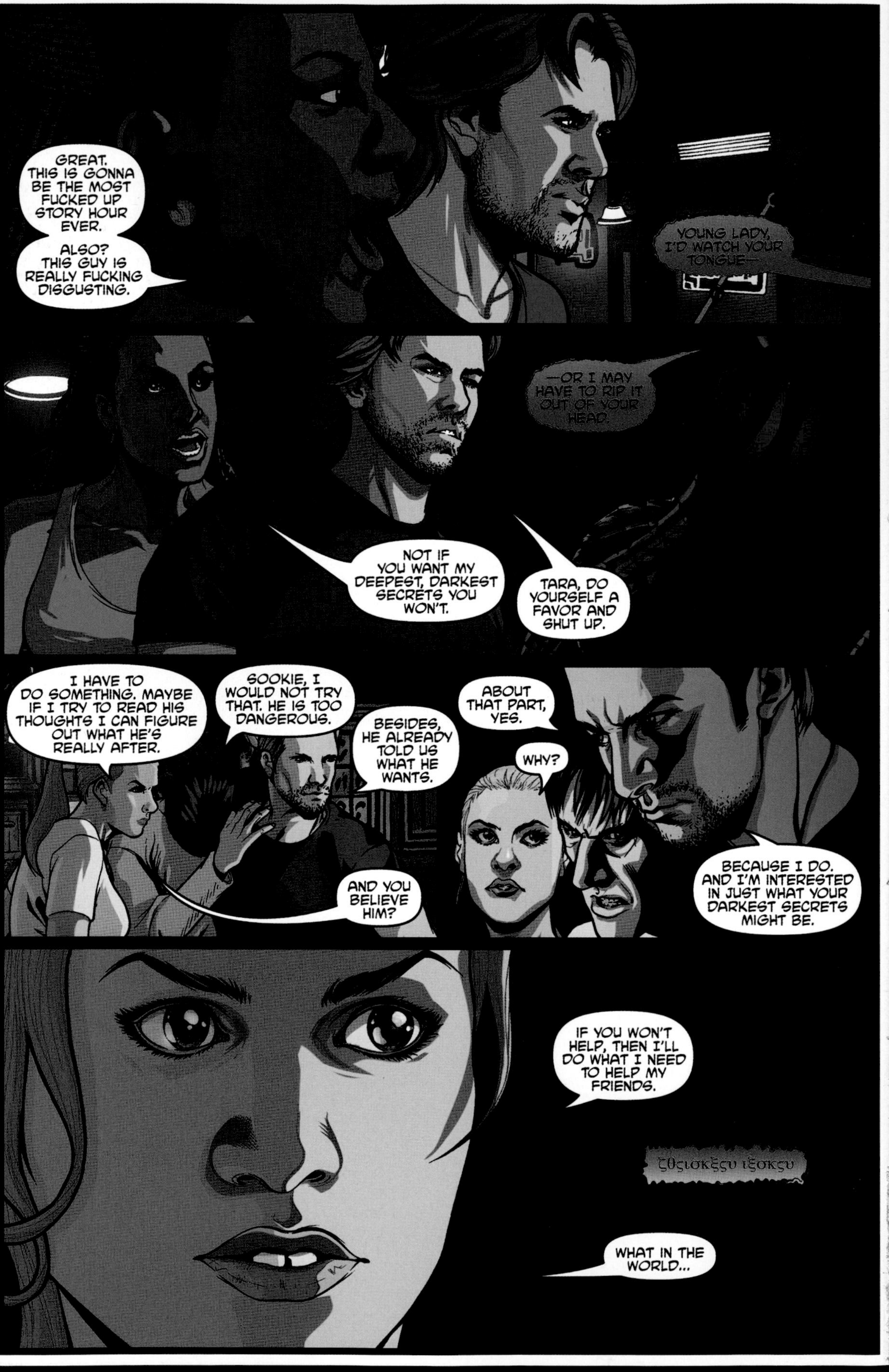
GREAT. THIS IS GONNA BE THE MOST FUCKED UP STORY HOUR EVER.
ALSO? THIS GUY IS REALLY FUCKING DISGUSTING.
YOUNG LADY, I'D WATCH YOUR TONGUE—
—OR I MAY HAVE TO RIP IT OUT OF YOUR HEAD.
NOT IF YOU WANT MY DEEPEST, DARKEST SECRETS YOU WON'T.
TARA, DO YOURSELF A FAVOR AND SHUT UP.
I HAVE TO DO SOMETHING. MAYBE IF I TRY TO READ HIS THOUGHTS I CAN FIGURE OUT WHAT HE'S REALLY AFTER.
SOOKIE, I WOULD NOT TRY THAT. HE IS TOO DANGEROUS.
BESIDES, HE ALREADY TOLD US WHAT HE WANTS.
AND YOU BELIEVE HIM?
ABOUT THAT PART, YES.
WHY?
BECAUSE I DO. AND I'M INTERESTED IN JUST WHAT YOUR DARKEST SECRETS MIGHT BE.
IF YOU WON'T HELP, THEN I'LL DO WHAT I NEED TO HELP MY FRIENDS.
ζθςισκξςυ ιξσκςυ
WHAT IN THE WORLD...

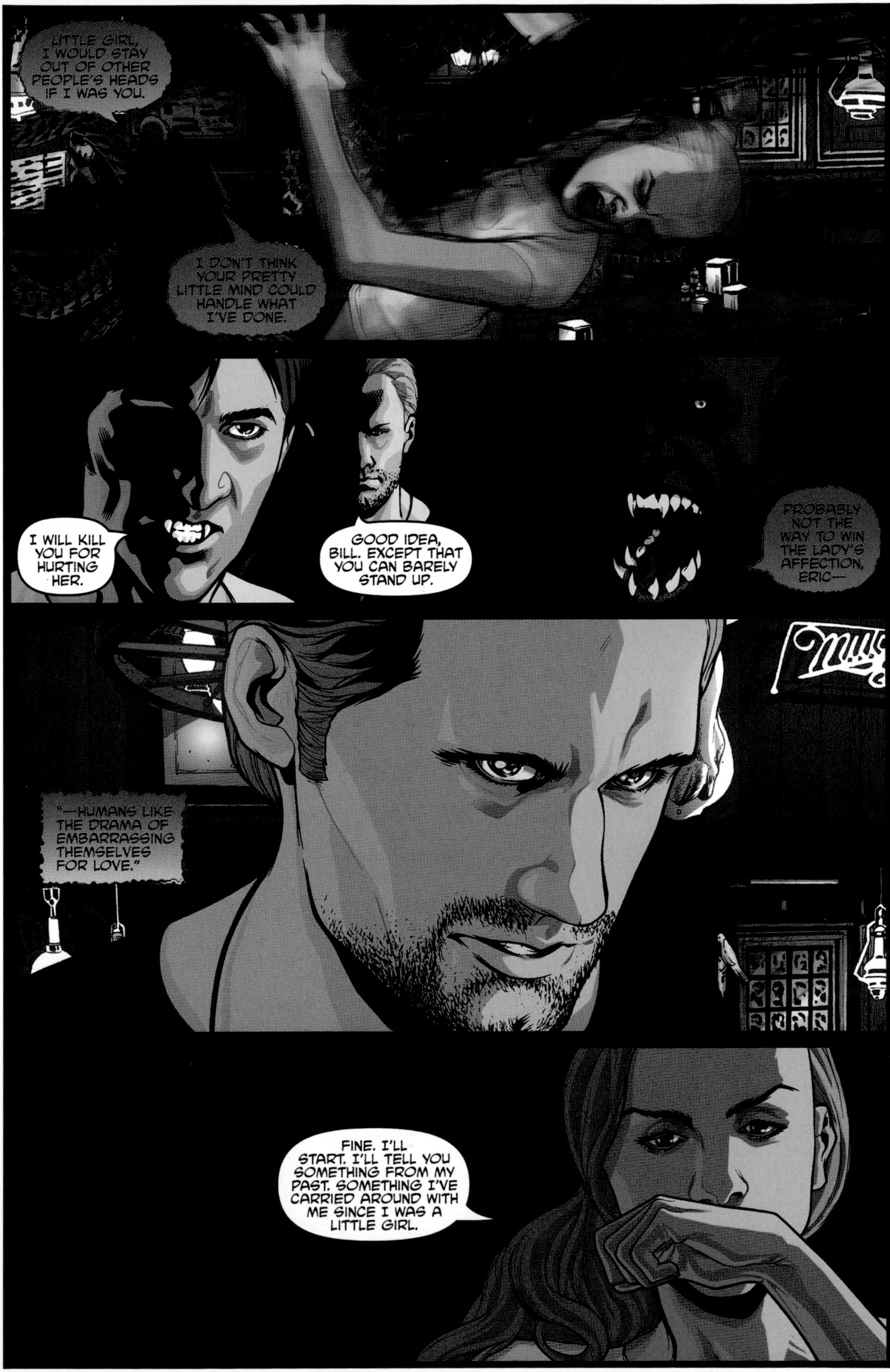
LITTLE GIRL, I WOULD STAY OUT OF OTHER PEOPLE'S HEADS IF I WAS YOU.
I DON'T THINK YOUR PRETTY LITTLE MIND COULD HANDLE WHAT I'VE DONE.
I WILL KILL YOU FOR HURTING HER.
GOOD IDEA, BILL. EXCEPT THAT YOU CAN BARELY STAND UP.
PROBABLY NOT THE WAY TO WIN THE LADY'S AFFECTION, ERIC—
"—HUMANS LIKE THE DRAMA OF EMBARRASSING THEMSELVES FOR LOVE."
FINE. I'LL START. I'LL TELL YOU SOMETHING FROM MY PAST. SOMETHING I'VE CARRIED AROUND WITH ME SINCE I WAS A LITTLE GIRL.

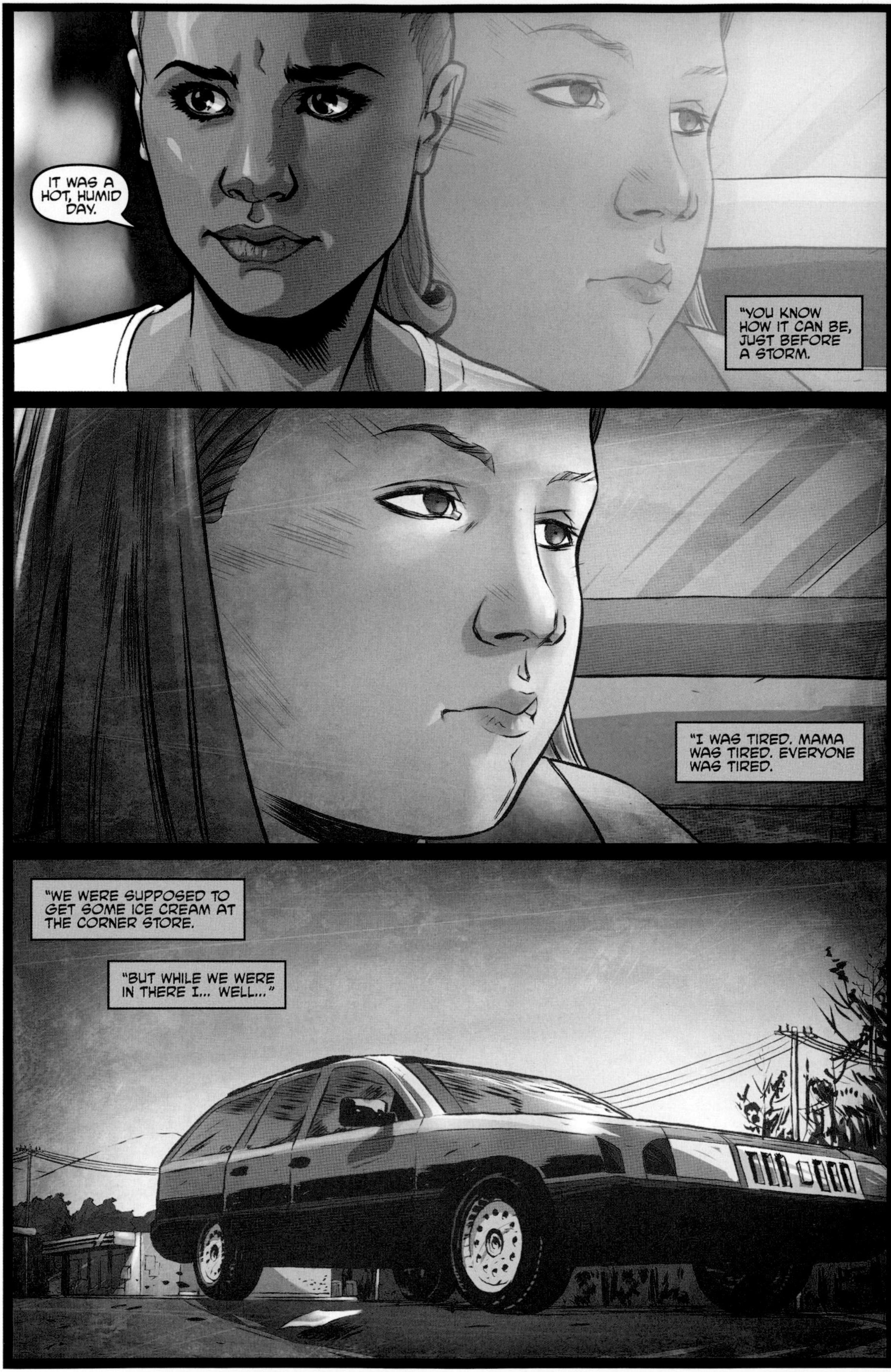
IT WAS A HOT, HUMID DAY.
"YOU KNOW HOW IT CAN BE, JUST BEFORE A STORM.
"I WAS TIRED. MAMA WAS TIRED. EVERYONE WAS TIRED.
"WE WERE SUPPOSED TO GET SOME ICE CREAM AT THE CORNER STORE.
"BUT WHILE WE WERE IN THERE I... WELL..."

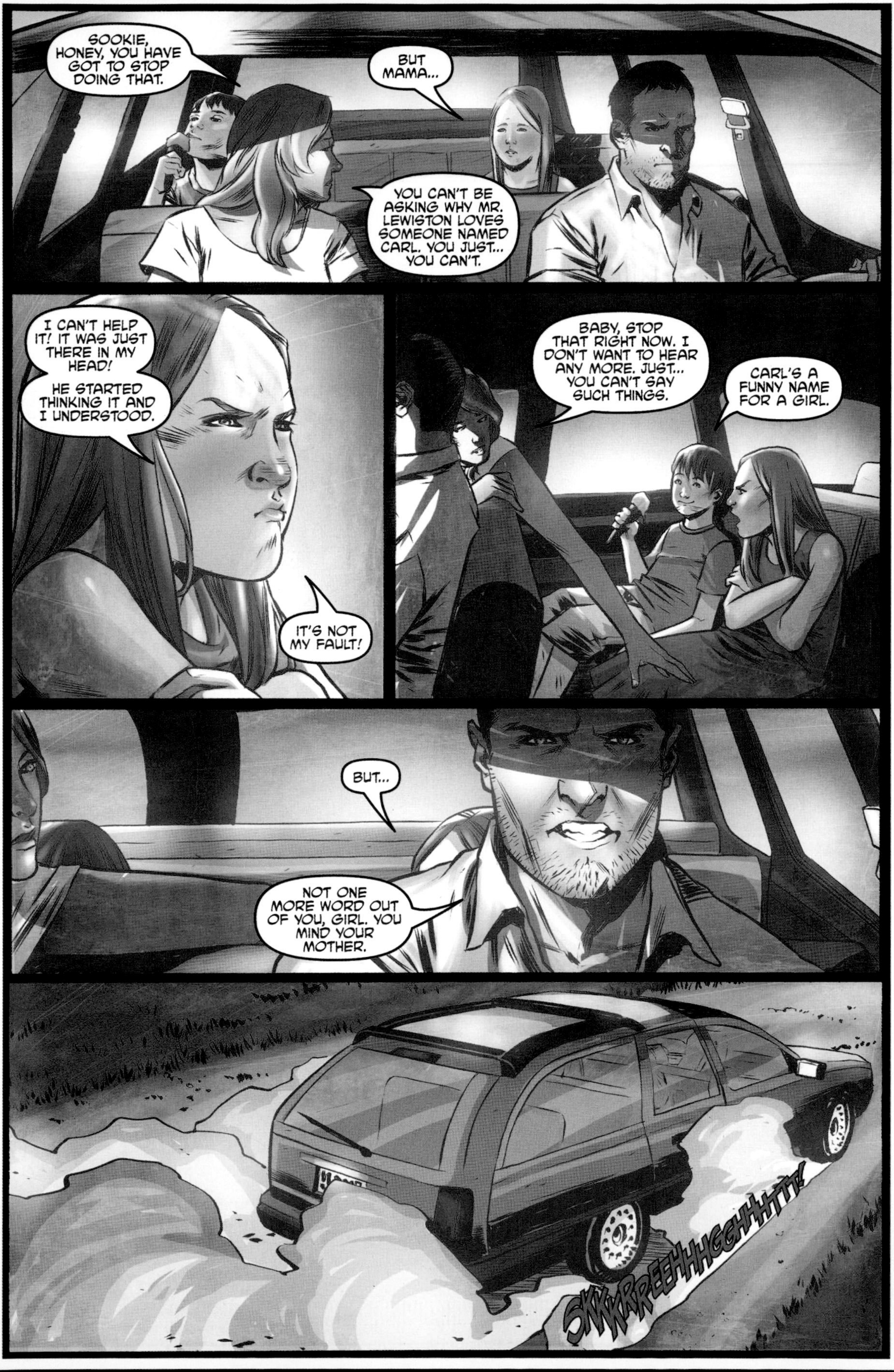
SOOKIE, HONEY, YOU HAVE GOT TO STOP DOING THAT.
BUT MAMA...
YOU CAN'T BE ASKING WHY MR. LEWISTON LOVES SOMEONE NAMED CARL. YOU JUST... YOU CAN'T.
I CAN'T HELP IT! IT WAS JUST THERE IN MY HEAD!
HE STARTED THINKING IT AND I UNDERSTOOD.
IT'S NOT MY FAULT!
BABY, STOP THAT RIGHT NOW. I DON'T WANT TO HEAR ANY MORE. JUST... YOU CAN'T SAY SUCH THINGS.
CARL'S A FUNNY NAME FOR A GIRL.
BUT...
NOT ONE MORE WORD OUT OF YOU, GIRL. YOU MIND YOUR MOTHER.
SKKKRREEHHHGGHHHTTT!

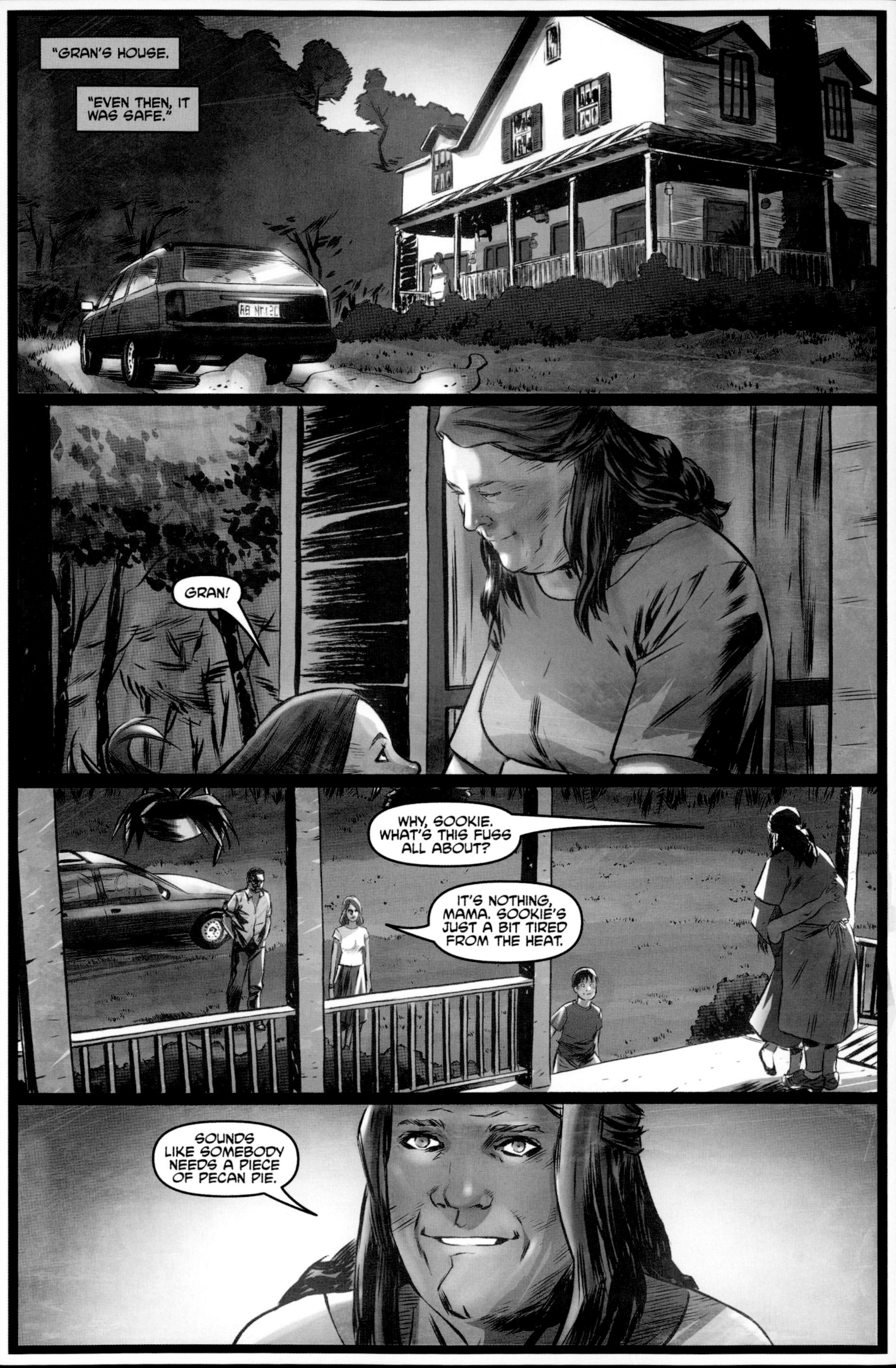
"GRAN'S HOUSE.
"EVEN THEN, IT WAS SAFE."
GRAN!
WHY, SOOKIE. WHAT'S THIS FUSS ALL ABOUT?
IT'S NOTHING, MAMA. SOOKIE'S JUST A BIT TIRED FROM THE HEAT.
SOUNDS LIKE SOMEBODY NEEDS A PIECE OF PECAN PIE.

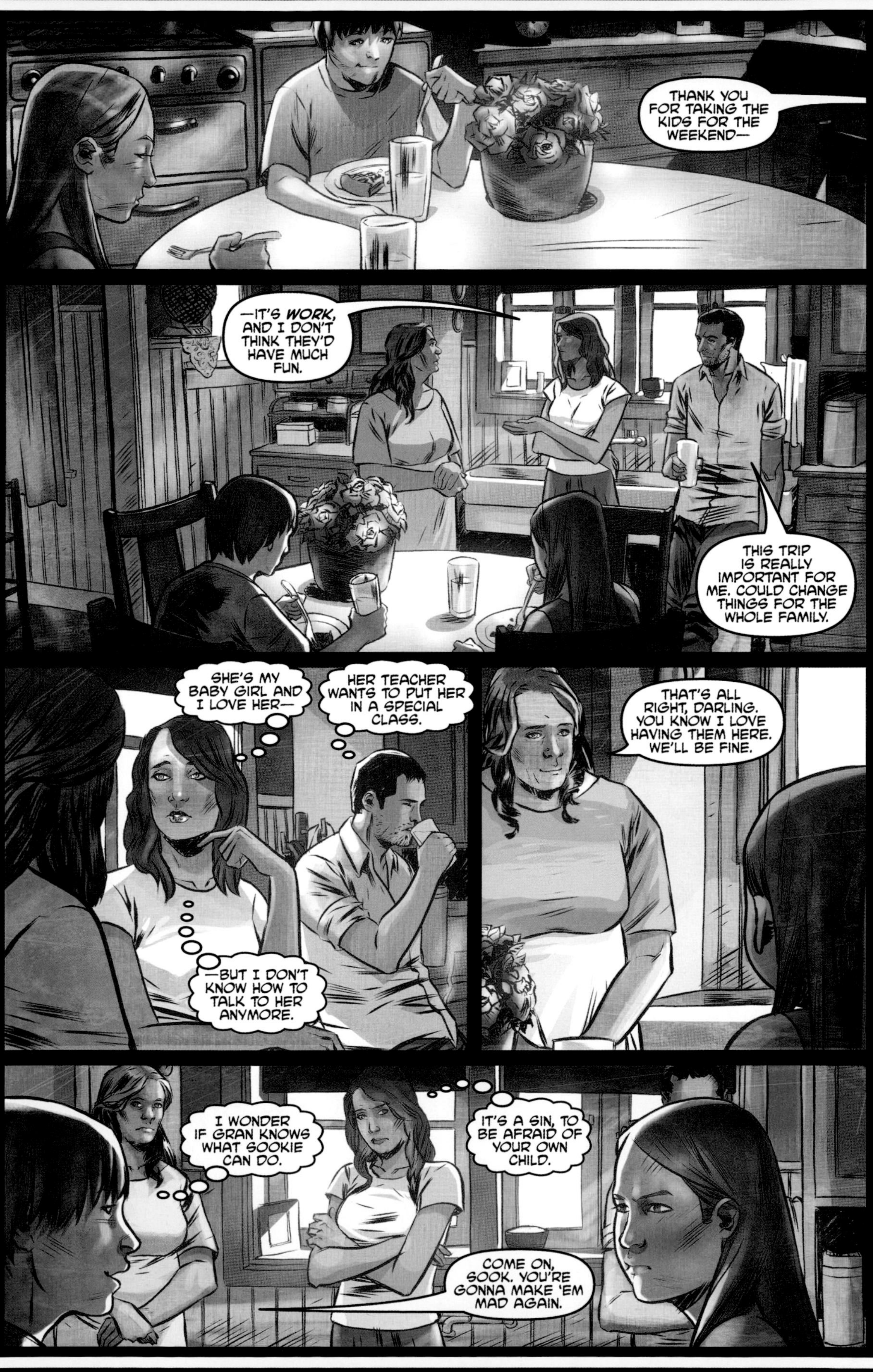
THANK YOU FOR TAKING THE KIDS FOR THE WEEKEND—
—IT'S *WORK*, AND I DON'T THINK THEY'D HAVE MUCH FUN.
THIS TRIP IS REALLY IMPORTANT FOR ME. COULD CHANGE THINGS FOR THE WHOLE FAMILY.
SHE'S MY BABY GIRL AND I LOVE HER—
HER TEACHER WANTS TO PUT HER IN A SPECIAL CLASS.
—BUT I DON'T KNOW HOW TO TALK TO HER ANYMORE.
THAT'S ALL RIGHT, DARLING. YOU KNOW I LOVE HAVING THEM HERE. WE'LL BE FINE.
I WONDER IF GRAN KNOWS WHAT SOOKIE CAN DO.
IT'S A SIN, TO BE AFRAID OF YOUR OWN CHILD.
COME ON, SOOK. YOU'RE GONNA MAKE 'EM MAD AGAIN.

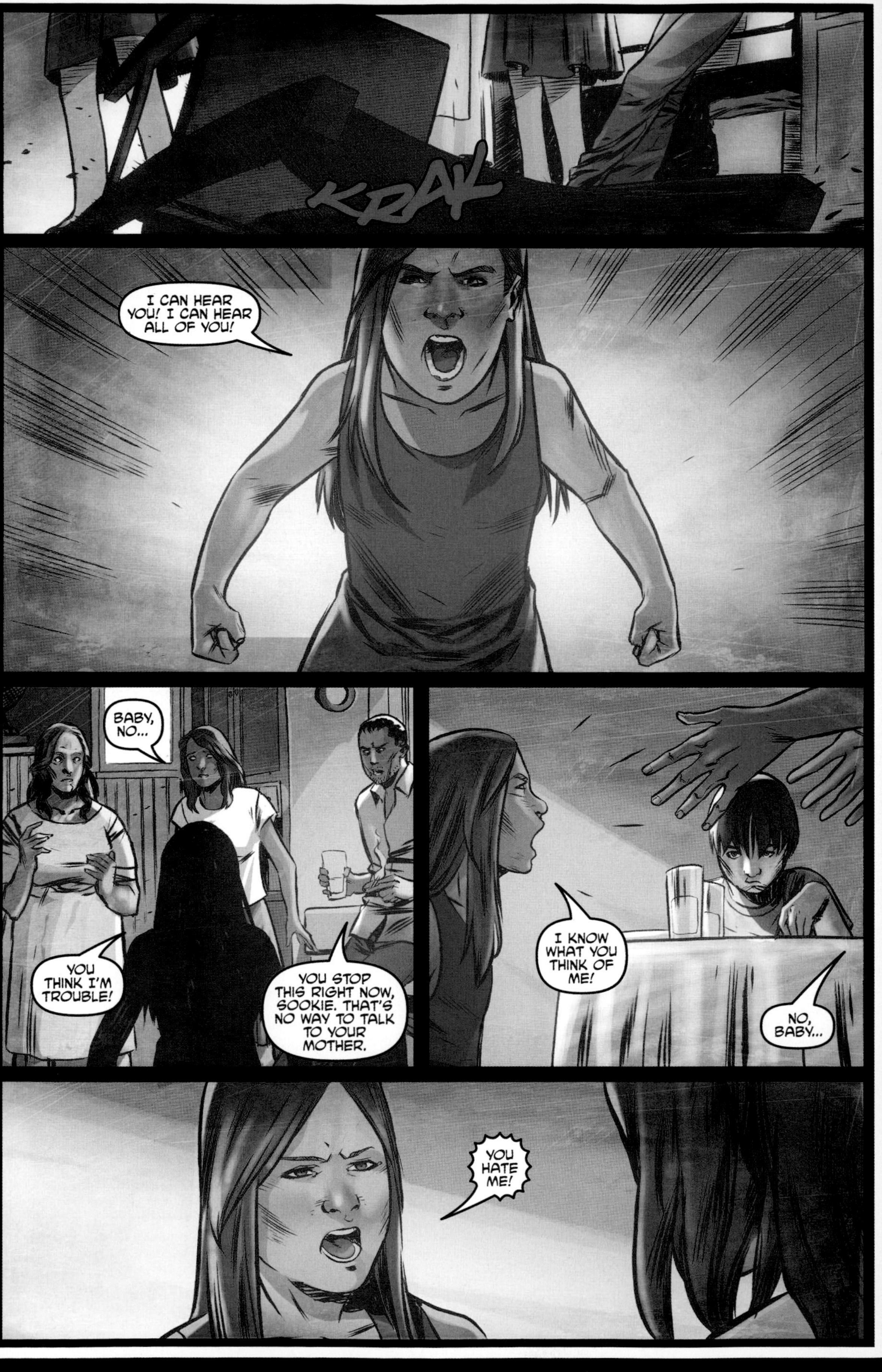
KRAK
I CAN HEAR YOU! I CAN HEAR ALL OF YOU!
BABY, NO...
YOU THINK I'M TROUBLE!
YOU STOP THIS RIGHT NOW, SOOKIE. THAT'S NO WAY TO TALK TO YOUR MOTHER.
I KNOW WHAT YOU THINK OF ME!
NO, BABY...
YOU HATE ME!

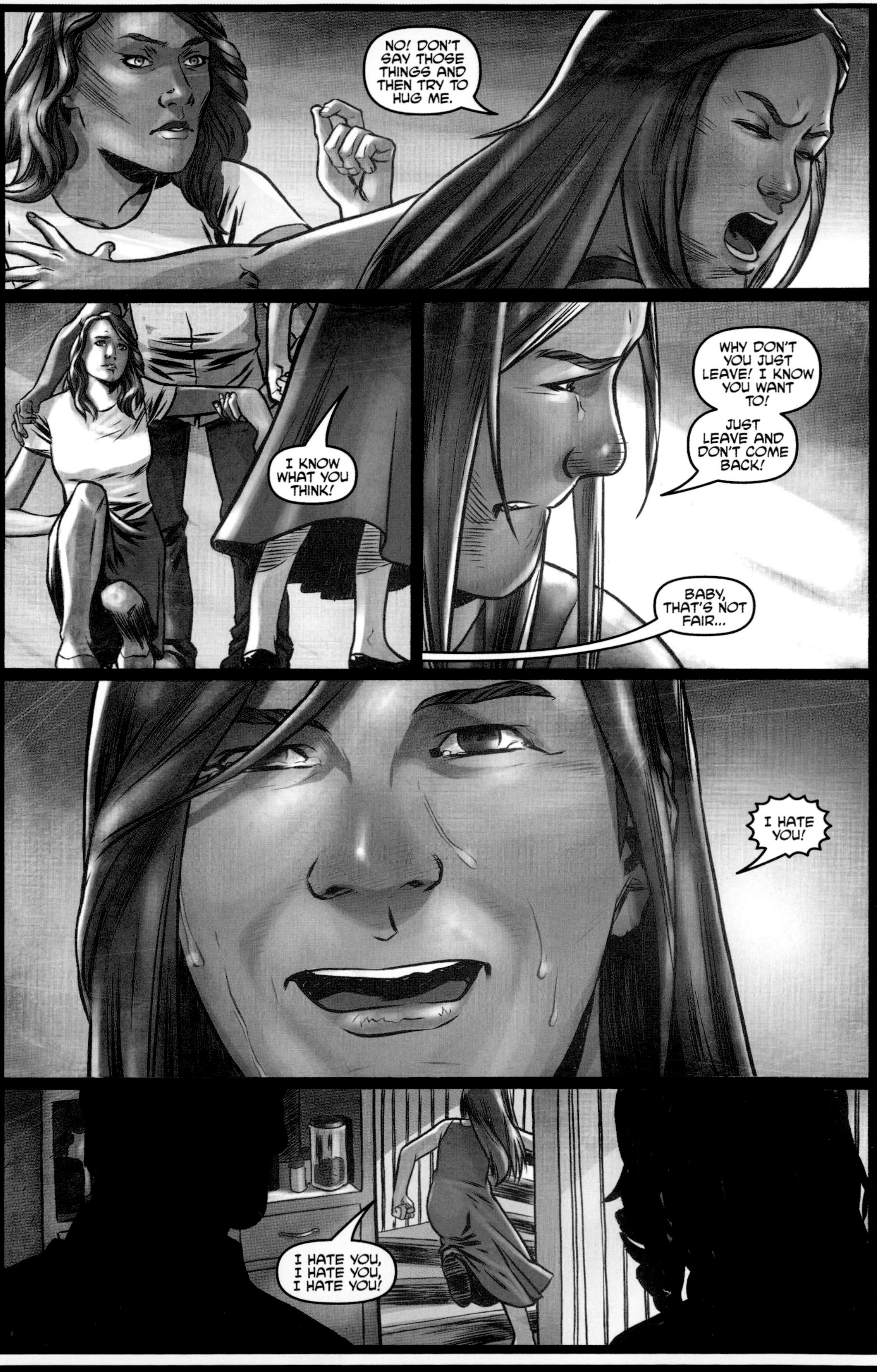
NO! DON'T SAY THOSE THINGS AND THEN TRY TO HUG ME.
I KNOW WHAT YOU THINK!
WHY DON'T YOU JUST LEAVE! I KNOW YOU WANT TO!
JUST LEAVE AND DON'T COME BACK!
BABY, THAT'S NOT FAIR...
I HATE YOU!
I HATE YOU, I HATE YOU, I HATE YOU!

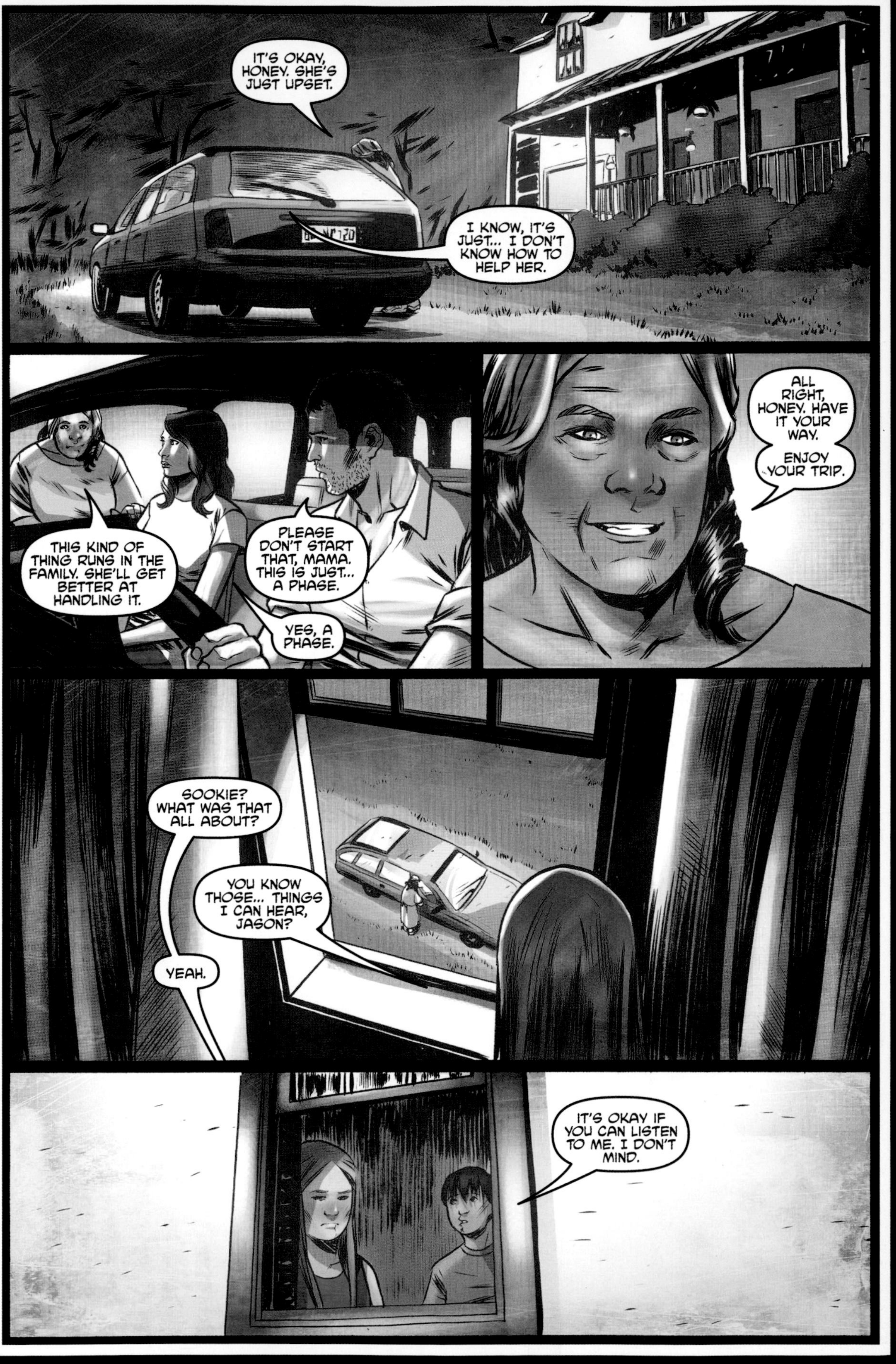
IT'S OKAY, HONEY. SHE'S JUST UPSET.
I KNOW, IT'S JUST... I DON'T KNOW HOW TO HELP HER.
THIS KIND OF THING RUNS IN THE FAMILY. SHE'LL GET BETTER AT HANDLING IT.
PLEASE DON'T START THAT, MAMA. THIS IS JUST... A PHASE.
YES, A PHASE.
ALL RIGHT, HONEY. HAVE IT YOUR WAY.
ENJOY YOUR TRIP.
SOOKIE? WHAT WAS THAT ALL ABOUT?
YOU KNOW THOSE... THINGS I CAN HEAR, JASON?
YEAH.
IT'S OKAY IF YOU CAN LISTEN TO ME. I DON'T MIND.

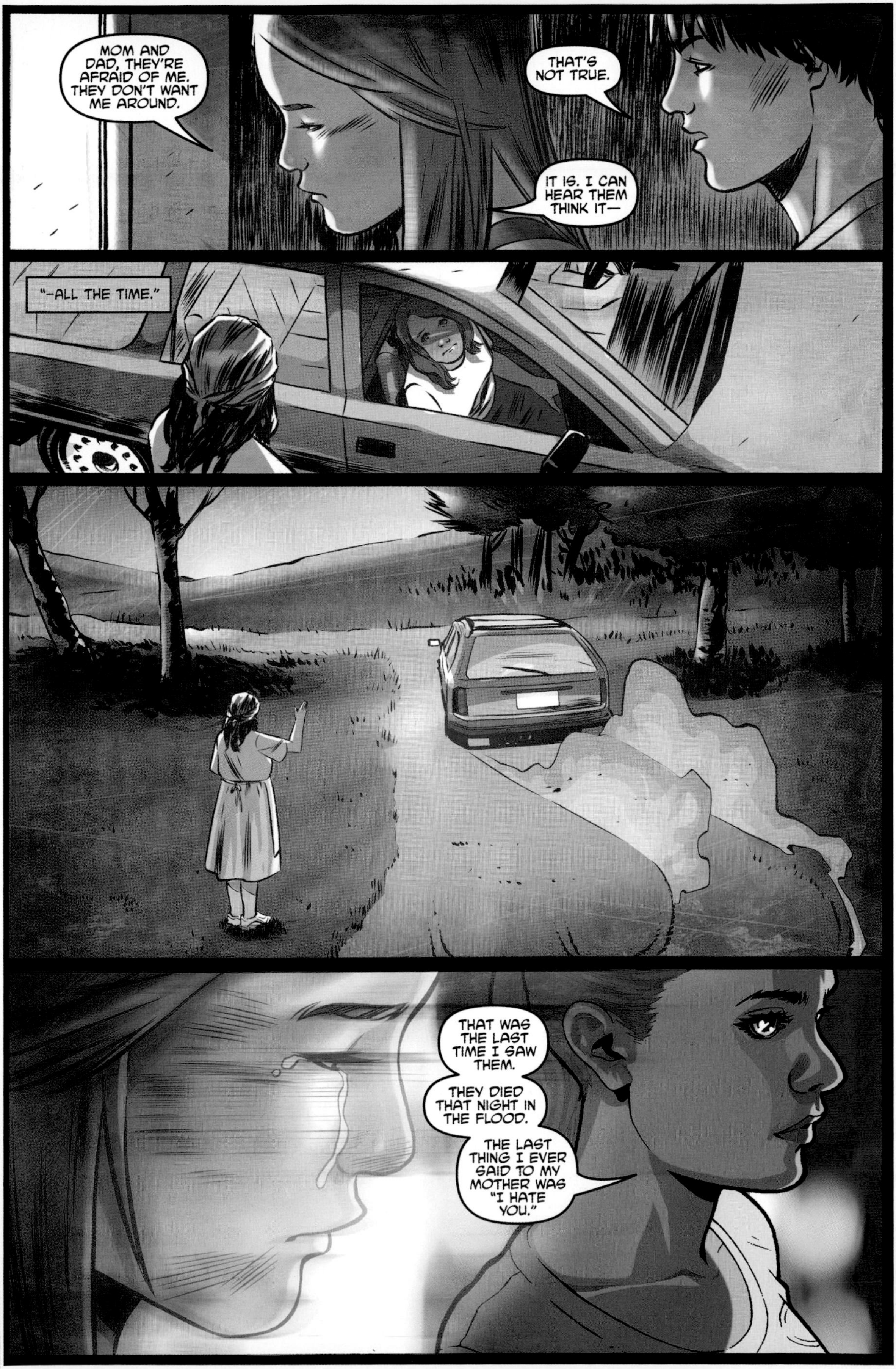
MOM AND DAD, THEY'RE AFRAID OF ME. THEY DON'T WANT ME AROUND.
THAT'S NOT TRUE.
IT IS. I CAN HEAR THEM THINK IT—
"—ALL THE TIME."
THAT WAS THE LAST TIME I SAW THEM.
THEY DIED THAT NIGHT IN THE FLOOD.
THE LAST THING I EVER SAID TO MY MOTHER WAS "I HATE YOU."

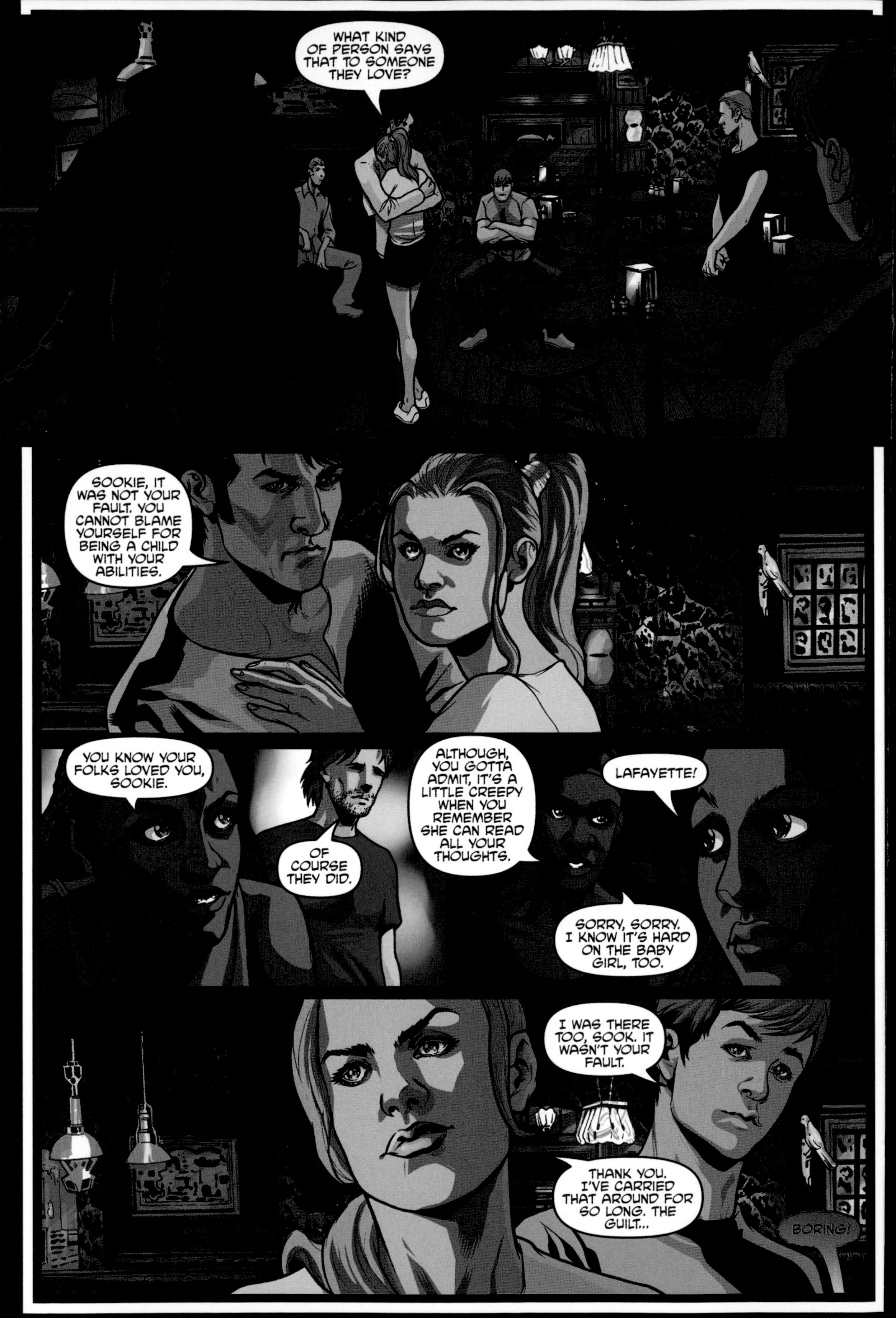
WHAT KIND OF PERSON SAYS THAT TO SOMEONE THEY LOVE?
SOOKIE, IT WAS NOT YOUR FAULT. YOU CANNOT BLAME YOURSELF FOR BEING A CHILD WITH YOUR ABILITIES.
YOU KNOW YOUR FOLKS LOVED YOU, SOOKIE.
OF COURSE THEY DID.
ALTHOUGH, YOU GOTTA ADMIT, IT'S A LITTLE CREEPY WHEN YOU REMEMBER SHE CAN READ ALL YOUR THOUGHTS.
LAFAYETTE!
SORRY, SORRY. I KNOW IT'S HARD ON THE BABY GIRL, TOO.
I WAS THERE TOO, SOOK. IT WASN'T YOUR FAULT.
THANK YOU. I'VE CARRIED THAT AROUND FOR SO LONG. THE GUILT...
BORING!

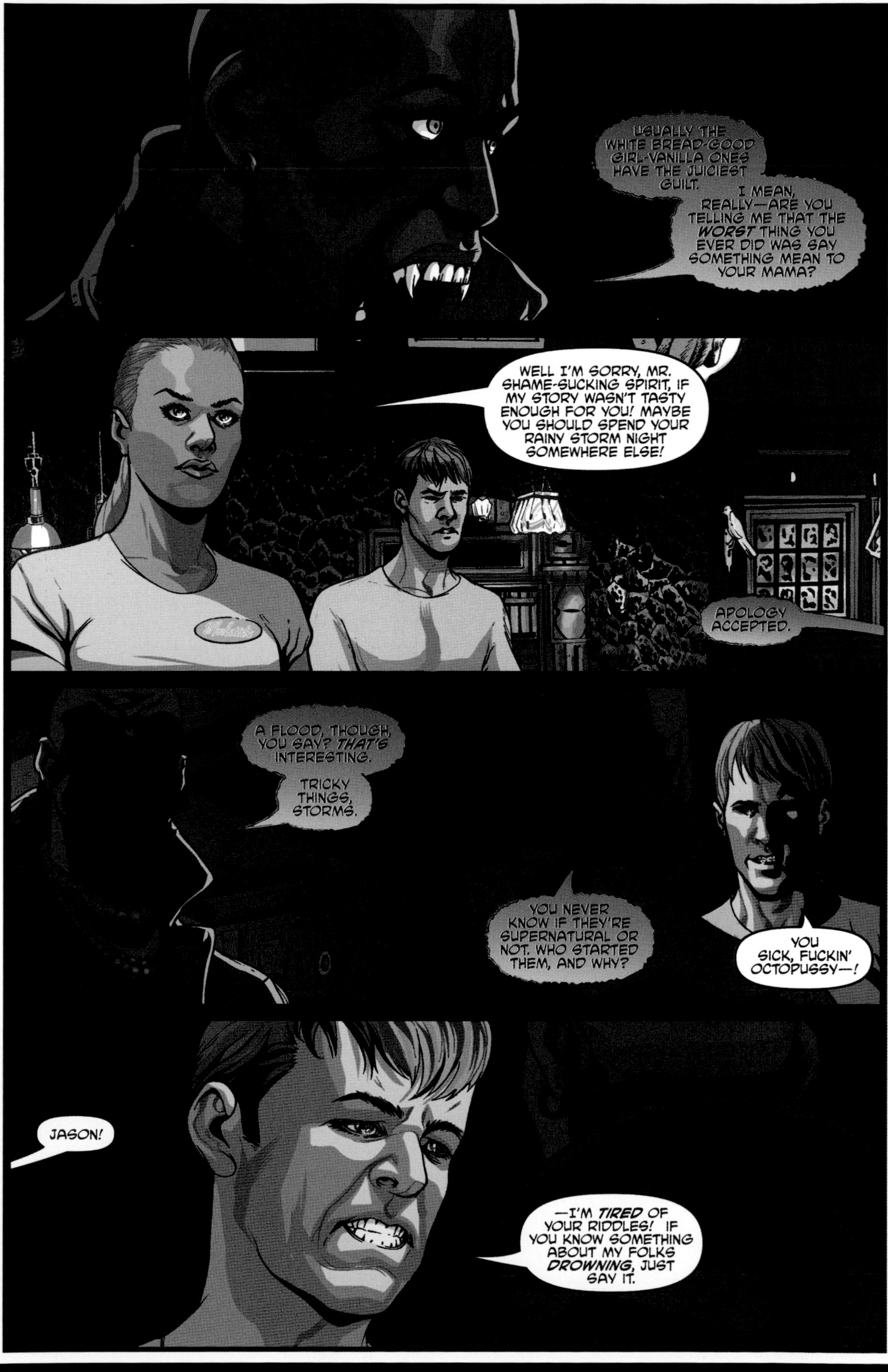
USUALLY THE WHITE BREAD-GOOD GIRL-VANILLA ONES HAVE THE JUICIEST GUILT.
I MEAN, REALLY—ARE YOU TELLING ME THAT THE *WORST* THING YOU EVER DID WAS SAY SOMETHING MEAN TO YOUR MAMA?
WELL I'M SORRY, MR. SHAME-SUCKING SPIRIT, IF MY STORY WASN'T TASTY ENOUGH FOR YOU! MAYBE YOU SHOULD SPEND YOUR RAINY STORM NIGHT SOMEWHERE ELSE!
APOLOGY ACCEPTED.
A FLOOD, THOUGH, YOU SAY? *THAT'S* INTERESTING.
TRICKY THINGS, STORMS.
YOU NEVER KNOW IF THEY'RE SUPERNATURAL OR NOT. WHO STARTED THEM, AND WHY?
YOU SICK, FUCKIN' OCTOPUSSY—!
JASON!
—I'M *TIRED* OF YOUR RIDDLES! IF YOU KNOW SOMETHING ABOUT MY FOLKS *DROWNING*, JUST SAY IT.

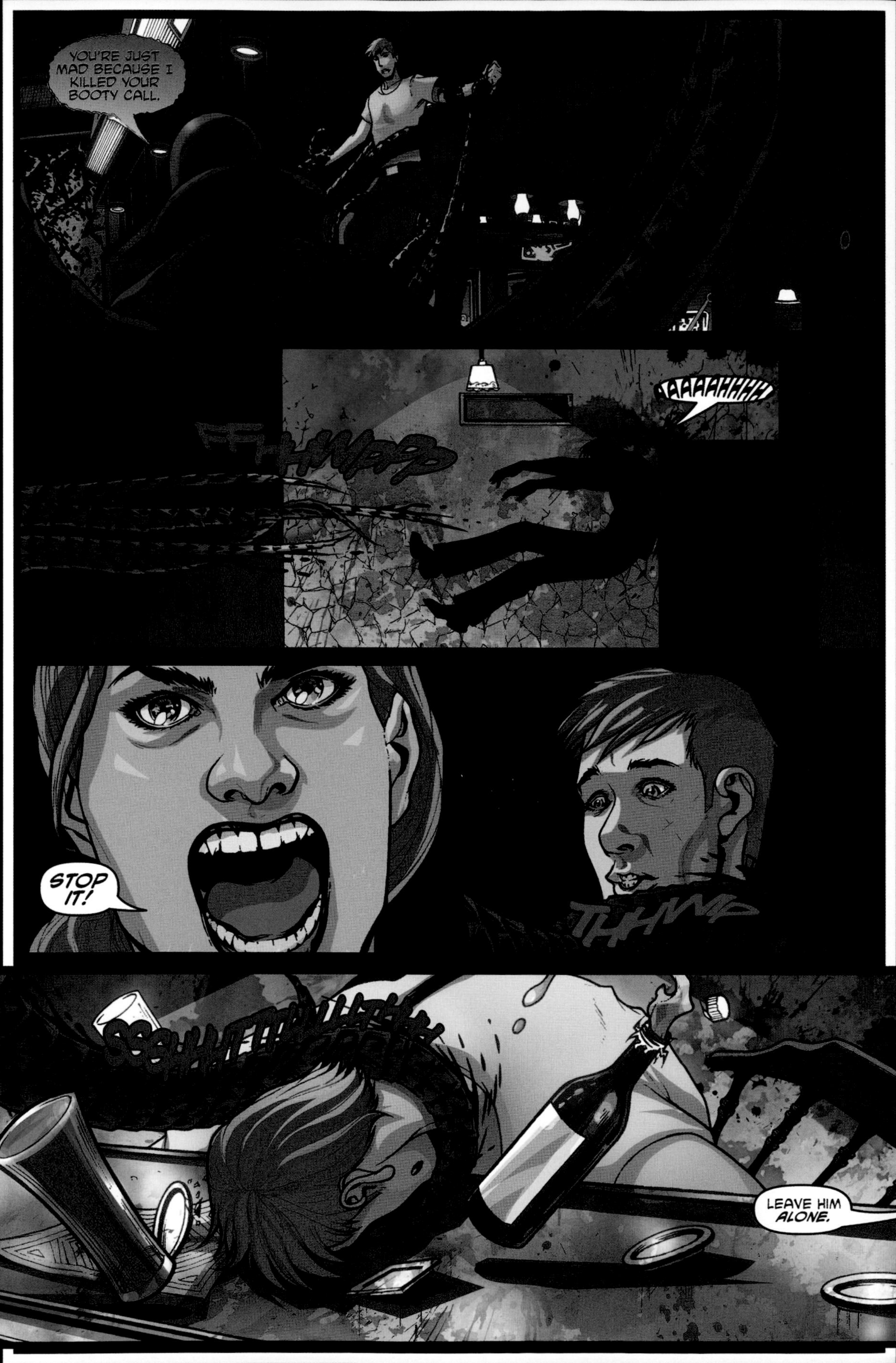
YOU'RE JUST MAD BECAUSE I KILLED YOUR BOOTY CALL.
STOP IT!
LEAVE HIM ALONE.

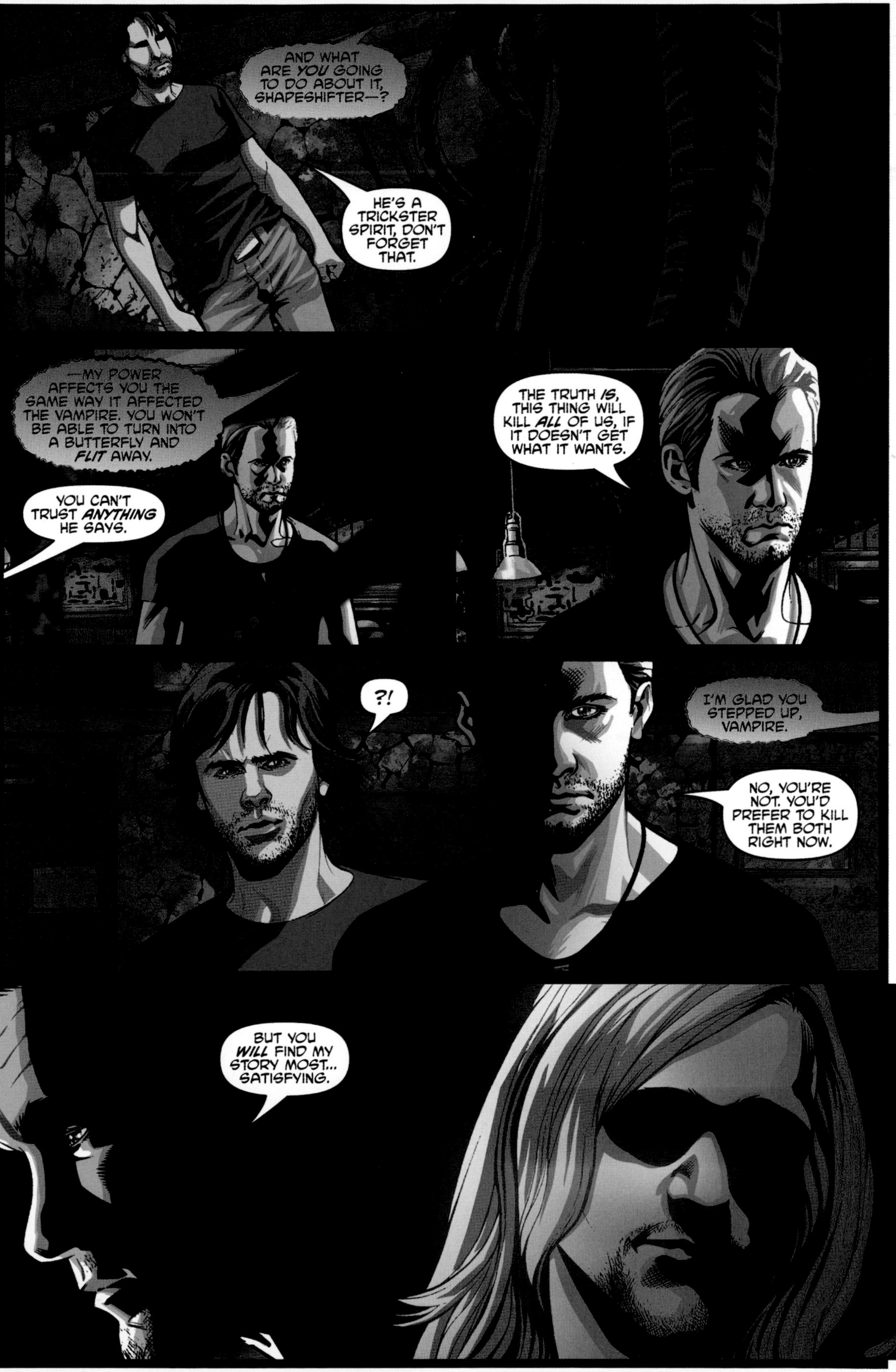
AND WHAT ARE *YOU* GOING TO DO ABOUT IT, SHAPESHIFTER—?
HE'S A TRICKSTER SPIRIT, DON'T FORGET THAT.
—MY POWER AFFECTS YOU THE SAME WAY IT AFFECTED THE VAMPIRE. YOU WON'T BE ABLE TO TURN INTO A BUTTERFLY AND *FLIT* AWAY.
YOU CAN'T TRUST *ANYTHING* HE SAYS.
THE TRUTH *IS*, THIS THING WILL KILL *ALL* OF US, IF IT DOESN'T GET WHAT IT WANTS.
?!
I'M GLAD YOU STEPPED UP, VAMPIRE.
NO, YOU'RE NOT. YOU'D PREFER TO KILL THEM BOTH RIGHT NOW.
BUT YOU *WILL* FIND MY STORY MOST... SATISFYING.

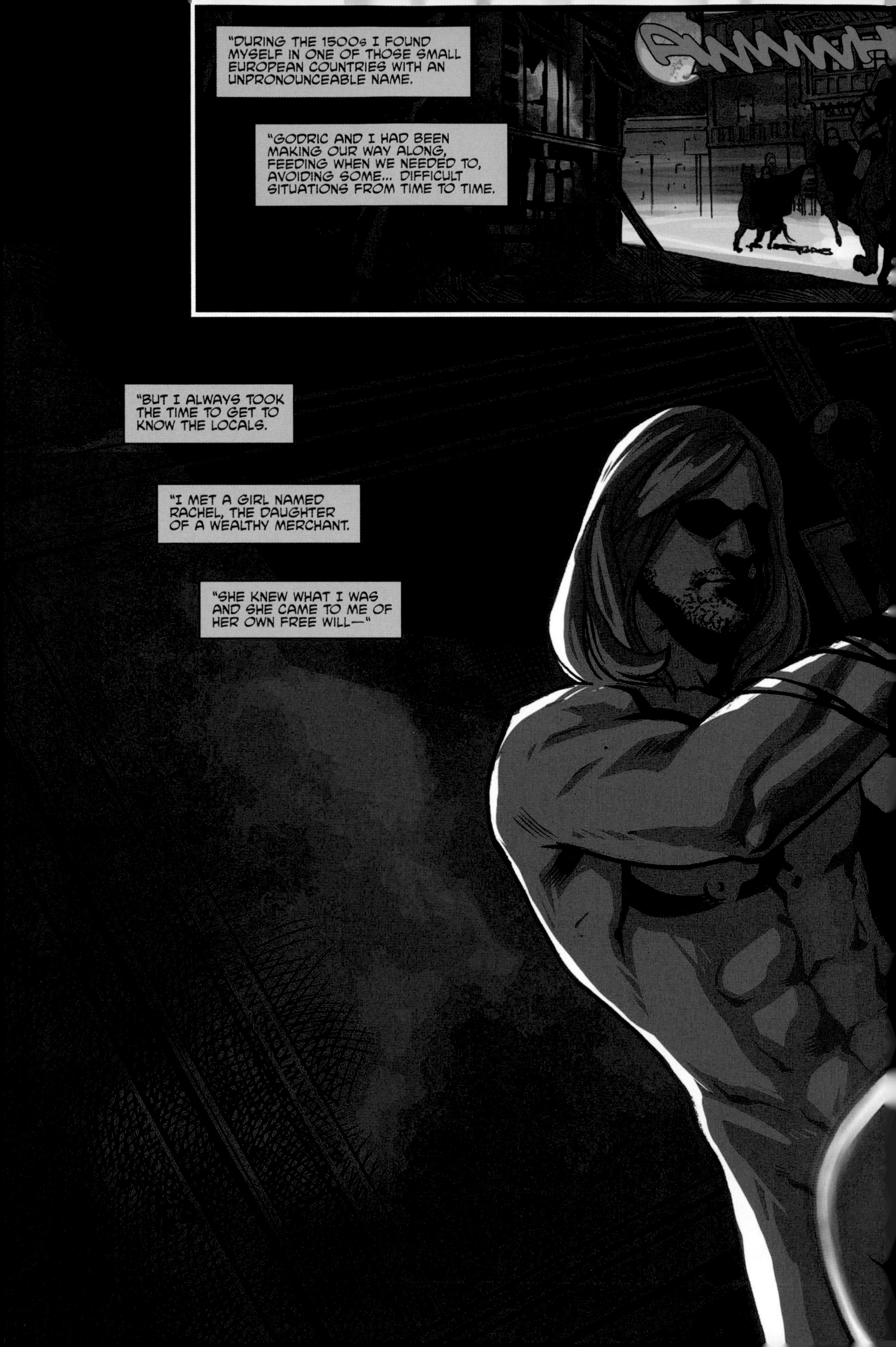
"DURING THE 1500s I FOUND MYSELF IN ONE OF THOSE SMALL EUROPEAN COUNTRIES WITH AN UNPRONOUNCEABLE NAME.
"GODRIC AND I HAD BEEN MAKING OUR WAY ALONG, FEEDING WHEN WE NEEDED TO, AVOIDING SOME... DIFFICULT SITUATIONS FROM TIME TO TIME.
"BUT I ALWAYS TOOK THE TIME TO GET TO KNOW THE LOCALS.
"I MET A GIRL NAMED RACHEL, THE DAUGHTER OF A WEALTHY MERCHANT.
"SHE KNEW WHAT I WAS AND SHE CAME TO ME OF HER OWN FREE WILL—"

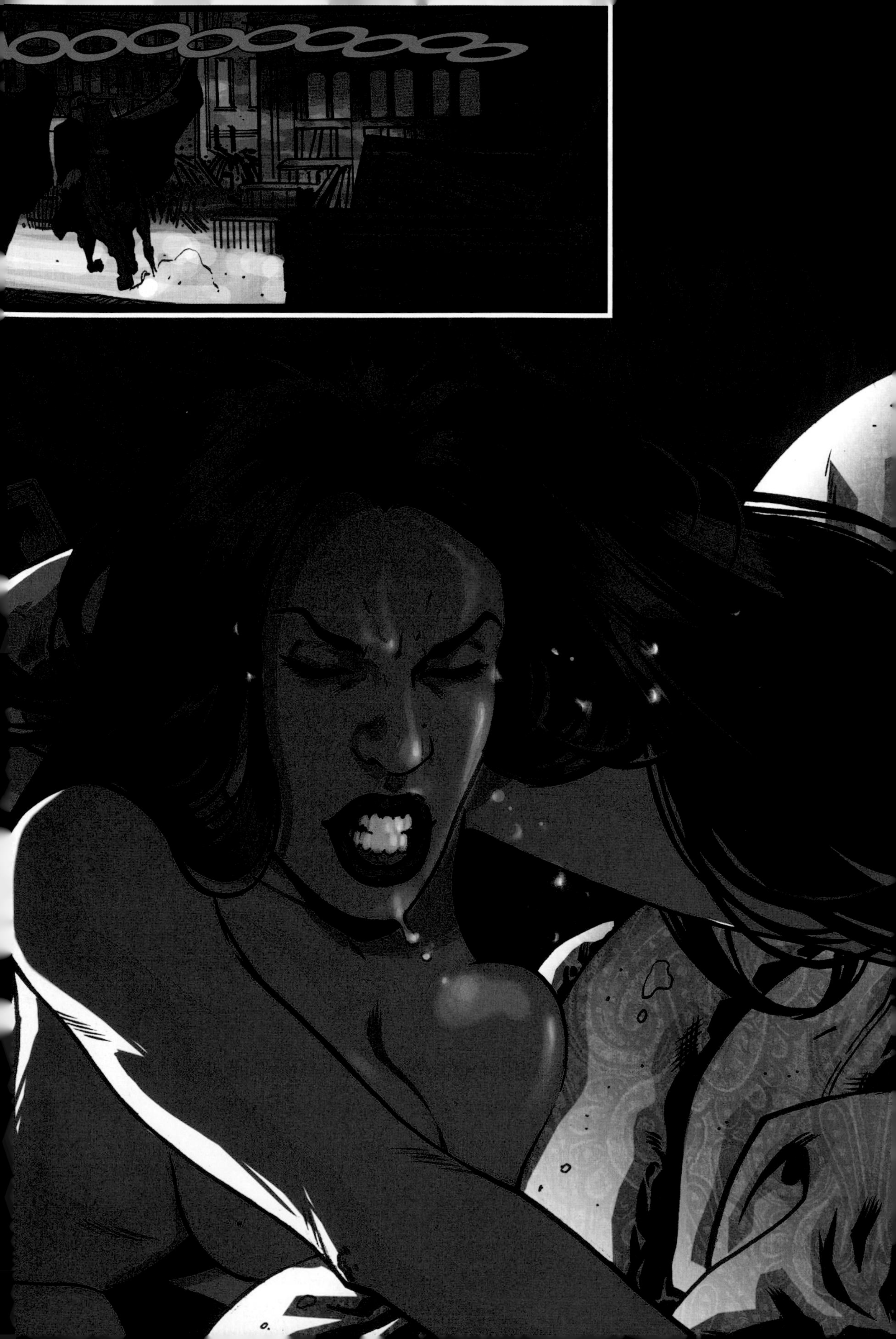

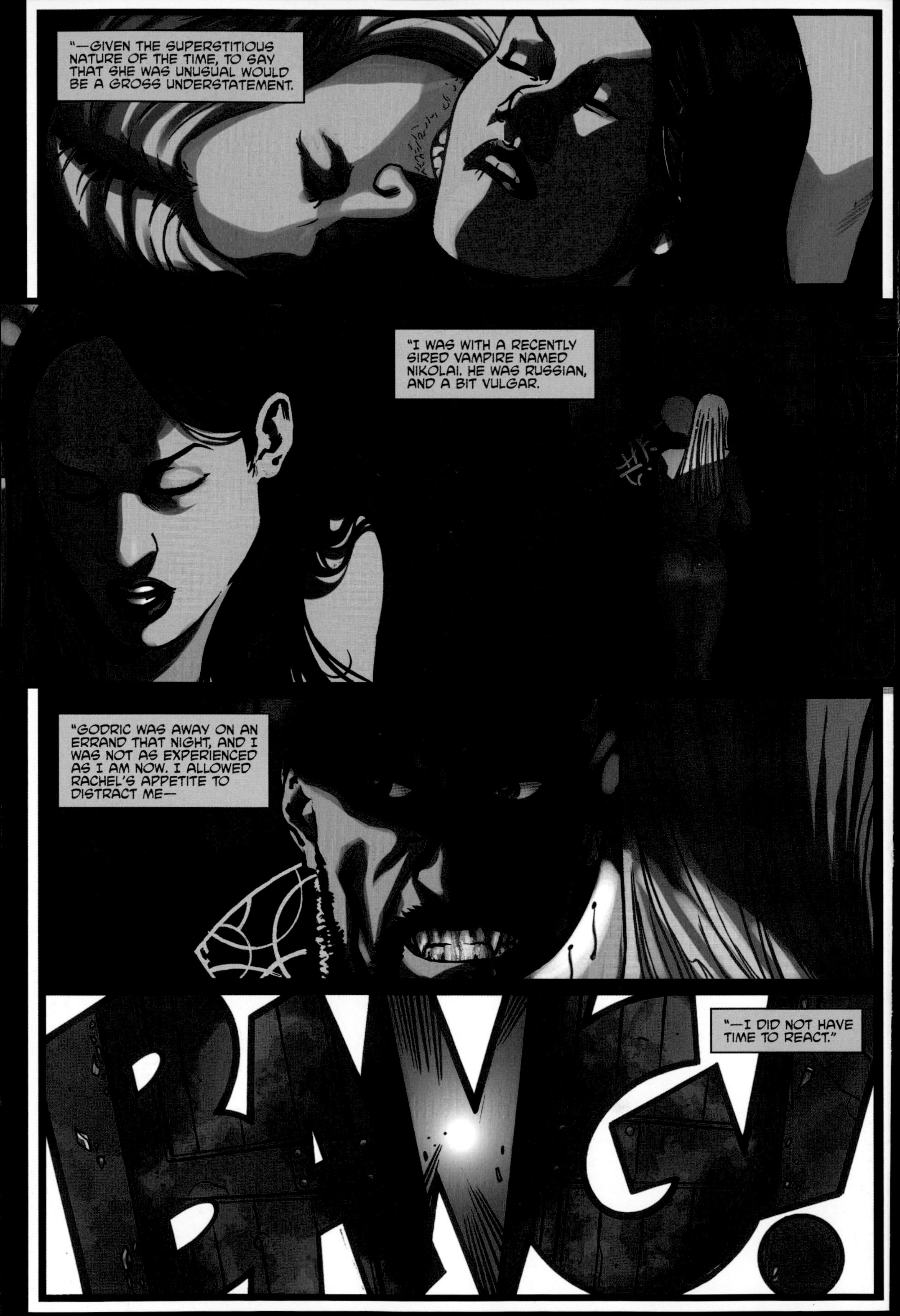
"—GIVEN THE SUPERSTITIOUS NATURE OF THE TIME, TO SAY THAT SHE WAS UNUSUAL WOULD BE A GROSS UNDERSTATEMENT.
"I WAS WITH A RECENTLY SIRED VAMPIRE NAMED NIKOLAI. HE WAS RUSSIAN, AND A BIT VULGAR.
"GODRIC WAS AWAY ON AN ERRAND THAT NIGHT, AND I WAS NOT AS EXPERIENCED AS I AM NOW. I ALLOWED RACHEL'S APPETITE TO DISTRACT ME—
"—I DID NOT HAVE TIME TO REACT."

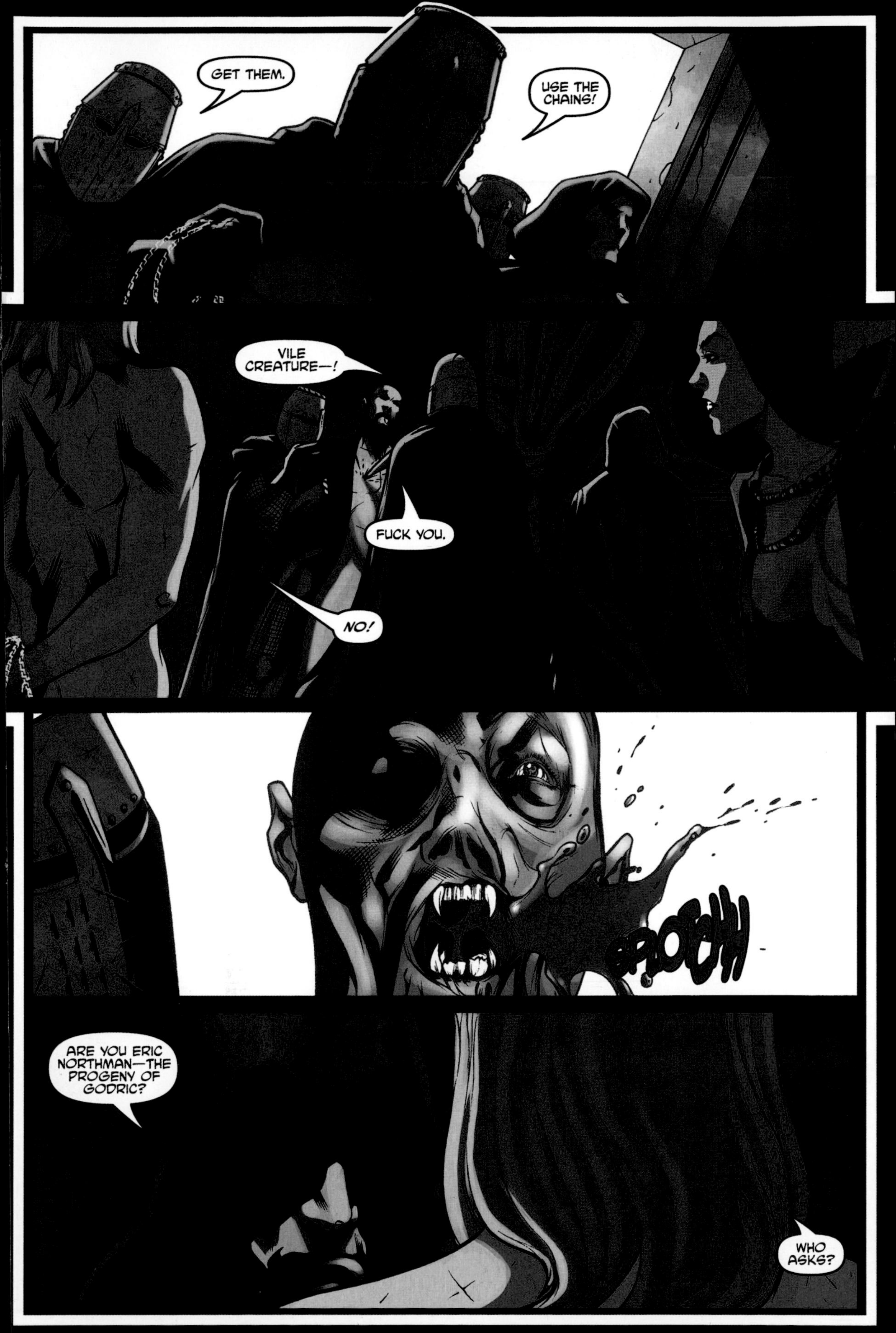
GET THEM.
USE THE CHAINS!
VILE CREATURE—!
FUCK YOU.
NO!
SPLOTCHH
ARE YOU ERIC NORTHMAN—THE PROGENY OF GODRIC?
WHO ASKS?

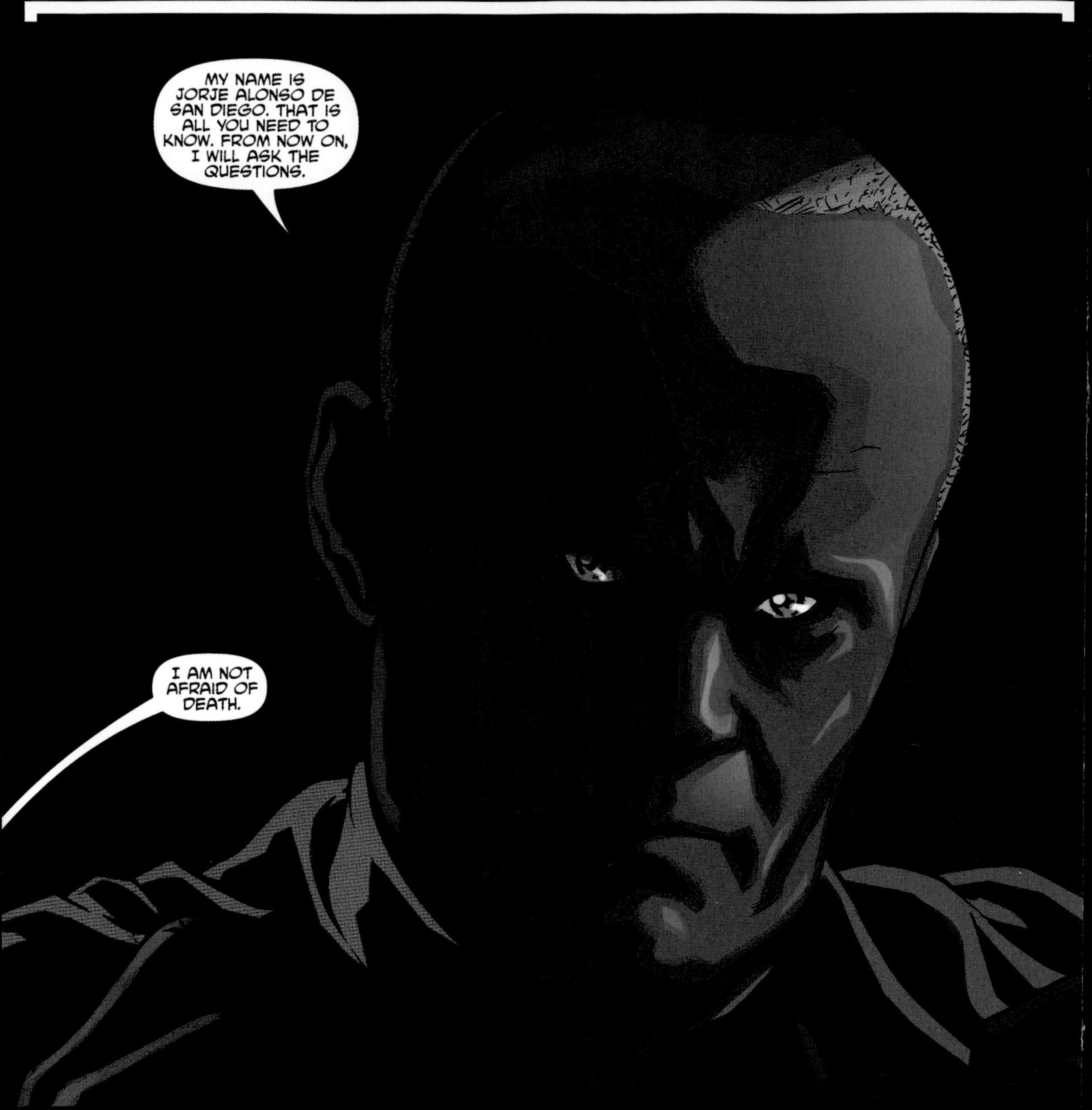
MY NAME IS JORJE ALONSO DE SAN DIEGO. THAT IS ALL YOU NEED TO KNOW. FROM NOW ON, I WILL ASK THE QUESTIONS.
I AM NOT AFRAID OF DEATH.

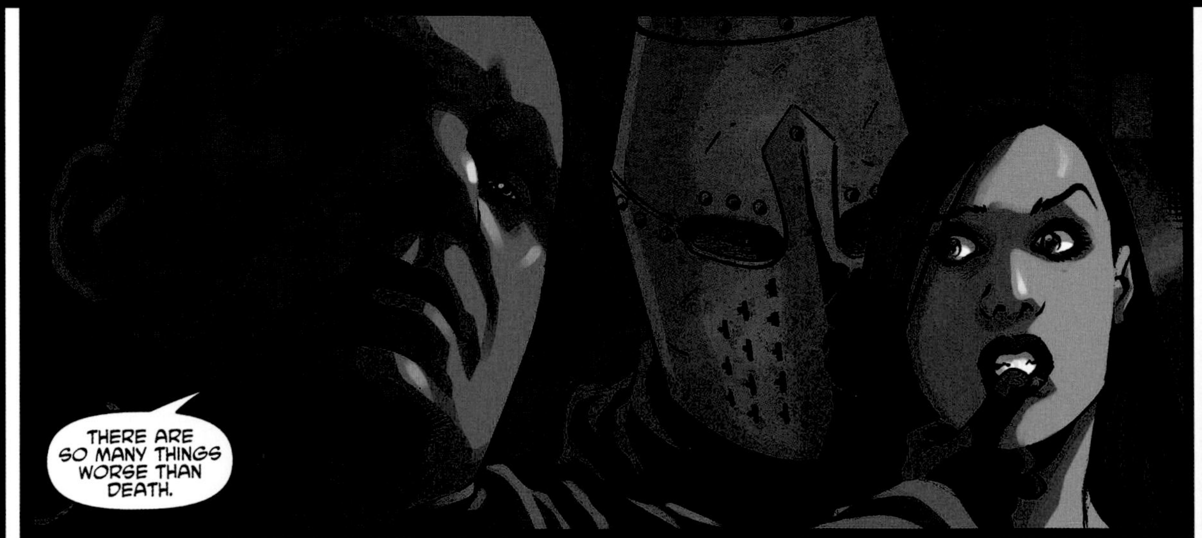
THERE ARE SO MANY THINGS WORSE THAN DEATH.

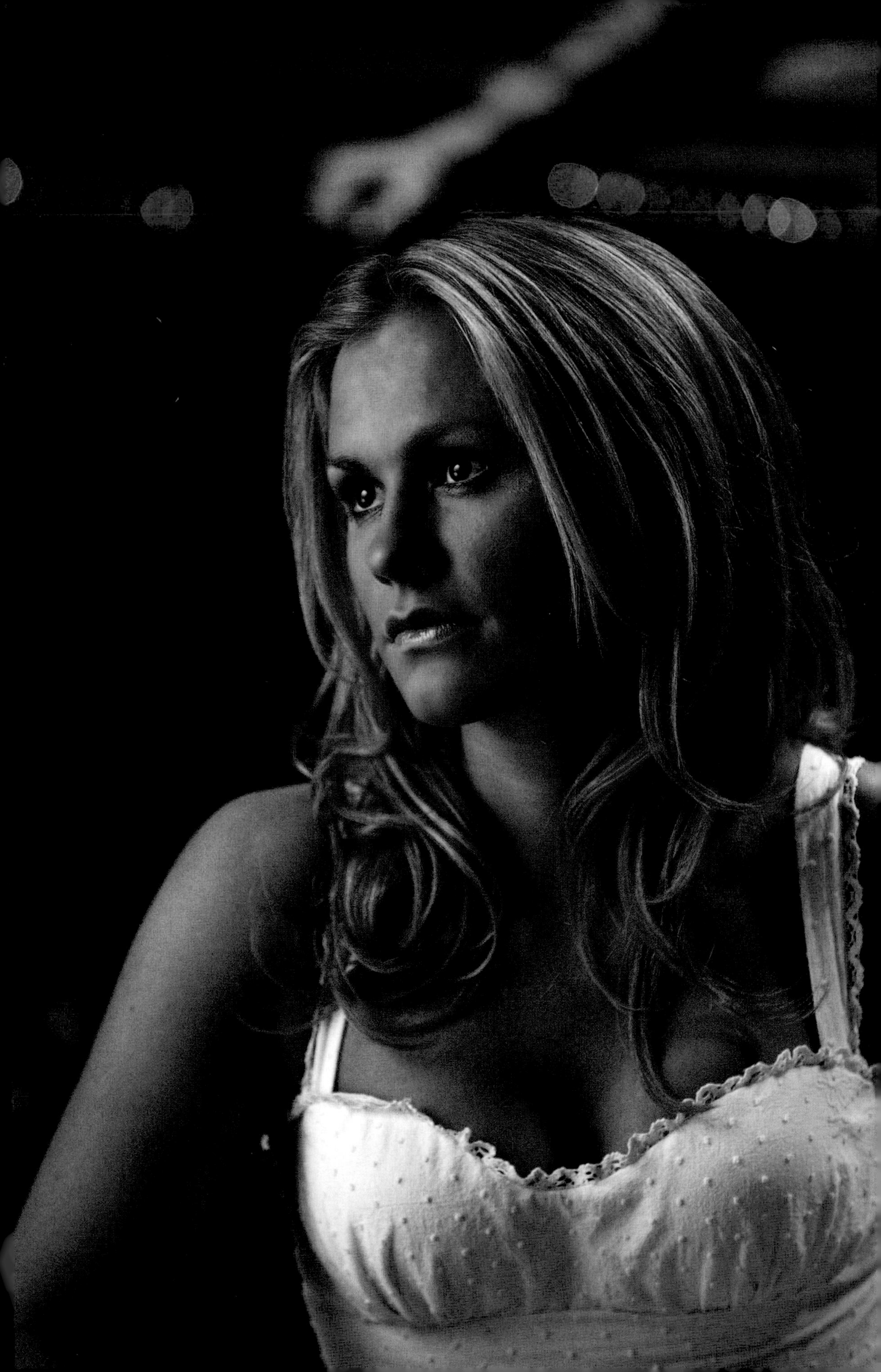

CHAPTER

art by DAVID MESSINA
colors by GIOVANNA NIRO

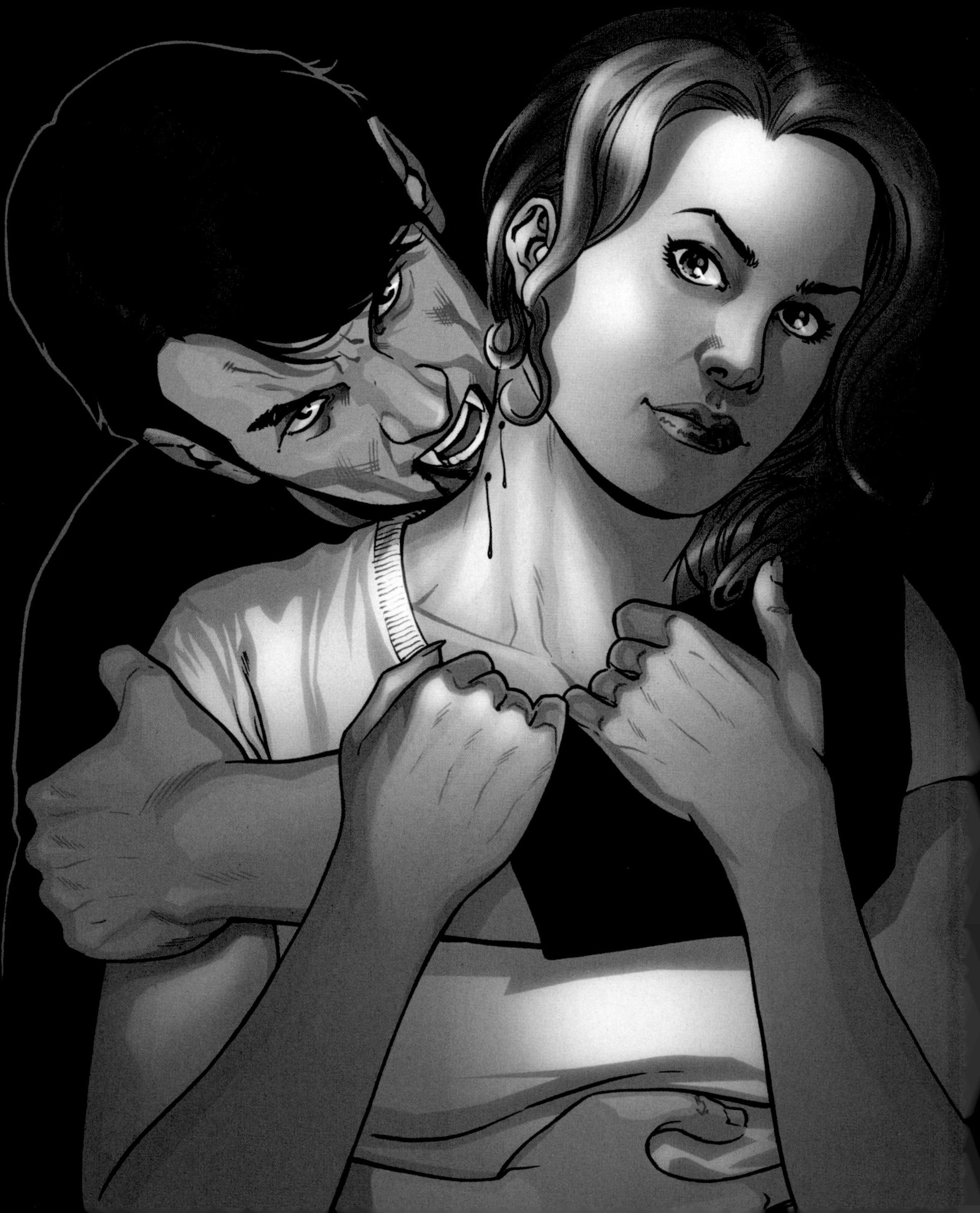

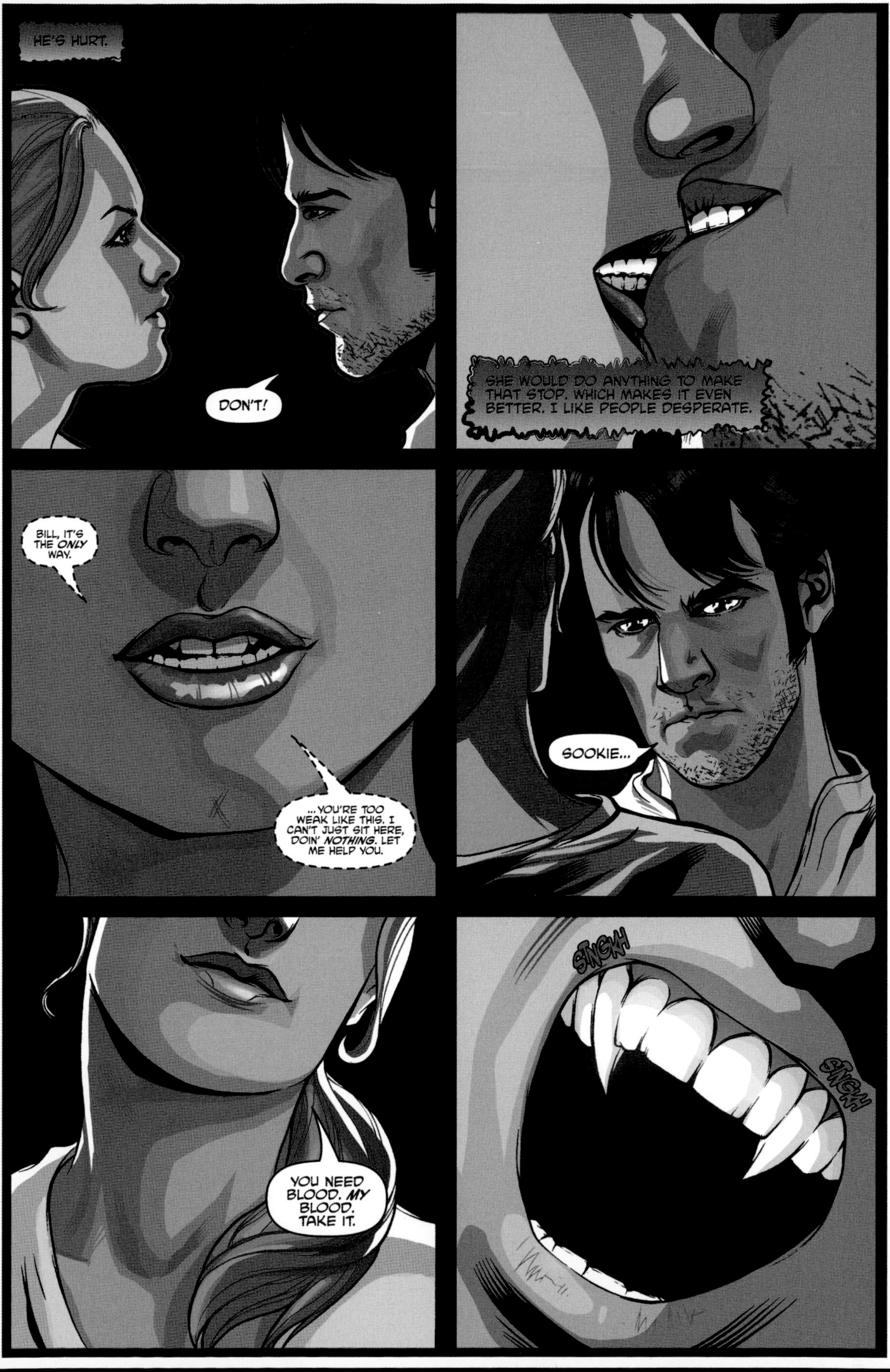
HE'S HURT.
DON'T!
SHE WOULD DO ANYTHING TO MAKE THAT STOP. WHICH MAKES IT EVEN BETTER. I LIKE PEOPLE DESPERATE.
BILL, IT'S THE *ONLY* WAY.
...YOU'RE TOO WEAK LIKE THIS. I CAN'T JUST SIT HERE, DOIN' *NOTHING*. LET ME HELP YOU.
SOOKIE...
YOU NEED BLOOD. *MY* BLOOD. TAKE IT.
SNGKH
SNGKH

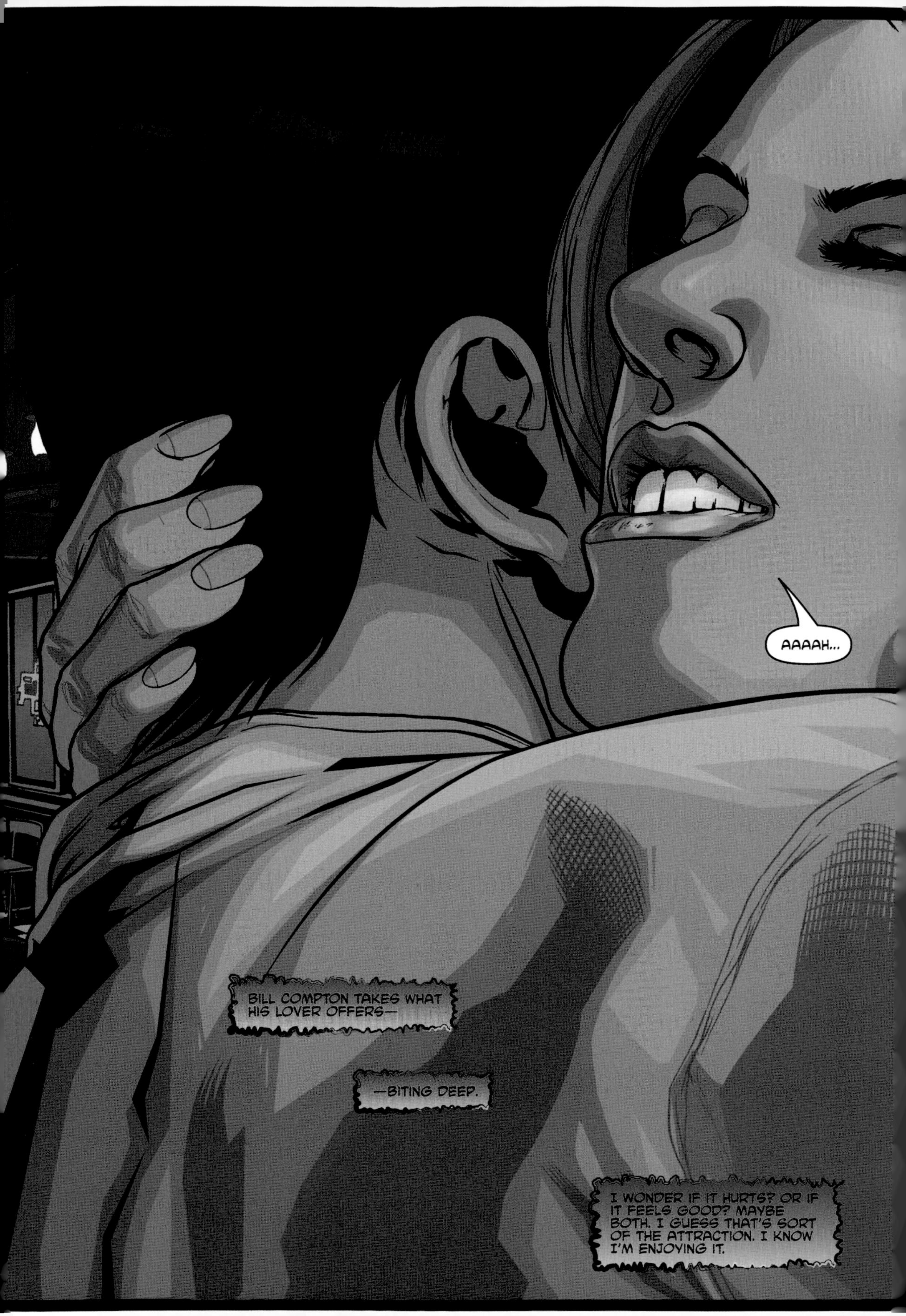
AAAAH...
BILL COMPTON TAKES WHAT HIS LOVER OFFERS—
—BITING DEEP.
I WONDER IF IT HURTS? OR IF IT FEELS GOOD? MAYBE BOTH. I GUESS THAT'S SORT OF THE ATTRACTION. I KNOW I'M ENJOYING IT.

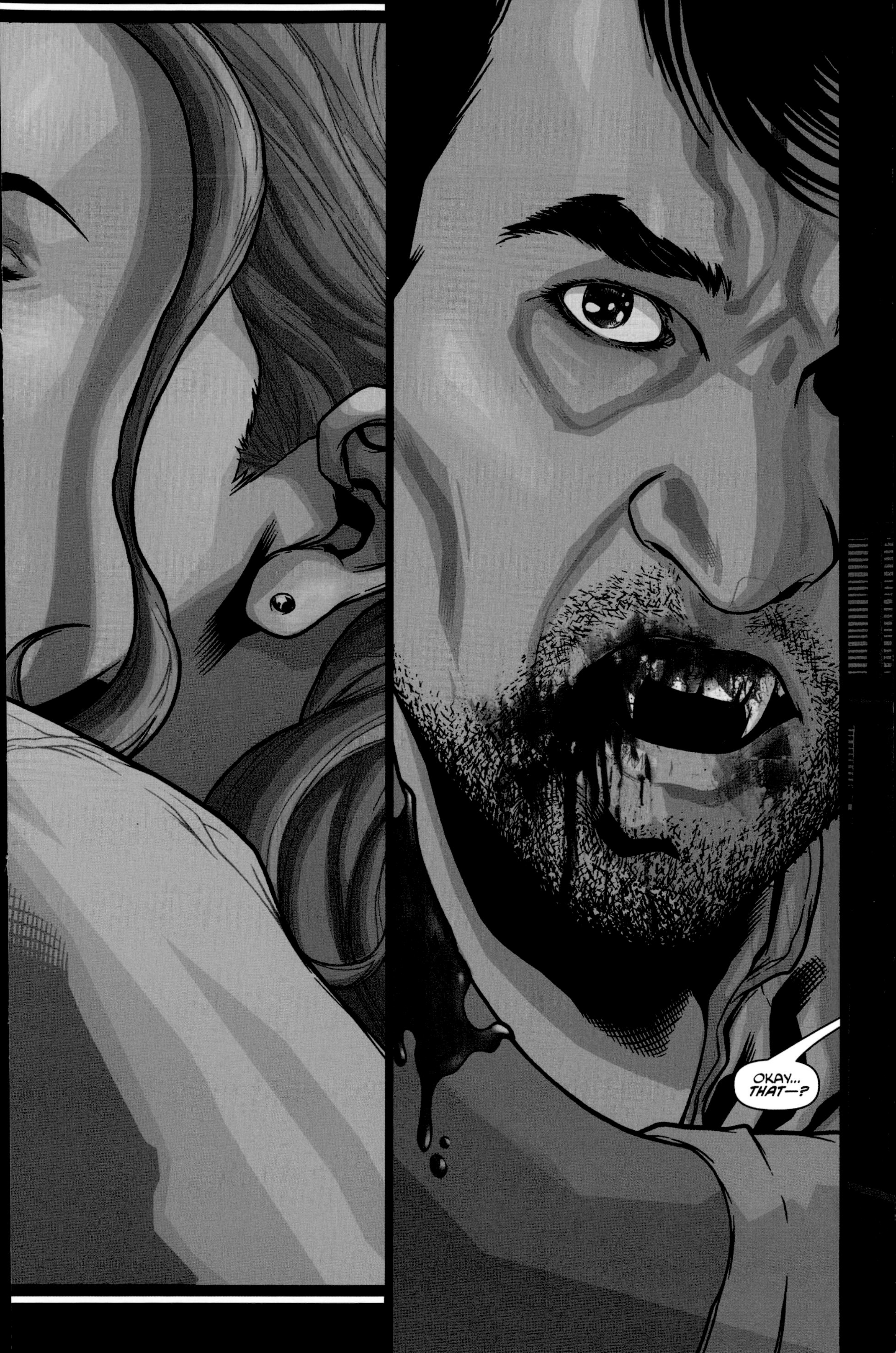
OKAY... THAT—?

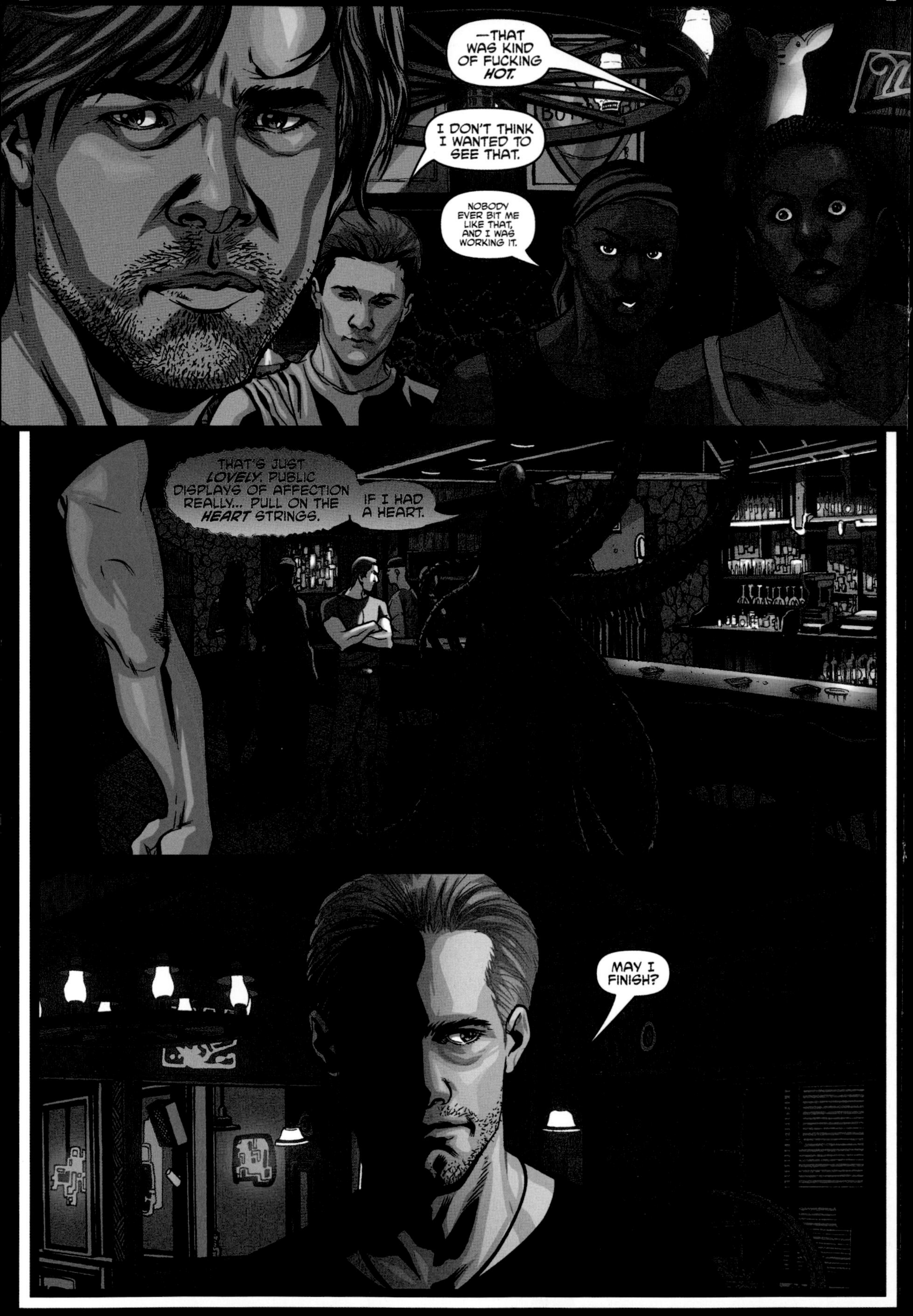
—THAT WAS KIND OF FUCKING *HOT.*
I DON'T THINK I WANTED TO SEE THAT.
NOBODY EVER BIT ME LIKE THAT, AND I WAS WORKING IT.
THAT'S JUST *LOVELY.* PUBLIC DISPLAYS OF AFFECTION REALLY... PULL ON THE *HEART* STRINGS.
IF I HAD A HEART.
MAY I FINISH?

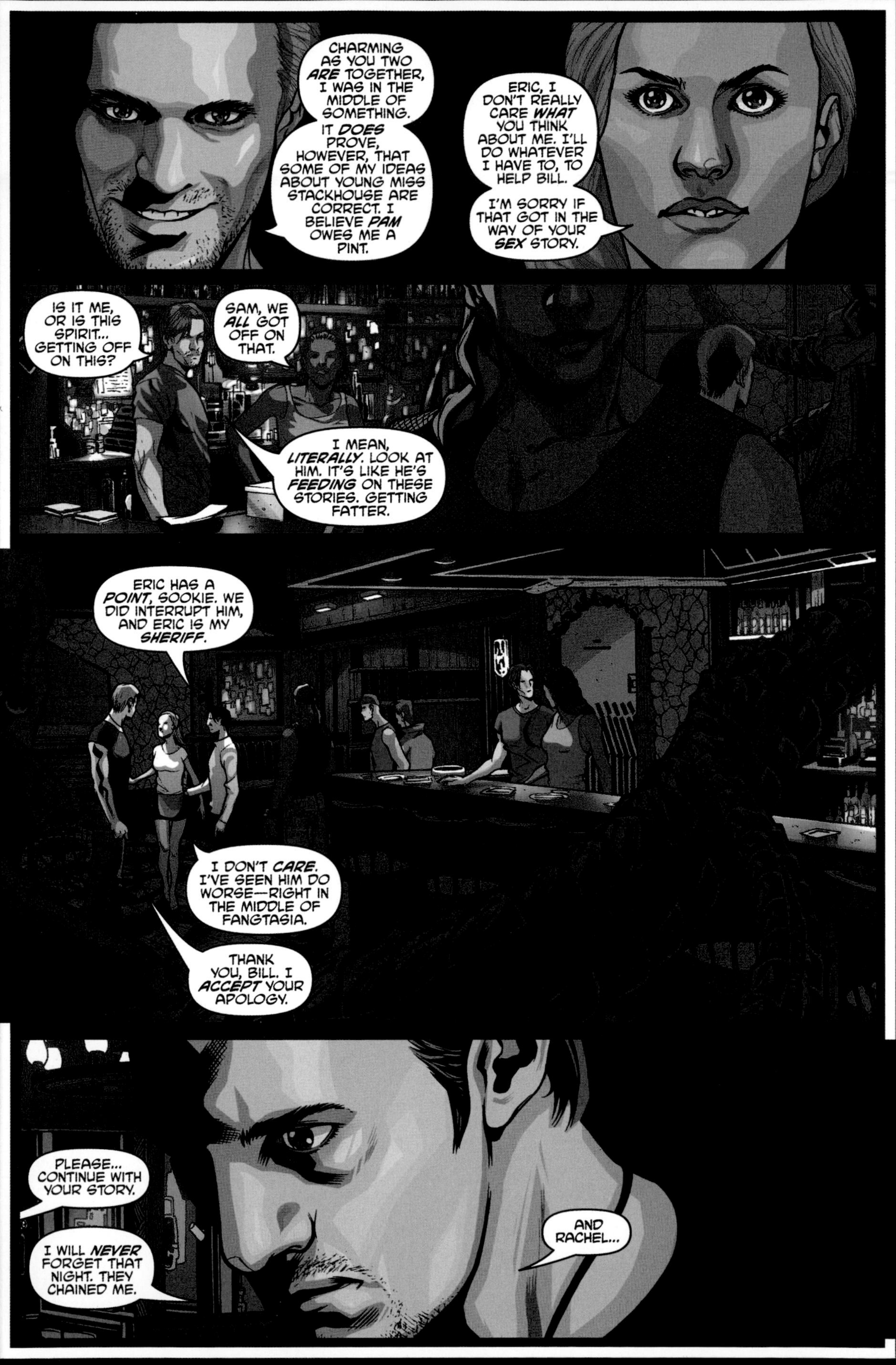
CHARMING AS YOU TWO ARE TOGETHER, I WAS IN THE MIDDLE OF SOMETHING.
IT DOES PROVE, HOWEVER, THAT SOME OF MY IDEAS ABOUT YOUNG MISS STACKHOUSE ARE CORRECT. I BELIEVE PAM OWES ME A PINT.
ERIC, I DON'T REALLY CARE WHAT YOU THINK ABOUT ME. I'LL DO WHATEVER I HAVE TO, TO HELP BILL.
I'M SORRY IF THAT GOT IN THE WAY OF YOUR SEX STORY.
IS IT ME, OR IS THIS SPIRIT... GETTING OFF ON THIS?
SAM, WE ALL GOT OFF ON THAT.
I MEAN, LITERALLY. LOOK AT HIM. IT'S LIKE HE'S FEEDING ON THESE STORIES. GETTING FATTER.
ERIC HAS A POINT, SOOKIE. WE DID INTERRUPT HIM, AND ERIC IS MY SHERIFF.
I DON'T CARE. I'VE SEEN HIM DO WORSE--RIGHT IN THE MIDDLE OF FANGTASIA.
THANK YOU, BILL. I ACCEPT YOUR APOLOGY.
PLEASE... CONTINUE WITH YOUR STORY.
I WILL NEVER FORGET THAT NIGHT. THEY CHAINED ME.
AND RACHEL...

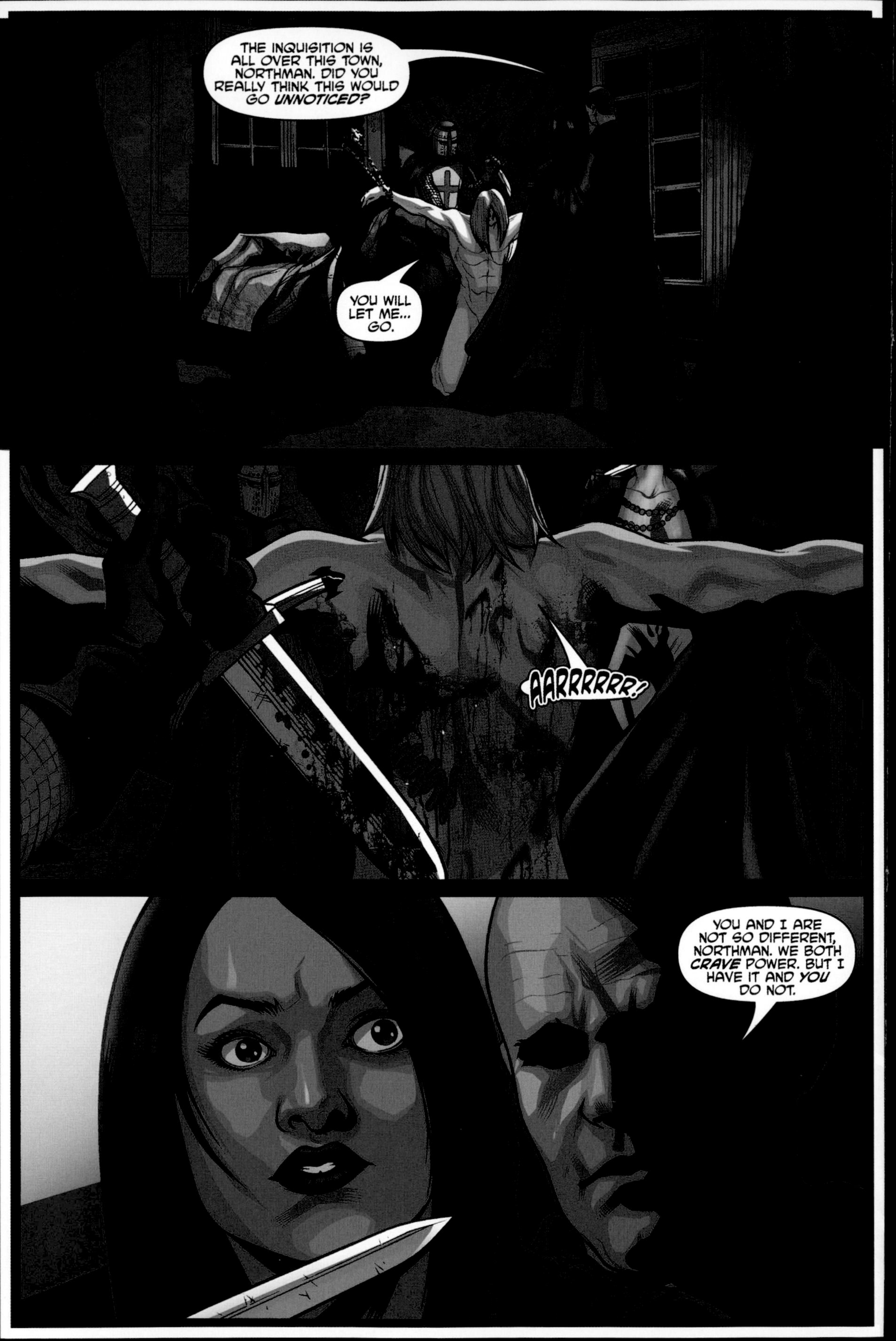
THE INQUISITION IS ALL OVER THIS TOWN, NORTHMAN. DID YOU REALLY THINK THIS WOULD GO *UNNOTICED?*
YOU WILL LET ME... GO.
AARRRRRR!
YOU AND I ARE NOT SO DIFFERENT, NORTHMAN. WE BOTH *CRAVE* POWER. BUT I HAVE IT AND *YOU* DO NOT.

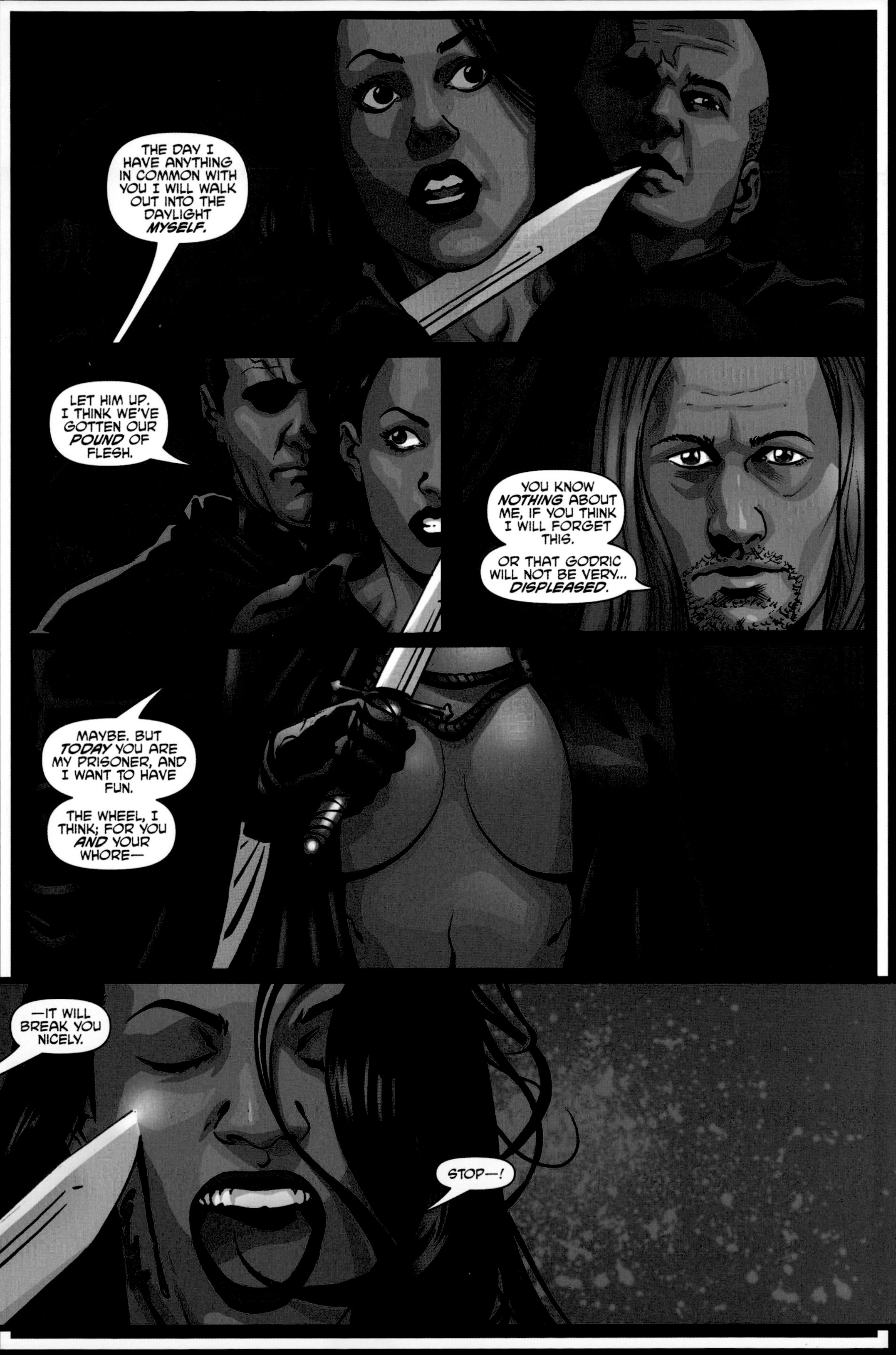
THE DAY I HAVE ANYTHING IN COMMON WITH YOU I WILL WALK OUT INTO THE DAYLIGHT *MYSELF.*
LET HIM UP. I THINK WE'VE GOTTEN OUR *POUND* OF FLESH.
YOU KNOW *NOTHING* ABOUT ME, IF YOU THINK I WILL FORGET THIS.
OR THAT GODRIC WILL NOT BE VERY... *DISPLEASED*.
MAYBE. BUT *TODAY* YOU ARE MY PRISONER, AND I WANT TO HAVE FUN.
THE WHEEL, I THINK; FOR YOU *AND* YOUR WHORE—
—IT WILL BREAK YOU NICELY.
STOP—!

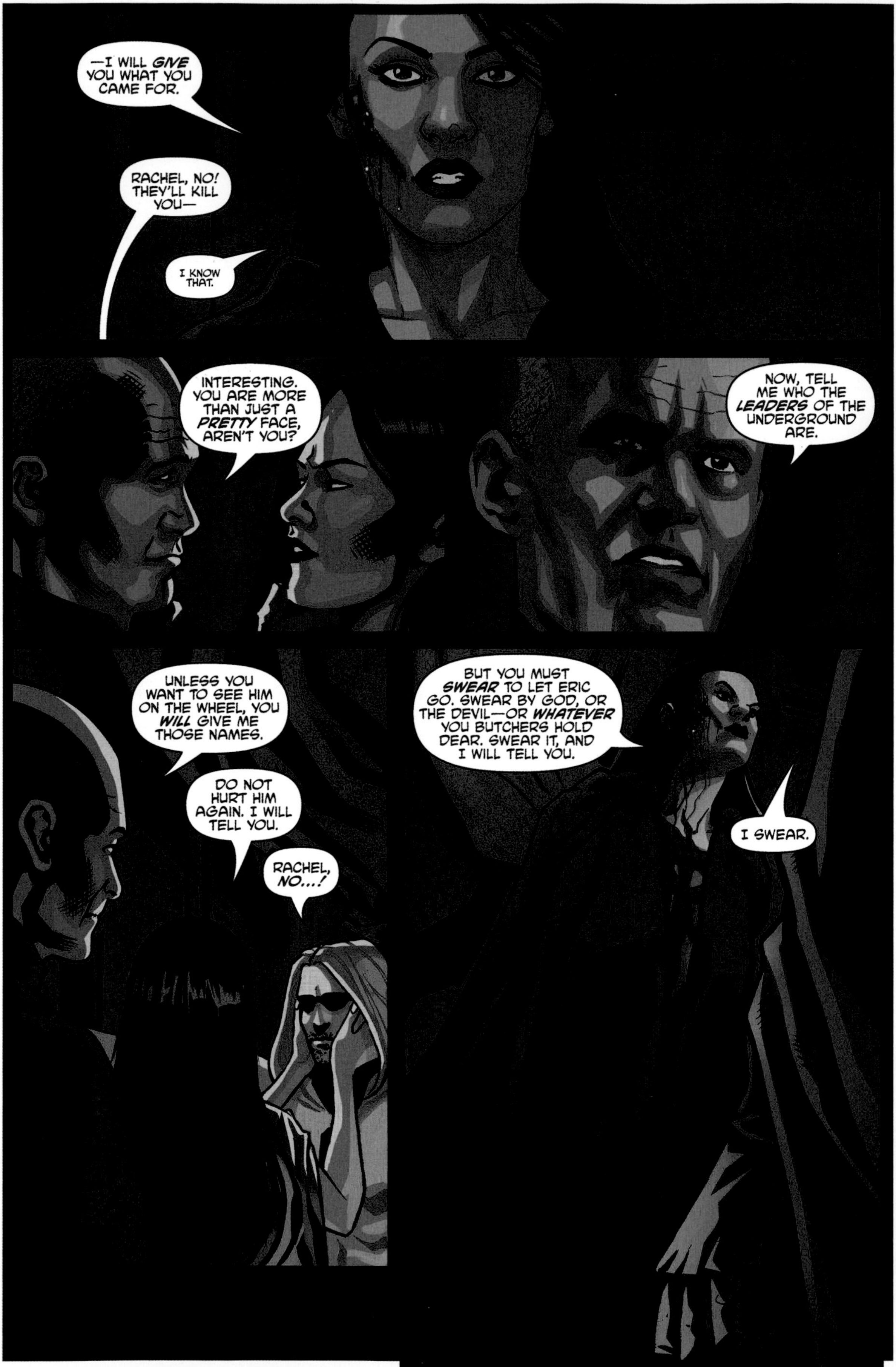
—I WILL GIVE YOU WHAT YOU CAME FOR.
RACHEL, NO! THEY'LL KILL YOU—
I KNOW THAT.
INTERESTING. YOU ARE MORE THAN JUST A PRETTY FACE, AREN'T YOU?
NOW, TELL ME WHO THE LEADERS OF THE UNDERGROUND ARE.
UNLESS YOU WANT TO SEE HIM ON THE WHEEL, YOU WILL GIVE ME THOSE NAMES.
DO NOT HURT HIM AGAIN. I WILL TELL YOU.
RACHEL, NO...!
BUT YOU MUST SWEAR TO LET ERIC GO. SWEAR BY GOD, OR THE DEVIL—OR WHATEVER YOU BUTCHERS HOLD DEAR. SWEAR IT, AND I WILL TELL YOU.
I SWEAR.

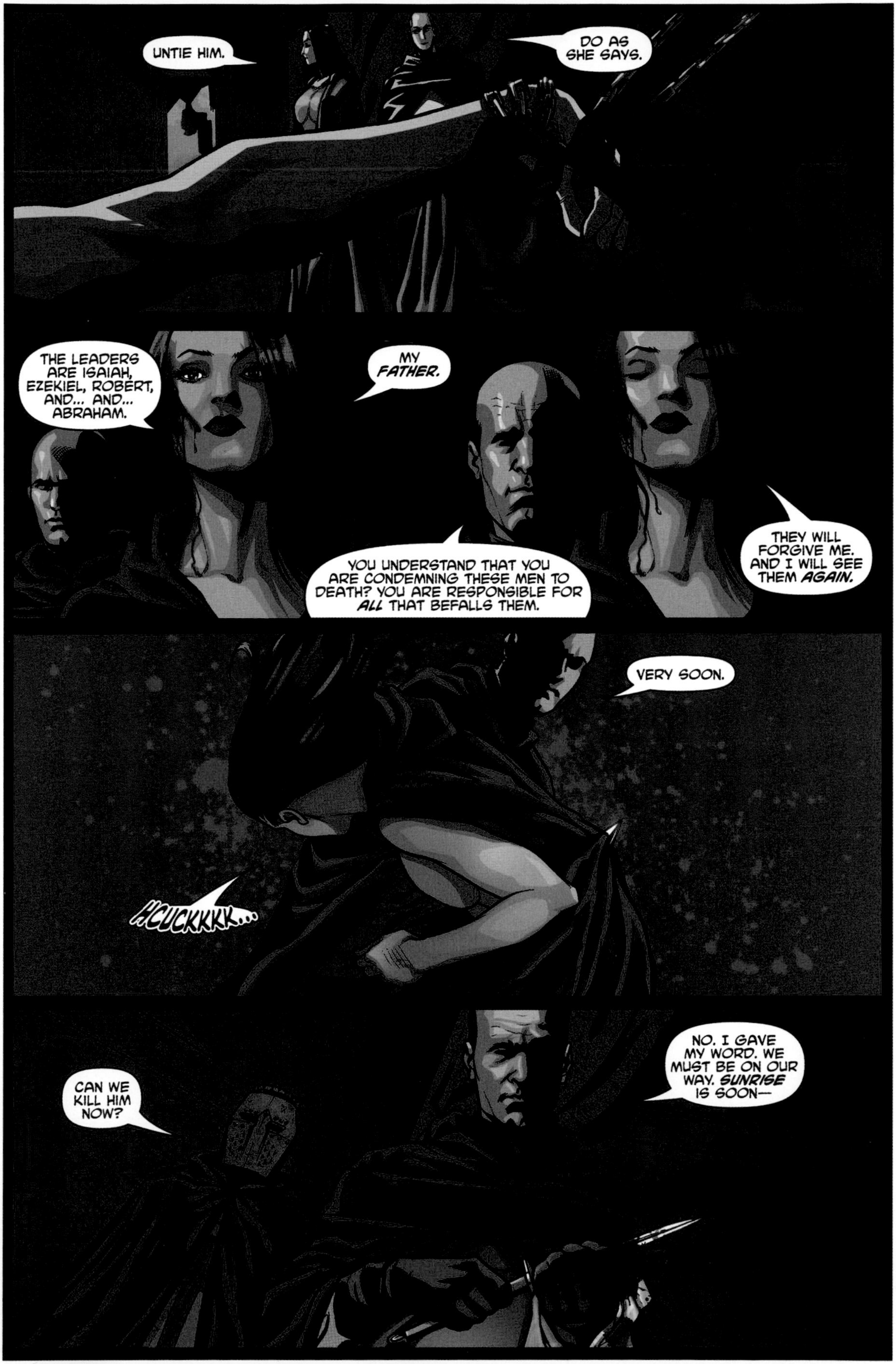
UNTIE HIM.
DO AS SHE SAYS.
THE LEADERS ARE ISAIAH, EZEKIEL, ROBERT, AND... AND... ABRAHAM.
MY *FATHER.*
YOU UNDERSTAND THAT YOU ARE CONDEMNING THESE MEN TO DEATH? YOU ARE RESPONSIBLE FOR *ALL* THAT BEFALLS THEM.
THEY WILL FORGIVE ME. AND I WILL SEE THEM *AGAIN.*
VERY SOON.
HCUCKKKK...
CAN WE KILL HIM NOW?
NO. I GAVE MY WORD. WE MUST BE ON OUR WAY. *SUNRISE* IS SOON—

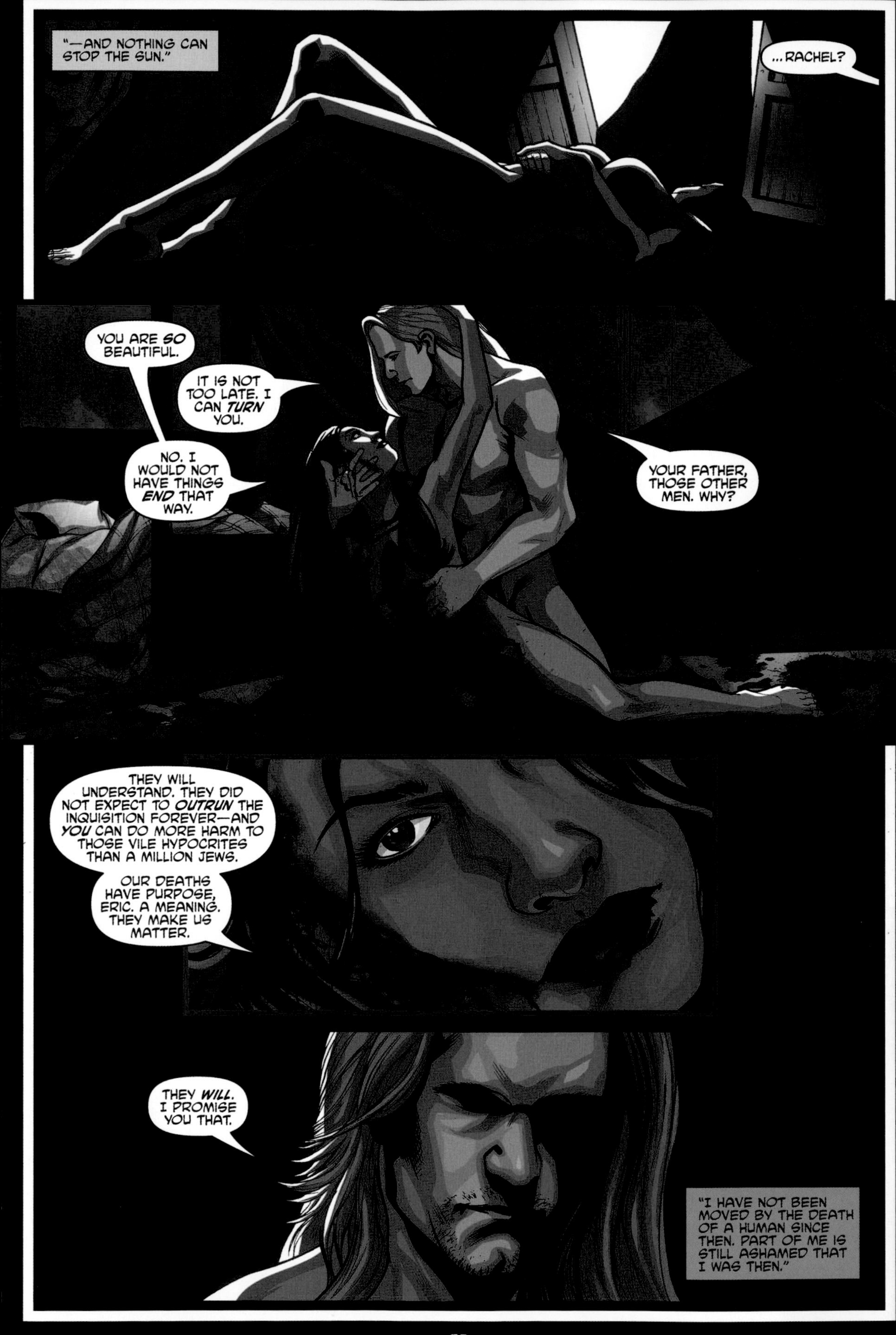
"—AND NOTHING CAN STOP THE SUN."
...RACHEL?
YOU ARE SO BEAUTIFUL.
IT IS NOT TOO LATE. I CAN TURN YOU.
NO. I WOULD NOT HAVE THINGS END THAT WAY.
YOUR FATHER, THOSE OTHER MEN. WHY?
THEY WILL UNDERSTAND. THEY DID NOT EXPECT TO OUTRUN THE INQUISITION FOREVER—AND YOU CAN DO MORE HARM TO THOSE VILE HYPOCRITES THAN A MILLION JEWS.
OUR DEATHS HAVE PURPOSE, ERIC. A MEANING. THEY MAKE US MATTER.
THEY WILL. I PROMISE YOU THAT.
"I HAVE NOT BEEN MOVED BY THE DEATH OF A HUMAN SINCE THEN. PART OF ME IS STILL ASHAMED THAT I WAS THEN."

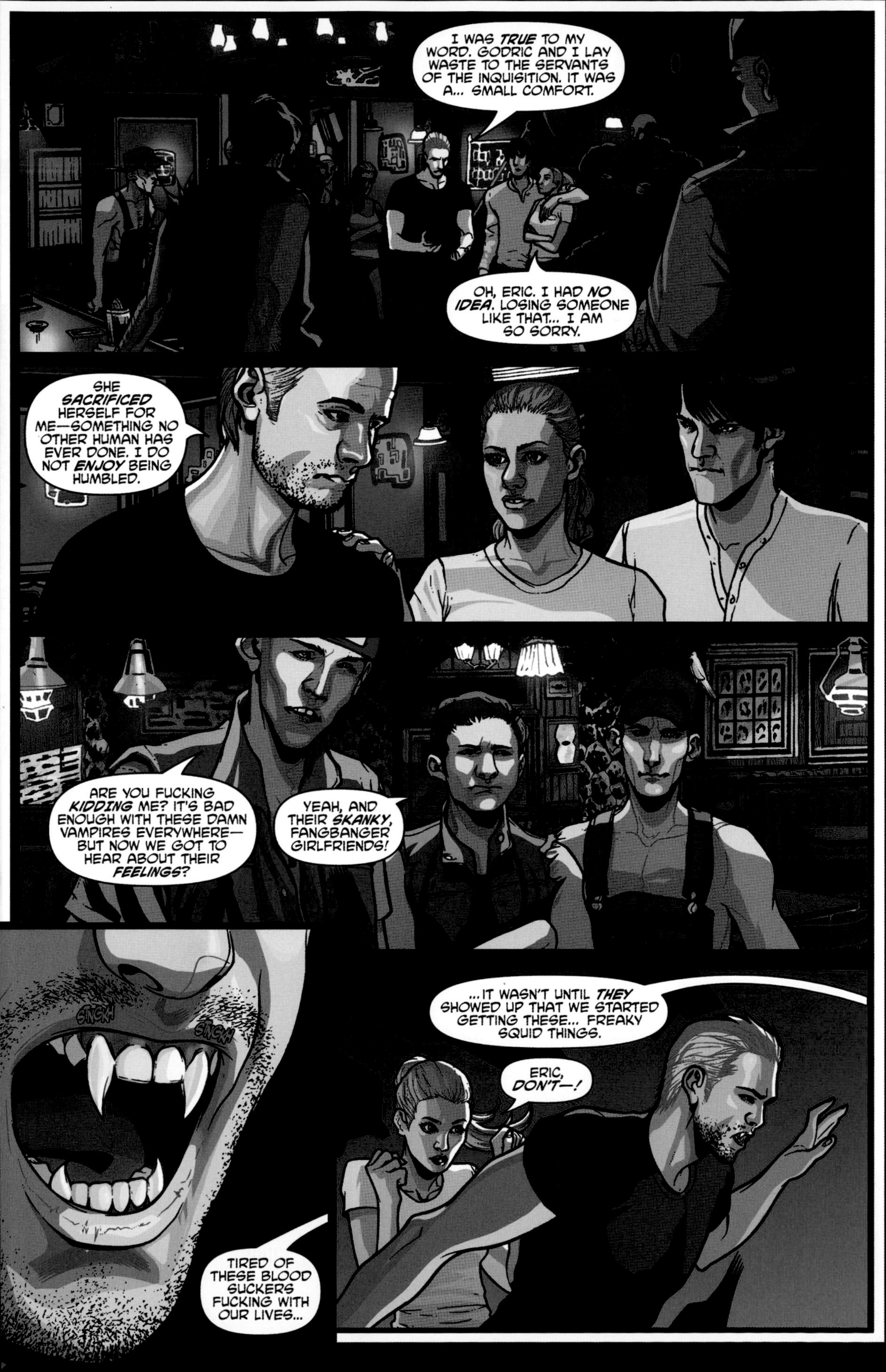
I WAS TRUE TO MY WORD. GODRIC AND I LAY WASTE TO THE SERVANTS OF THE INQUISITION. IT WAS A... SMALL COMFORT.
OH, ERIC. I HAD NO IDEA. LOSING SOMEONE LIKE THAT... I AM SO SORRY.
SHE SACRIFICED HERSELF FOR ME—SOMETHING NO OTHER HUMAN HAS EVER DONE. I DO NOT ENJOY BEING HUMBLED.
ARE YOU FUCKING KIDDING ME? IT'S BAD ENOUGH WITH THESE DAMN VAMPIRES EVERYWHERE—BUT NOW WE GOT TO HEAR ABOUT THEIR FEELINGS?
YEAH, AND THEIR SKANKY, FANGBANGER GIRLFRIENDS!
TIRED OF THESE BLOOD SUCKERS FUCKING WITH OUR LIVES...
...IT WASN'T UNTIL THEY SHOWED UP THAT WE STARTED GETTING THESE... FREAKY SQUID THINGS.
ERIC, DON'T—!

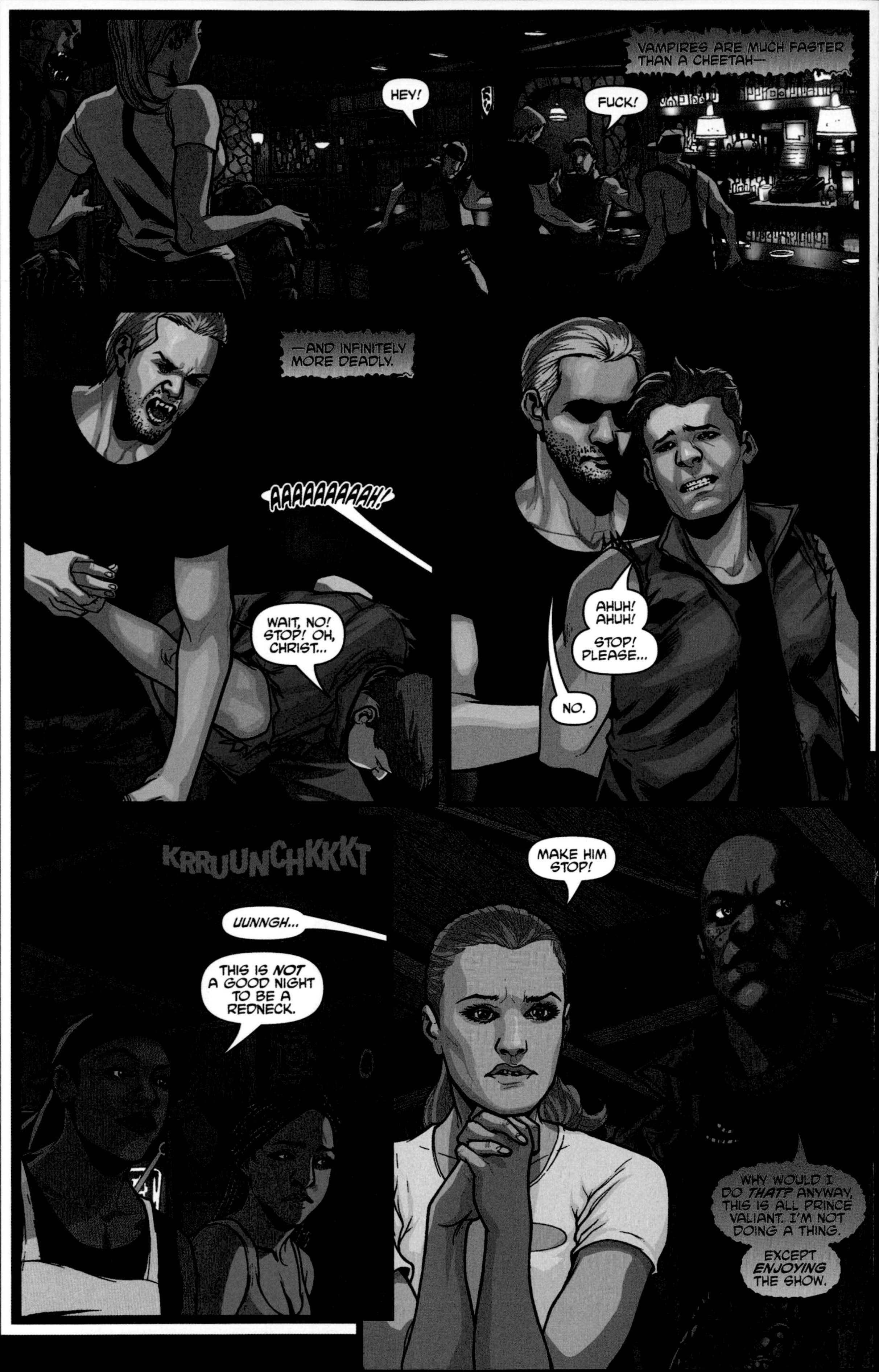
VAMPIRES ARE MUCH FASTER THAN A CHEETAH—
HEY!
FUCK!
—AND INFINITELY MORE DEADLY.
AAAAAAAAAH!
WAIT, NO! STOP! OH, CHRIST...
AHUH! AHUH!
STOP! PLEASE...
NO.
KRRUUNCHKKKT
UUNNGH...
THIS IS NOT A GOOD NIGHT TO BE A REDNECK.
MAKE HIM STOP!
WHY WOULD I DO THAT? ANYWAY, THIS IS ALL PRINCE VALIANT. I'M NOT DOING A THING.
EXCEPT ENJOYING THE SHOW.

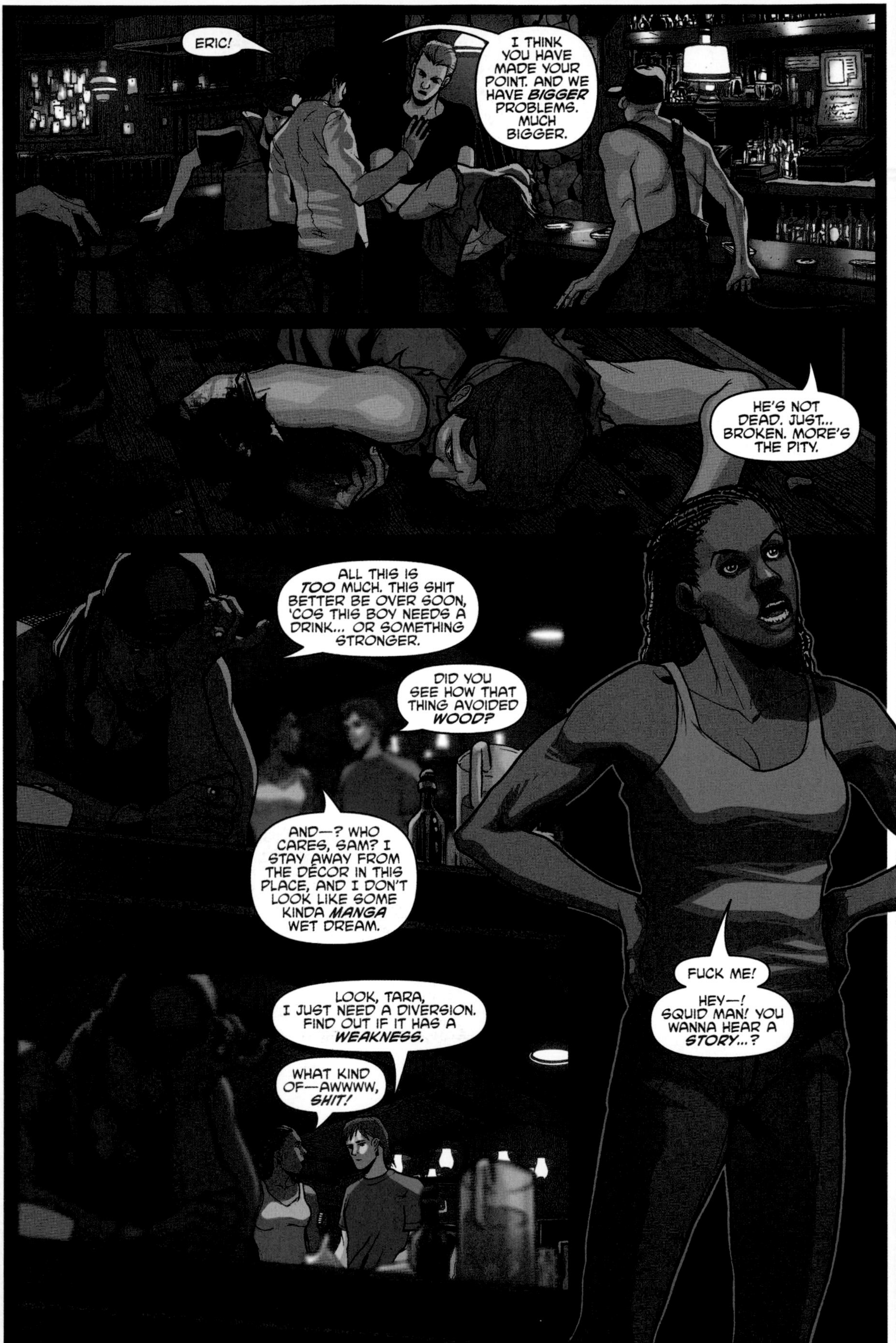
ERIC!
I THINK YOU HAVE MADE YOUR POINT. AND WE HAVE *BIGGER* PROBLEMS. MUCH BIGGER.
HE'S NOT DEAD. JUST... BROKEN. MORE'S THE PITY.
ALL THIS IS *TOO* MUCH. THIS SHIT BETTER BE OVER SOON, 'COS THIS BOY NEEDS A DRINK... OR SOMETHING STRONGER.
DID YOU SEE HOW THAT THING AVOIDED *WOOD?*
AND—? WHO CARES, SAM? I STAY AWAY FROM THE DÉCOR IN THIS PLACE, AND I DON'T LOOK LIKE SOME KINDA *MANGA* WET DREAM.
LOOK, TARA, I JUST NEED A DIVERSION. FIND OUT IF IT HAS A *WEAKNESS.*
WHAT KIND OF—AWWWW, *SHIT!*
FUCK ME!
HEY—! SQUID MAN! YOU WANNA HEAR A *STORY*...?

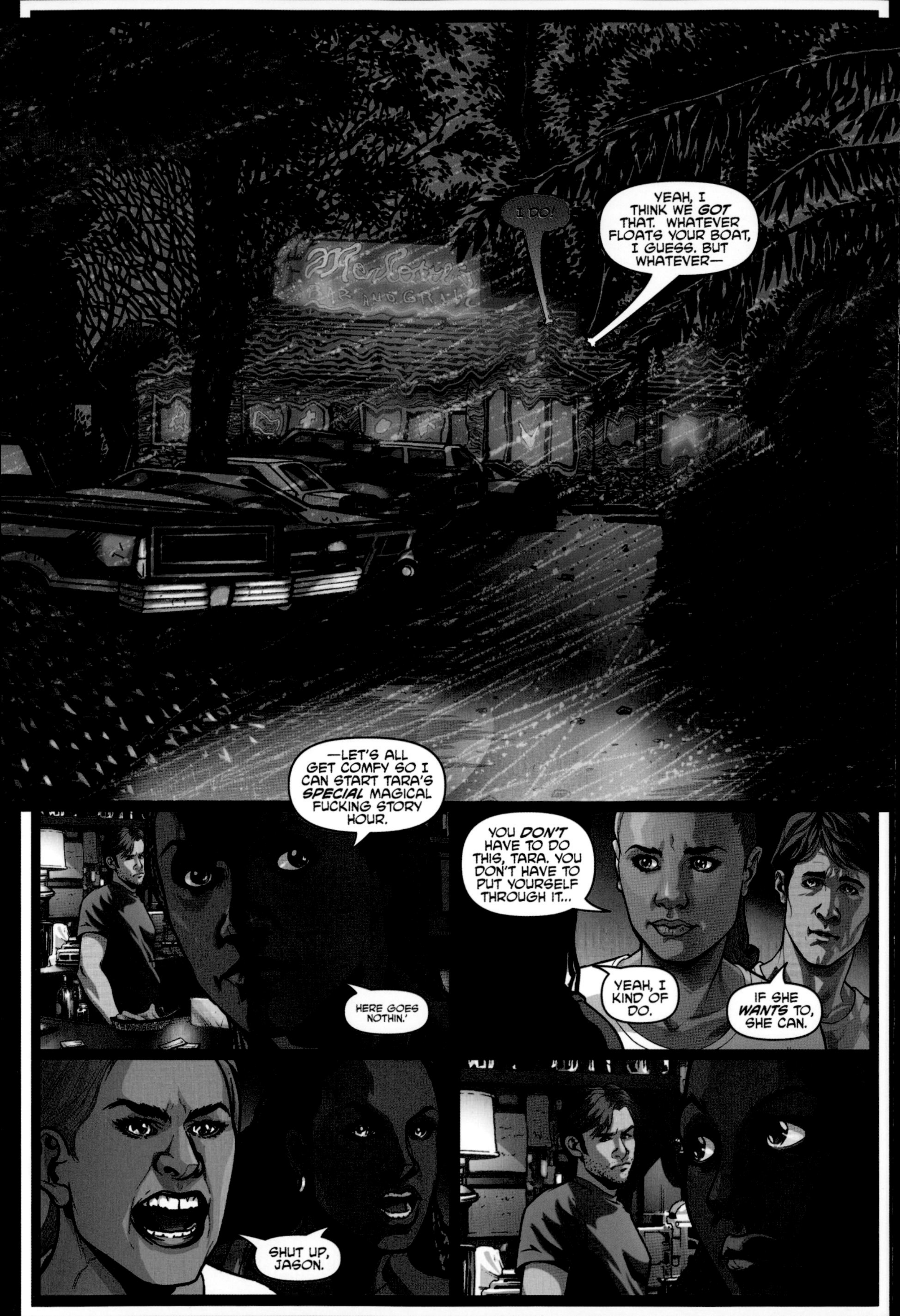

I DO!
YEAH, I THINK WE GOT THAT. WHATEVER FLOATS YOUR BOAT, I GUESS. BUT WHATEVER—
—LET'S ALL GET COMFY SO I CAN START TARA'S SPECIAL MAGICAL FUCKING STORY HOUR.
HERE GOES NOTHIN.'
YOU DON'T HAVE TO DO THIS, TARA. YOU DON'T HAVE TO PUT YOURSELF THROUGH IT...
YEAH, I KIND OF DO.
IF SHE WANTS TO, SHE CAN.
SHUT UP, JASON.

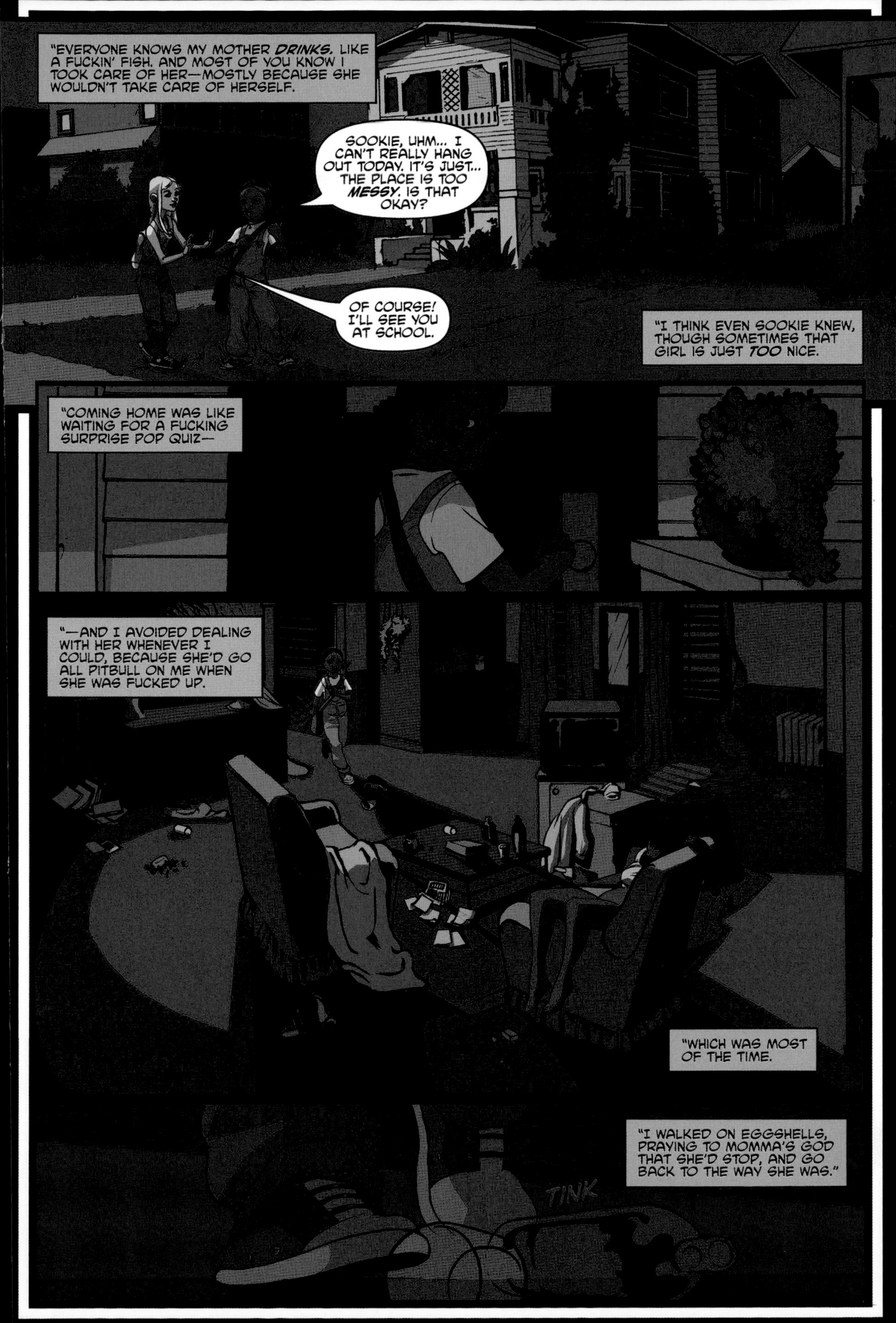
"EVERYONE KNOWS MY MOTHER DRINKS. LIKE A FUCKIN' FISH. AND MOST OF YOU KNOW I TOOK CARE OF HER—MOSTLY BECAUSE SHE WOULDN'T TAKE CARE OF HERSELF.
SOOKIE, UHM... I CAN'T REALLY HANG OUT TODAY. IT'S JUST... THE PLACE IS TOO MESSY. IS THAT OKAY?
OF COURSE! I'LL SEE YOU AT SCHOOL.
"I THINK EVEN SOOKIE KNEW, THOUGH SOMETIMES THAT GIRL IS JUST TOO NICE.
"COMING HOME WAS LIKE WAITING FOR A FUCKING SURPRISE POP QUIZ—
"—AND I AVOIDED DEALING WITH HER WHENEVER I COULD, BECAUSE SHE'D GO ALL PITBULL ON ME WHEN SHE WAS FUCKED UP.
"WHICH WAS MOST OF THE TIME.
"I WALKED ON EGGSHELLS, PRAYING TO MOMMA'S GOD THAT SHE'D STOP, AND GO BACK TO THE WAY SHE WAS."
TINK

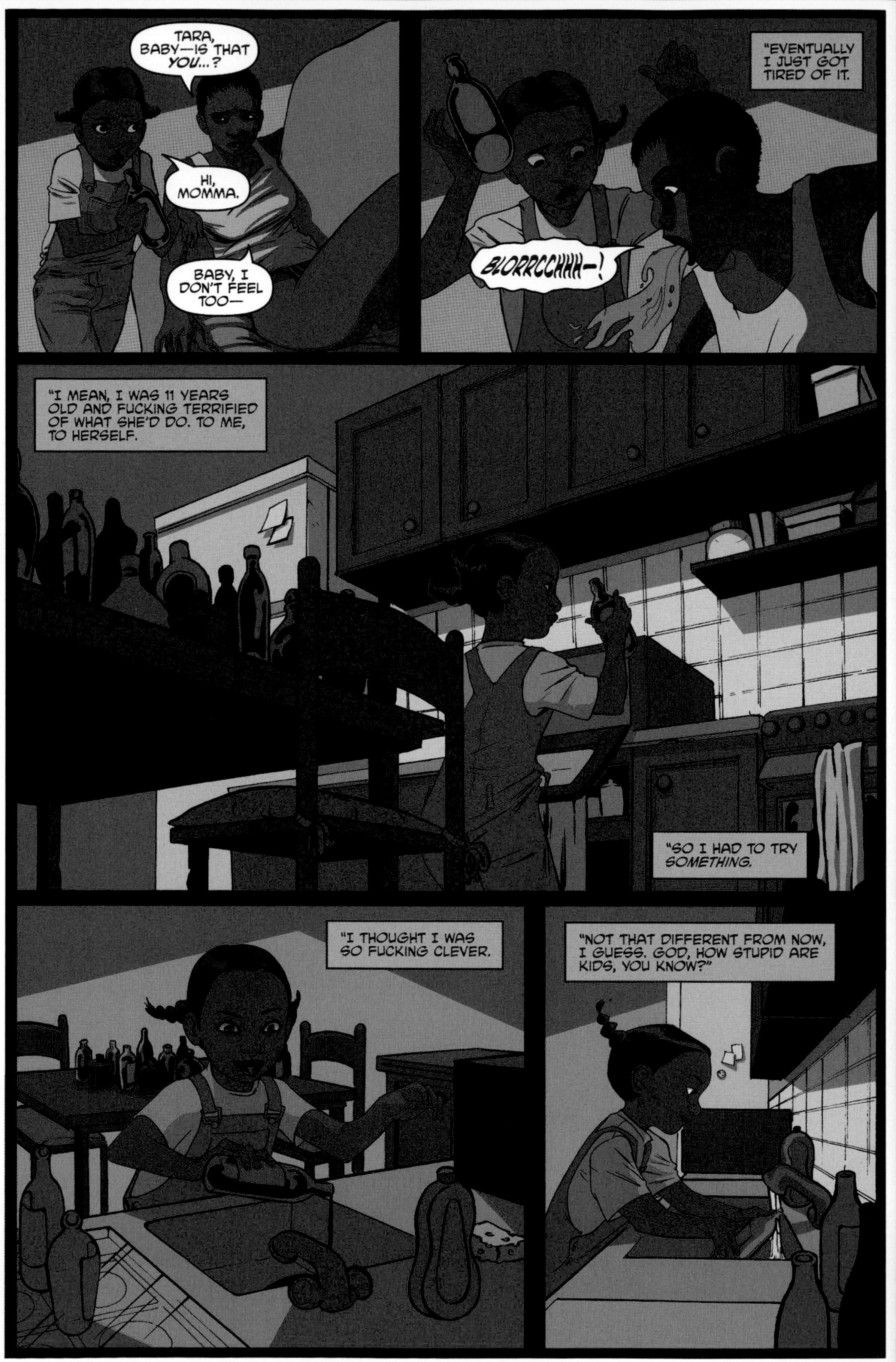
TARA, BABY—IS THAT *YOU*...?
HI, MOMMA.
BABY, I DON'T FEEL TOO—
"EVENTUALLY I JUST GOT TIRED OF IT.
BLORRCCHHH—!
"I MEAN, I WAS 11 YEARS OLD AND FUCKING TERRIFIED OF WHAT SHE'D DO. TO ME, TO HERSELF.
"SO I HAD TO TRY *SOMETHING.*
"I THOUGHT I WAS SO FUCKING CLEVER.
"NOT THAT DIFFERENT FROM NOW, I GUESS. GOD, HOW STUPID ARE KIDS, YOU KNOW?"

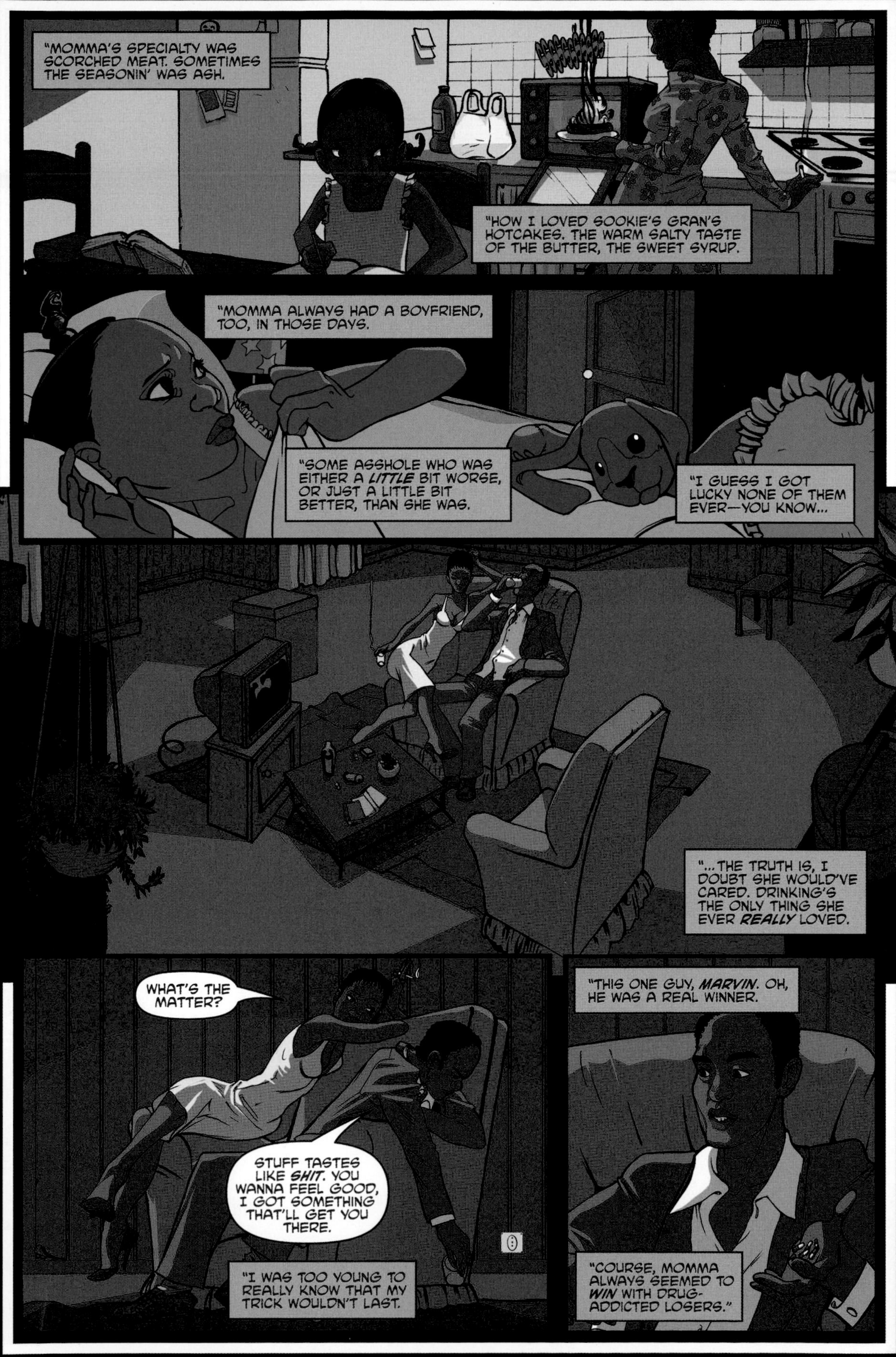
"MOMMA'S SPECIALTY WAS SCORCHED MEAT. SOMETIMES THE SEASONIN' WAS ASH.
"HOW I LOVED SOOKIE'S GRAN'S HOTCAKES. THE WARM SALTY TASTE OF THE BUTTER, THE SWEET SYRUP.
"MOMMA ALWAYS HAD A BOYFRIEND, TOO, IN THOSE DAYS.
"SOME ASSHOLE WHO WAS EITHER A *LITTLE* BIT WORSE, OR JUST A LITTLE BIT BETTER, THAN SHE WAS.
"I GUESS I GOT LUCKY NONE OF THEM EVER—YOU KNOW...
"...THE TRUTH IS, I DOUBT SHE WOULD'VE CARED. DRINKING'S THE ONLY THING SHE EVER *REALLY* LOVED.
WHAT'S THE MATTER?
STUFF TASTES LIKE *SHIT*. YOU WANNA FEEL GOOD, I GOT SOMETHING THAT'LL GET YOU THERE.
"I WAS TOO YOUNG TO REALLY KNOW THAT MY TRICK WOULDN'T LAST.
"THIS ONE GUY, *MARVIN*. OH, HE WAS A REAL WINNER.
"COURSE, MOMMA ALWAYS SEEMED TO *WIN* WITH DRUG-ADDICTED LOSERS."

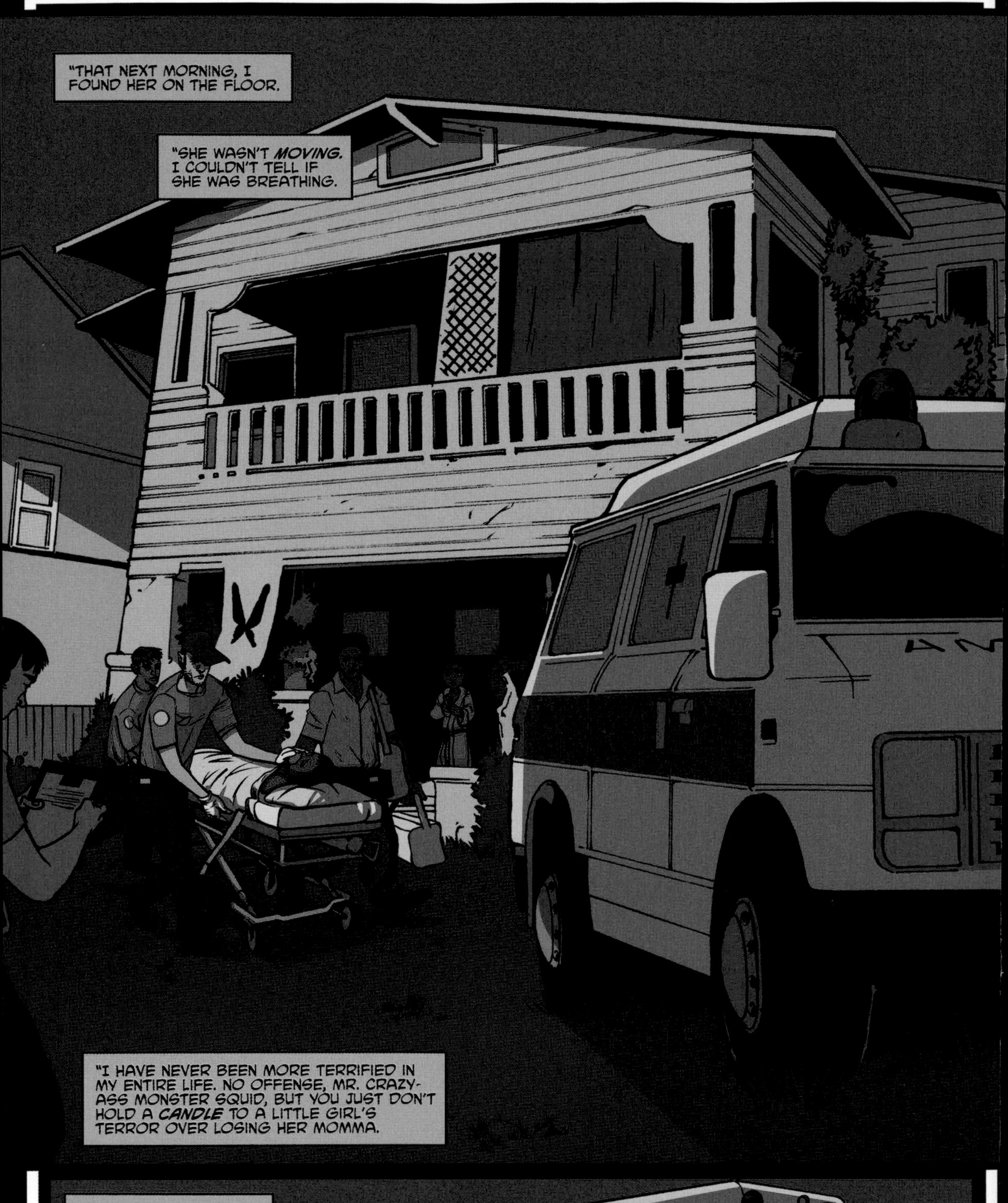
"THAT NEXT MORNING, I FOUND HER ON THE FLOOR.
"SHE WASN'T *MOVING.* I COULDN'T TELL IF SHE WAS BREATHING.
"I HAVE NEVER BEEN MORE TERRIFIED IN MY ENTIRE LIFE. NO OFFENSE, MR. CRAZY-ASS MONSTER SQUID, BUT YOU JUST DON'T HOLD A *CANDLE* TO A LITTLE GIRL'S TERROR OVER LOSING HER MOMMA.

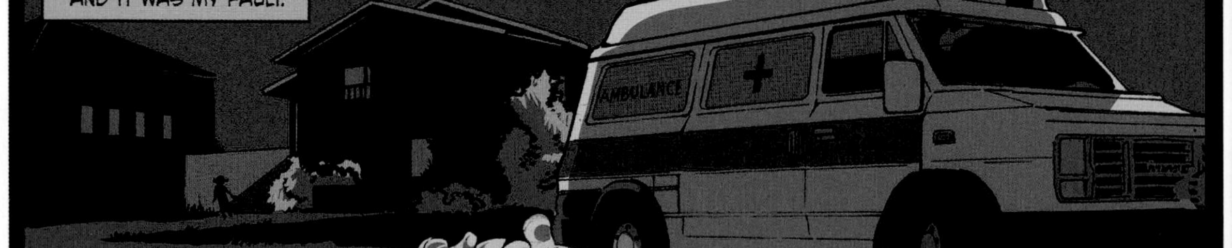
"AND IT WAS MY FAULT."
AMBULANCE

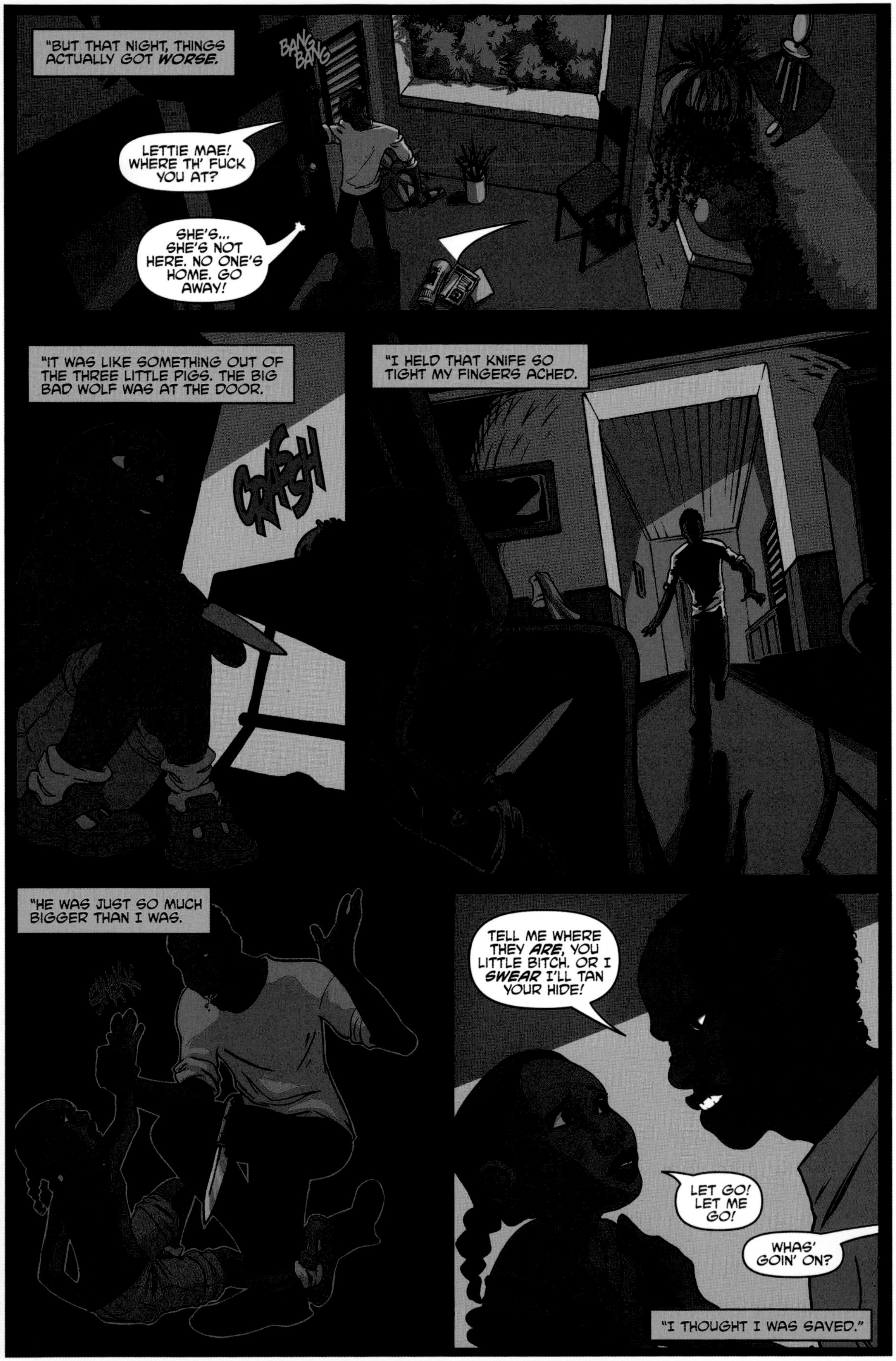
"BUT THAT NIGHT, THINGS ACTUALLY GOT *WORSE.*
BANG BANG
LETTIE MAE! WHERE TH' FUCK YOU AT?
SHE'S... SHE'S NOT HERE. NO ONE'S HOME. GO AWAY!
"IT WAS LIKE SOMETHING OUT OF THE THREE LITTLE PIGS. THE BIG BAD WOLF WAS AT THE DOOR.
CRASH
"I HELD THAT KNIFE SO TIGHT MY FINGERS ACHED.
"HE WAS JUST SO MUCH BIGGER THAN I WAS.
TELL ME WHERE THEY *ARE*, YOU LITTLE BITCH. OR I *SWEAR* I'LL TAN YOUR HIDE!
LET GO! LET ME GO!
WHAS' GOIN' ON?
"I THOUGHT I WAS SAVED."

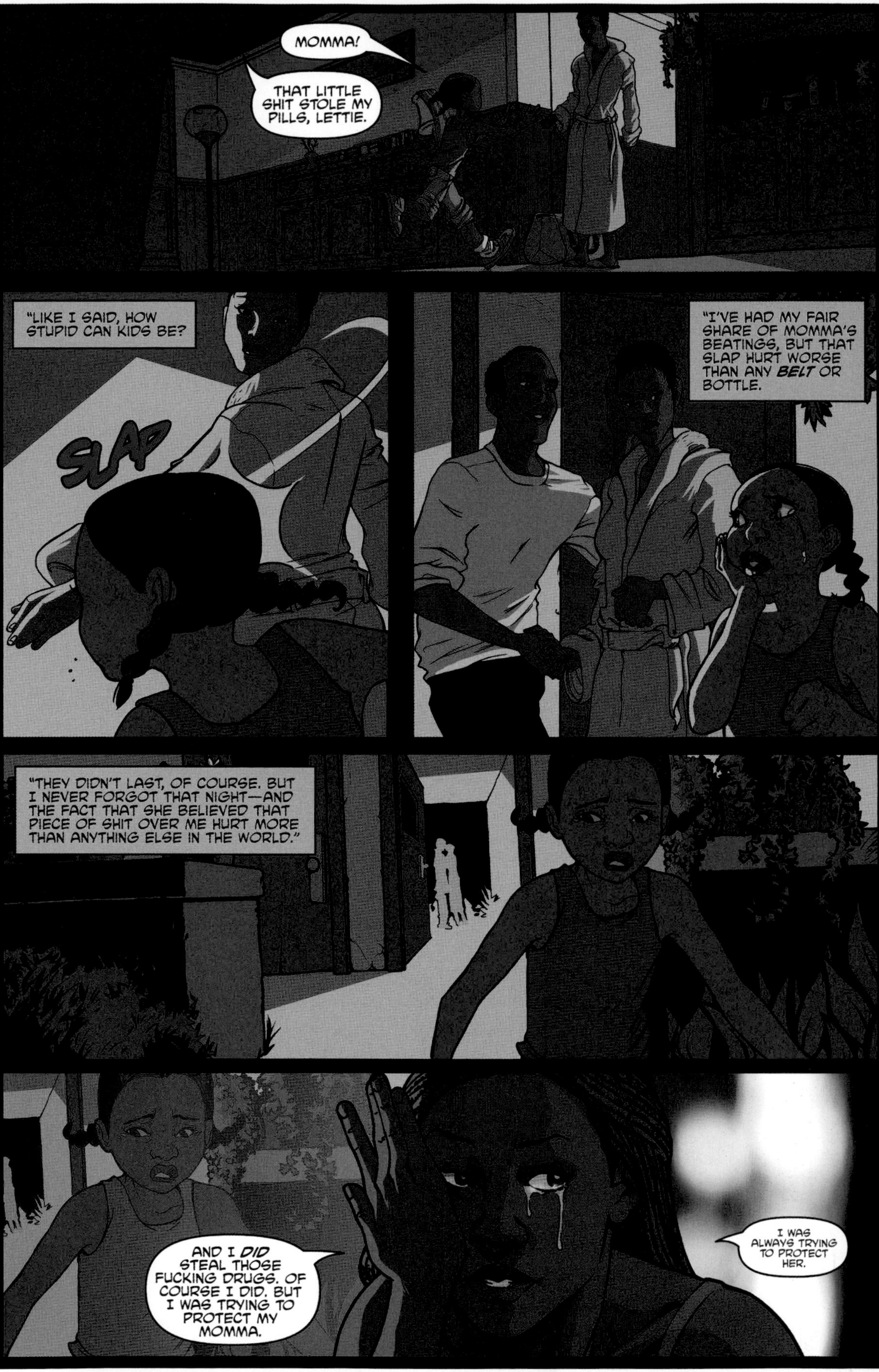
MOMMA!
THAT LITTLE SHIT STOLE MY PILLS, LETTIE.
"LIKE I SAID, HOW STUPID CAN KIDS BE?
SLAP
"I'VE HAD MY FAIR SHARE OF MOMMA'S BEATINGS, BUT THAT SLAP HURT WORSE THAN ANY *BELT* OR BOTTLE.
"THEY DIDN'T LAST, OF COURSE. BUT I NEVER FORGOT THAT NIGHT—AND THE FACT THAT SHE BELIEVED THAT PIECE OF SHIT OVER ME HURT MORE THAN ANYTHING ELSE IN THE WORLD."
AND I *DID* STEAL THOSE FUCKING DRUGS. OF COURSE I DID. BUT I WAS TRYING TO PROTECT MY MOMMA.
I WAS ALWAYS TRYING TO PROTECT HER.

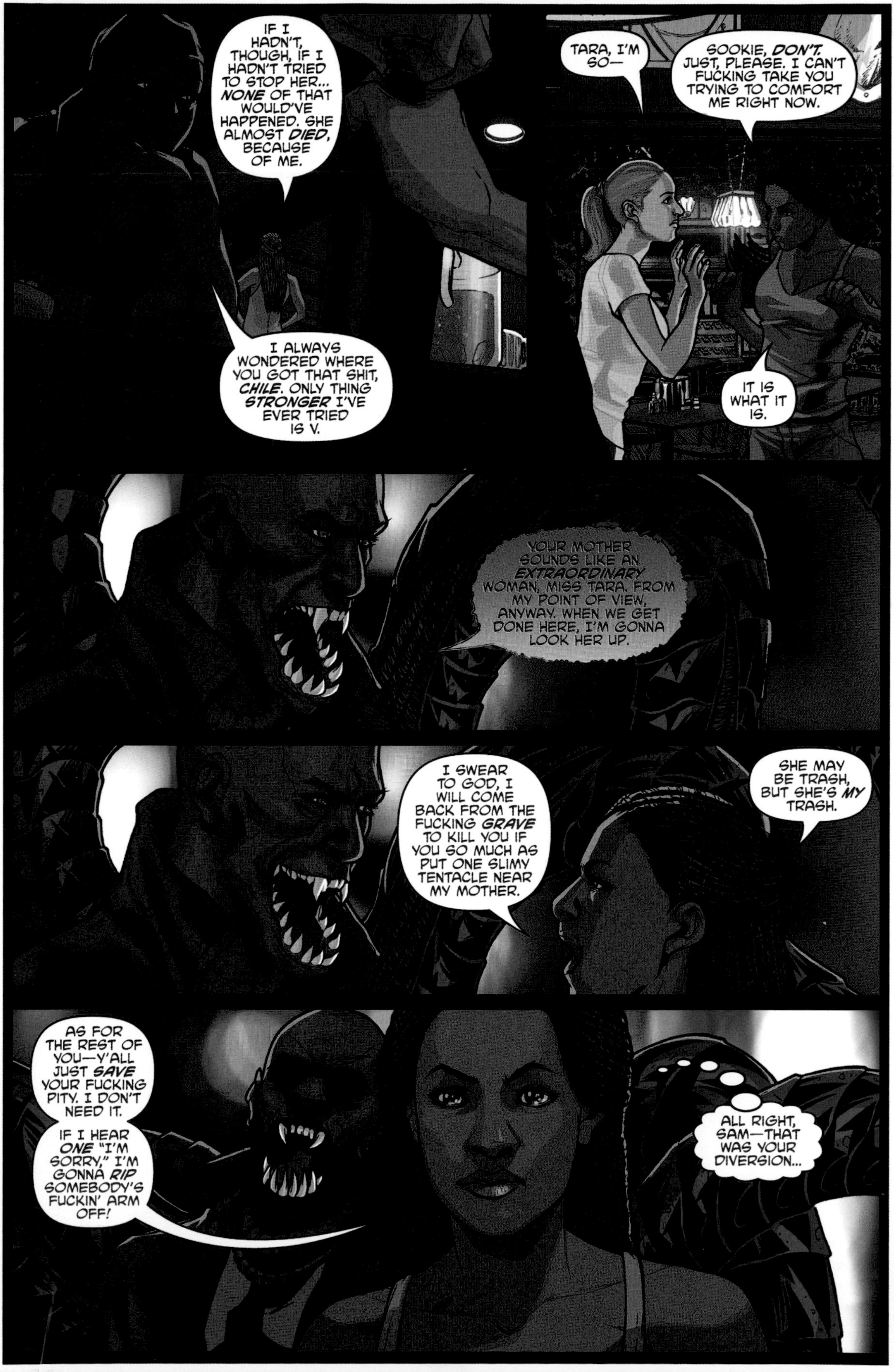
IF I HADN'T, THOUGH, IF I HADN'T TRIED TO STOP HER... NONE OF THAT WOULD'VE HAPPENED. SHE ALMOST DIED, BECAUSE OF ME.
I ALWAYS WONDERED WHERE YOU GOT THAT SHIT, CHILE. ONLY THING STRONGER I'VE EVER TRIED IS V.
TARA, I'M SO—
SOOKIE, DON'T. JUST, PLEASE. I CAN'T FUCKING TAKE YOU TRYING TO COMFORT ME RIGHT NOW.
IT IS WHAT IT IS.
YOUR MOTHER SOUNDS LIKE AN EXTRAORDINARY WOMAN, MISS TARA. FROM MY POINT OF VIEW, ANYWAY. WHEN WE GET DONE HERE, I'M GONNA LOOK HER UP.
I SWEAR TO GOD, I WILL COME BACK FROM THE FUCKING GRAVE TO KILL YOU IF YOU SO MUCH AS PUT ONE SLIMY TENTACLE NEAR MY MOTHER.
SHE MAY BE TRASH, BUT SHE'S MY TRASH.
AS FOR THE REST OF YOU—Y'ALL JUST SAVE YOUR FUCKING PITY. I DON'T NEED IT.
IF I HEAR ONE "I'M SORRY," I'M GONNA RIP SOMEBODY'S FUCKIN' ARM OFF!
ALL RIGHT, SAM—THAT WAS YOUR DIVERSION...

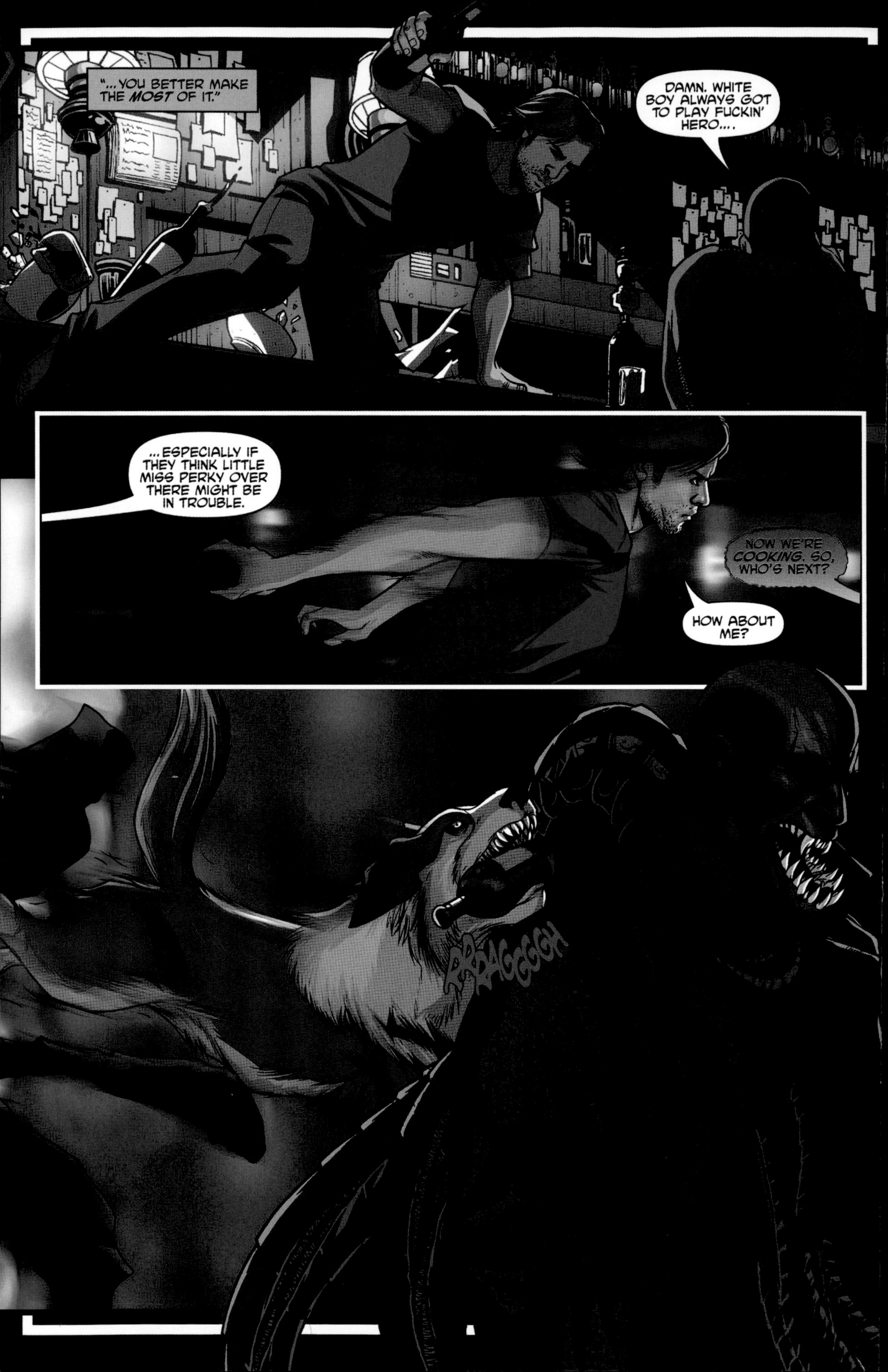
"...YOU BETTER MAKE THE *MOST* OF IT."
DAMN. WHITE BOY ALWAYS GOT TO PLAY FUCKIN' HERO....
...ESPECIALLY IF THEY THINK LITTLE MISS PERKY OVER THERE MIGHT BE IN TROUBLE.
NOW WE'RE *COOKING*. SO, WHO'S NEXT?
HOW ABOUT ME?
RRRAAGGGGH

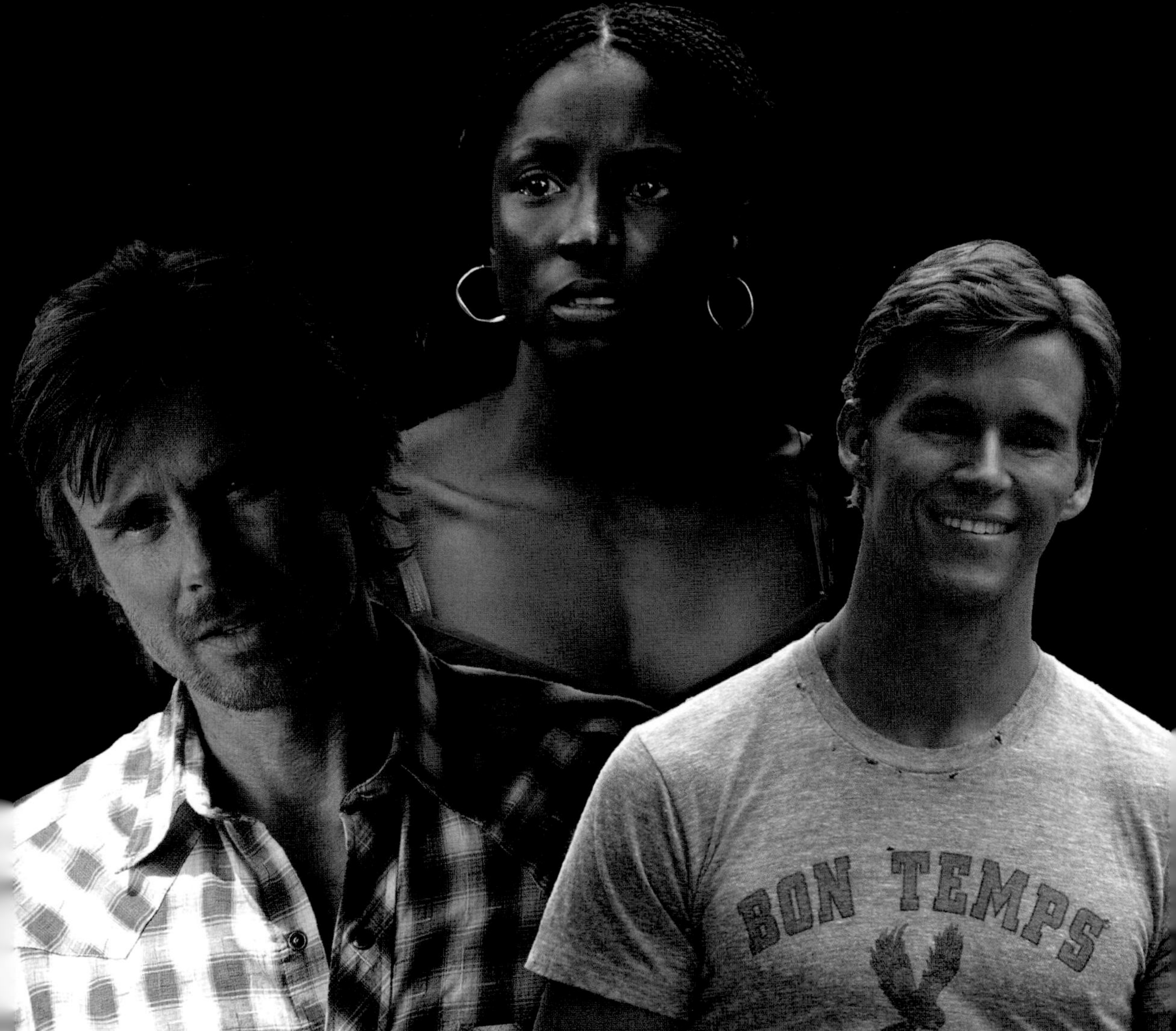
BON TEMPS
FOOTBALL

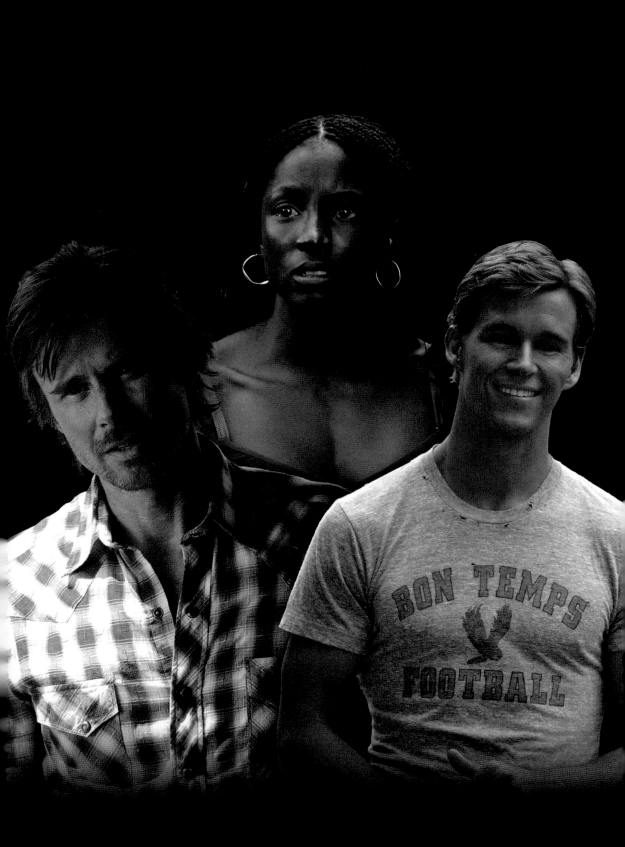

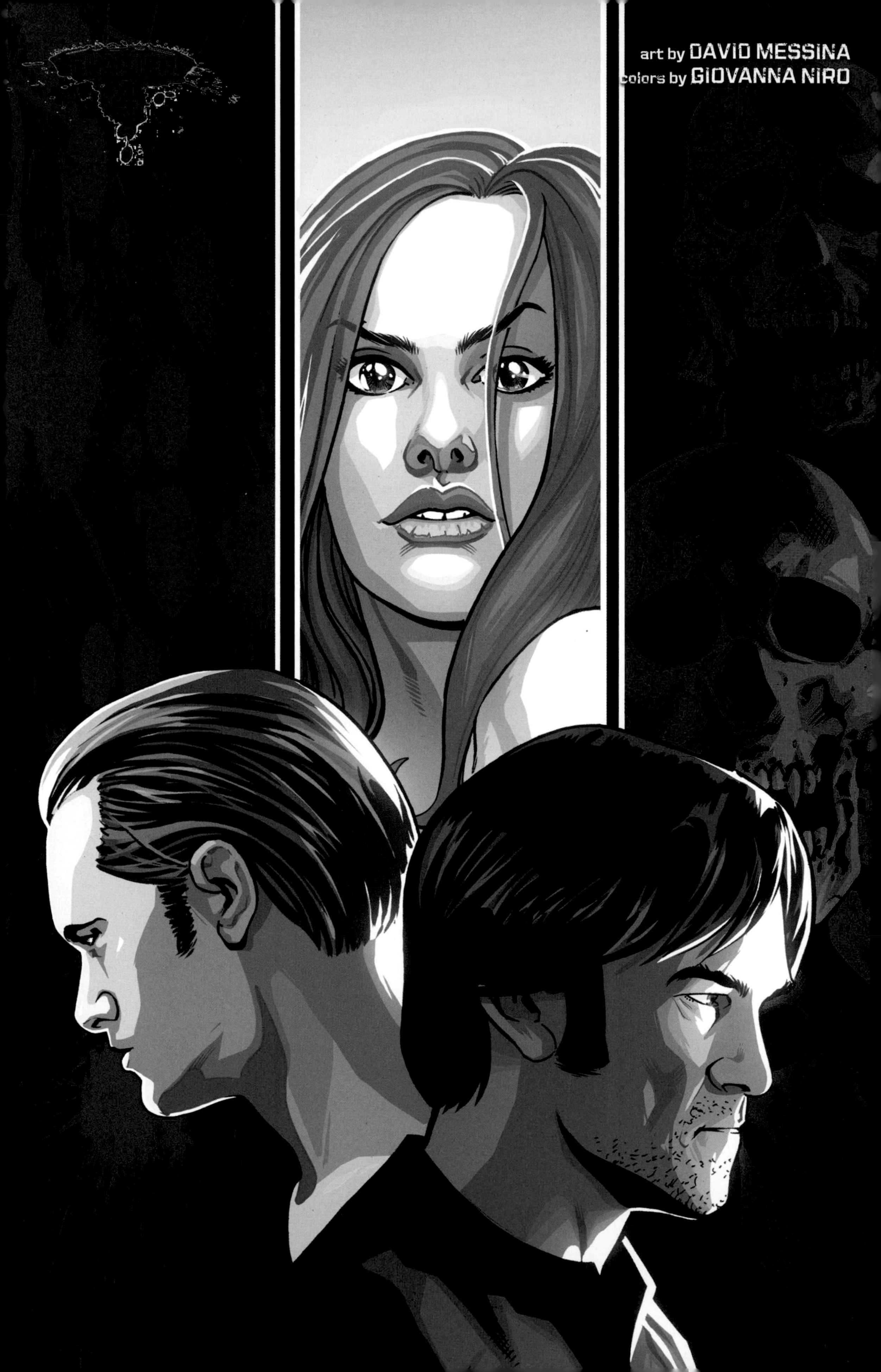
art by DAVID MESSINA
colors by GIOVANNA NIRO

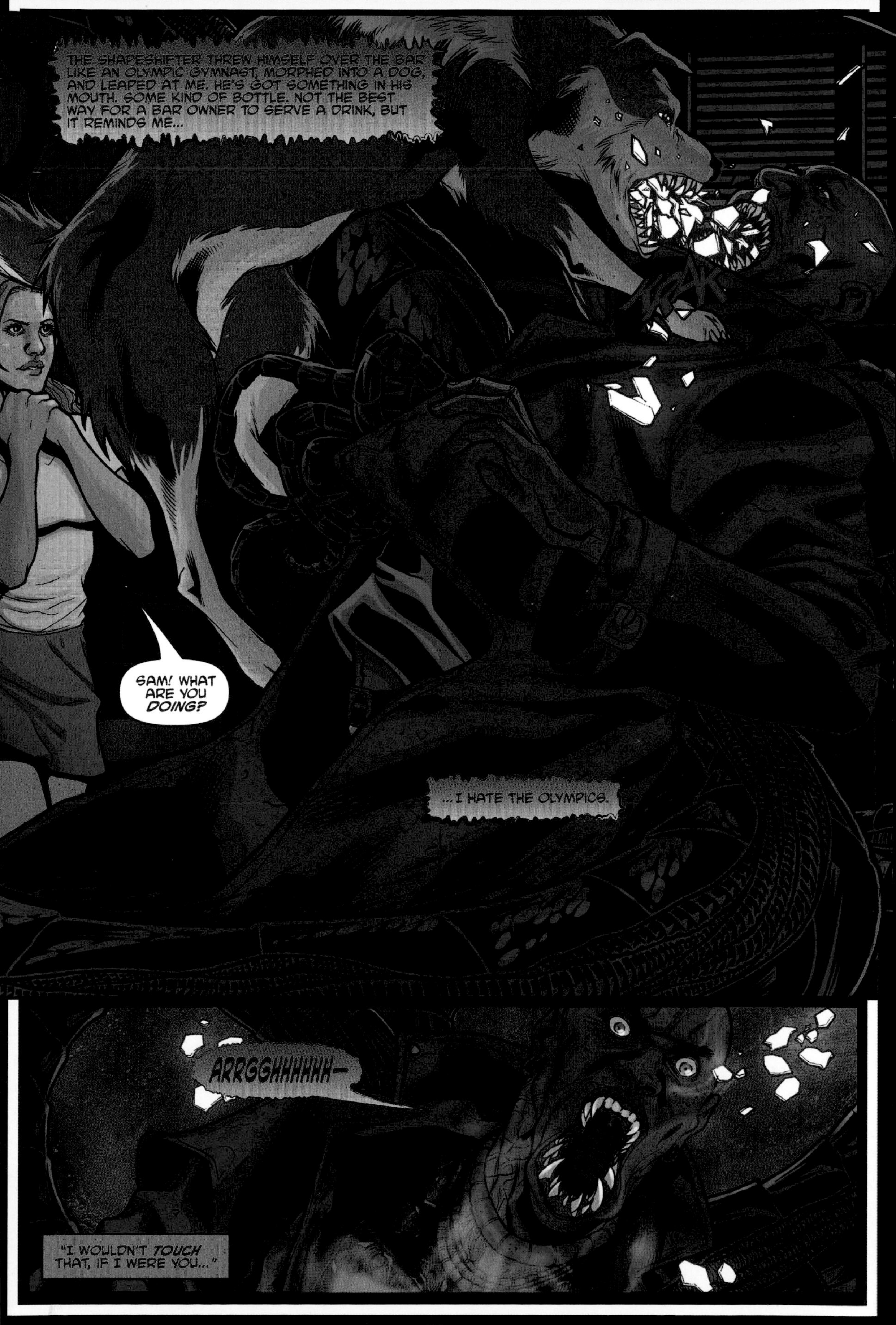
THE SHAPESHIFTER THREW HIMSELF OVER THE BAR LIKE AN OLYMPIC GYMNAST, MORPHED INTO A DOG, AND LEAPED AT ME. HE'S GOT SOMETHING IN HIS MOUTH. SOME KIND OF BOTTLE. NOT THE BEST WAY FOR A BAR OWNER TO SERVE A DRINK, BUT IT REMINDS ME...
SAM! WHAT ARE YOU *DOING?*
...I HATE THE OLYMPICS.
ARRGGHHHHHH—
"I WOULDN'T *TOUCH* THAT, IF I WERE YOU..."

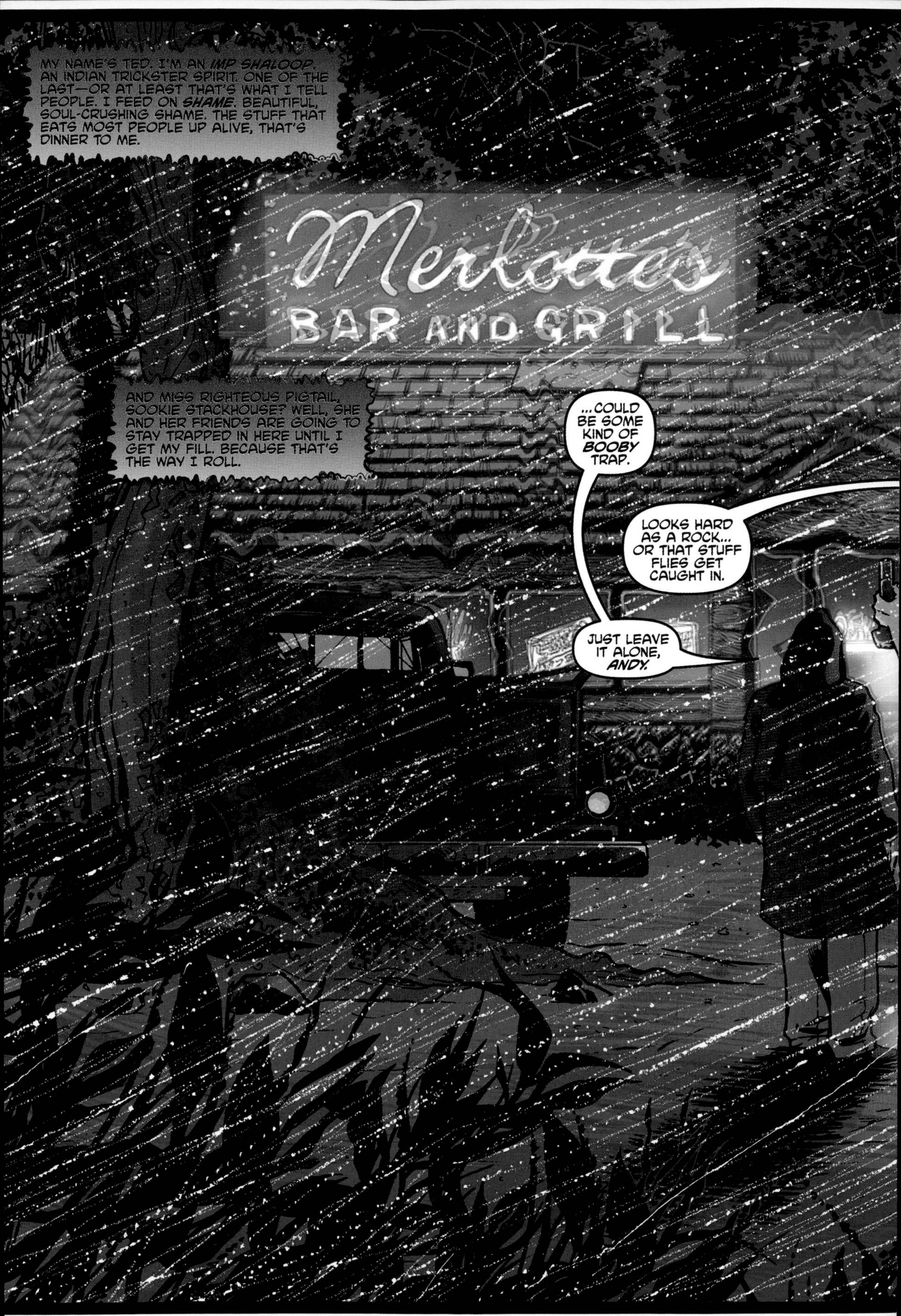
MY NAME'S TED. I'M AN *IMP SHALOOP*. AN INDIAN TRICKSTER SPIRIT. ONE OF THE LAST—OR AT LEAST THAT'S WHAT I TELL PEOPLE. I FEED ON *SHAME*. BEAUTIFUL, SOUL-CRUSHING SHAME. THE STUFF THAT EATS MOST PEOPLE UP ALIVE, THAT'S DINNER TO ME.
Merlotte's
BAR AND GRILL
AND MISS RIGHTEOUS PIGTAIL, SOOKIE STACKHOUSE? WELL, SHE AND HER FRIENDS ARE GOING TO STAY TRAPPED IN HERE UNTIL I GET MY FILL. BECAUSE THAT'S THE WAY I ROLL.
...COULD BE SOME KIND OF *BOOBY* TRAP.
LOOKS HARD AS A ROCK... OR THAT STUFF FLIES GET CAUGHT IN.
JUST LEAVE IT ALONE, *ANDY*.

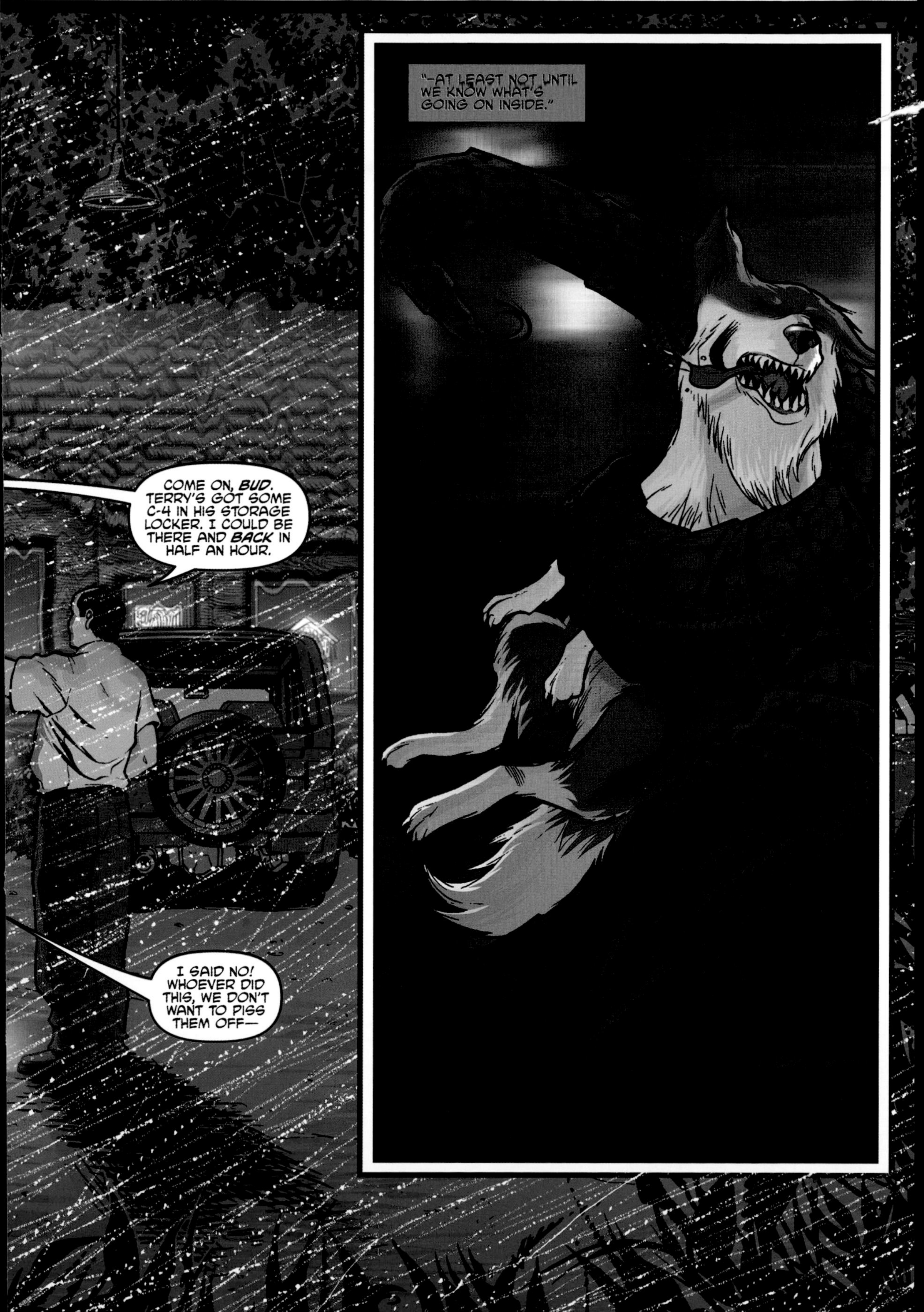
COME ON, BUD. TERRY'S GOT SOME C-4 IN HIS STORAGE LOCKER. I COULD BE THERE AND BACK IN HALF AN HOUR.
I SAID NO! WHOEVER DID THIS, WE DON'T WANT TO PISS THEM OFF—
"—AT LEAST NOT UNTIL WE KNOW WHAT'S GOING ON INSIDE."

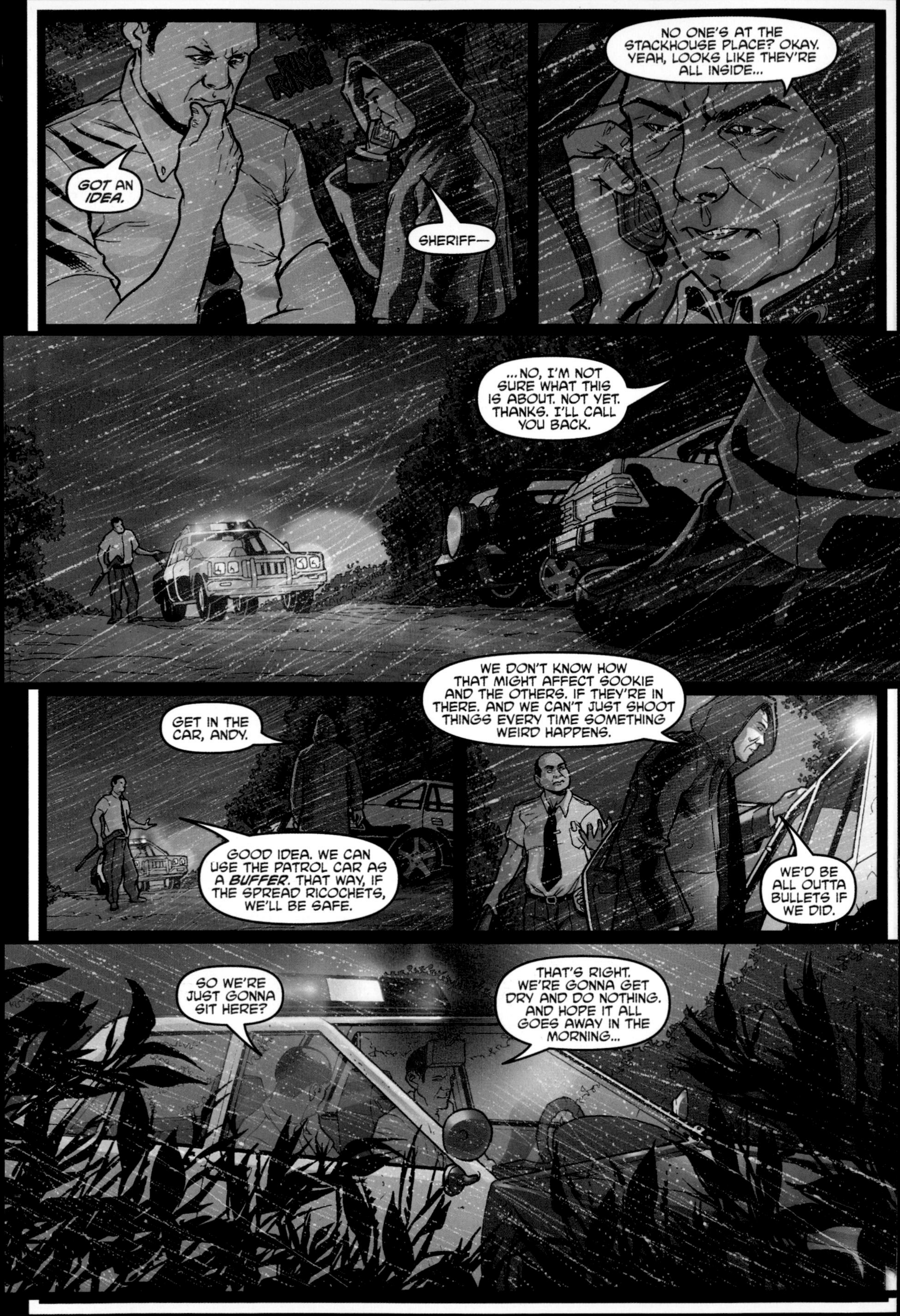
GOT AN IDEA.
SHERIFF—
NO ONE'S AT THE STACKHOUSE PLACE? OKAY. YEAH, LOOKS LIKE THEY'RE ALL INSIDE...
...NO, I'M NOT SURE WHAT THIS IS ABOUT. NOT YET. THANKS. I'LL CALL YOU BACK.
GET IN THE CAR, ANDY.
GOOD IDEA. WE CAN USE THE PATROL CAR AS A *BUFFER*. THAT WAY, IF THE SPREAD RICOCHETS, WE'LL BE SAFE.
WE DON'T KNOW HOW THAT MIGHT AFFECT SOOKIE AND THE OTHERS. IF THEY'RE IN THERE. AND WE CAN'T JUST SHOOT THINGS EVERY TIME SOMETHING WEIRD HAPPENS.
WE'D BE ALL OUTTA BULLETS IF WE DID.
SO WE'RE JUST GONNA SIT HERE?
THAT'S RIGHT. WE'RE GONNA GET DRY AND DO NOTHING. AND HOPE IT ALL GOES AWAY IN THE MORNING...

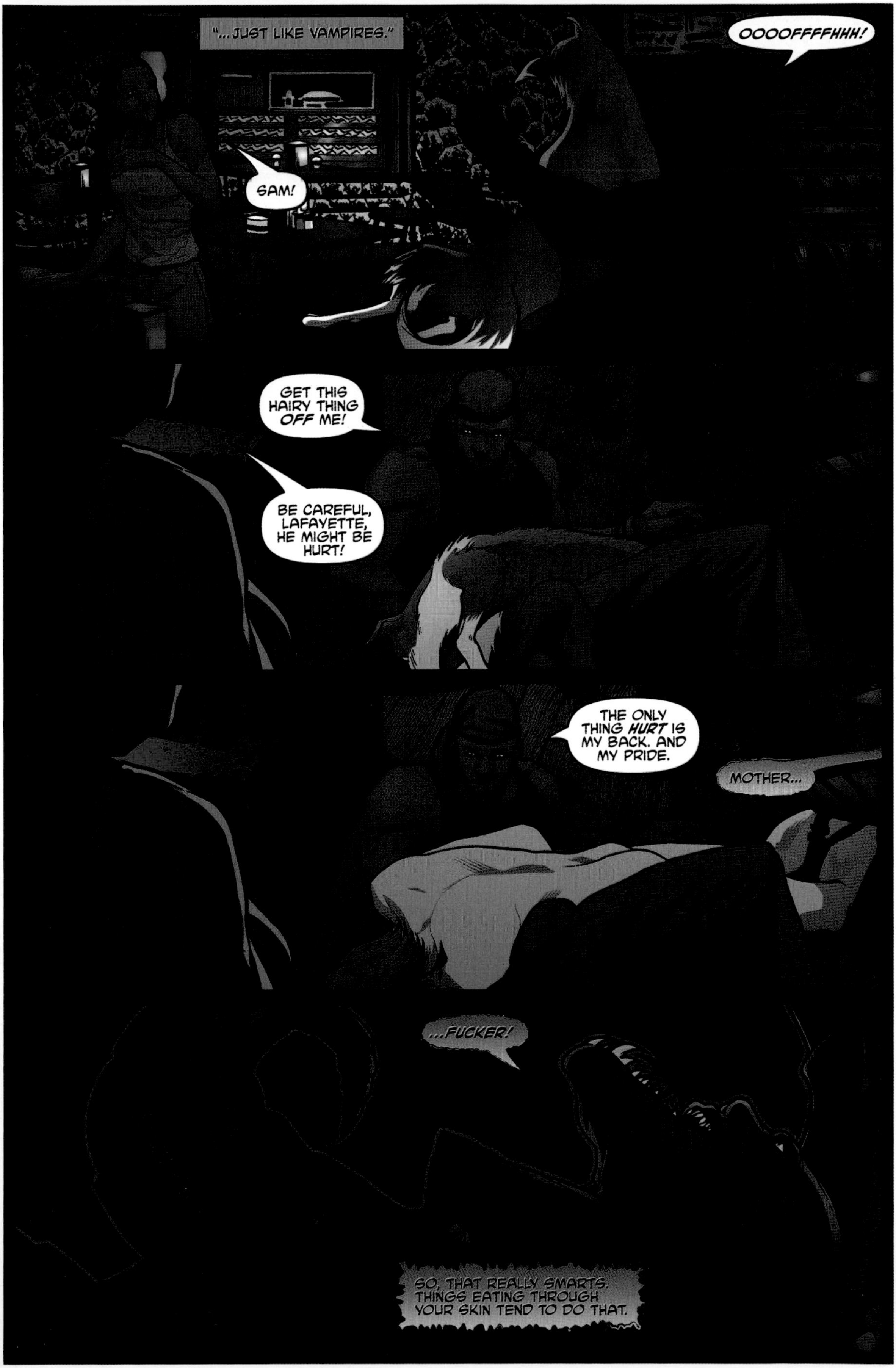
"...JUST LIKE VAMPIRES."
OOOOFFFFHHH!
SAM!
GET THIS HAIRY THING OFF ME!
BE CAREFUL, LAFAYETTE, HE MIGHT BE HURT!
THE ONLY THING HURT IS MY BACK. AND MY PRIDE.
MOTHER...
...FUCKER!
SO, THAT REALLY SMARTS. THINGS EATING THROUGH YOUR SKIN TEND TO DO THAT.

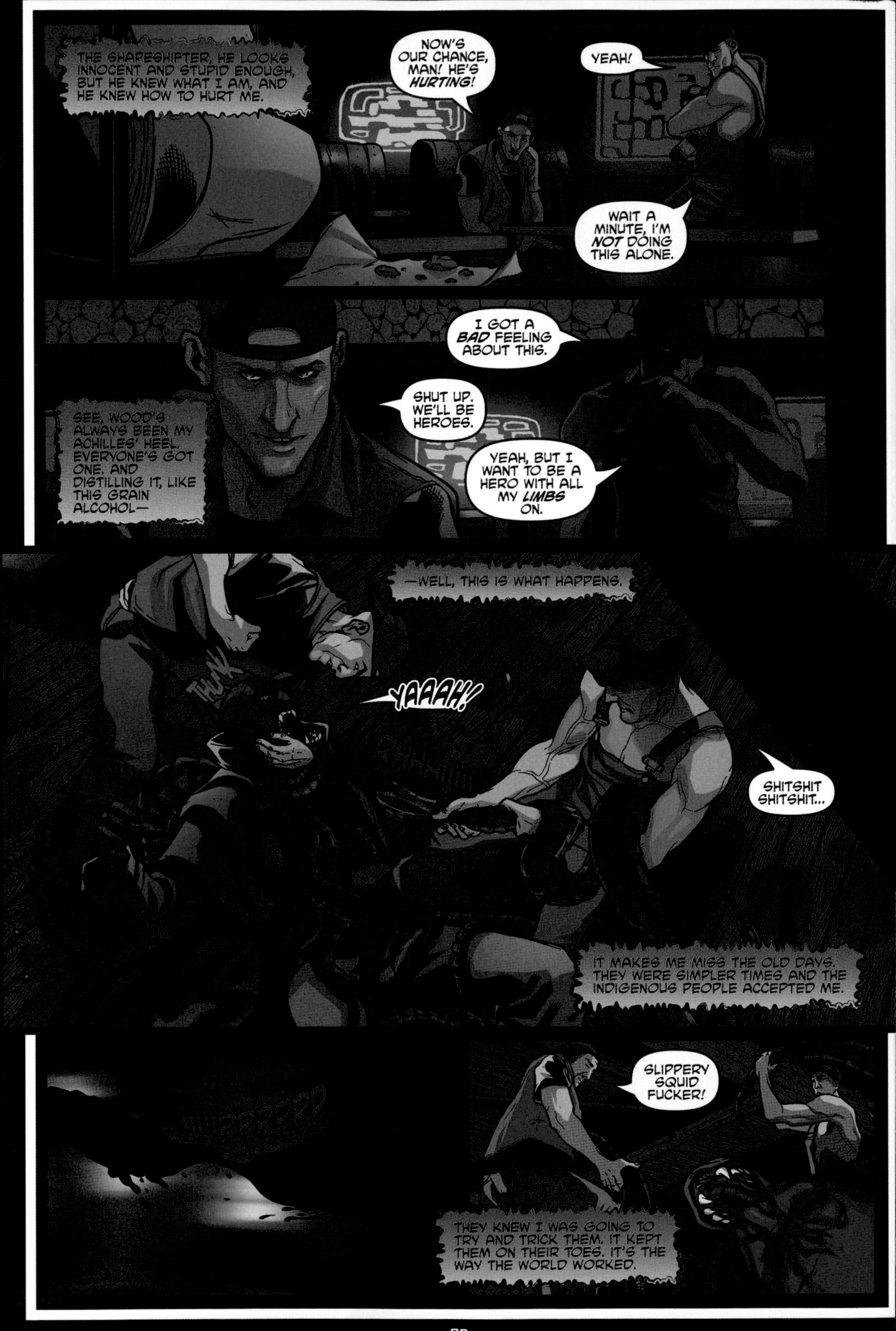
THE SHAPESHIFTER, HE LOOKS INNOCENT AND STUPID ENOUGH, BUT HE KNEW WHAT I AM, AND HE KNEW HOW TO HURT ME.
NOW'S OUR CHANCE, MAN! HE'S HURTING!
YEAH!
WAIT A MINUTE, I'M NOT DOING THIS ALONE.
I GOT A BAD FEELING ABOUT THIS.
SEE, WOOD'S ALWAYS BEEN MY ACHILLES' HEEL. EVERYONE'S GOT ONE. AND DISTILLING IT, LIKE THIS GRAIN ALCOHOL—
SHUT UP. WE'LL BE HEROES.
YEAH, BUT I WANT TO BE A HERO WITH ALL MY LIMBS ON.
—WELL, THIS IS WHAT HAPPENS.
YAAAH!
SHITSHIT SHITSHIT...
IT MAKES ME MISS THE OLD DAYS. THEY WERE SIMPLER TIMES AND THE INDIGENOUS PEOPLE ACCEPTED ME.
SLIPPERY SQUID FUCKER!
THEY KNEW I WAS GOING TO TRY AND TRICK THEM. IT KEPT THEM ON THEIR TOES. IT'S THE WAY THE WORLD WORKED.

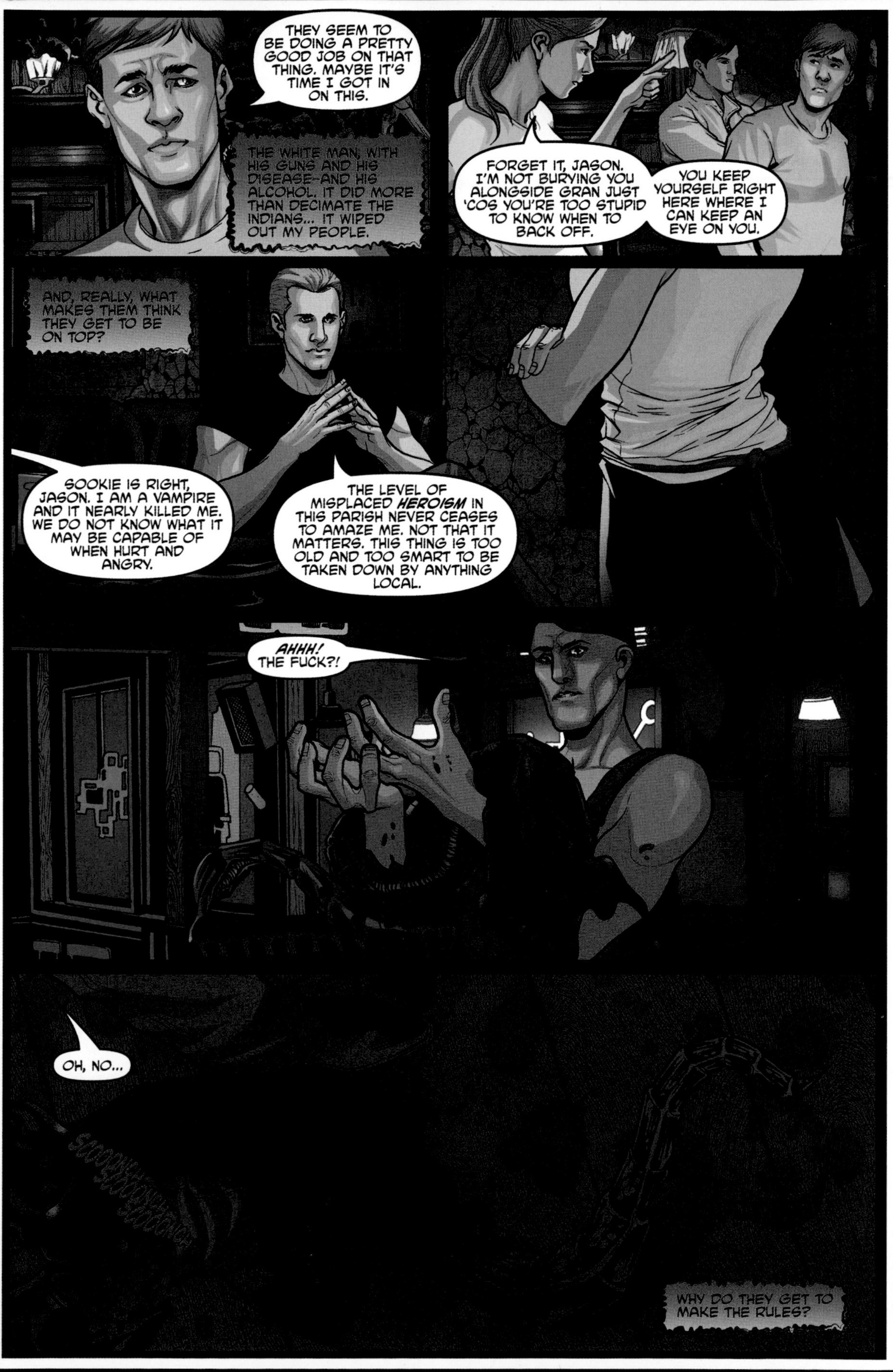
THEY SEEM TO BE DOING A PRETTY GOOD JOB ON THAT THING. MAYBE IT'S TIME I GOT IN ON THIS.
THE WHITE MAN, WITH HIS GUNS AND HIS DISEASE--AND HIS ALCOHOL. IT DID MORE THAN DECIMATE THE INDIANS... IT WIPED OUT MY PEOPLE.
FORGET IT, JASON. I'M NOT BURYING YOU ALONGSIDE GRAN JUST 'COS YOU'RE TOO STUPID TO KNOW WHEN TO BACK OFF.
YOU KEEP YOURSELF RIGHT HERE WHERE I CAN KEEP AN EYE ON YOU.
AND, REALLY, WHAT MAKES THEM THINK THEY GET TO BE ON TOP?
SOOKIE IS RIGHT, JASON. I AM A VAMPIRE AND IT NEARLY KILLED ME. WE DO NOT KNOW WHAT IT MAY BE CAPABLE OF WHEN HURT AND ANGRY.
THE LEVEL OF MISPLACED HEROISM IN THIS PARISH NEVER CEASES TO AMAZE ME. NOT THAT IT MATTERS. THIS THING IS TOO OLD AND TOO SMART TO BE TAKEN DOWN BY ANYTHING LOCAL.
AHHH! THE FUCK?!
OH, NO...
WHY DO THEY GET TO MAKE THE RULES?

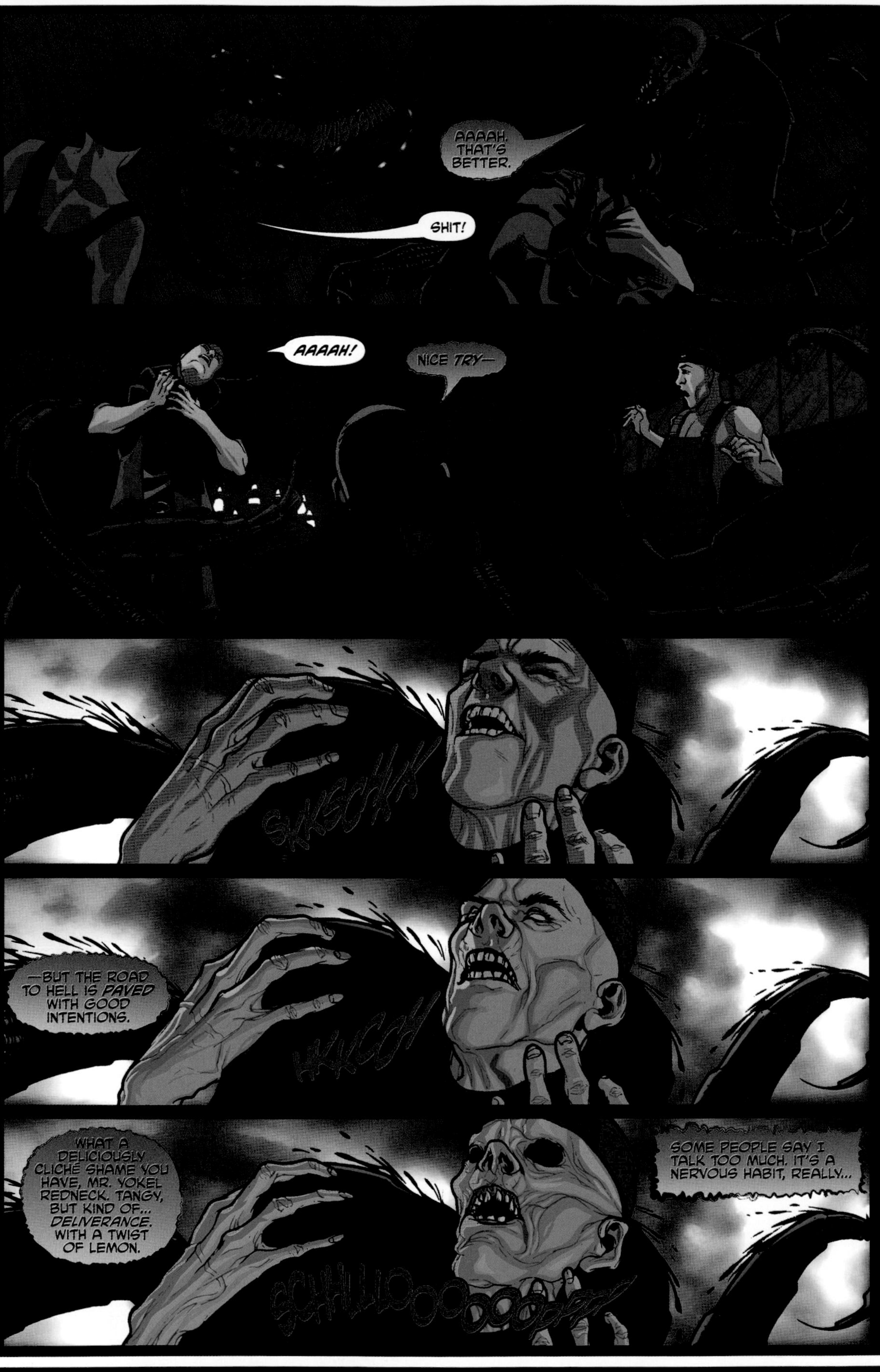
AAAAH. THAT'S BETTER.
SHIT!
AAAAH!
NICE *TRY*—
—BUT THE ROAD TO HELL IS *PAVED* WITH GOOD INTENTIONS.
WHAT A DELICIOUSLY CLICHÉ SHAME YOU HAVE, MR. YOKEL REDNECK. TANGY, BUT KIND OF... *DELIVERANCE*. WITH A TWIST OF LEMON.
SOME PEOPLE SAY I TALK TOO MUCH. IT'S A NERVOUS HABIT, REALLY...

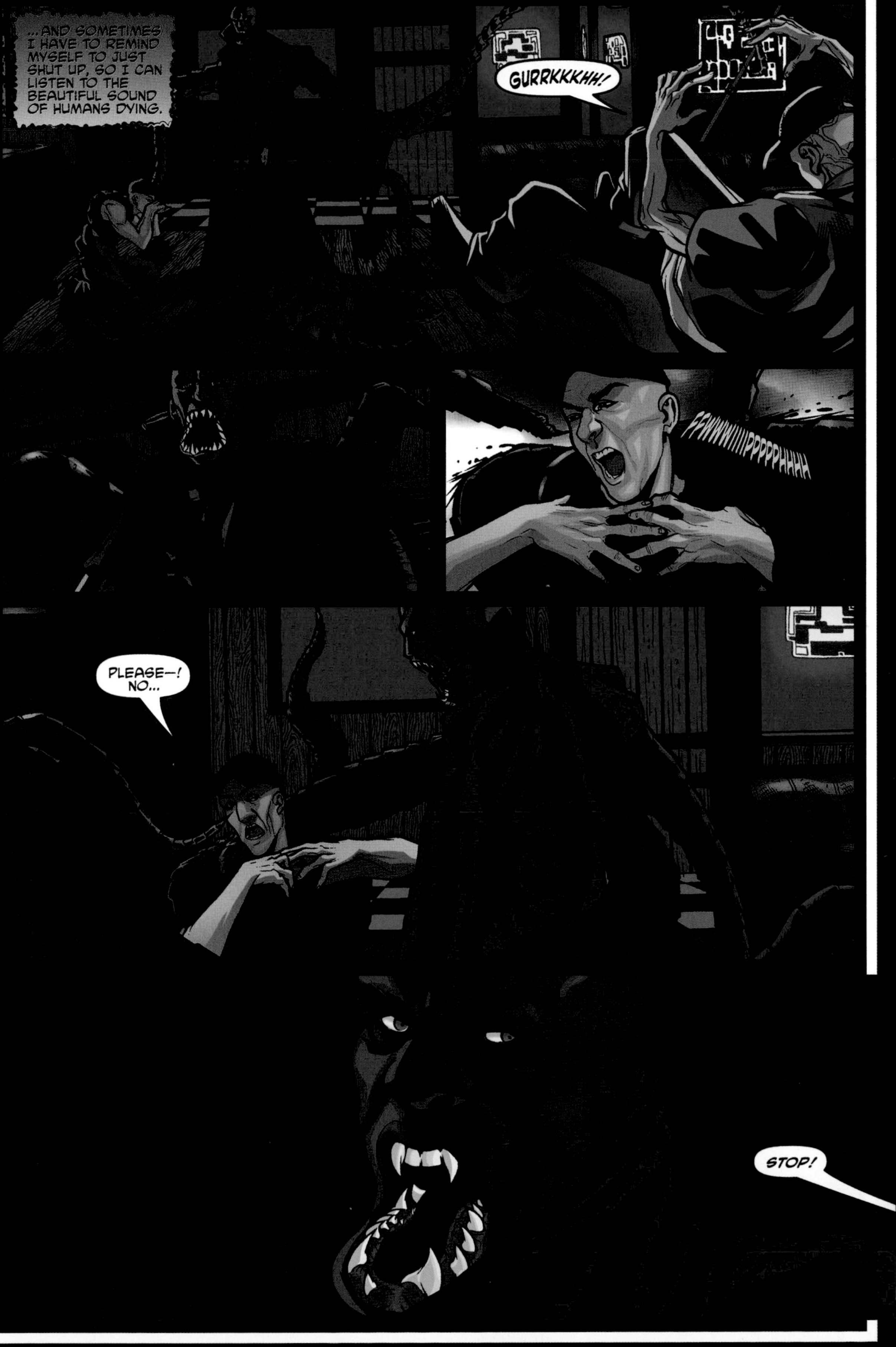
...AND SOMETIMES I HAVE TO REMIND MYSELF TO JUST SHUT UP, SO I CAN LISTEN TO THE BEAUTIFUL SOUND OF HUMANS DYING.
GURRKKKHH!
FFWWWIIIIPPPPHHHH
PLEASE--! NO...
STOP!

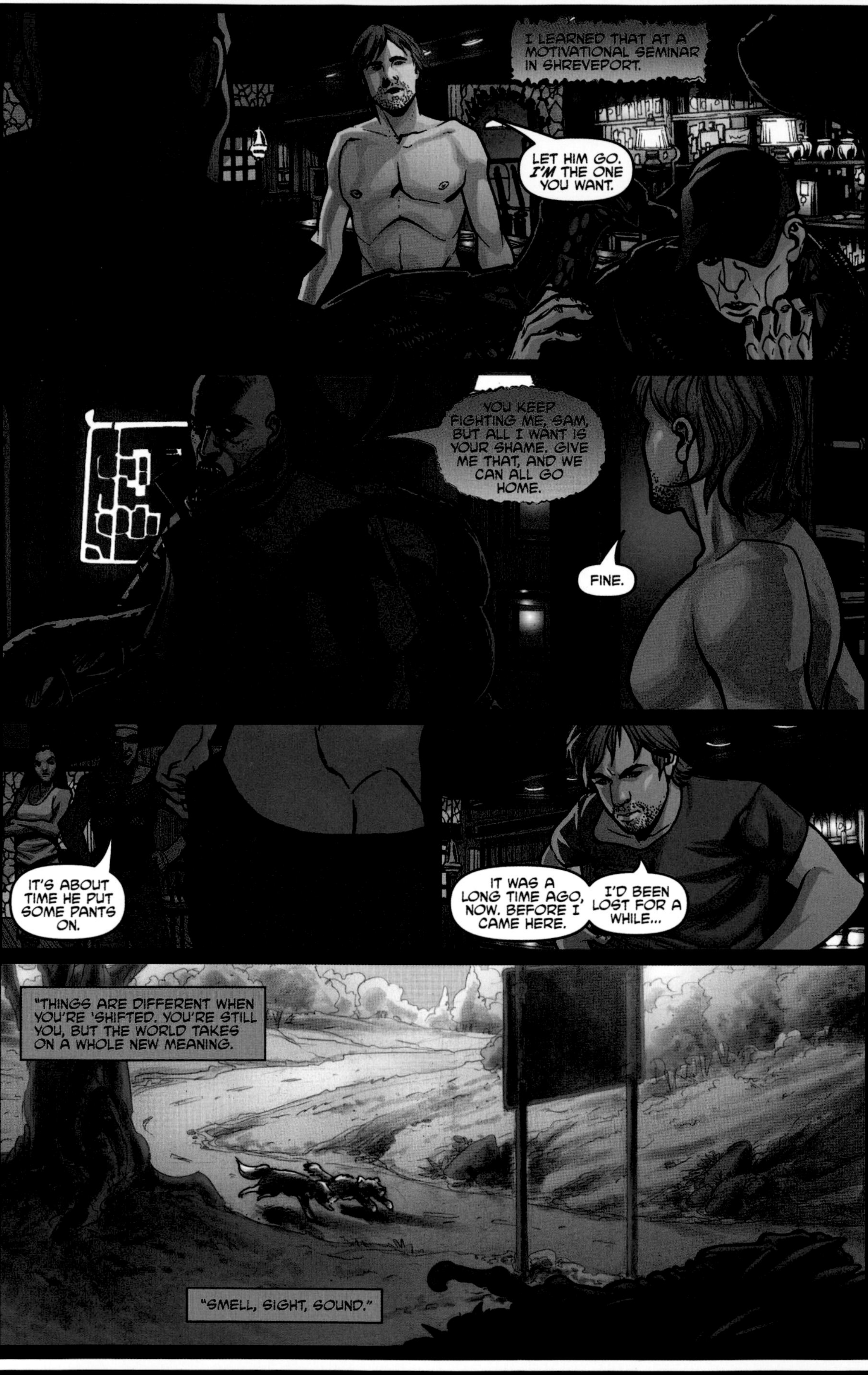
I LEARNED THAT AT A MOTIVATIONAL SEMINAR IN SHREVEPORT.
LET HIM GO. I'M THE ONE YOU WANT.
YOU KEEP FIGHTING ME, SAM, BUT ALL I WANT IS YOUR SHAME. GIVE ME THAT, AND WE CAN ALL GO HOME.
FINE.
IT'S ABOUT TIME HE PUT SOME PANTS ON.
IT WAS A LONG TIME AGO, NOW. BEFORE I CAME HERE.
I'D BEEN LOST FOR A WHILE...
"THINGS ARE DIFFERENT WHEN YOU'RE 'SHIFTED. YOU'RE STILL YOU, BUT THE WORLD TAKES ON A WHOLE NEW MEANING.
"SMELL, SIGHT, SOUND."

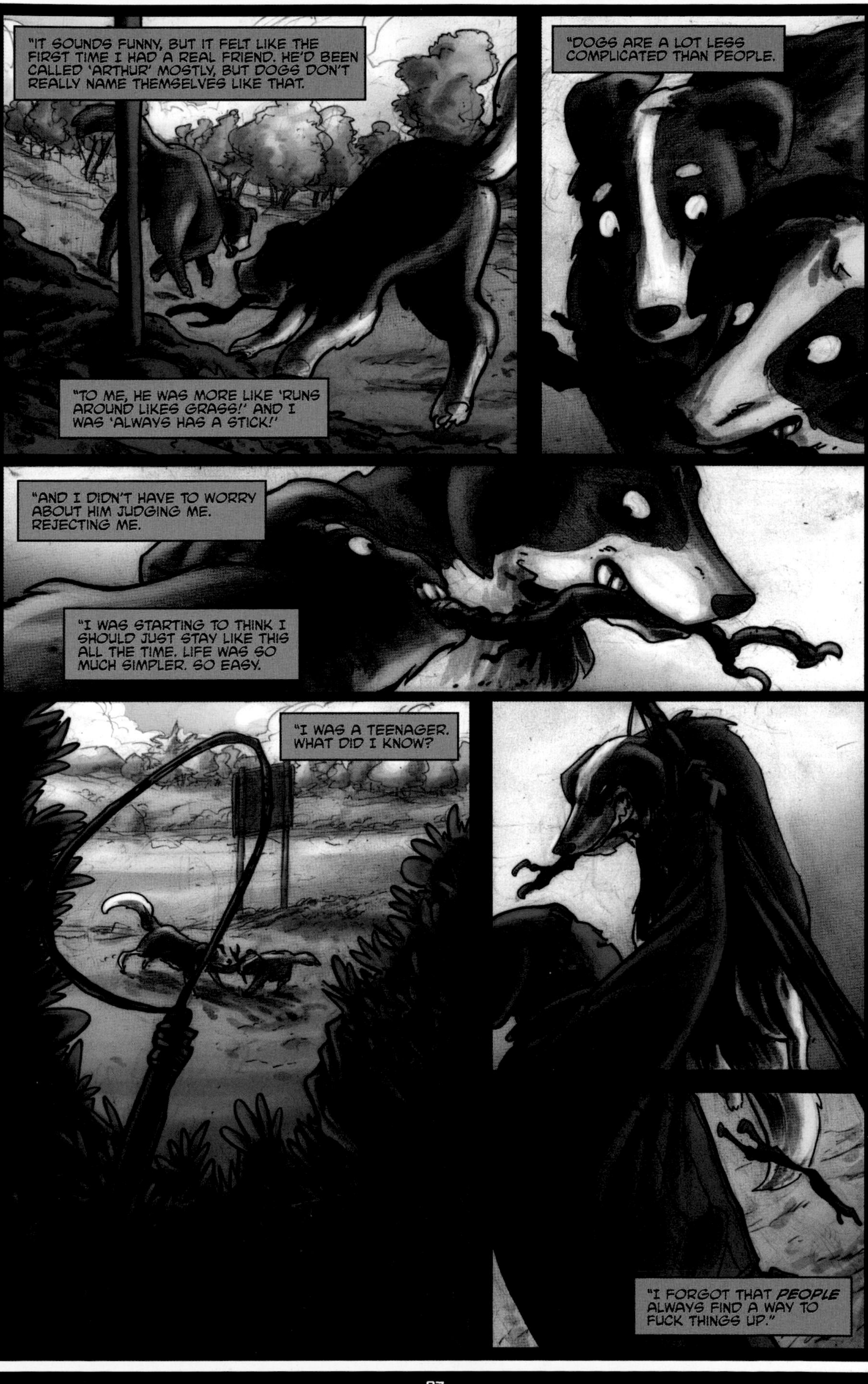
"IT SOUNDS FUNNY, BUT IT FELT LIKE THE FIRST TIME I HAD A REAL FRIEND. HE'D BEEN CALLED 'ARTHUR' MOSTLY, BUT DOGS DON'T REALLY NAME THEMSELVES LIKE THAT.
"TO ME, HE WAS MORE LIKE 'RUNS AROUND LIKES GRASS!' AND I WAS 'ALWAYS HAS A STICK!'
"DOGS ARE A LOT LESS COMPLICATED THAN PEOPLE.
"AND I DIDN'T HAVE TO WORRY ABOUT HIM JUDGING ME. REJECTING ME.
"I WAS STARTING TO THINK I SHOULD JUST STAY LIKE THIS ALL THE TIME. LIFE WAS SO MUCH SIMPLER. SO EASY.
"I WAS A TEENAGER. WHAT DID I KNOW?
"I FORGOT THAT *PEOPLE* ALWAYS FIND A WAY TO FUCK THINGS UP."

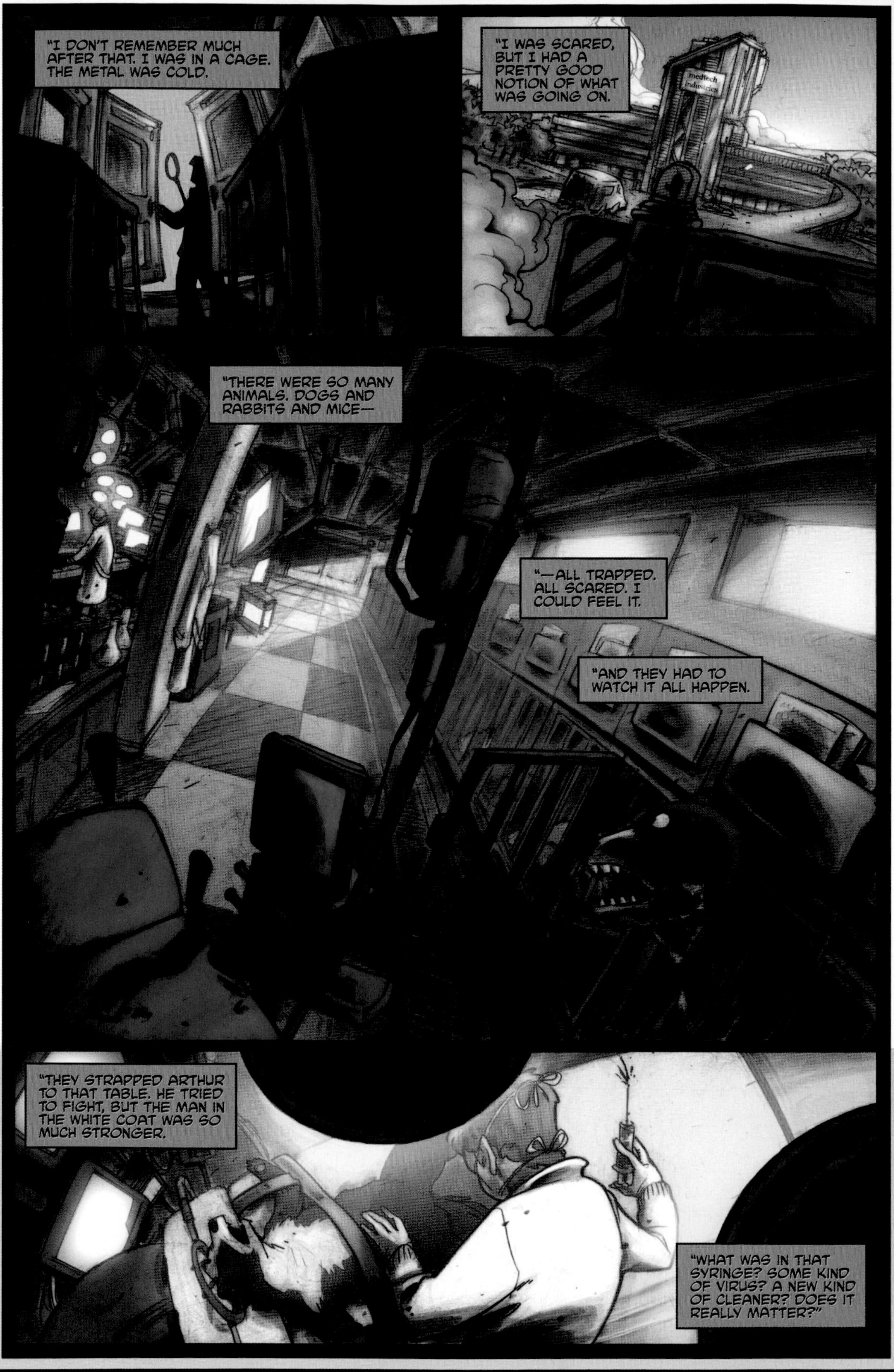
"I DON'T REMEMBER MUCH AFTER THAT. I WAS IN A CAGE. THE METAL WAS COLD.
"I WAS SCARED, BUT I HAD A PRETTY GOOD NOTION OF WHAT WAS GOING ON.
medtech industries
"THERE WERE SO MANY ANIMALS. DOGS AND RABBITS AND MICE—
"—ALL TRAPPED. ALL SCARED. I COULD FEEL IT.
"AND THEY HAD TO WATCH IT ALL HAPPEN.
"THEY STRAPPED ARTHUR TO THAT TABLE. HE TRIED TO FIGHT, BUT THE MAN IN THE WHITE COAT WAS SO MUCH STRONGER.
"WHAT WAS IN THAT SYRINGE? SOME KIND OF VIRUS? A NEW KIND OF CLEANER? DOES IT REALLY MATTER?"

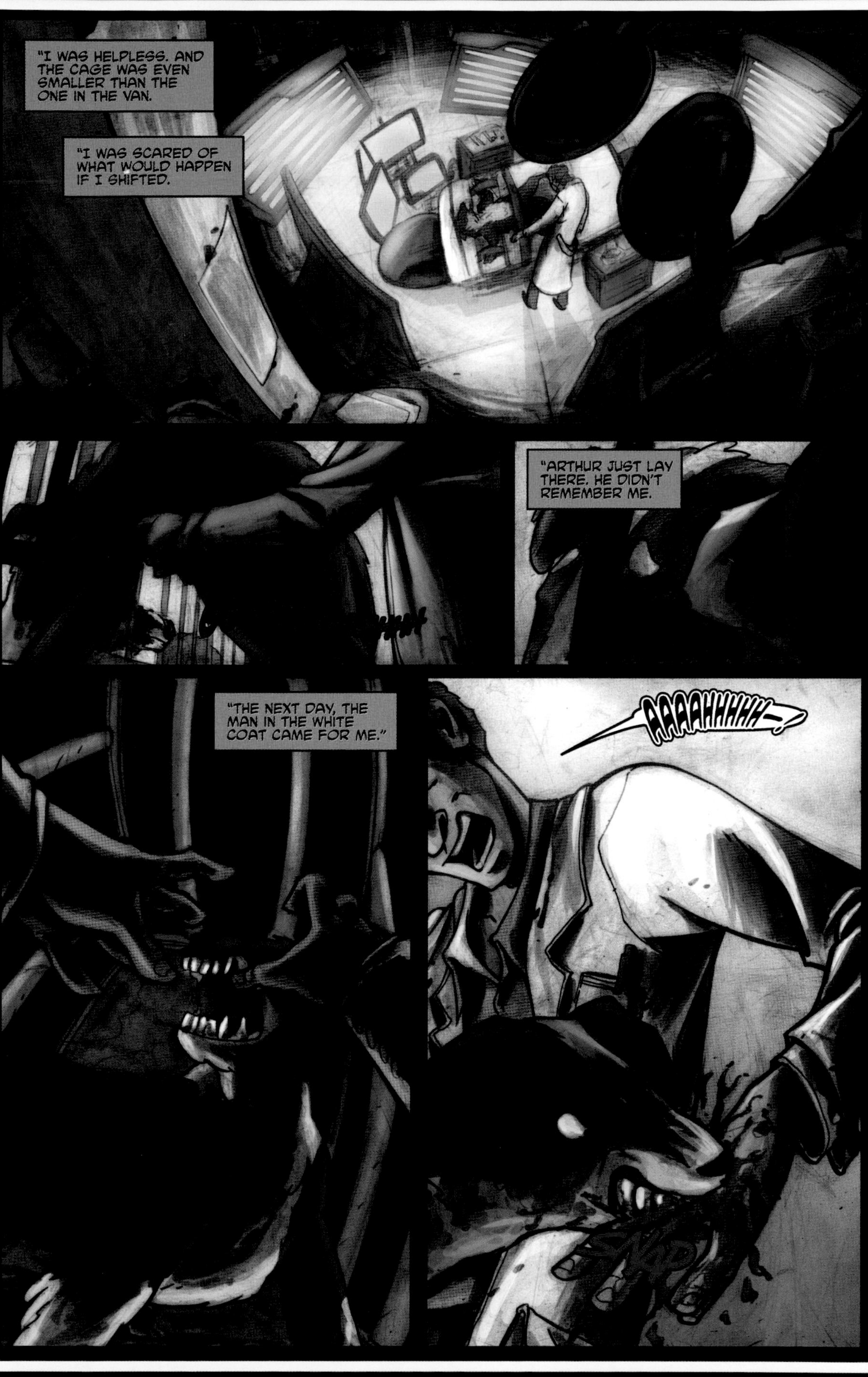
"I WAS HELPLESS. AND THE CAGE WAS EVEN SMALLER THAN THE ONE IN THE VAN.
"I WAS SCARED OF WHAT WOULD HAPPEN IF I SHIFTED.
"ARTHUR JUST LAY THERE. HE DIDN'T REMEMBER ME.
"THE NEXT DAY, THE MAN IN THE WHITE COAT CAME FOR ME."
AAAAHHHHH—!

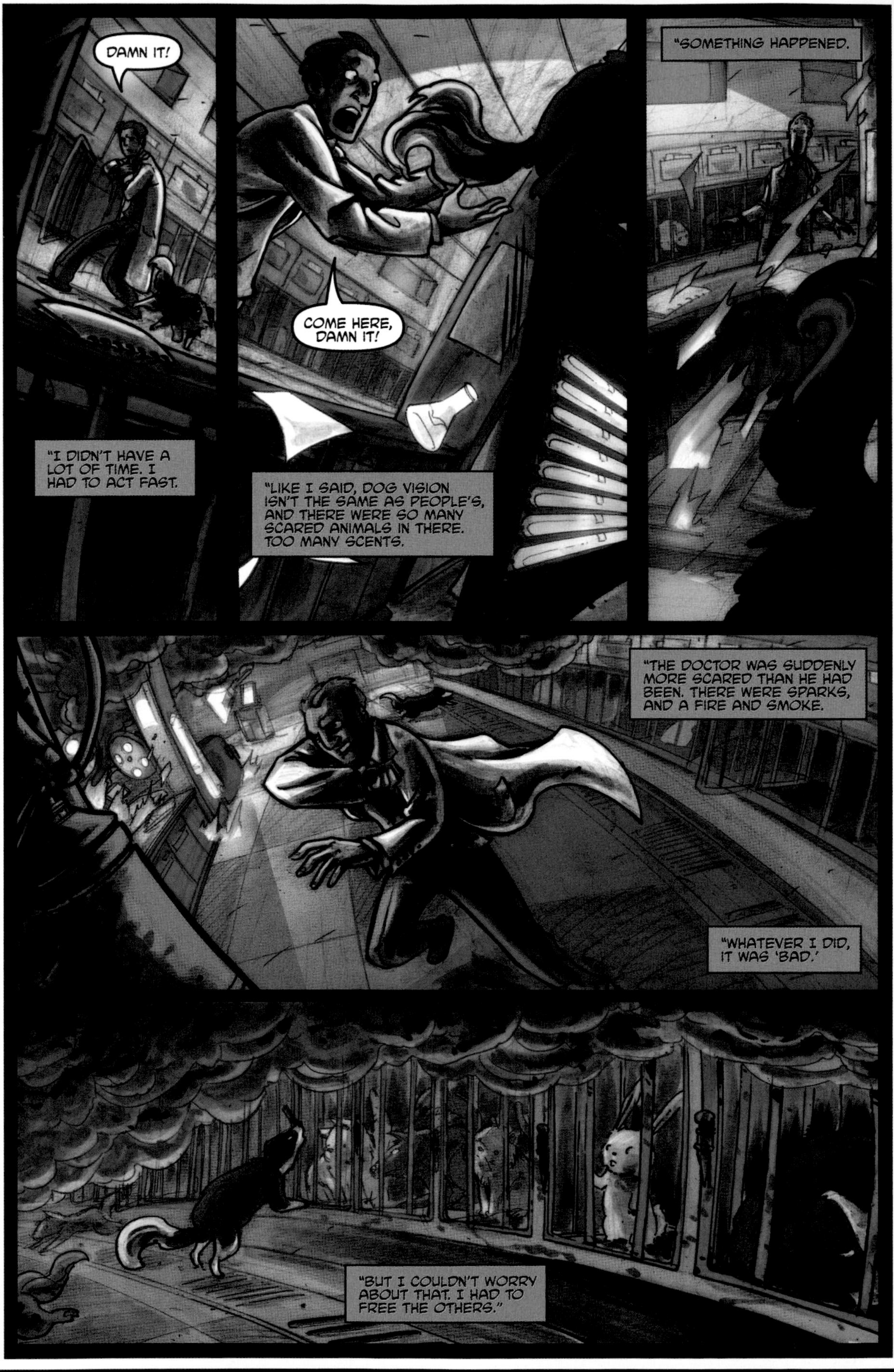
DAMN IT!
COME HERE, DAMN IT!
"SOMETHING HAPPENED.
"I DIDN'T HAVE A LOT OF TIME. I HAD TO ACT FAST.
"LIKE I SAID, DOG VISION ISN'T THE SAME AS PEOPLE'S, AND THERE WERE SO MANY SCARED ANIMALS IN THERE. TOO MANY SCENTS.
"THE DOCTOR WAS SUDDENLY MORE SCARED THAN HE HAD BEEN. THERE WERE SPARKS, AND A FIRE AND SMOKE.
"WHATEVER I DID, IT WAS 'BAD.'
"BUT I COULDN'T WORRY ABOUT THAT. I HAD TO FREE THE OTHERS."

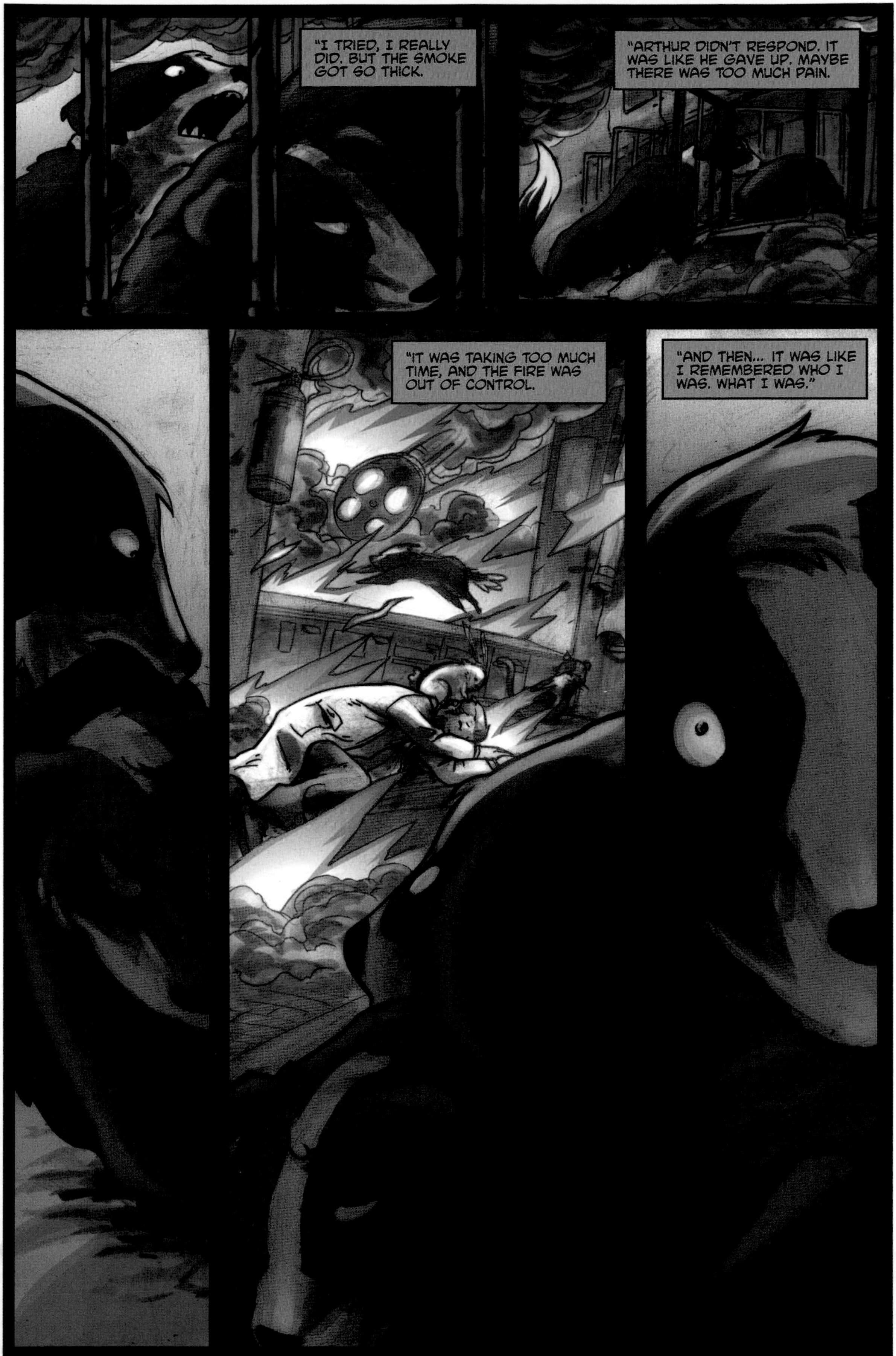
"I TRIED, I REALLY DID. BUT THE SMOKE GOT SO THICK.
"ARTHUR DIDN'T RESPOND. IT WAS LIKE HE GAVE UP. MAYBE THERE WAS TOO MUCH PAIN.
"IT WAS TAKING TOO MUCH TIME, AND THE FIRE WAS OUT OF CONTROL.
"AND THEN... IT WAS LIKE I REMEMBERED WHO I WAS. WHAT I WAS."

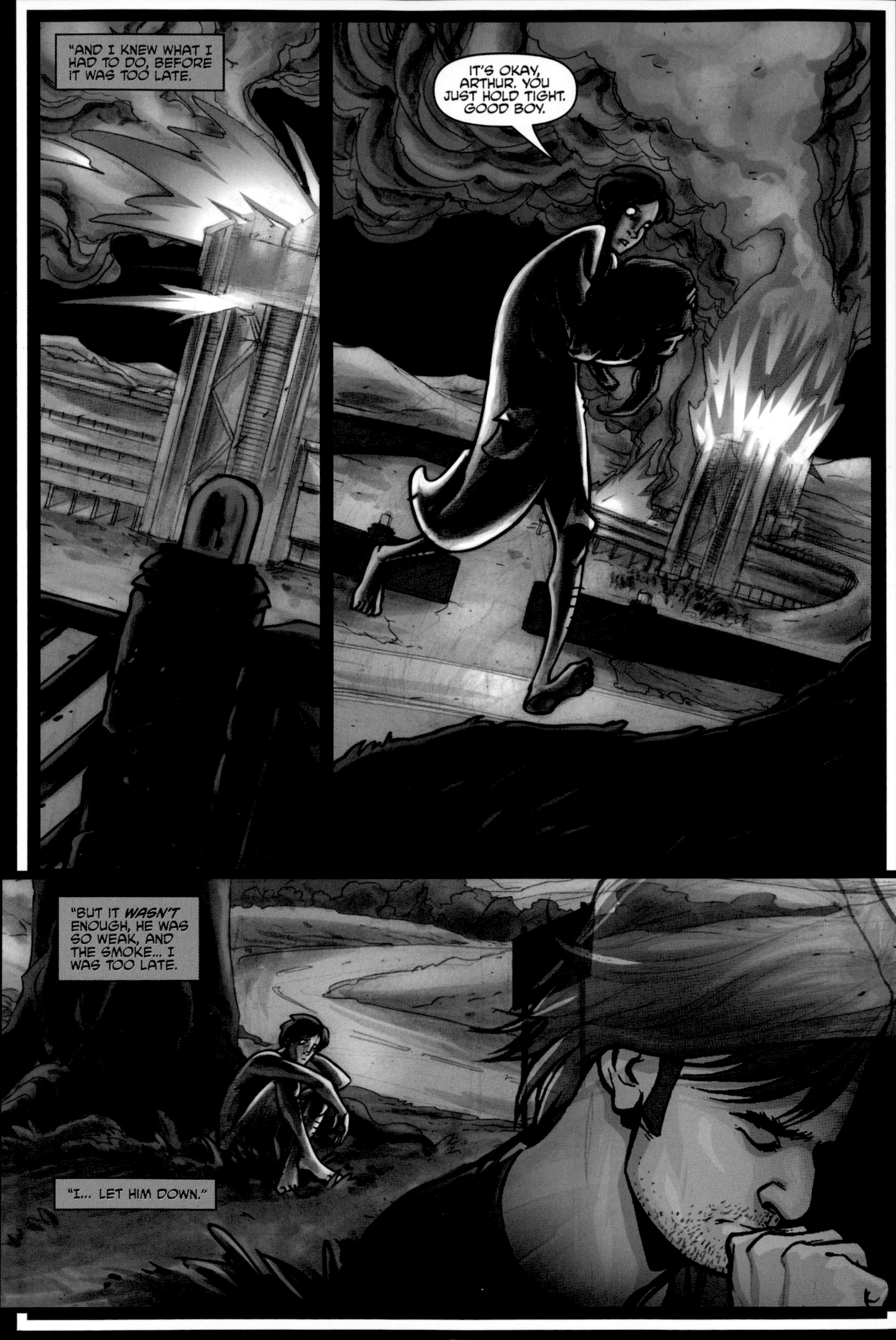
"AND I KNEW WHAT I HAD TO DO, BEFORE IT WAS TOO LATE.
IT'S OKAY, ARTHUR. YOU JUST HOLD TIGHT. GOOD BOY.
"BUT IT *WASN'T* ENOUGH, HE WAS SO WEAK, AND THE SMOKE... I WAS TOO LATE.
"I... LET HIM DOWN."

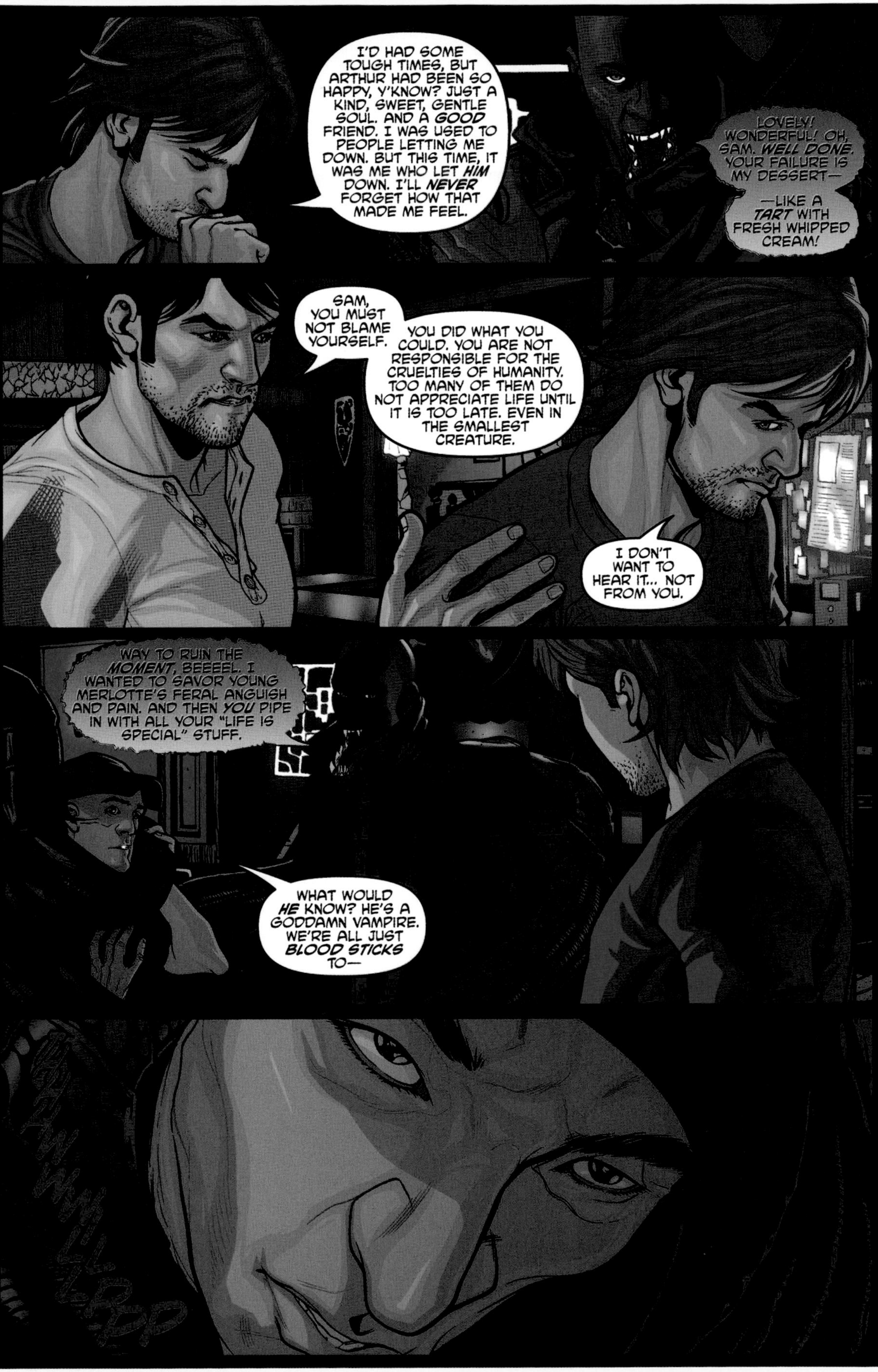
I'D HAD SOME TOUGH TIMES, BUT ARTHUR HAD BEEN SO HAPPY, Y'KNOW? JUST A KIND, SWEET, GENTLE SOUL. AND A GOOD FRIEND. I WAS USED TO PEOPLE LETTING ME DOWN. BUT THIS TIME, IT WAS ME WHO LET HIM DOWN. I'LL NEVER FORGET HOW THAT MADE ME FEEL.
LOVELY! WONDERFUL! OH, SAM. WELL DONE. YOUR FAILURE IS MY DESSERT—
—LIKE A TART WITH FRESH WHIPPED CREAM!
SAM, YOU MUST NOT BLAME YOURSELF.
YOU DID WHAT YOU COULD. YOU ARE NOT RESPONSIBLE FOR THE CRUELTIES OF HUMANITY. TOO MANY OF THEM DO NOT APPRECIATE LIFE UNTIL IT IS TOO LATE. EVEN IN THE SMALLEST CREATURE.
I DON'T WANT TO HEAR IT... NOT FROM YOU.
WAY TO RUIN THE MOMENT, BEEEEL. I WANTED TO SAVOR YOUNG MERLOTTE'S FERAL ANGUISH AND PAIN. AND THEN YOU PIPE IN WITH ALL YOUR "LIFE IS SPECIAL" STUFF.
WHAT WOULD HE KNOW? HE'S A GODDAMN VAMPIRE. WE'RE ALL JUST BLOOD STICKS TO—

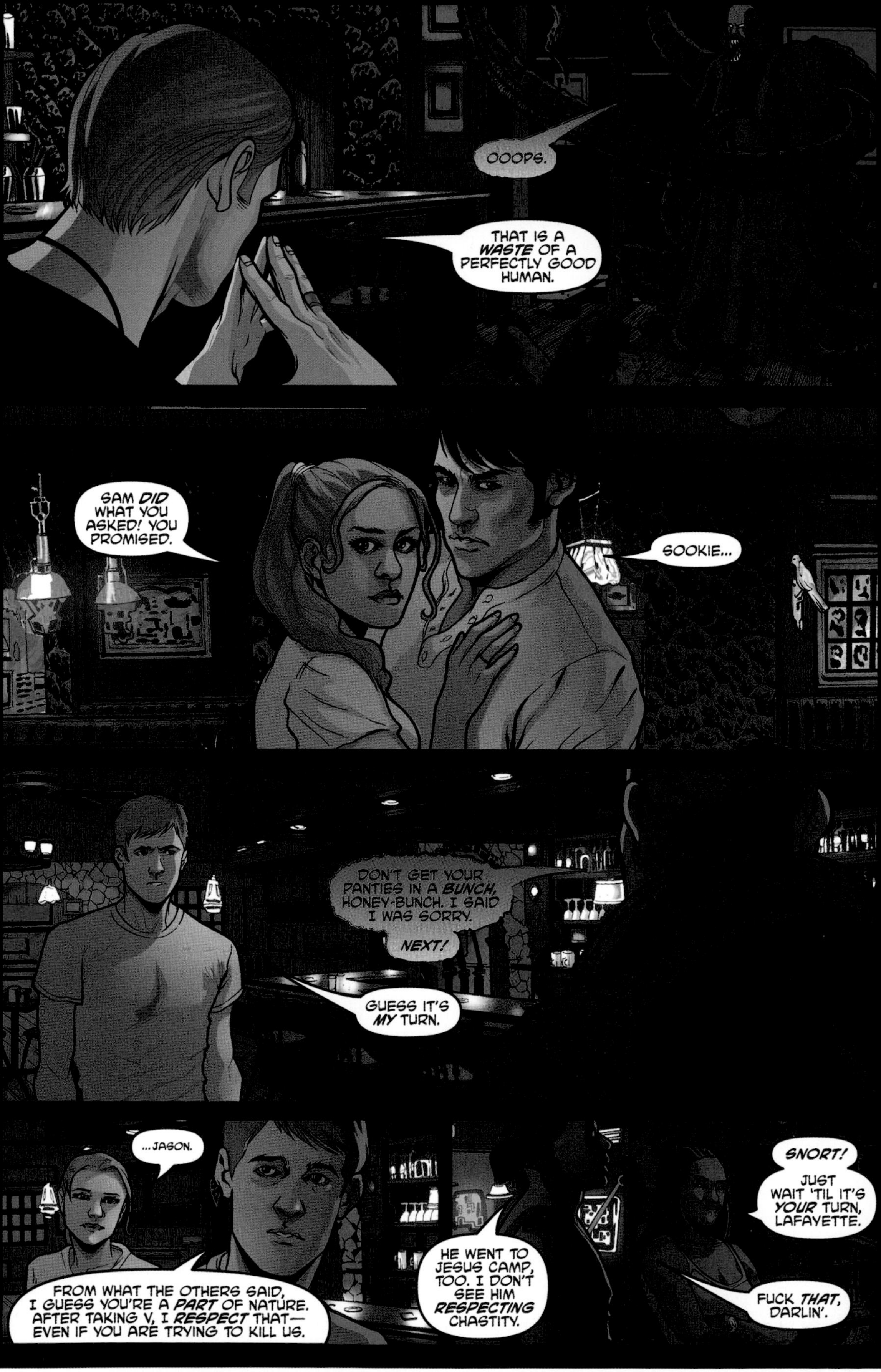
OOOPS.
THAT IS A WASTE OF A PERFECTLY GOOD HUMAN.
SAM DID WHAT YOU ASKED! YOU PROMISED.
SOOKIE...
DON'T GET YOUR PANTIES IN A BUNCH, HONEY-BUNCH. I SAID I WAS SORRY.
NEXT!
GUESS IT'S MY TURN.
...JASON.
FROM WHAT THE OTHERS SAID, I GUESS YOU'RE A PART OF NATURE. AFTER TAKING V, I RESPECT THAT— EVEN IF YOU ARE TRYING TO KILL US.
HE WENT TO JESUS CAMP, TOO. I DON'T SEE HIM RESPECTING CHASTITY.
SNORT!
JUST WAIT 'TIL IT'S YOUR TURN, LAFAYETTE.
FUCK THAT, DARLIN'.

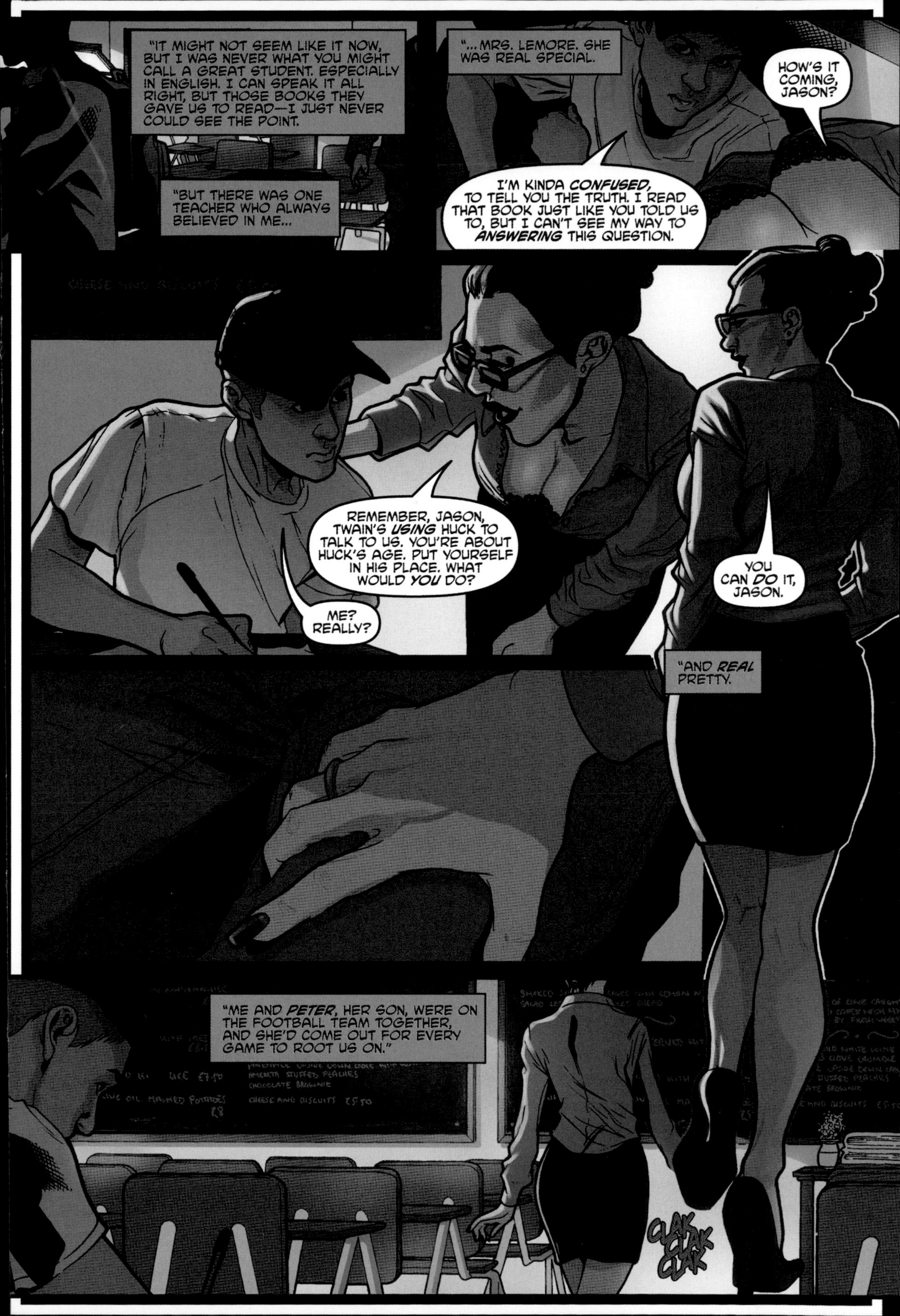
"IT MIGHT NOT SEEM LIKE IT NOW, BUT I WAS NEVER WHAT YOU MIGHT CALL A GREAT STUDENT. ESPECIALLY IN ENGLISH. I CAN SPEAK IT ALL RIGHT, BUT THOSE BOOKS THEY GAVE US TO READ—I JUST NEVER COULD SEE THE POINT.
"BUT THERE WAS ONE TEACHER WHO ALWAYS BELIEVED IN ME...
"...MRS. LEMORE. SHE WAS REAL SPECIAL.
HOW'S IT COMING, JASON?
I'M KINDA *CONFUSED*, TO TELL YOU THE TRUTH. I READ THAT BOOK JUST LIKE YOU TOLD US TO, BUT I CAN'T SEE MY WAY TO *ANSWERING* THIS QUESTION.
REMEMBER, JASON, TWAIN'S *USING* HUCK TO TALK TO US. YOU'RE ABOUT HUCK'S AGE. PUT YOURSELF IN HIS PLACE. WHAT WOULD *YOU* DO?
ME? REALLY?
YOU CAN *DO* IT, JASON.
"AND *REAL* PRETTY.
"ME AND *PETER*, HER SON, WERE ON THE FOOTBALL TEAM TOGETHER, AND SHE'D COME OUT FOR EVERY GAME TO ROOT US ON."
CLAK CLAK CLAK

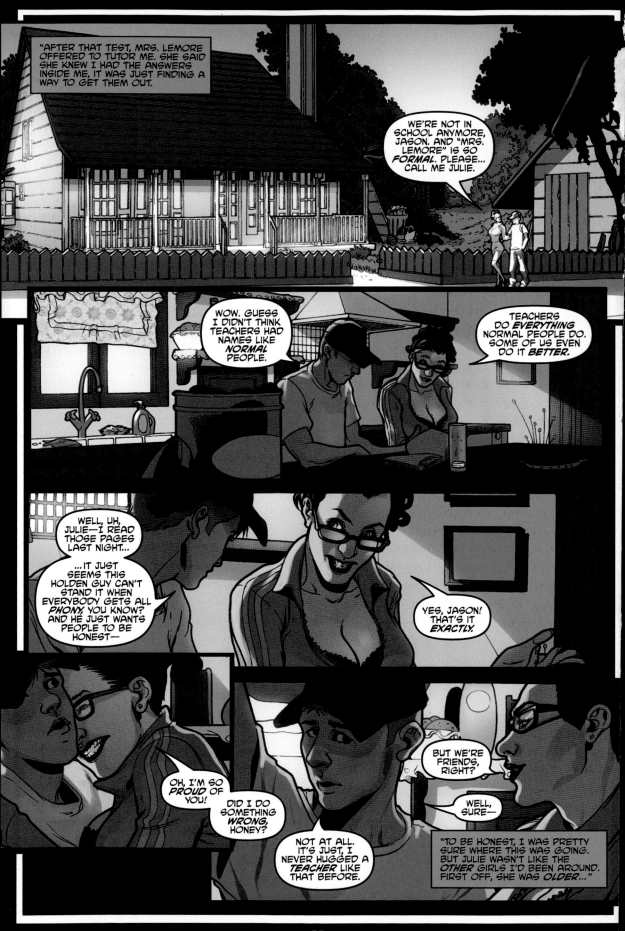

"AFTER THAT TEST, MRS. LEMORE OFFERED TO TUTOR ME. SHE SAID SHE KNEW I HAD THE ANSWERS INSIDE ME, IT WAS JUST FINDING A WAY TO GET THEM OUT.

WE'RE NOT IN SCHOOL ANYMORE, JASON. AND "MRS. LEMORE" IS SO *FORMAL.* PLEASE... CALL ME JULIE.

WOW. GUESS I DIDN'T THINK TEACHERS HAD NAMES LIKE *NORMAL* PEOPLE.

TEACHERS DO *EVERYTHING* NORMAL PEOPLE DO. SOME OF US EVEN DO IT *BETTER.*

WELL, UH, JULIE—I READ THOSE PAGES LAST NIGHT...

...IT JUST SEEMS THIS HOLDEN GUY CAN'T STAND IT WHEN EVERYBODY GETS ALL *PHONY,* YOU KNOW? AND HE JUST WANTS PEOPLE TO BE HONEST—

YES, JASON! THAT'S IT *EXACTLY.*

OH, I'M SO *PROUD* OF YOU!

DID I DO SOMETHING *WRONG,* HONEY?

NOT AT ALL. IT'S JUST, I NEVER HUGGED A *TEACHER* LIKE THAT BEFORE.

BUT WE'RE FRIENDS, RIGHT?

WELL, SURE—

"TO BE HONEST, I WAS PRETTY SURE WHERE THIS WAS GOING. BUT JULIE WASN'T LIKE THE *OTHER* GIRLS I'D BEEN AROUND. FIRST OFF, SHE WAS *OLDER*..."

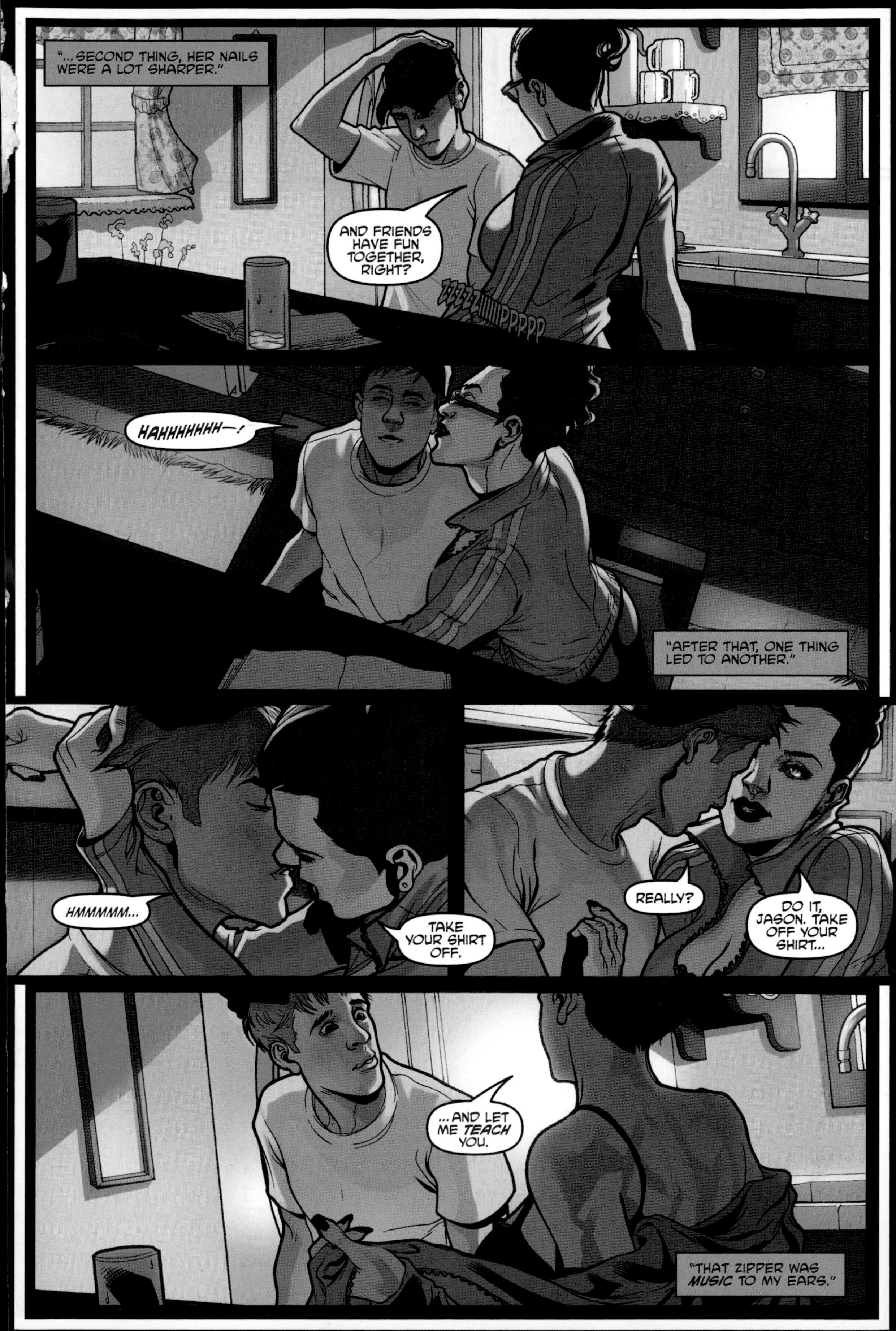
"...SECOND THING, HER NAILS WERE A LOT SHARPER."
AND FRIENDS HAVE FUN TOGETHER, RIGHT?
ZZZZZIIIIIIPPPPP
HAHHHHHHH--!
"AFTER THAT, ONE THING LED TO ANOTHER."
HMMMMM...
TAKE YOUR SHIRT OFF.
REALLY?
DO IT, JASON. TAKE OFF YOUR SHIRT...
...AND LET ME TEACH YOU.
"THAT ZIPPER WAS MUSIC TO MY EARS."

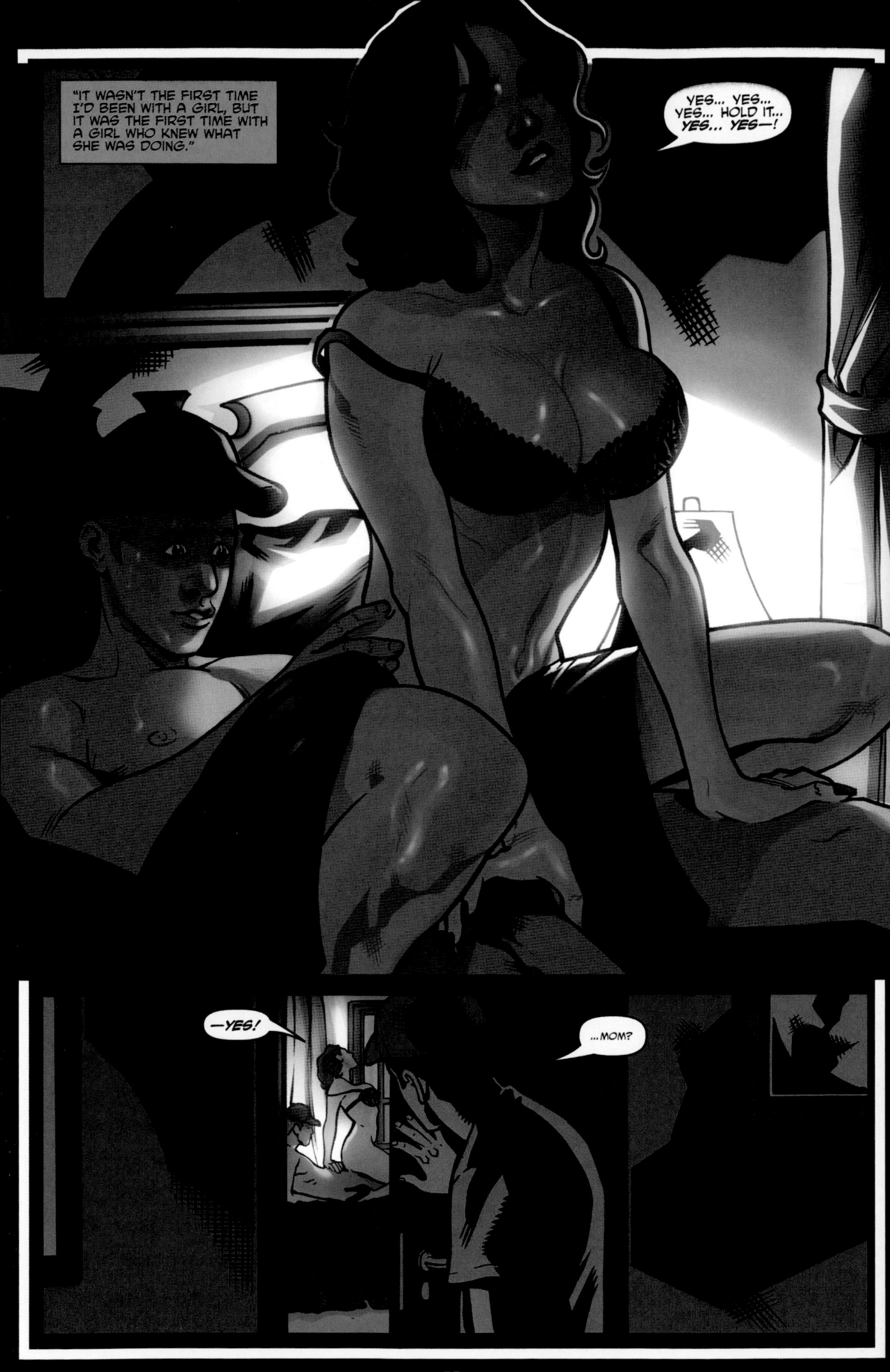
"IT WASN'T THE FIRST TIME I'D BEEN WITH A GIRL, BUT IT WAS THE FIRST TIME WITH A GIRL WHO KNEW WHAT SHE WAS DOING."
YES... YES... YES... HOLD IT... YES... YES—!
—YES!
...MOM?

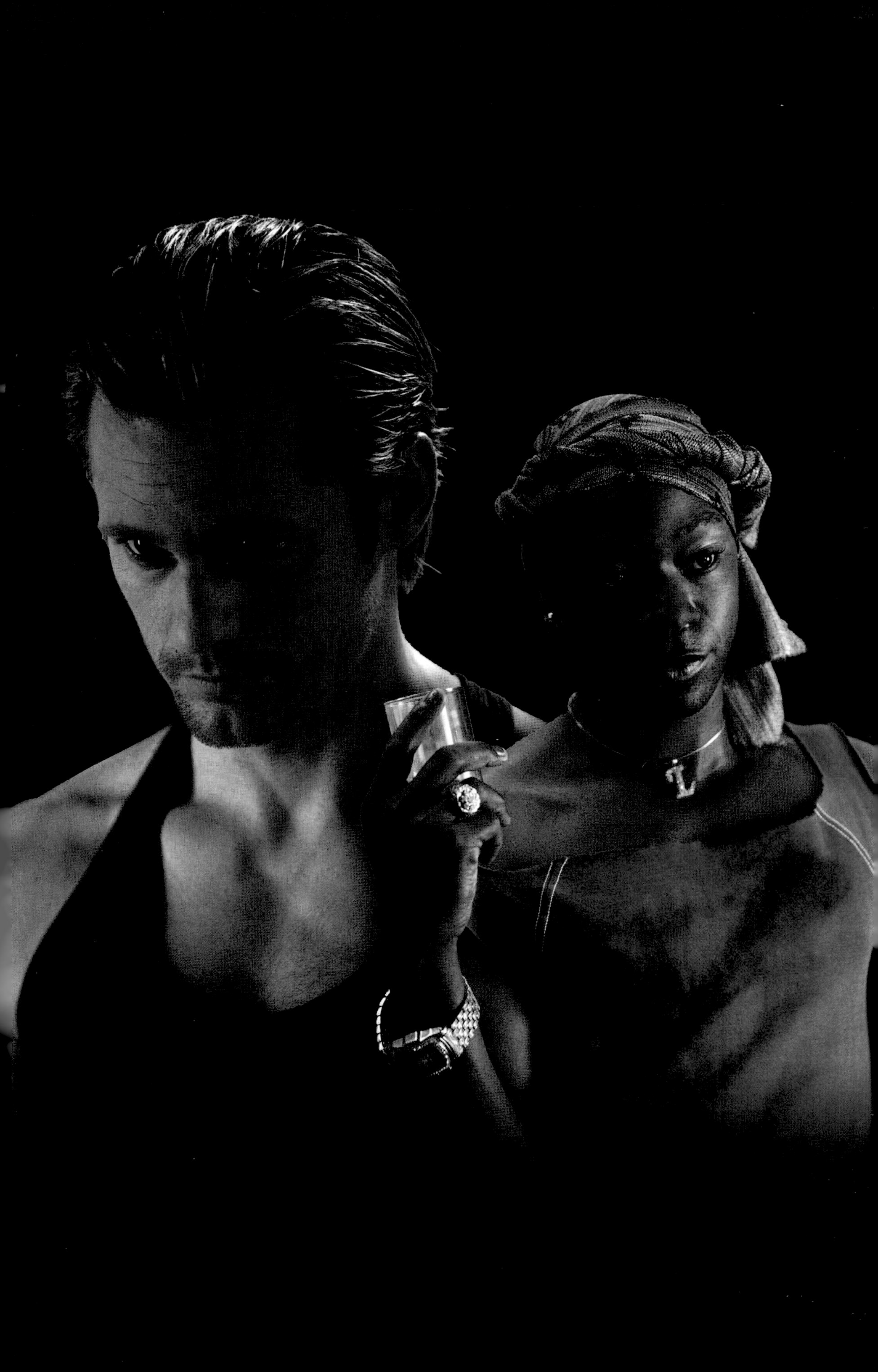

art by DAVID MESSINA
colors by GIOVANNA NIRO

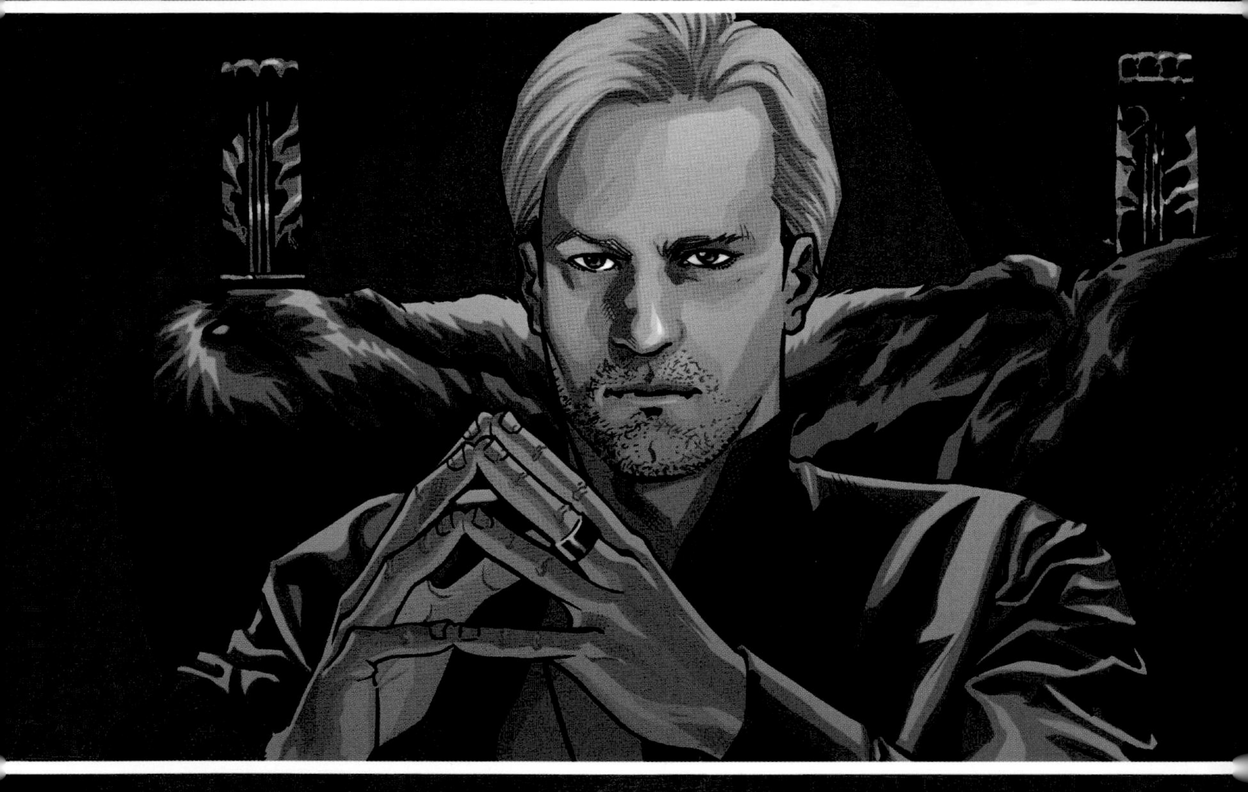

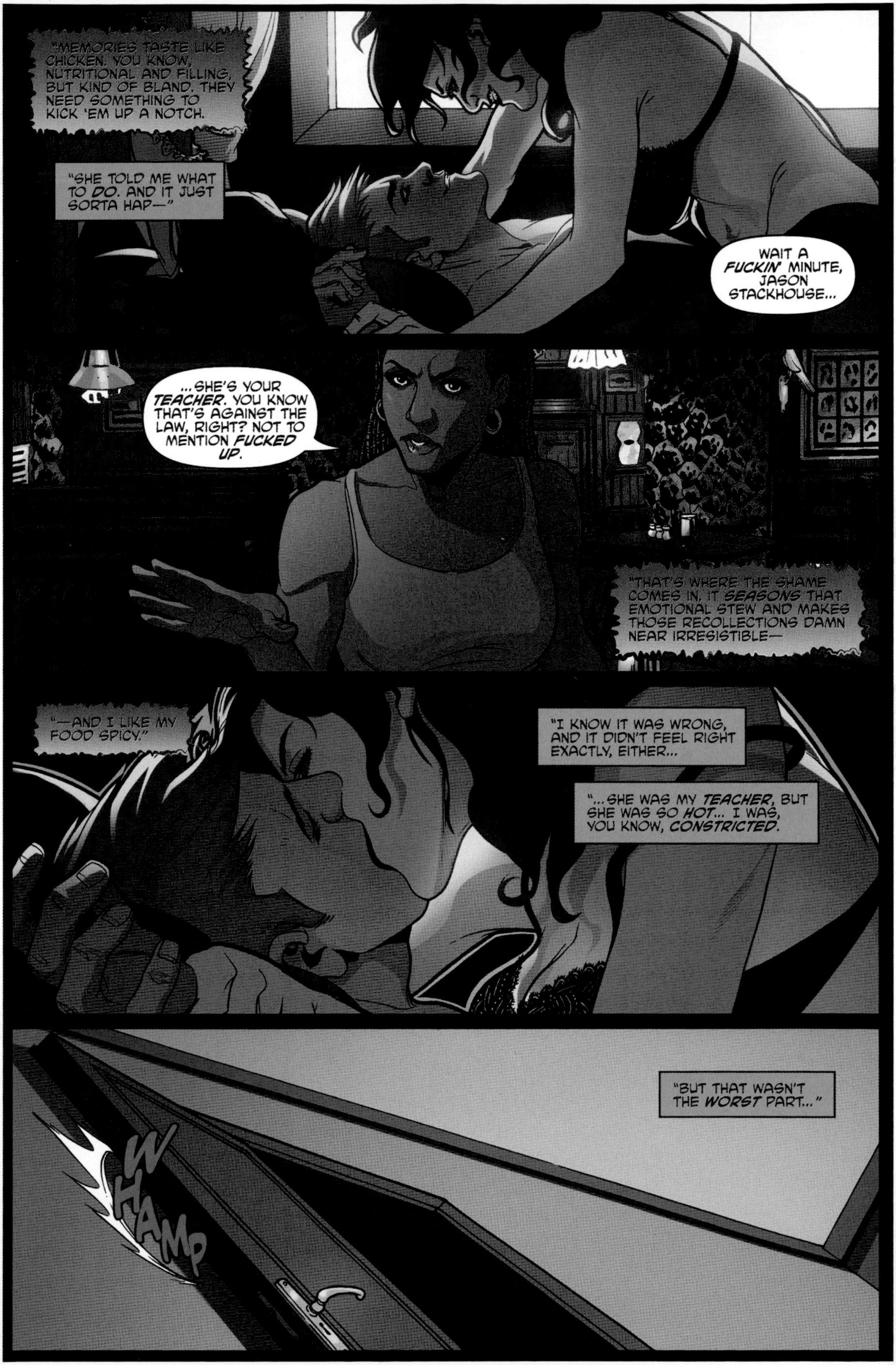

"MEMORIES TASTE LIKE CHICKEN. YOU KNOW, NUTRITIONAL AND FILLING, BUT KIND OF BLAND. THEY NEED SOMETHING TO KICK 'EM UP A NOTCH.
"SHE TOLD ME WHAT TO DO. AND IT JUST SORTA HAP—"
WAIT A FUCKIN' MINUTE, JASON STACKHOUSE...
...SHE'S YOUR TEACHER. YOU KNOW THAT'S AGAINST THE LAW, RIGHT? NOT TO MENTION FUCKED UP.
"THAT'S WHERE THE SHAME COMES IN. IT SEASONS THAT EMOTIONAL STEW AND MAKES THOSE RECOLLECTIONS DAMN NEAR IRRESISTIBLE—
"—AND I LIKE MY FOOD SPICY."
"I KNOW IT WAS WRONG, AND IT DIDN'T FEEL RIGHT EXACTLY, EITHER...
"...SHE WAS MY TEACHER, BUT SHE WAS SO HOT... I WAS, YOU KNOW, CONSTRICTED.
"BUT THAT WASN'T THE WORST PART..."
WHAMP

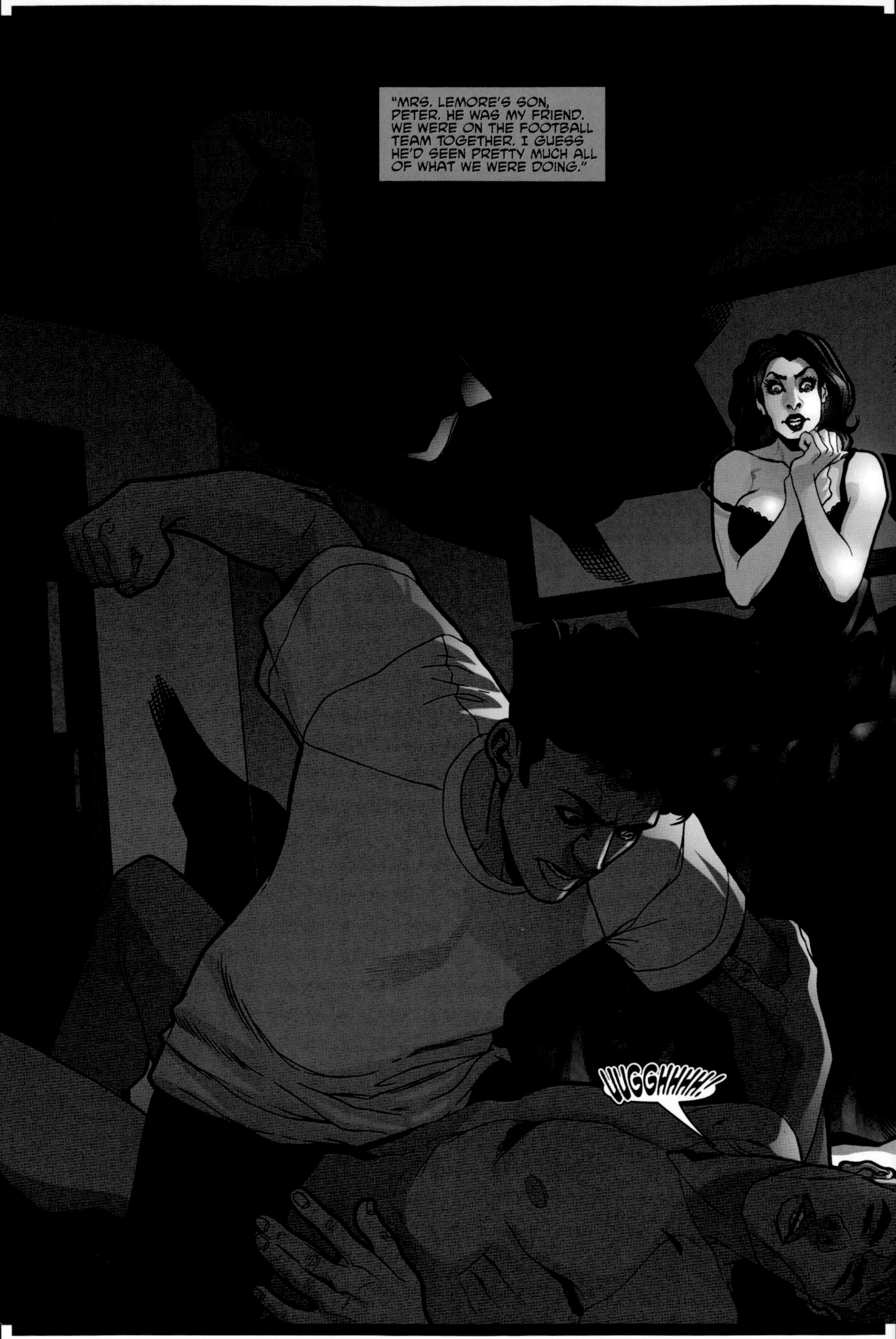
"MRS. LEMORE'S SON, PETER. HE WAS MY FRIEND. WE WERE ON THE FOOTBALL TEAM TOGETHER. I GUESS HE'D SEEN PRETTY MUCH ALL OF WHAT WE WERE DOING."
UUGGHHHH!

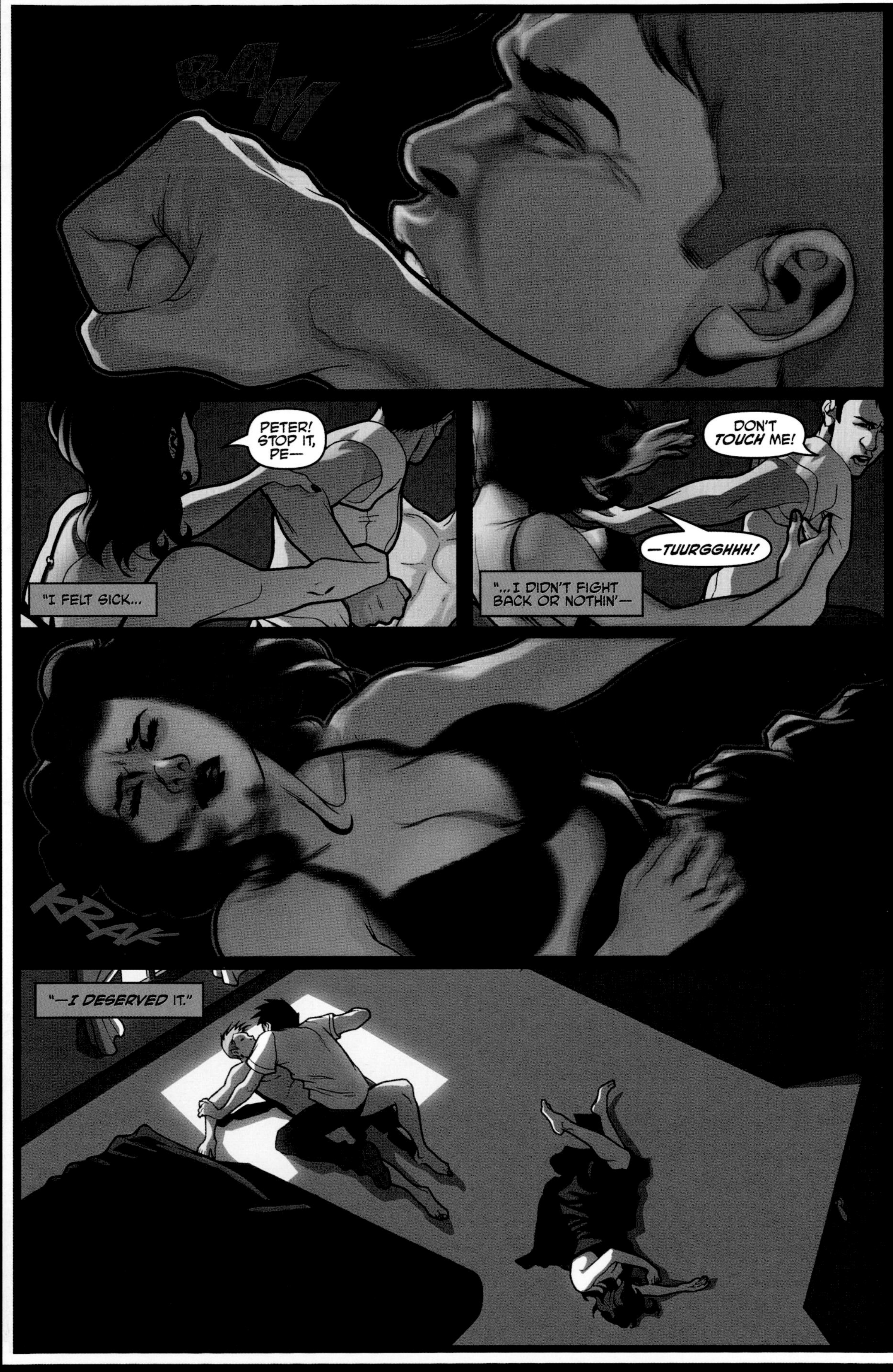
BAM
PETER! STOP IT, PE—
"I FELT SICK...
DON'T TOUCH ME!
—TUURGGHHH!
"...I DIDN'T FIGHT BACK OR NOTHIN'—
KRAK
"—I DESERVED IT."

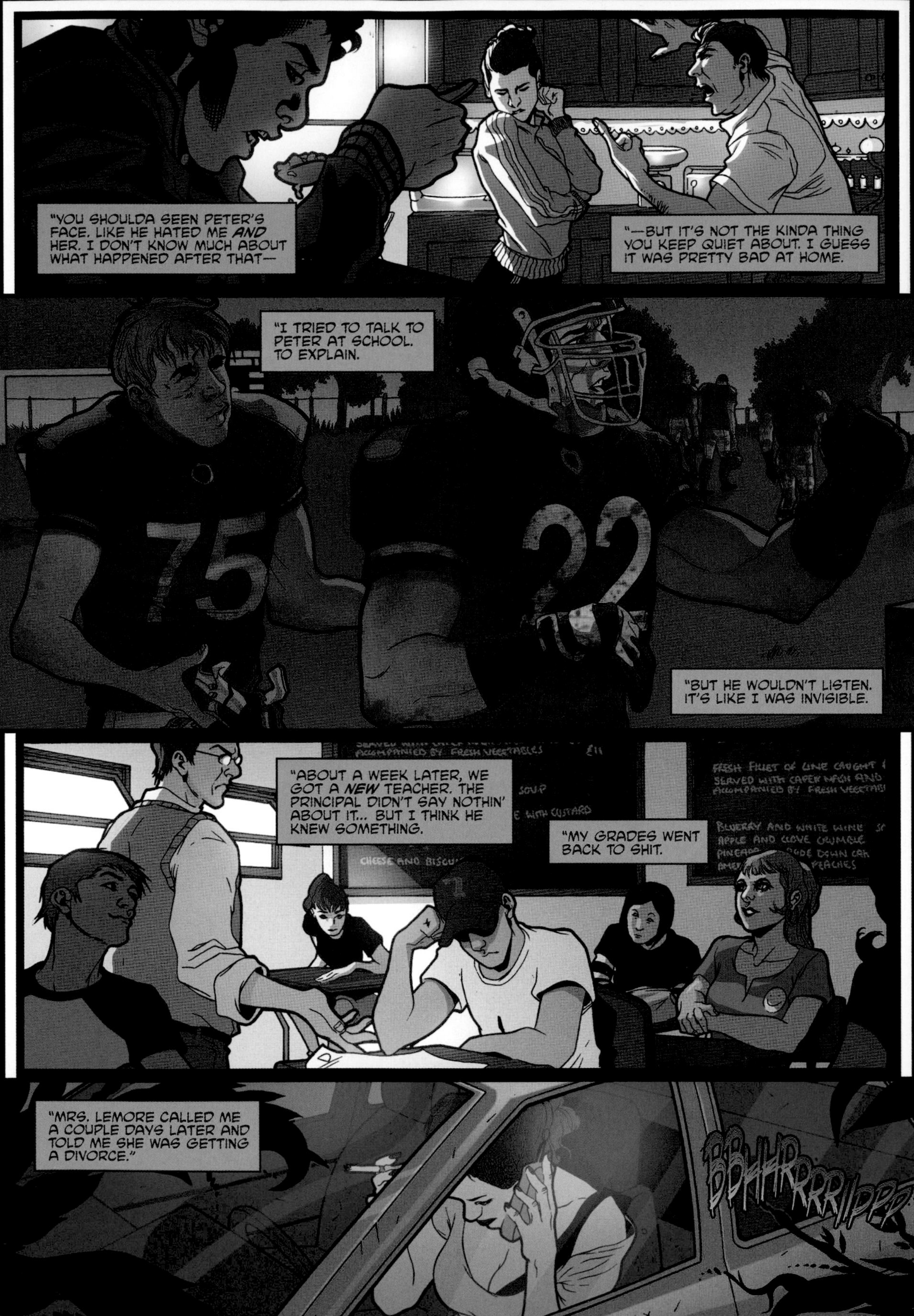
"YOU SHOULDA SEEN PETER'S FACE. LIKE HE HATED ME *AND* HER. I DON'T KNOW MUCH ABOUT WHAT HAPPENED AFTER THAT—
"—BUT IT'S NOT THE KINDA THING YOU KEEP QUIET ABOUT. I GUESS IT WAS PRETTY BAD AT HOME.
"I TRIED TO TALK TO PETER AT SCHOOL. TO EXPLAIN.
75
22
"BUT HE WOULDN'T LISTEN. IT'S LIKE I WAS INVISIBLE.
"ABOUT A WEEK LATER, WE GOT A *NEW* TEACHER. THE PRINCIPAL DIDN'T SAY NOTHIN' ABOUT IT... BUT I THINK HE KNEW SOMETHING.
"MY GRADES WENT BACK TO SHIT.
"MRS. LEMORE CALLED ME A COUPLE DAYS LATER AND TOLD ME SHE WAS GETTING A DIVORCE."

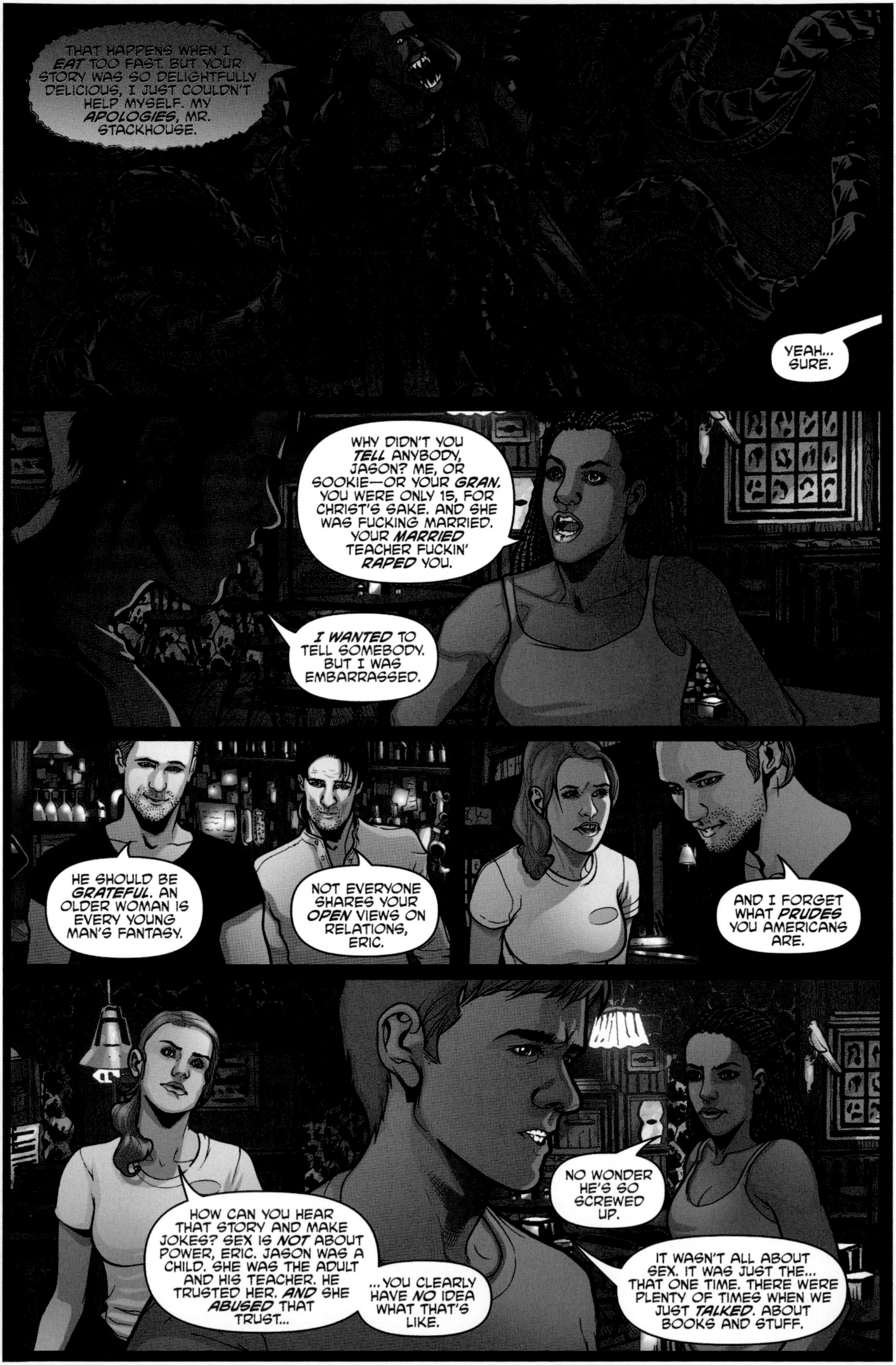
THAT HAPPENS WHEN I EAT TOO FAST. BUT YOUR STORY WAS SO DELIGHTFULLY DELICIOUS, I JUST COULDN'T HELP MYSELF. MY APOLOGIES, MR. STACKHOUSE.
YEAH... SURE.
WHY DIDN'T YOU TELL ANYBODY, JASON? ME, OR SOOKIE—OR YOUR GRAN. YOU WERE ONLY 15, FOR CHRIST'S SAKE. AND SHE WAS FUCKING MARRIED. YOUR MARRIED TEACHER FUCKIN' RAPED YOU.
I WANTED TO TELL SOMEBODY. BUT I WAS EMBARRASSED.
HE SHOULD BE GRATEFUL. AN OLDER WOMAN IS EVERY YOUNG MAN'S FANTASY.
NOT EVERYONE SHARES YOUR OPEN VIEWS ON RELATIONS, ERIC.
AND I FORGET WHAT PRUDES YOU AMERICANS ARE.
HOW CAN YOU HEAR THAT STORY AND MAKE JOKES? SEX IS NOT ABOUT POWER, ERIC. JASON WAS A CHILD. SHE WAS THE ADULT AND HIS TEACHER. HE TRUSTED HER. AND SHE ABUSED THAT TRUST...
...YOU CLEARLY HAVE NO IDEA WHAT THAT'S LIKE.
NO WONDER HE'S SO SCREWED UP.
IT WASN'T ALL ABOUT SEX. IT WAS JUST THE... THAT ONE TIME. THERE WERE PLENTY OF TIMES WHEN WE JUST TALKED. ABOUT BOOKS AND STUFF.

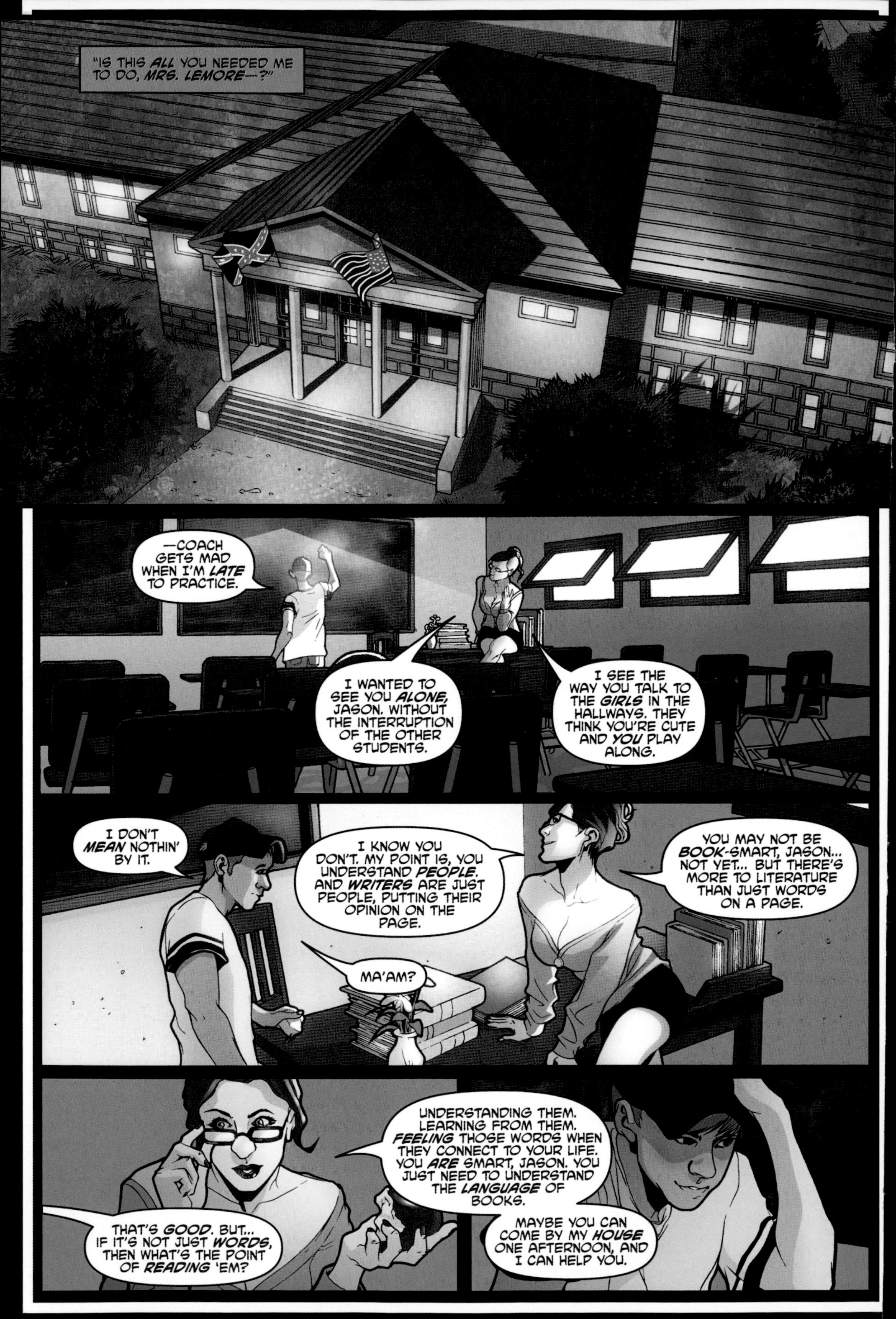
"IS THIS ALL YOU NEEDED ME TO DO, MRS. LEMORE—?"
—COACH GETS MAD WHEN I'M LATE TO PRACTICE.
I WANTED TO SEE YOU ALONE, JASON. WITHOUT THE INTERRUPTION OF THE OTHER STUDENTS.
I SEE THE WAY YOU TALK TO THE GIRLS IN THE HALLWAYS. THEY THINK YOU'RE CUTE AND YOU PLAY ALONG.
I DON'T MEAN NOTHIN' BY IT.
I KNOW YOU DON'T. MY POINT IS, YOU UNDERSTAND PEOPLE. AND WRITERS ARE JUST PEOPLE, PUTTING THEIR OPINION ON THE PAGE.
MA'AM?
YOU MAY NOT BE BOOK-SMART, JASON... NOT YET... BUT THERE'S MORE TO LITERATURE THAN JUST WORDS ON A PAGE.
THAT'S GOOD. BUT... IF IT'S NOT JUST WORDS, THEN WHAT'S THE POINT OF READING 'EM?
UNDERSTANDING THEM. LEARNING FROM THEM. FEELING THOSE WORDS WHEN THEY CONNECT TO YOUR LIFE. YOU ARE SMART, JASON. YOU JUST NEED TO UNDERSTAND THE LANGUAGE OF BOOKS.
MAYBE YOU CAN COME BY MY HOUSE ONE AFTERNOON, AND I CAN HELP YOU.

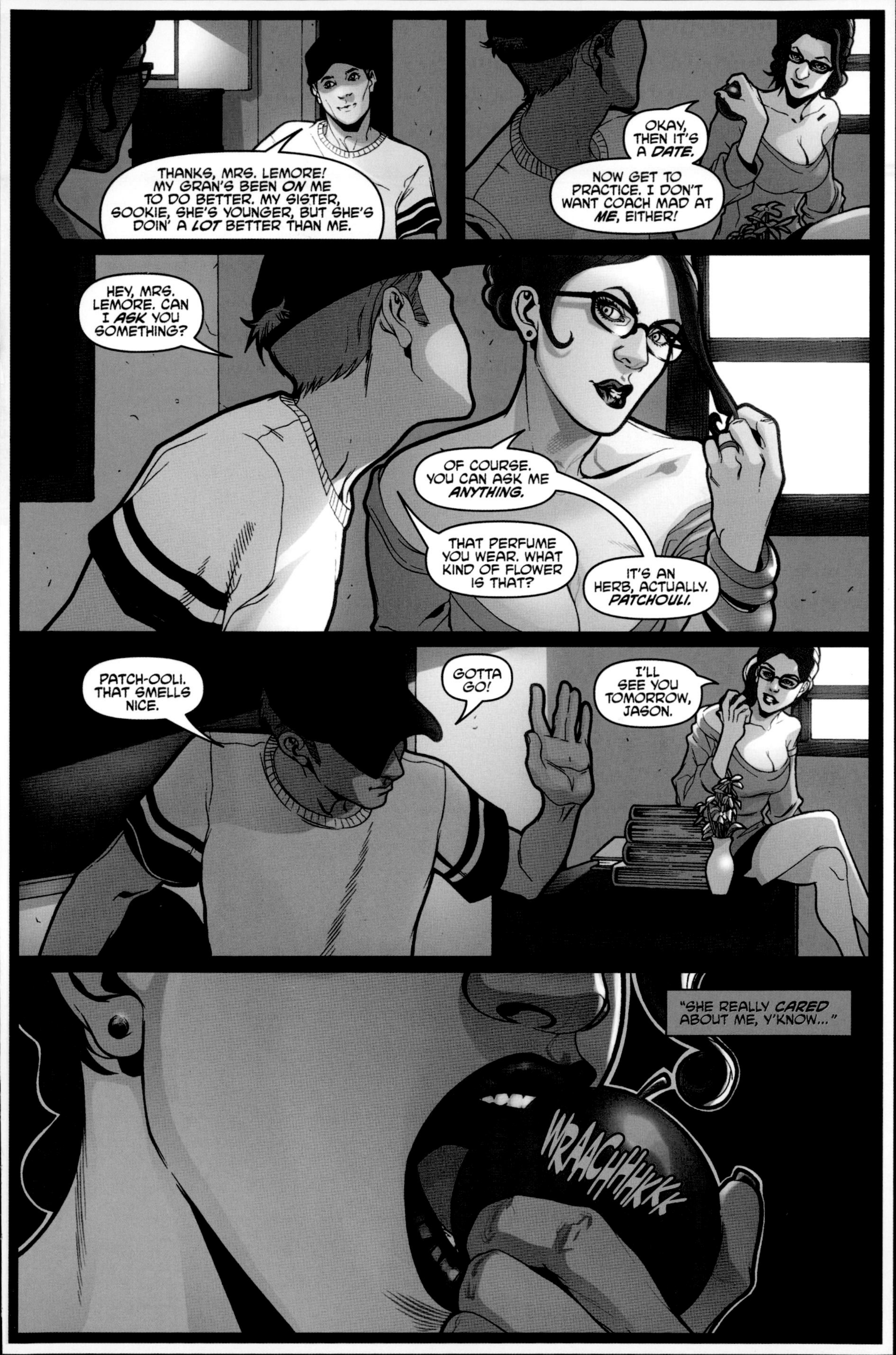
THANKS, MRS. LEMORE! MY GRAN'S BEEN ON ME TO DO BETTER. MY SISTER, SOOKIE, SHE'S YOUNGER, BUT SHE'S DOIN' A LOT BETTER THAN ME.
OKAY, THEN IT'S A DATE.
NOW GET TO PRACTICE. I DON'T WANT COACH MAD AT ME, EITHER!
HEY, MRS. LEMORE. CAN I ASK YOU SOMETHING?
OF COURSE. YOU CAN ASK ME ANYTHING.
THAT PERFUME YOU WEAR. WHAT KIND OF FLOWER IS THAT?
IT'S AN HERB, ACTUALLY. PATCHOULI.
PATCH-OOLI. THAT SMELLS NICE.
GOTTA GO!
I'LL SEE YOU TOMORROW, JASON.
"SHE REALLY CARED ABOUT ME, Y'KNOW..."
WRAACHHHKKK

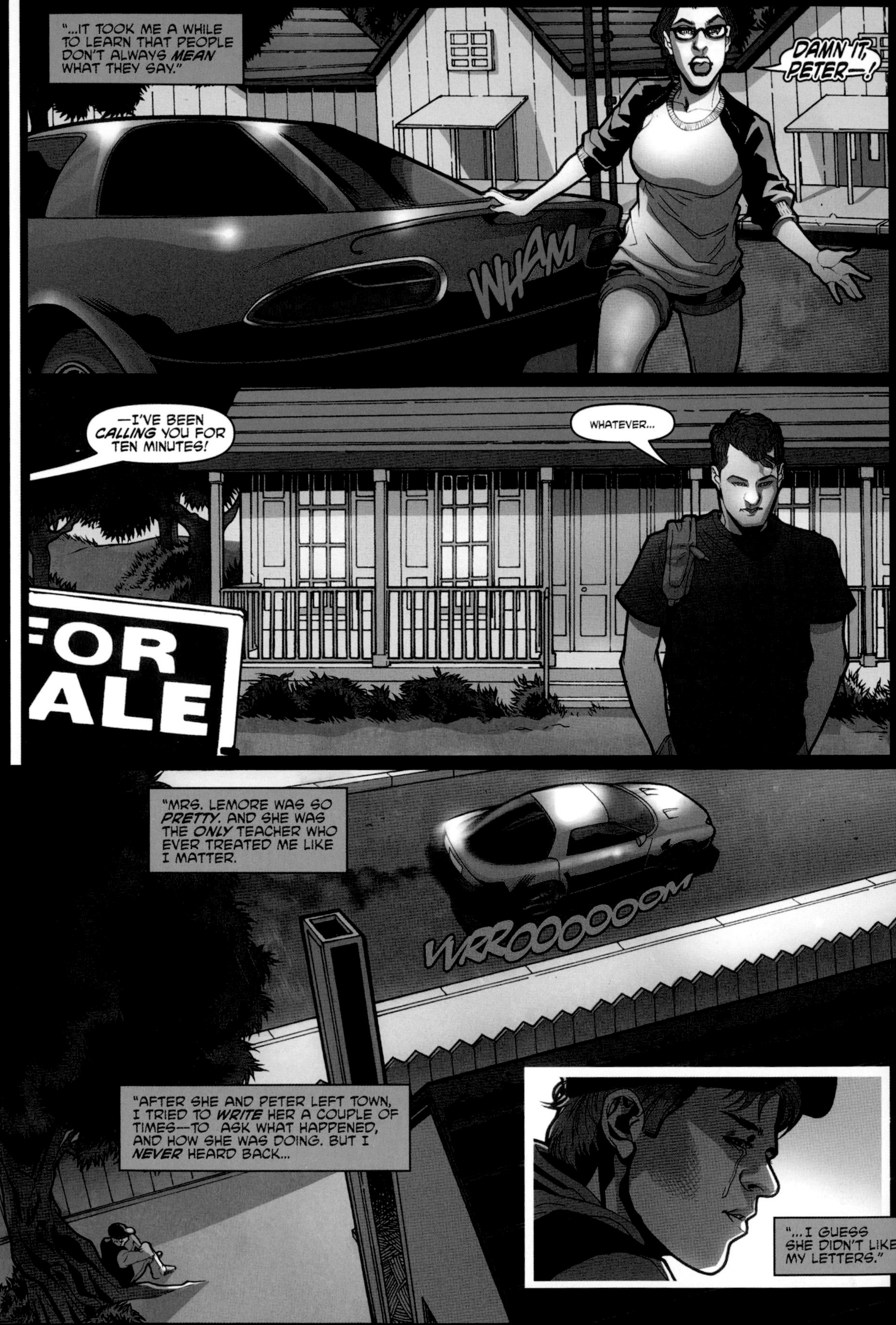
"...IT TOOK ME A WHILE TO LEARN THAT PEOPLE DON'T ALWAYS *MEAN* WHAT THEY SAY."
DAMN IT, PETER—!
WHAM
—I'VE BEEN *CALLING* YOU FOR TEN MINUTES!
WHATEVER...
FOR
ALE
"MRS. LEMORE WAS SO *PRETTY*. AND SHE WAS THE *ONLY* TEACHER WHO EVER TREATED ME LIKE I MATTER.
VRROOOOOOOOM
"AFTER SHE AND PETER LEFT TOWN, I TRIED TO *WRITE* HER A COUPLE OF TIMES—TO ASK WHAT HAPPENED, AND HOW SHE WAS DOING. BUT I *NEVER* HEARD BACK...
"...I GUESS SHE DIDN'T LIKE MY LETTERS."

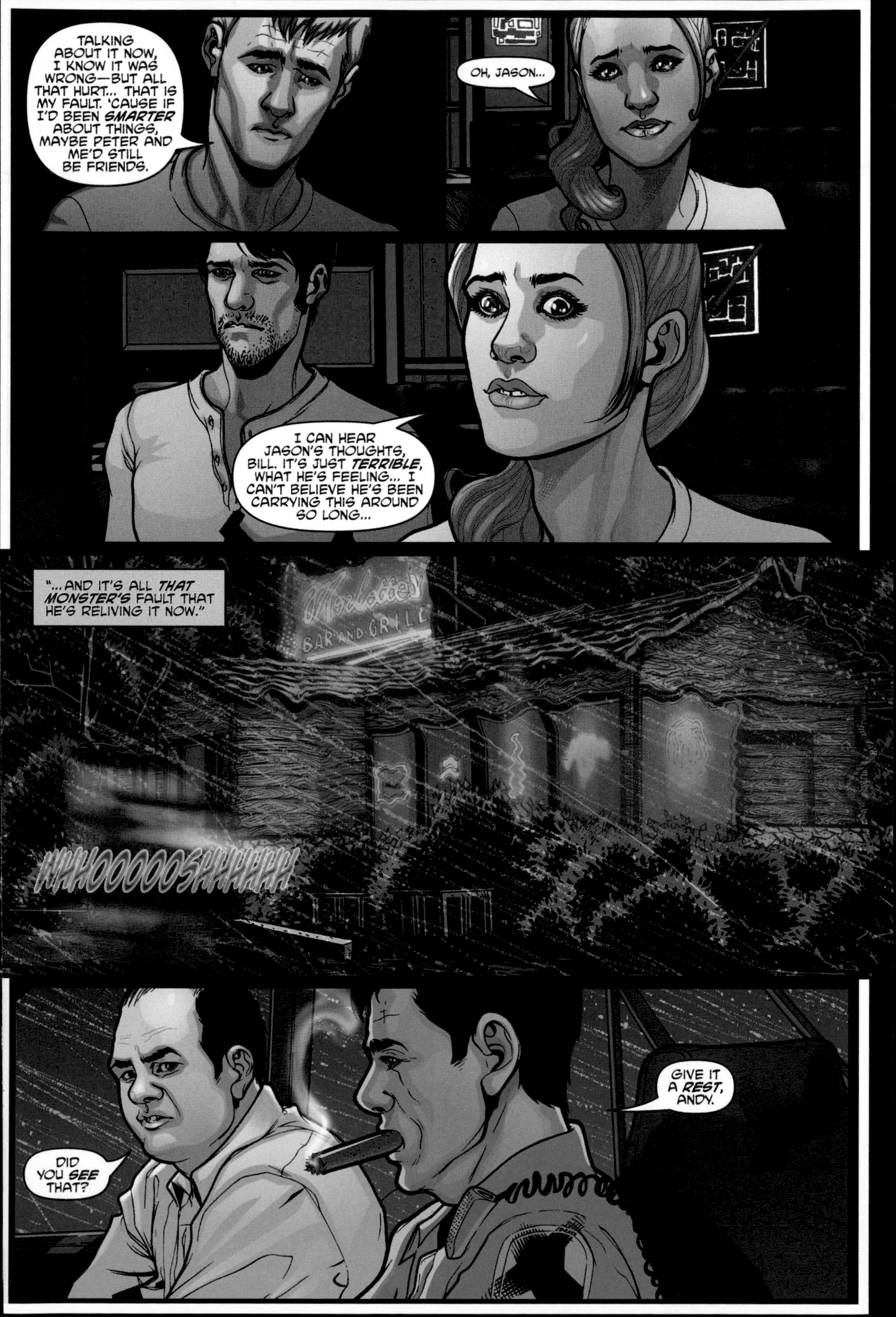
TALKING ABOUT IT NOW, I KNOW IT WAS WRONG—BUT ALL THAT HURT... THAT IS MY FAULT. 'CAUSE IF I'D BEEN *SMARTER* ABOUT THINGS, MAYBE PETER AND ME'D STILL BE FRIENDS.
OH, JASON...
I CAN HEAR JASON'S THOUGHTS, BILL. IT'S JUST *TERRIBLE*, WHAT HE'S FEELING... I CAN'T BELIEVE HE'S BEEN CARRYING THIS AROUND SO LONG...
"...AND IT'S ALL *THAT MONSTER'S* FAULT THAT HE'S RELIVING IT NOW."
Merlotte's
BAR AND GRILL
WHHOOOOOOSHHHHHH
DID YOU *SEE* THAT?
GIVE IT A *REST*, ANDY.

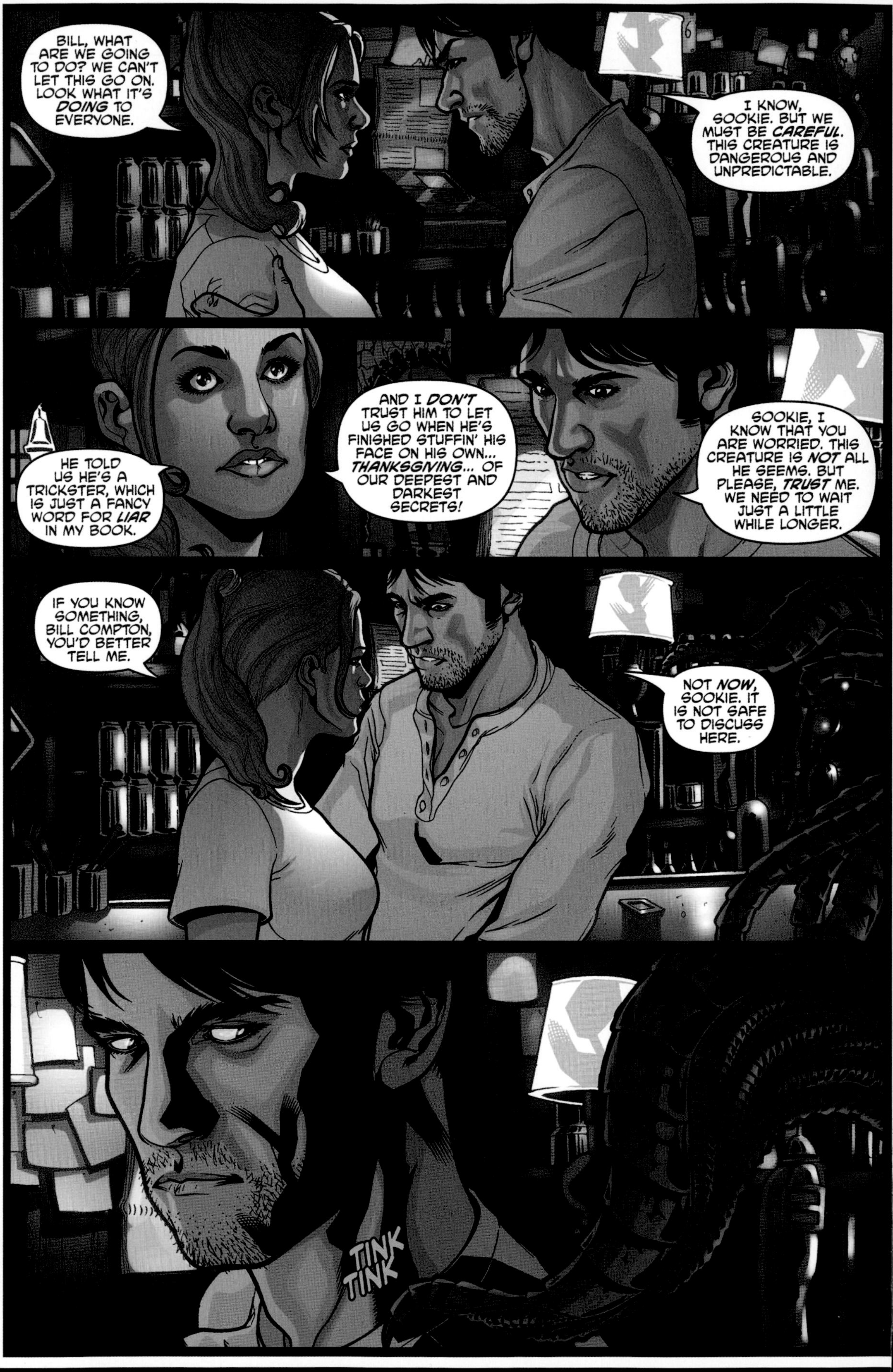
BILL, WHAT ARE WE GOING TO DO? WE CAN'T LET THIS GO ON. LOOK WHAT IT'S DOING TO EVERYONE.
I KNOW, SOOKIE. BUT WE MUST BE CAREFUL. THIS CREATURE IS DANGEROUS AND UNPREDICTABLE.
HE TOLD US HE'S A TRICKSTER, WHICH IS JUST A FANCY WORD FOR LIAR IN MY BOOK.
AND I DON'T TRUST HIM TO LET US GO WHEN HE'S FINISHED STUFFIN' HIS FACE ON HIS OWN... THANKSGIVING... OF OUR DEEPEST AND DARKEST SECRETS!
SOOKIE, I KNOW THAT YOU ARE WORRIED. THIS CREATURE IS NOT ALL HE SEEMS. BUT PLEASE, TRUST ME. WE NEED TO WAIT JUST A LITTLE WHILE LONGER.
IF YOU KNOW SOMETHING, BILL COMPTON, YOU'D BETTER TELL ME.
NOT NOW, SOOKIE. IT IS NOT SAFE TO DISCUSS HERE.
TINK TINK

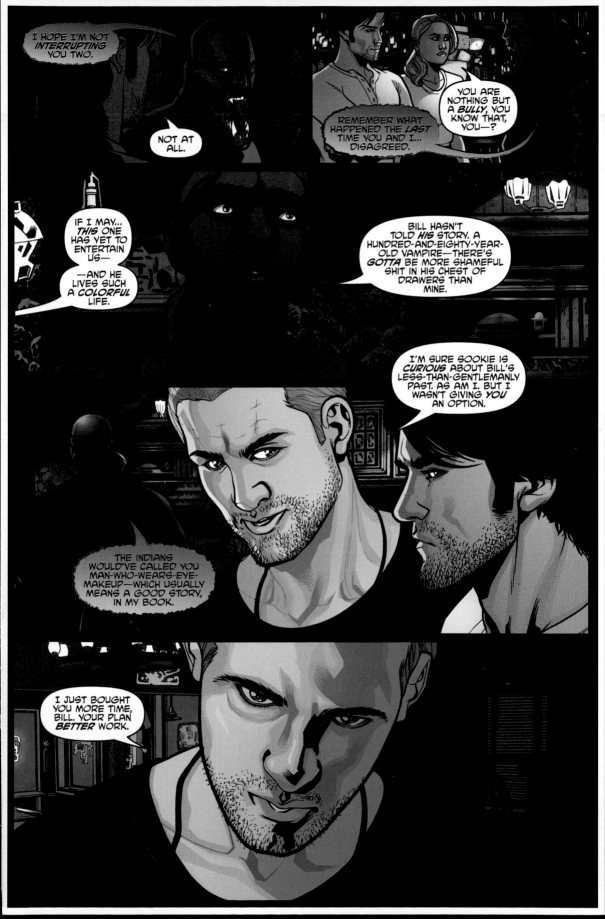

I HOPE I'M NOT *INTERRUPTING* YOU TWO.

NOT AT ALL.

REMEMBER WHAT HAPPENED THE *LAST* TIME YOU AND I... DISAGREED.

YOU ARE NOTHING BUT A *BULLY*, YOU KNOW THAT, YOU—?

IF I MAY... *THIS* ONE HAS YET TO ENTERTAIN US—

—AND HE LIVES SUCH A *COLORFUL* LIFE.

BILL HASN'T TOLD *HIS* STORY. A HUNDRED-AND-EIGHTY-YEAR-OLD VAMPIRE—THERE'S *GOTTA* BE MORE SHAMEFUL SHIT IN HIS CHEST OF DRAWERS THAN MINE.

I'M SURE SOOKIE IS *CURIOUS* ABOUT BILL'S LESS-THAN-GENTLEMANLY PAST. AS AM I. BUT I WASN'T GIVING *YOU* AN OPTION.

THE INDIANS WOULD'VE CALLED YOU MAN-WHO-WEARS-EYE-MAKEUP—WHICH USUALLY MEANS A GOOD STORY, IN MY BOOK.

I JUST BOUGHT YOU MORE TIME, BILL. YOUR PLAN *BETTER* WORK.

- 111 -

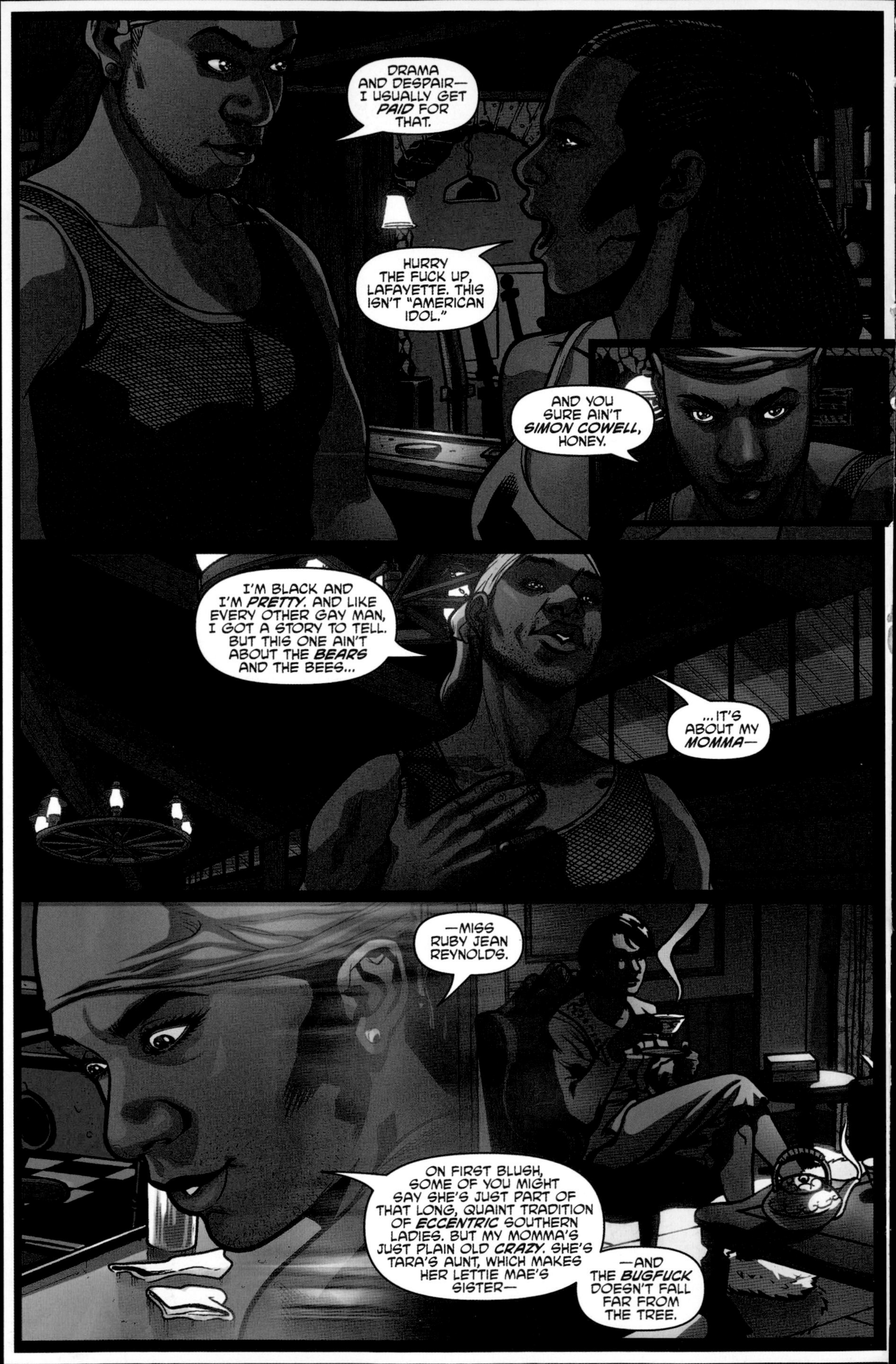
DRAMA AND DESPAIR— I USUALLY GET *PAID* FOR THAT.
HURRY THE FUCK UP, LAFAYETTE. THIS ISN'T "AMERICAN IDOL."
AND YOU SURE AIN'T *SIMON COWELL*, HONEY.
I'M BLACK AND I'M *PRETTY*. AND LIKE EVERY OTHER GAY MAN, I GOT A STORY TO TELL. BUT THIS ONE AIN'T ABOUT THE *BEARS* AND THE BEES...
...IT'S ABOUT MY *MOMMA*—
—MISS RUBY JEAN REYNOLDS.
ON FIRST BLUSH, SOME OF YOU MIGHT SAY SHE'S JUST PART OF THAT LONG, QUAINT TRADITION OF *ECCENTRIC* SOUTHERN LADIES. BUT MY MOMMA'S JUST PLAIN OLD *CRAZY*. SHE'S TARA'S AUNT, WHICH MAKES HER LETTIE MAE'S SISTER—
—AND THE *BUGFUCK* DOESN'T FALL FAR FROM THE TREE.

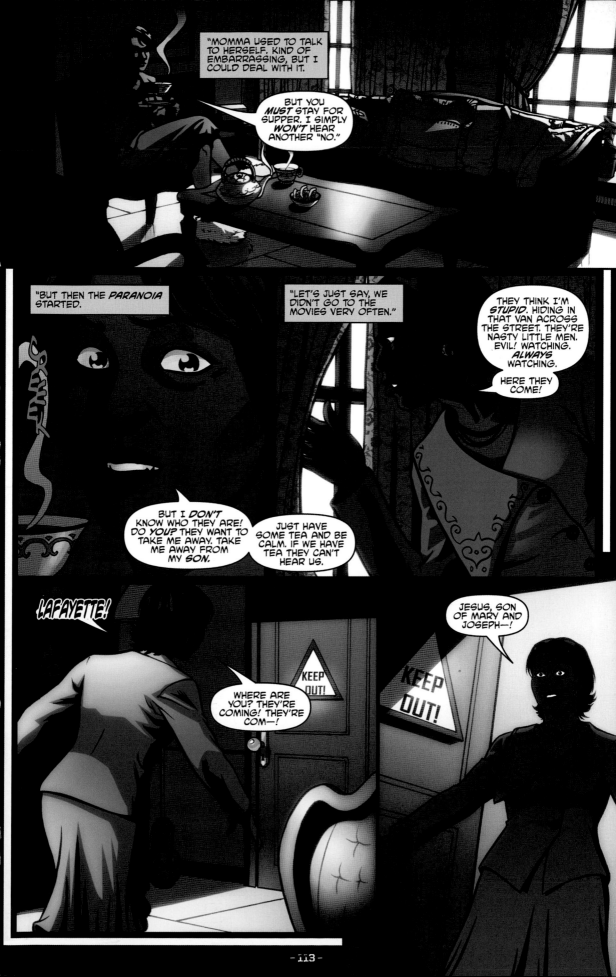

"MOMMA USED TO TALK TO HERSELF. KIND OF EMBARRASSING, BUT I COULD DEAL WITH IT.

BUT YOU *MUST* STAY FOR SUPPER. I SIMPLY *WON'T* HEAR ANOTHER "NO."

"BUT THEN THE *PARANOIA* STARTED.

"LET'S JUST SAY, WE DIDN'T GO TO THE MOVIES VERY OFTEN."

THEY THINK I'M *STUPID*. HIDING IN THAT VAN ACROSS THE STREET. THEY'RE NASTY LITTLE MEN. EVIL! WATCHING. *ALWAYS* WATCHING.

HERE THEY COME!

BUT I *DON'T* KNOW WHO THEY ARE! DO *YOU?* THEY WANT TO TAKE ME AWAY. TAKE ME AWAY FROM MY *SON*.

JUST HAVE SOME TEA AND BE CALM. IF WE HAVE TEA THEY CAN'T HEAR US.

LAFAYETTE!

WHERE ARE YOU? THEY'RE COMING! THEY'RE COM—!

KEEP OUT!

JESUS, SON OF MARY AND JOSEPH—!

KEEP OUT!

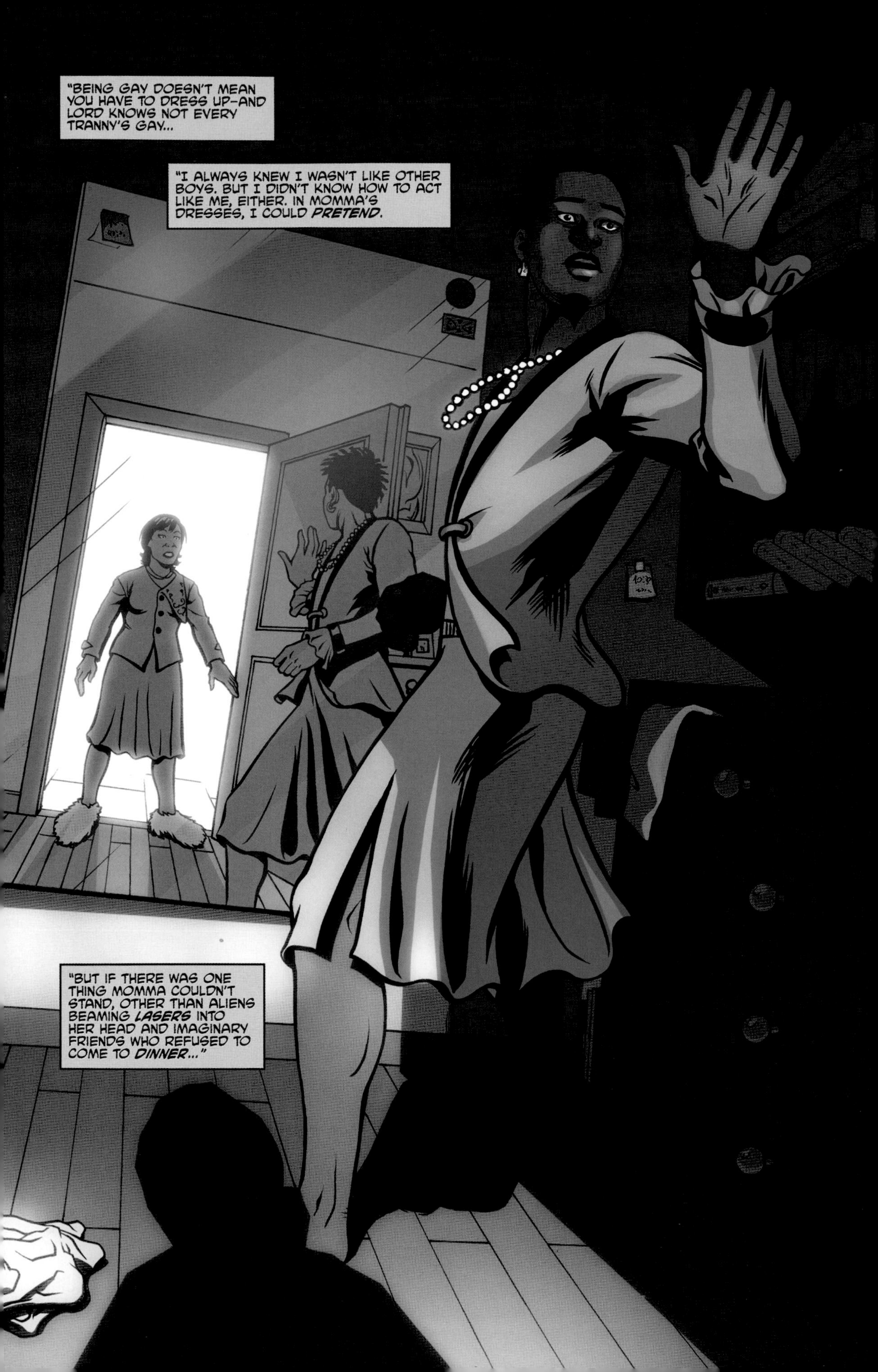
"BEING GAY DOESN'T MEAN YOU HAVE TO DRESS UP--AND LORD KNOWS NOT EVERY TRANNY'S GAY...
"I ALWAYS KNEW I WASN'T LIKE OTHER BOYS. BUT I DIDN'T KNOW HOW TO ACT LIKE ME, EITHER. IN MOMMA'S DRESSES, I COULD *PRETEND*.
"BUT IF THERE WAS ONE THING MOMMA COULDN'T STAND, OTHER THAN ALIENS BEAMING *LASERS* INTO HER HEAD AND IMAGINARY FRIENDS WHO REFUSED TO COME TO *DINNER*..."

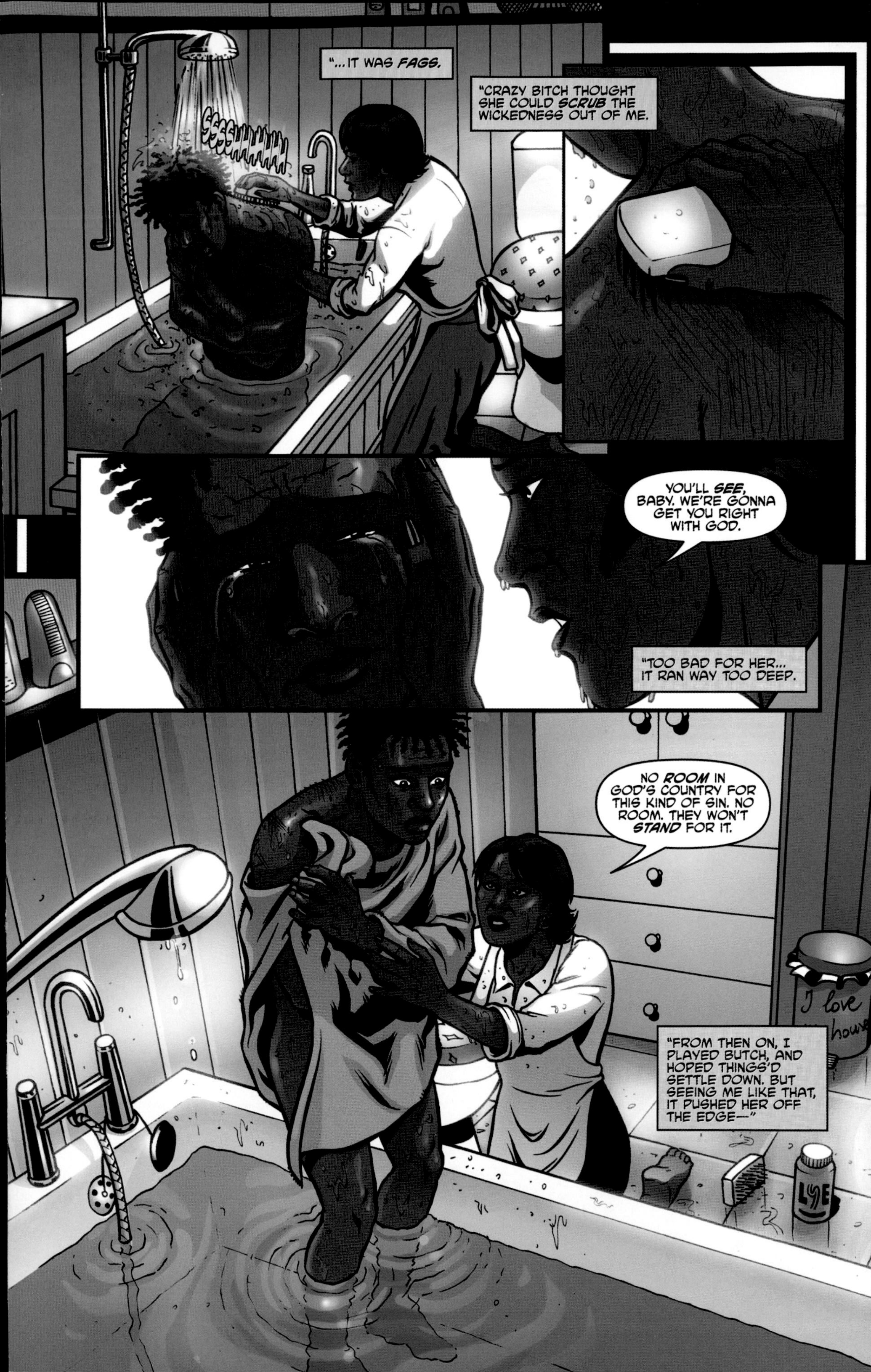
"...IT WAS FAGS.
SSSSHHHHHHH
"CRAZY BITCH THOUGHT SHE COULD SCRUB THE WICKEDNESS OUT OF ME.
YOU'LL SEE, BABY. WE'RE GONNA GET YOU RIGHT WITH GOD.
"TOO BAD FOR HER... IT RAN WAY TOO DEEP.
NO ROOM IN GOD'S COUNTRY FOR THIS KIND OF SIN. NO ROOM. THEY WON'T STAND FOR IT.
"FROM THEN ON, I PLAYED BUTCH, AND HOPED THINGS'D SETTLE DOWN. BUT SEEING ME LIKE THAT, IT PUSHED HER OFF THE EDGE--"
LYE

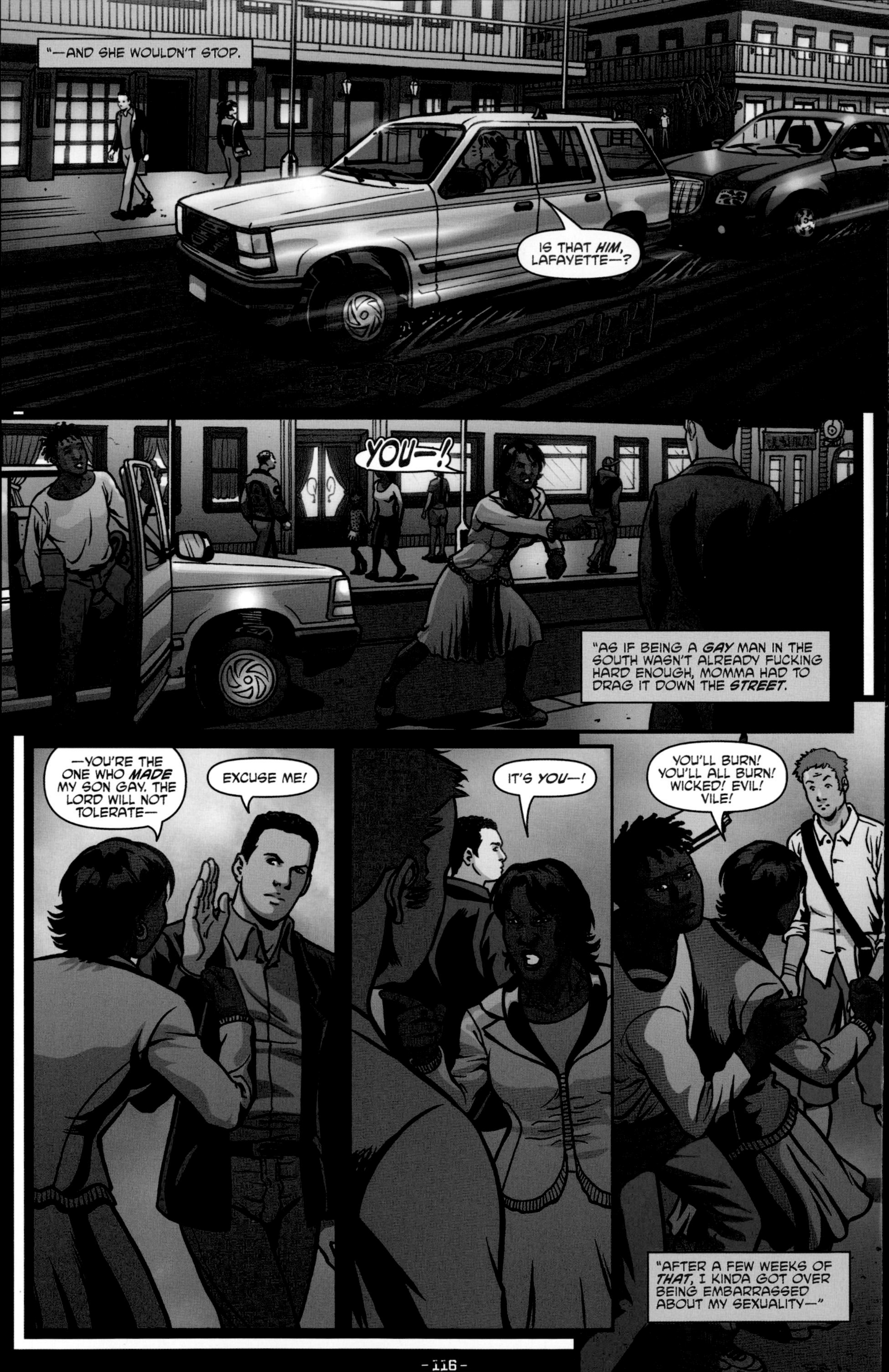
"—AND SHE WOULDN'T STOP.
IS THAT *HIM*, LAFAYETTE—?
YOU—!
"AS IF BEING A *GAY* MAN IN THE SOUTH WASN'T ALREADY FUCKING HARD ENOUGH, MOMMA HAD TO DRAG IT DOWN THE *STREET*.
—YOU'RE THE ONE WHO *MADE* MY SON GAY. THE LORD WILL NOT TOLERATE—
EXCUSE ME!
IT'S *YOU*—!
YOU'LL BURN! YOU'LL ALL BURN! WICKED! EVIL! VILE!
"AFTER A FEW WEEKS OF *THAT*, I KINDA GOT OVER BEING EMBARRASSED ABOUT MY SEXUALITY—"

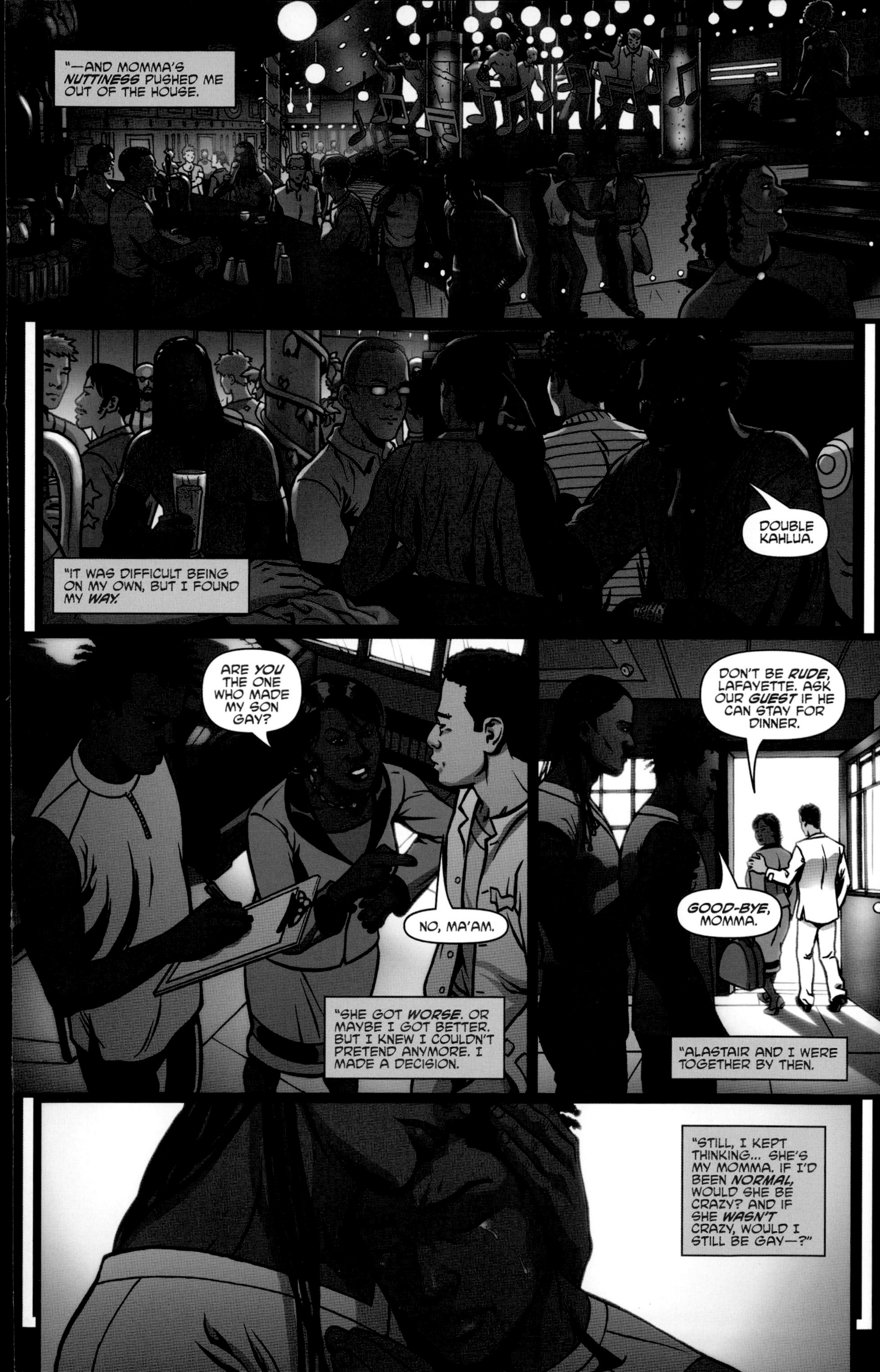
"—AND MOMMA'S *NUTTINESS* PUSHED ME OUT OF THE HOUSE.
DOUBLE KAHLUA.
"IT WAS DIFFICULT BEING ON MY OWN, BUT I FOUND MY *WAY.*
ARE *YOU* THE ONE WHO MADE MY SON GAY?
NO, MA'AM.
"SHE GOT *WORSE*. OR MAYBE I GOT BETTER. BUT I KNEW I COULDN'T PRETEND ANYMORE. I MADE A DECISION.
DON'T BE *RUDE*, LAFAYETTE. ASK OUR *GUEST* IF HE CAN STAY FOR DINNER.
GOOD-BYE, MOMMA.
"ALASTAIR AND I WERE TOGETHER BY THEN.
"STILL, I KEPT THINKING... SHE'S MY MOMMA. IF I'D BEEN *NORMAL,* WOULD SHE BE CRAZY? AND IF SHE *WASN'T* CRAZY, WOULD I STILL BE GAY—?"

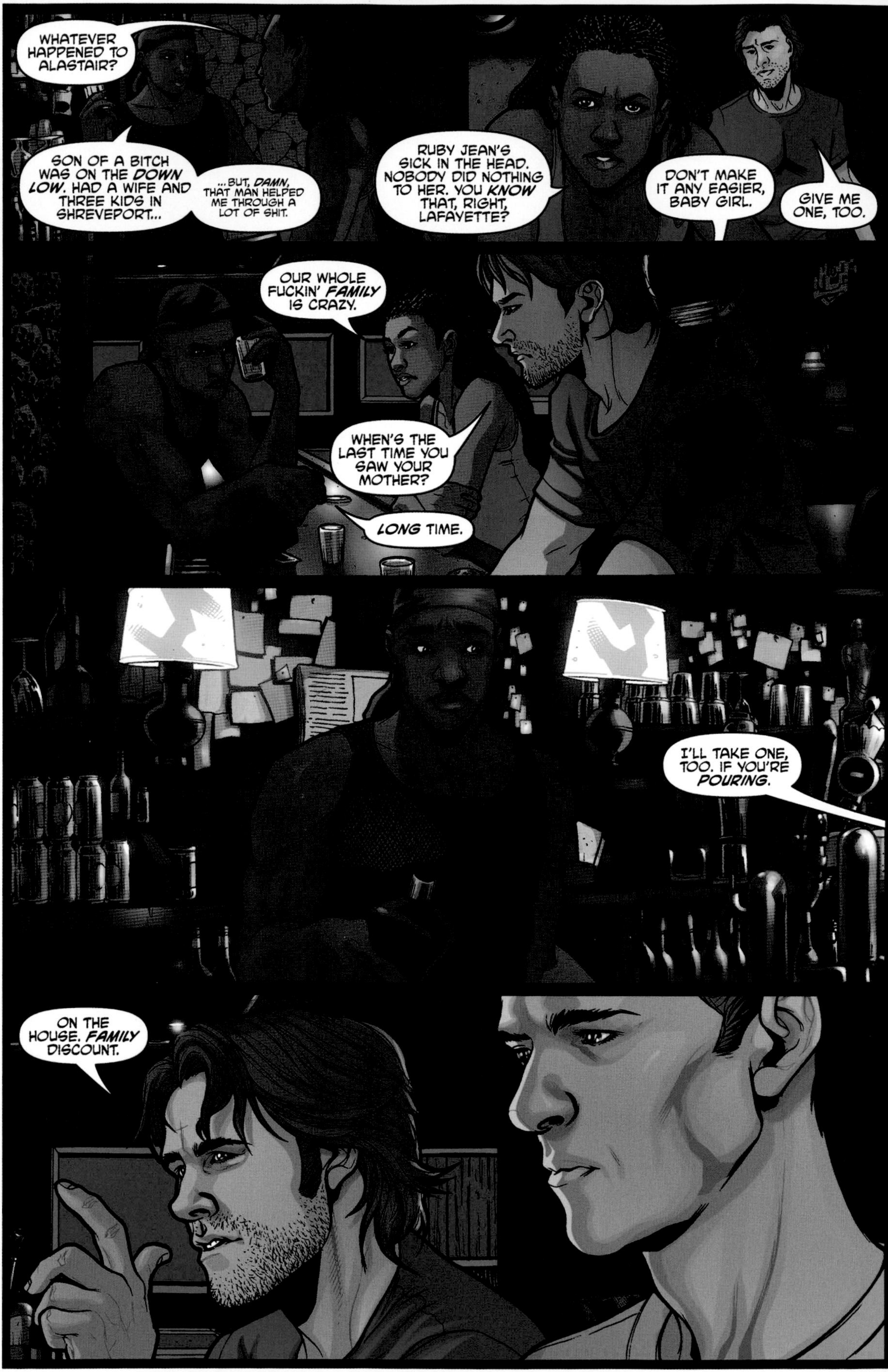
WHATEVER HAPPENED TO ALASTAIR?
SON OF A BITCH WAS ON THE *DOWN LOW*. HAD A WIFE AND THREE KIDS IN SHREVEPORT...
...BUT, *DAMN*, THAT MAN HELPED ME THROUGH A LOT OF SHIT.
RUBY JEAN'S SICK IN THE HEAD. NOBODY DID NOTHING TO HER. YOU *KNOW* THAT, RIGHT, LAFAYETTE?
DON'T MAKE IT ANY EASIER, BABY GIRL.
GIVE ME ONE, TOO.
OUR WHOLE FUCKIN' *FAMILY* IS CRAZY.
WHEN'S THE LAST TIME YOU SAW YOUR MOTHER?
LONG TIME.
I'LL TAKE ONE, TOO. IF YOU'RE *POURING*.
ON THE HOUSE. *FAMILY* DISCOUNT.

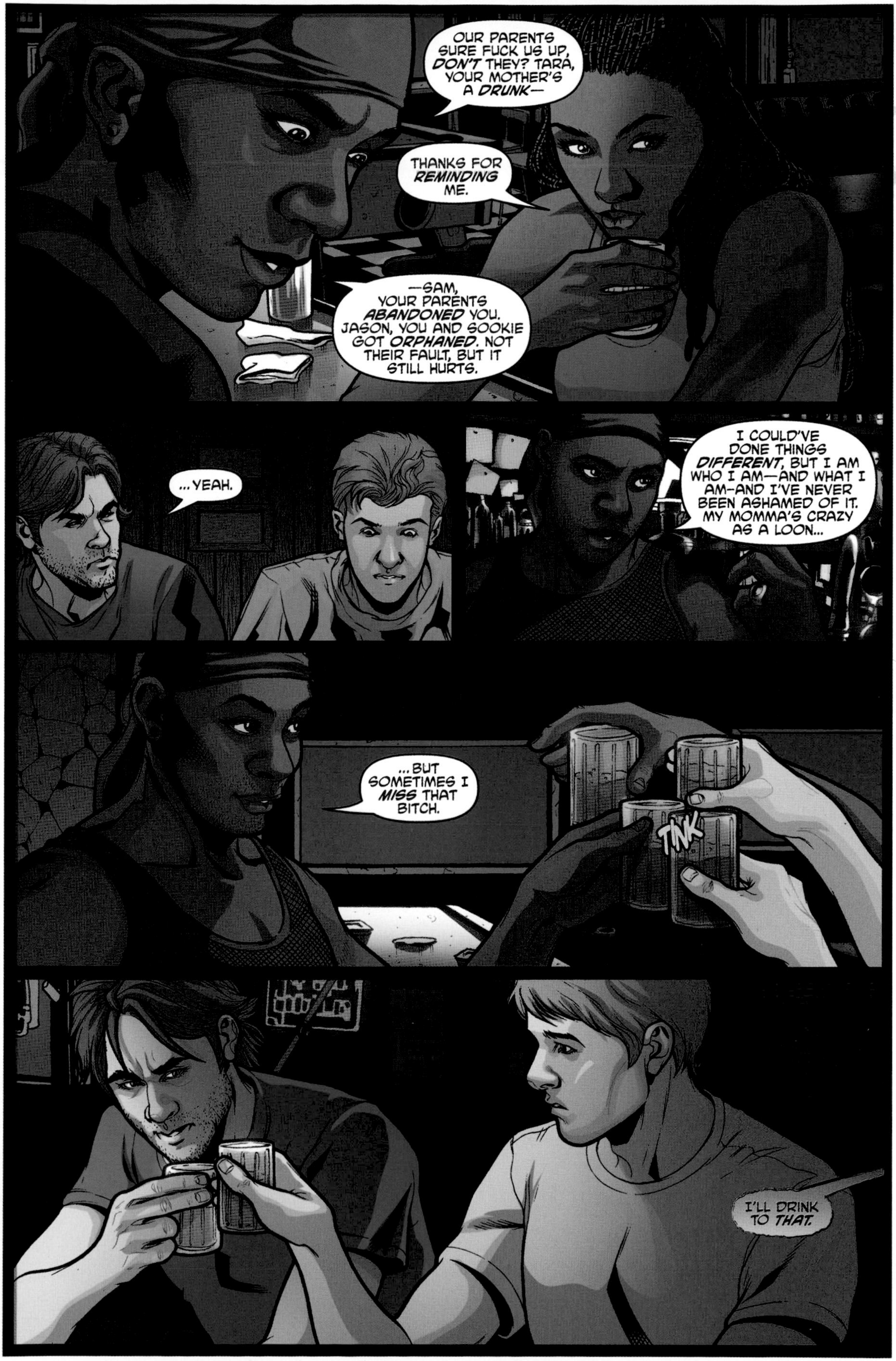
OUR PARENTS SURE FUCK US UP, DON'T THEY? TARA, YOUR MOTHER'S A DRUNK—
THANKS FOR REMINDING ME.
—SAM, YOUR PARENTS ABANDONED YOU. JASON, YOU AND SOOKIE GOT ORPHANED. NOT THEIR FAULT, BUT IT STILL HURTS.
...YEAH.
I COULD'VE DONE THINGS DIFFERENT, BUT I AM WHO I AM—AND WHAT I AM—AND I'VE NEVER BEEN ASHAMED OF IT. MY MOMMA'S CRAZY AS A LOON...
...BUT SOMETIMES I MISS THAT BITCH.
TINK
I'LL DRINK TO THAT.

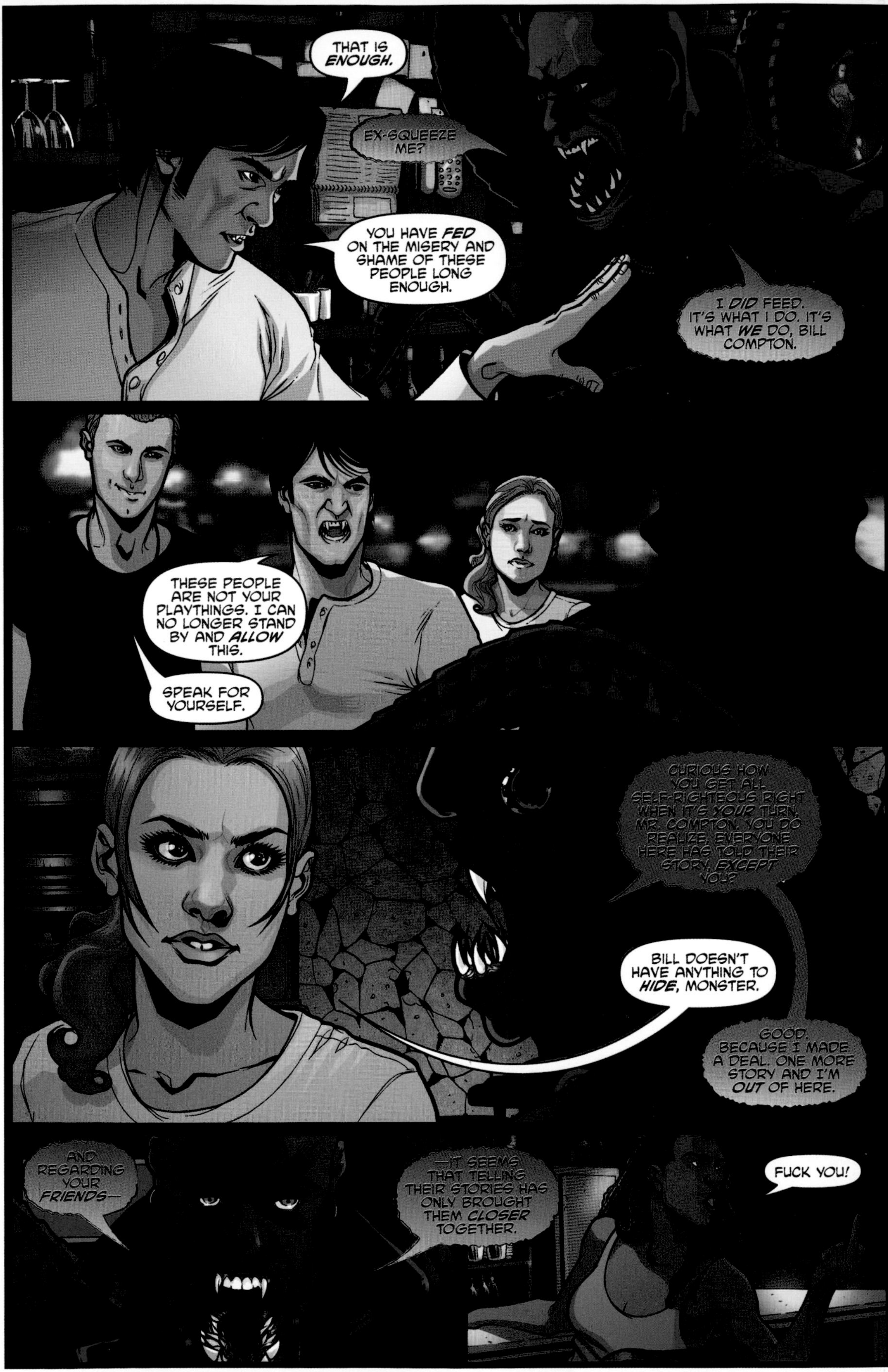
THAT IS ENOUGH.
EX-SQUEEZE ME?
YOU HAVE FED ON THE MISERY AND SHAME OF THESE PEOPLE LONG ENOUGH.
I DID FEED. IT'S WHAT I DO. IT'S WHAT WE DO, BILL COMPTON.
THESE PEOPLE ARE NOT YOUR PLAYTHINGS. I CAN NO LONGER STAND BY AND ALLOW THIS.
SPEAK FOR YOURSELF.
CURIOUS HOW YOU GET ALL SELF-RIGHTEOUS RIGHT WHEN IT'S YOUR TURN, MR. COMPTON. YOU DO REALIZE, EVERYONE HERE HAS TOLD THEIR STORY, EXCEPT YOU?
BILL DOESN'T HAVE ANYTHING TO HIDE, MONSTER.
GOOD. BECAUSE I MADE A DEAL. ONE MORE STORY AND I'M OUT OF HERE.
AND REGARDING YOUR FRIENDS—
—IT SEEMS THAT TELLING THEIR STORIES HAS ONLY BROUGHT THEM CLOSER TOGETHER.
FUCK YOU!

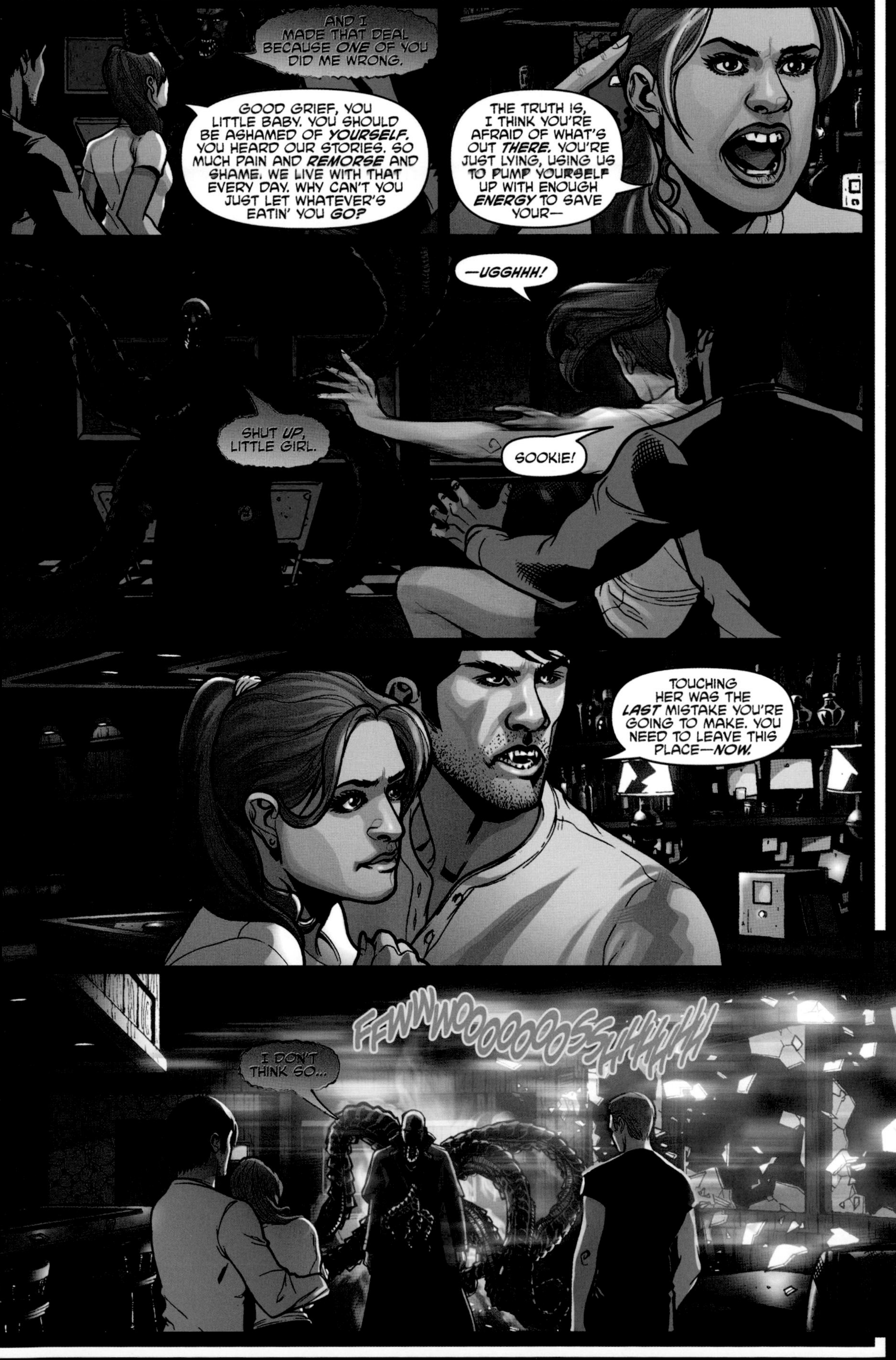
AND I MADE THAT DEAL BECAUSE ONE OF YOU DID ME WRONG.
GOOD GRIEF, YOU LITTLE BABY. YOU SHOULD BE ASHAMED OF YOURSELF. YOU HEARD OUR STORIES. SO MUCH PAIN AND REMORSE AND SHAME. WE LIVE WITH THAT EVERY DAY. WHY CAN'T YOU JUST LET WHATEVER'S EATIN' YOU GO?
THE TRUTH IS, I THINK YOU'RE AFRAID OF WHAT'S OUT THERE. YOU'RE JUST LYING, USING US TO PUMP YOURSELF UP WITH ENOUGH ENERGY TO SAVE YOUR—
—UGGHHH!
SHUT UP, LITTLE GIRL.
SOOKIE!
TOUCHING HER WAS THE LAST MISTAKE YOU'RE GOING TO MAKE. YOU NEED TO LEAVE THIS PLACE—NOW.
FFWWWOOOOOOOSSHHHHH!!
I DON'T THINK SO...

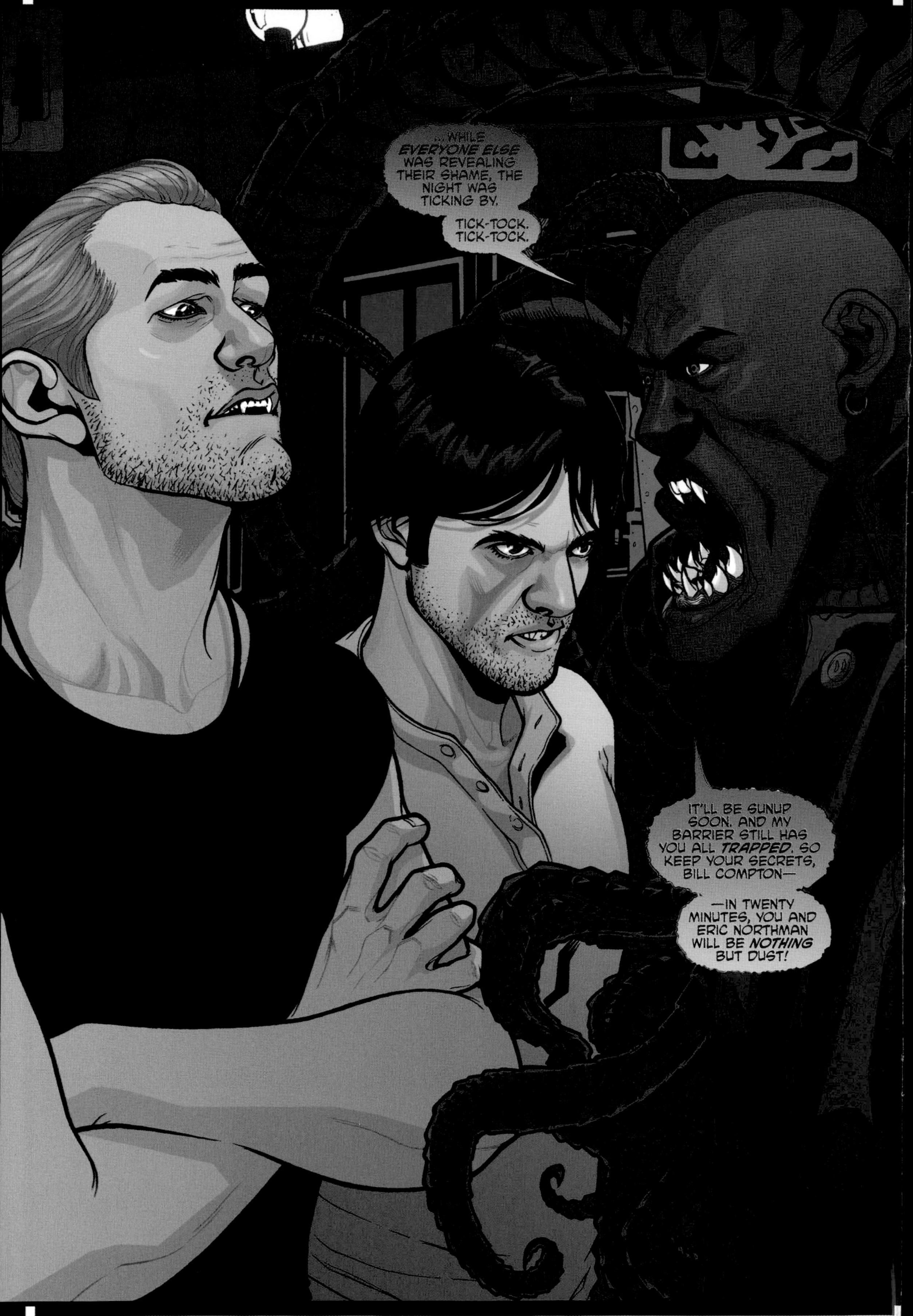
...WHILE EVERYONE ELSE WAS REVEALING THEIR SHAME, THE NIGHT WAS TICKING BY.
TICK-TOCK. TICK-TOCK.
IT'LL BE SUNUP SOON. AND MY BARRIER STILL HAS YOU ALL TRAPPED. SO KEEP YOUR SECRETS, BILL COMPTON—
—IN TWENTY MINUTES, YOU AND ERIC NORTHMAN WILL BE NOTHING BUT DUST!

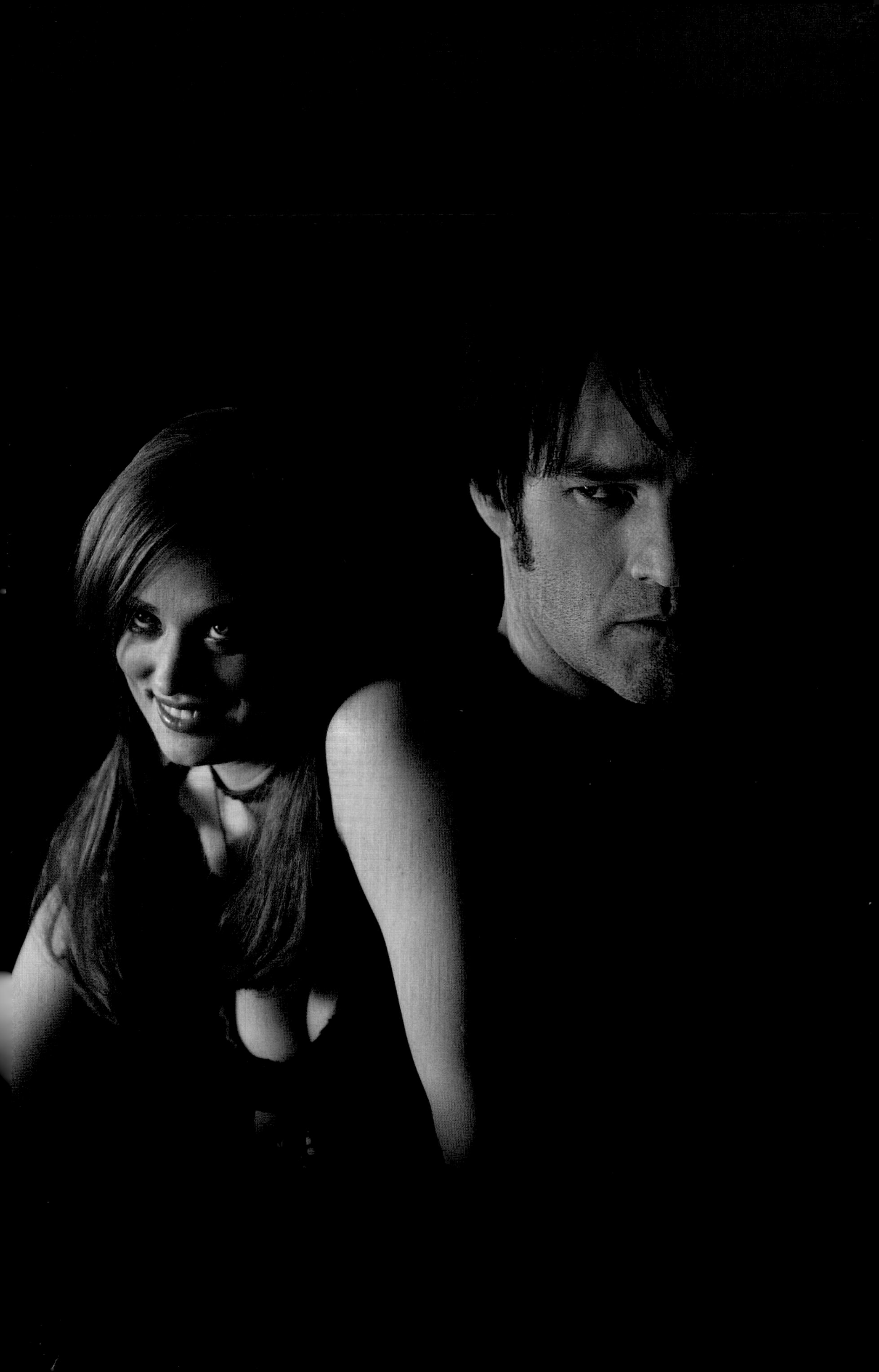

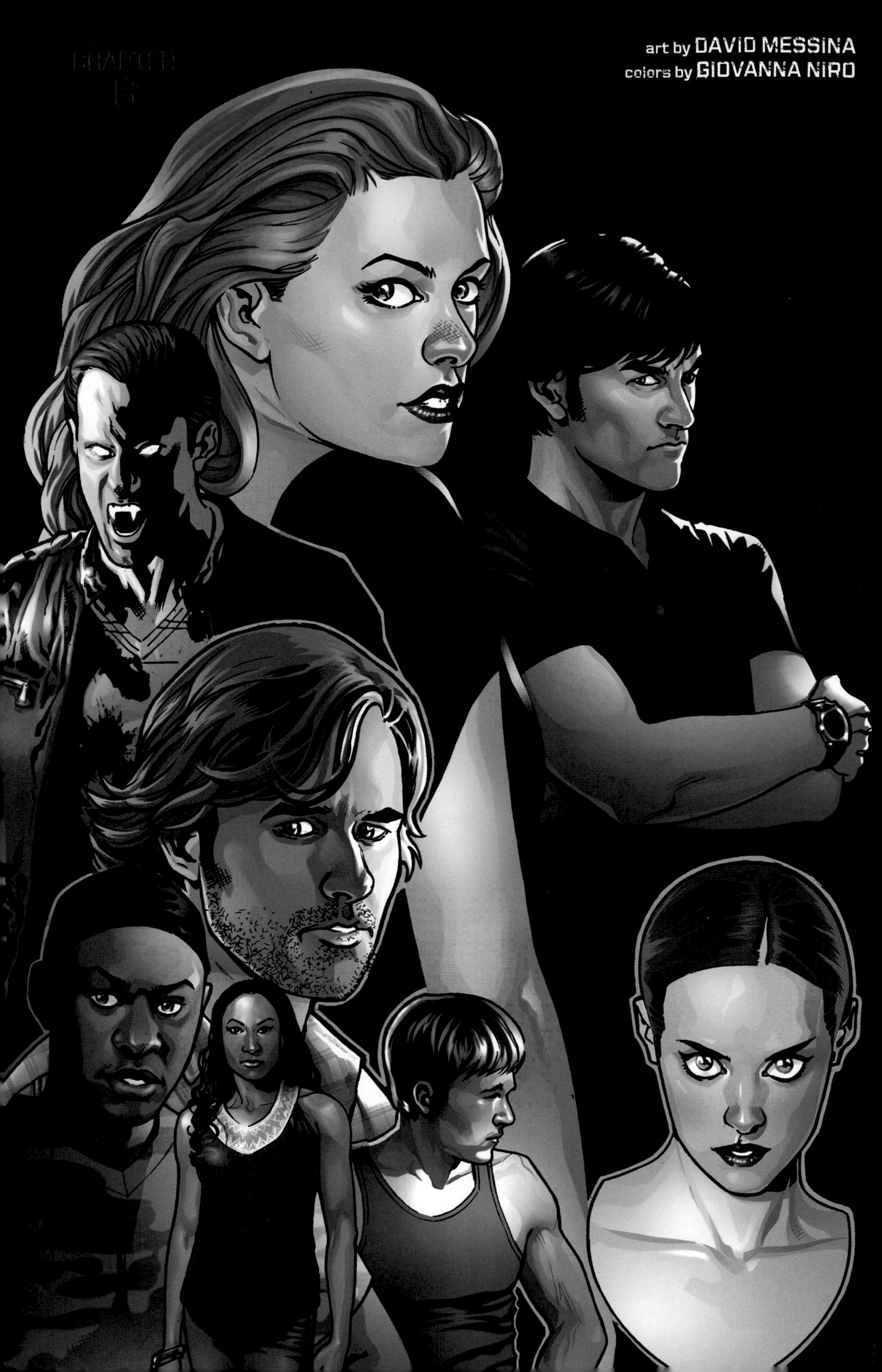
CHAPTER

art by DAVID MESSINA
colors by GIOVANNA NIRO

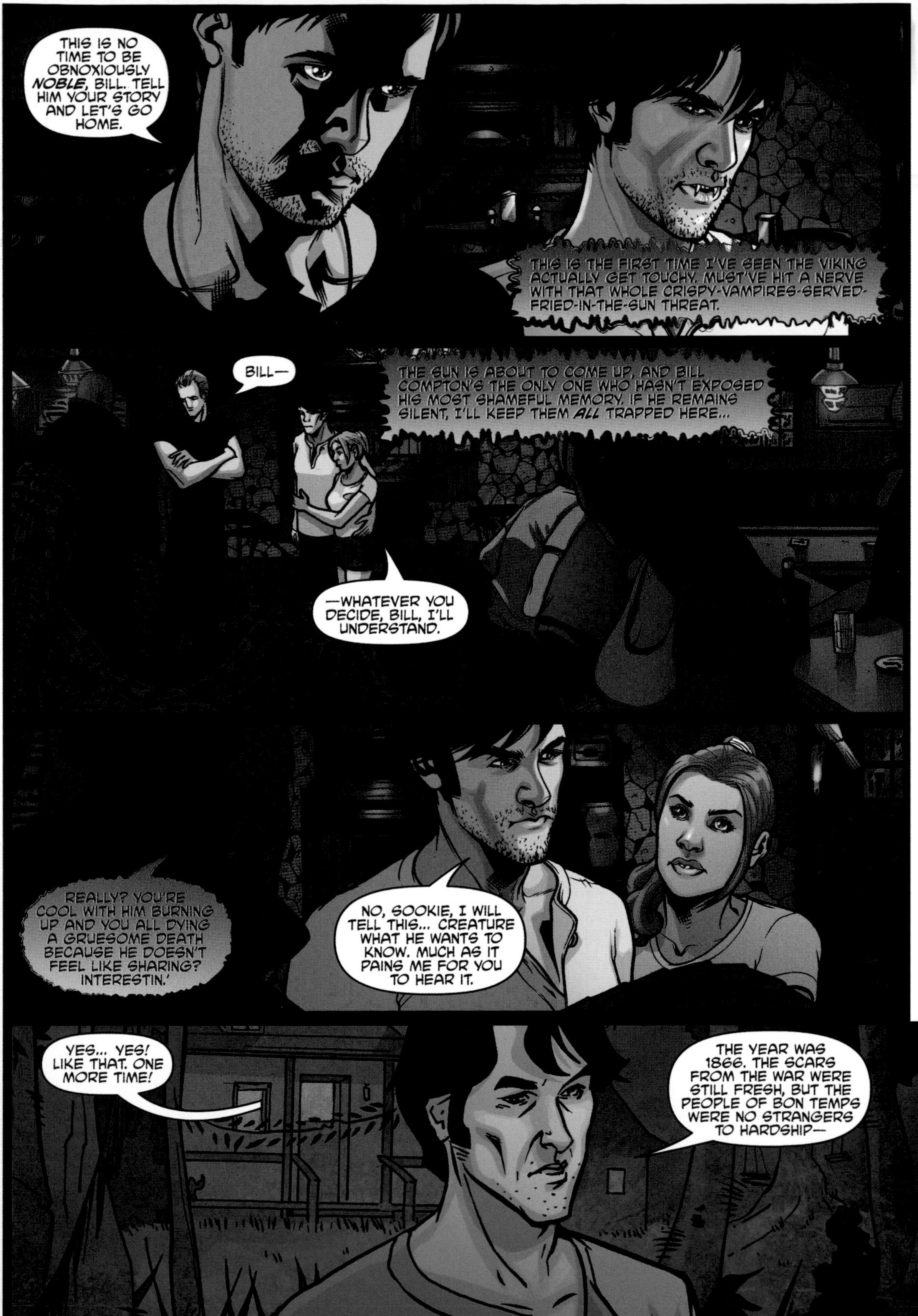
THIS IS NO TIME TO BE OBNOXIOUSLY NOBLE, BILL. TELL HIM YOUR STORY AND LET'S GO HOME.
THIS IS THE FIRST TIME I'VE SEEN THE VIKING ACTUALLY GET TOUCHY. MUST'VE HIT A NERVE WITH THAT WHOLE CRISPY-VAMPIRES-SERVED-FRIED-IN-THE-SUN THREAT.
BILL—
THE SUN IS ABOUT TO COME UP, AND BILL COMPTON'S THE ONLY ONE WHO HASN'T EXPOSED HIS MOST SHAMEFUL MEMORY. IF HE REMAINS SILENT, I'LL KEEP THEM ALL TRAPPED HERE...
—WHATEVER YOU DECIDE, BILL, I'LL UNDERSTAND.
REALLY? YOU'RE COOL WITH HIM BURNING UP AND YOU ALL DYING A GRUESOME DEATH BECAUSE HE DOESN'T FEEL LIKE SHARING? INTERESTIN.'
NO, SOOKIE, I WILL TELL THIS... CREATURE WHAT HE WANTS TO KNOW. MUCH AS IT PAINS ME FOR YOU TO HEAR IT.
YES... YES! LIKE THAT. ONE MORE TIME!
THE YEAR WAS 1866. THE SCARS FROM THE WAR WERE STILL FRESH, BUT THE PEOPLE OF BON TEMPS WERE NO STRANGERS TO HARDSHIP—

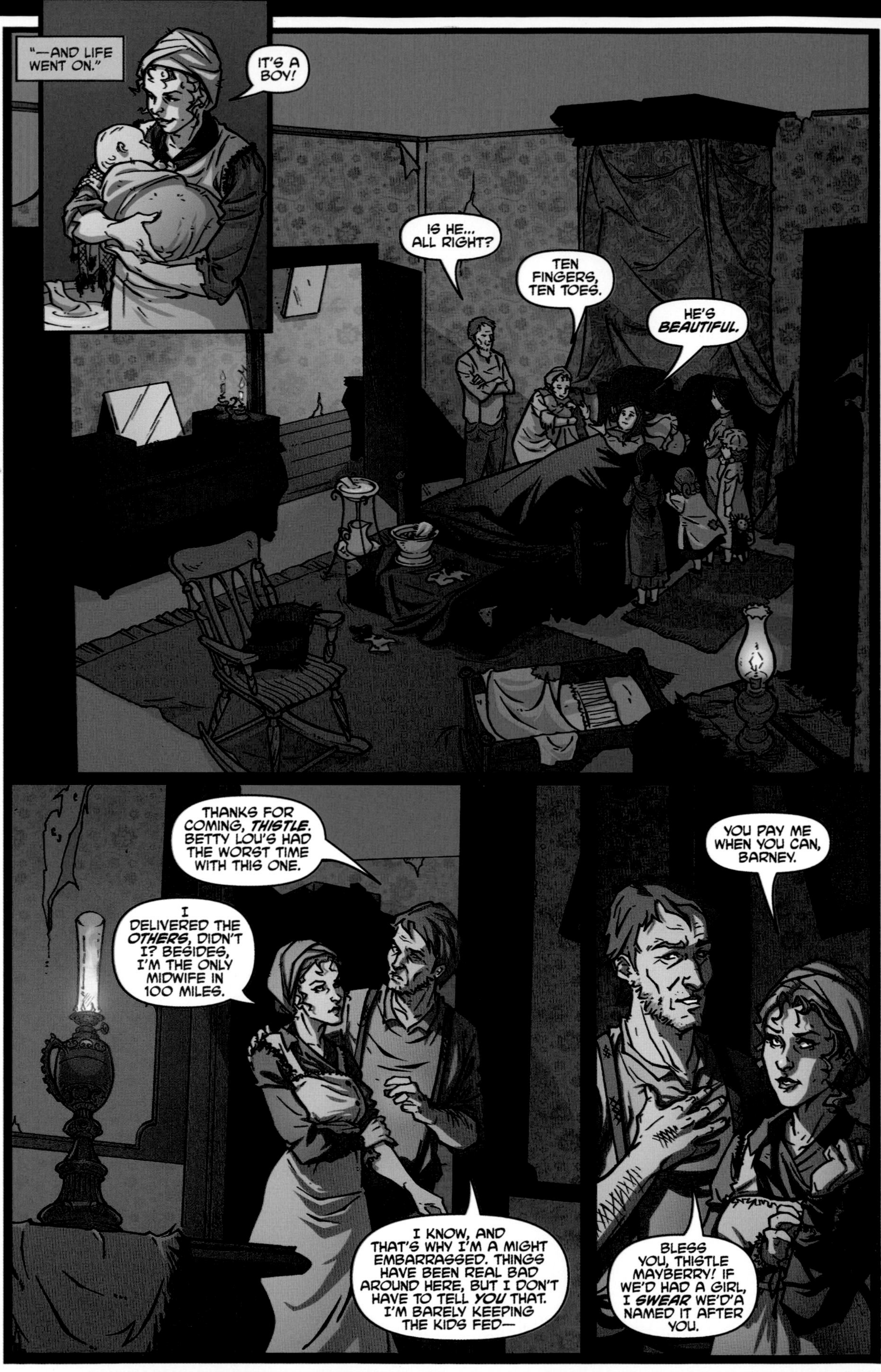
"—AND LIFE WENT ON."
IT'S A BOY!
IS HE... ALL RIGHT?
TEN FINGERS, TEN TOES.
HE'S *BEAUTIFUL.*
THANKS FOR COMING, *THISTLE*. BETTY LOU'S HAD THE WORST TIME WITH THIS ONE.
I DELIVERED THE *OTHERS*, DIDN'T I? BESIDES, I'M THE ONLY MIDWIFE IN 100 MILES.
I KNOW, AND THAT'S WHY I'M A MIGHT EMBARRASSED. THINGS HAVE BEEN REAL BAD AROUND HERE, BUT I DON'T HAVE TO TELL *YOU* THAT. I'M BARELY KEEPING THE KIDS FED—
YOU PAY ME WHEN YOU CAN, BARNEY.
BLESS YOU, THISTLE MAYBERRY! IF WE'D HAD A GIRL, I *SWEAR* WE'D'A NAMED IT AFTER YOU.

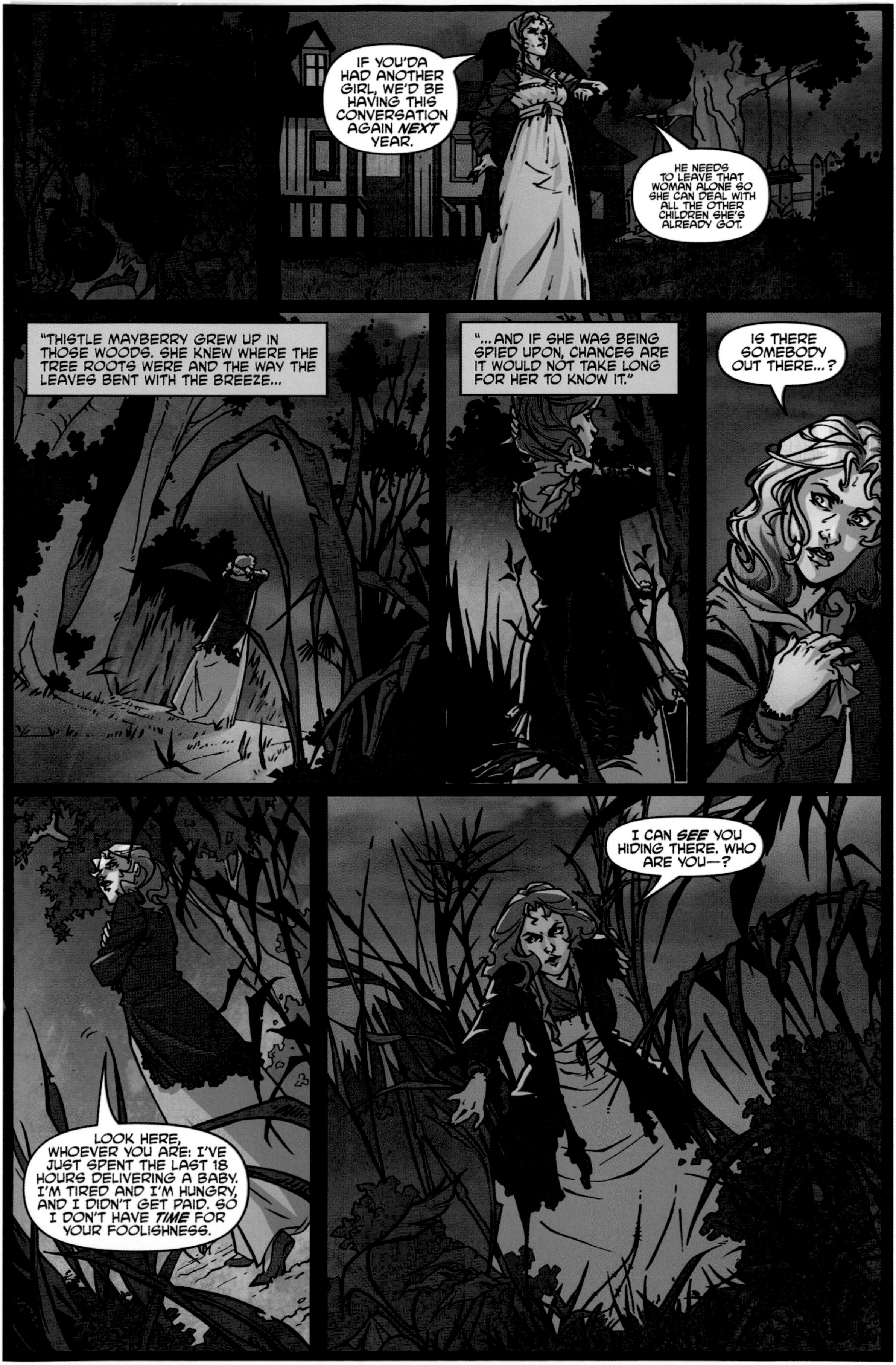
IF YOU'DA HAD ANOTHER GIRL, WE'D BE HAVING THIS CONVERSATION AGAIN *NEXT* YEAR.
HE NEEDS TO LEAVE THAT WOMAN ALONE SO SHE CAN DEAL WITH ALL THE OTHER CHILDREN SHE'S ALREADY GOT.
"THISTLE MAYBERRY GREW UP IN THOSE WOODS. SHE KNEW WHERE THE TREE ROOTS WERE AND THE WAY THE LEAVES BENT WITH THE BREEZE...
"...AND IF SHE WAS BEING SPIED UPON, CHANCES ARE IT WOULD NOT TAKE LONG FOR HER TO KNOW IT."
IS THERE SOMEBODY OUT THERE...?
LOOK HERE, WHOEVER YOU ARE: I'VE JUST SPENT THE LAST 18 HOURS DELIVERING A BABY. I'M TIRED AND I'M HUNGRY, AND I DIDN'T GET PAID. SO I DON'T HAVE *TIME* FOR YOUR FOOLISHNESS.
I CAN *SEE* YOU HIDING THERE. WHO ARE YOU--?

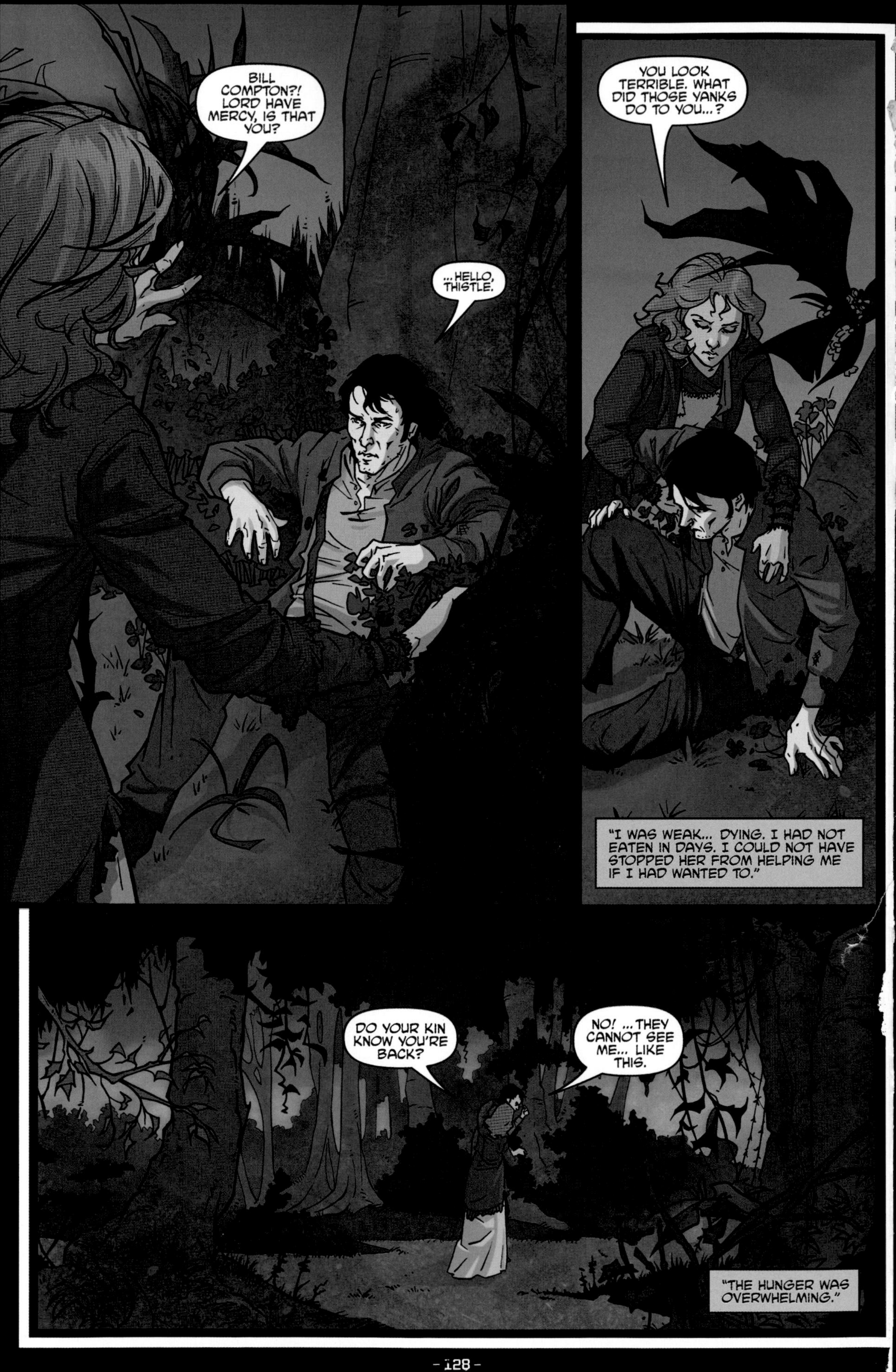
BILL COMPTON?! LORD HAVE MERCY, IS THAT YOU?
...HELLO, THISTLE.
YOU LOOK TERRIBLE. WHAT DID THOSE YANKS DO TO YOU...?
"I WAS WEAK... DYING. I HAD NOT EATEN IN DAYS. I COULD NOT HAVE STOPPED HER FROM HELPING ME IF I HAD WANTED TO."
DO YOUR KIN KNOW YOU'RE BACK?
NO! ...THEY CANNOT SEE ME... LIKE THIS.
"THE HUNGER WAS OVERWHELMING."

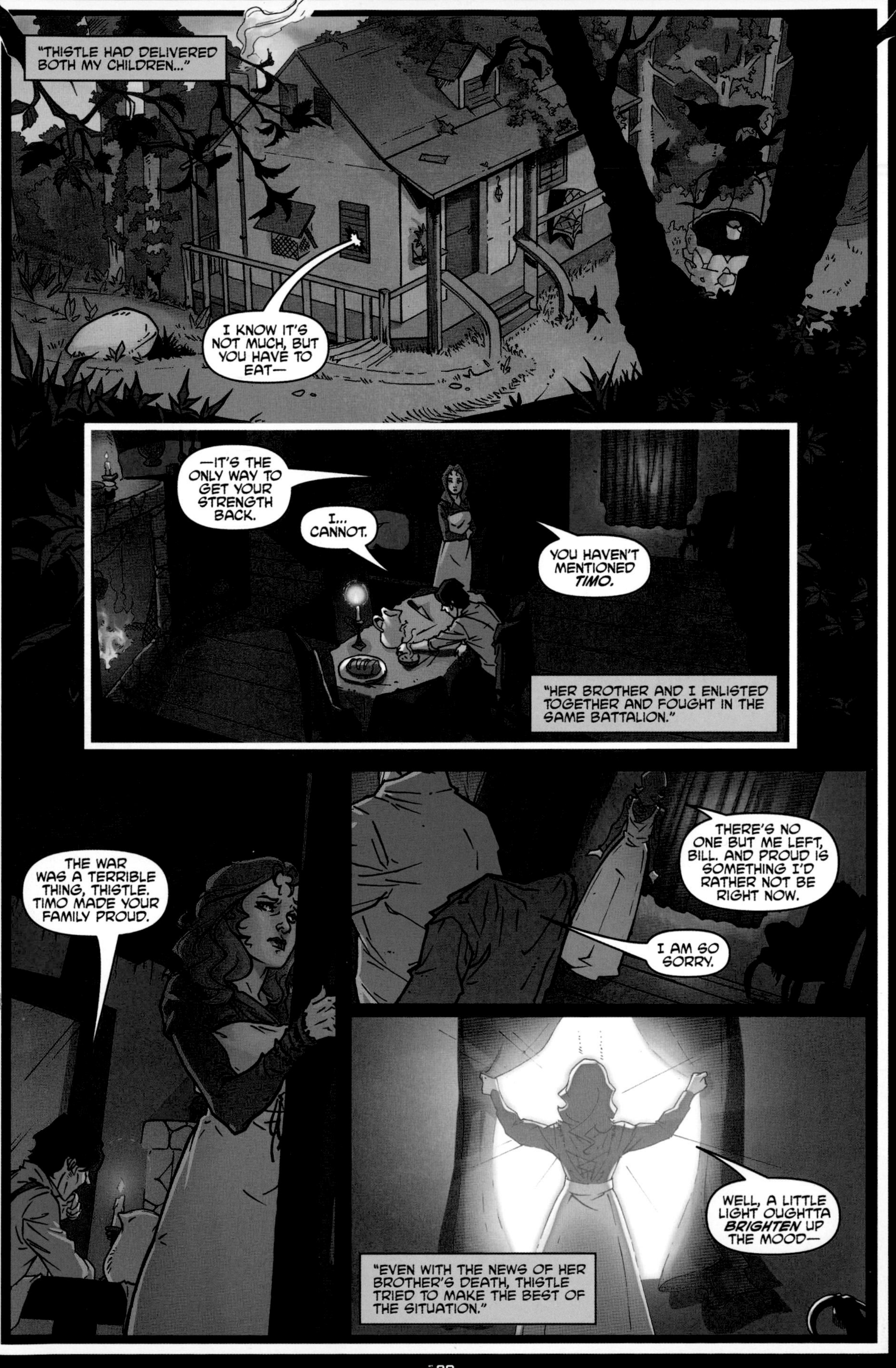
"THISTLE HAD DELIVERED BOTH MY CHILDREN..."
I KNOW IT'S NOT MUCH, BUT YOU HAVE TO EAT—
—IT'S THE ONLY WAY TO GET YOUR STRENGTH BACK.
I... CANNOT.
YOU HAVEN'T MENTIONED *TIMO.*
"HER BROTHER AND I ENLISTED TOGETHER AND FOUGHT IN THE SAME BATTALION."
THE WAR WAS A TERRIBLE THING, THISTLE. TIMO MADE YOUR FAMILY PROUD.
THERE'S NO ONE BUT ME LEFT, BILL. AND PROUD IS SOMETHING I'D RATHER NOT BE RIGHT NOW.
I AM SO SORRY.
WELL, A LITTLE LIGHT OUGHTTA *BRIGHTEN* UP THE MOOD—
"EVEN WITH THE NEWS OF HER BROTHER'S DEATH, THISTLE TRIED TO MAKE THE BEST OF THE SITUATION."

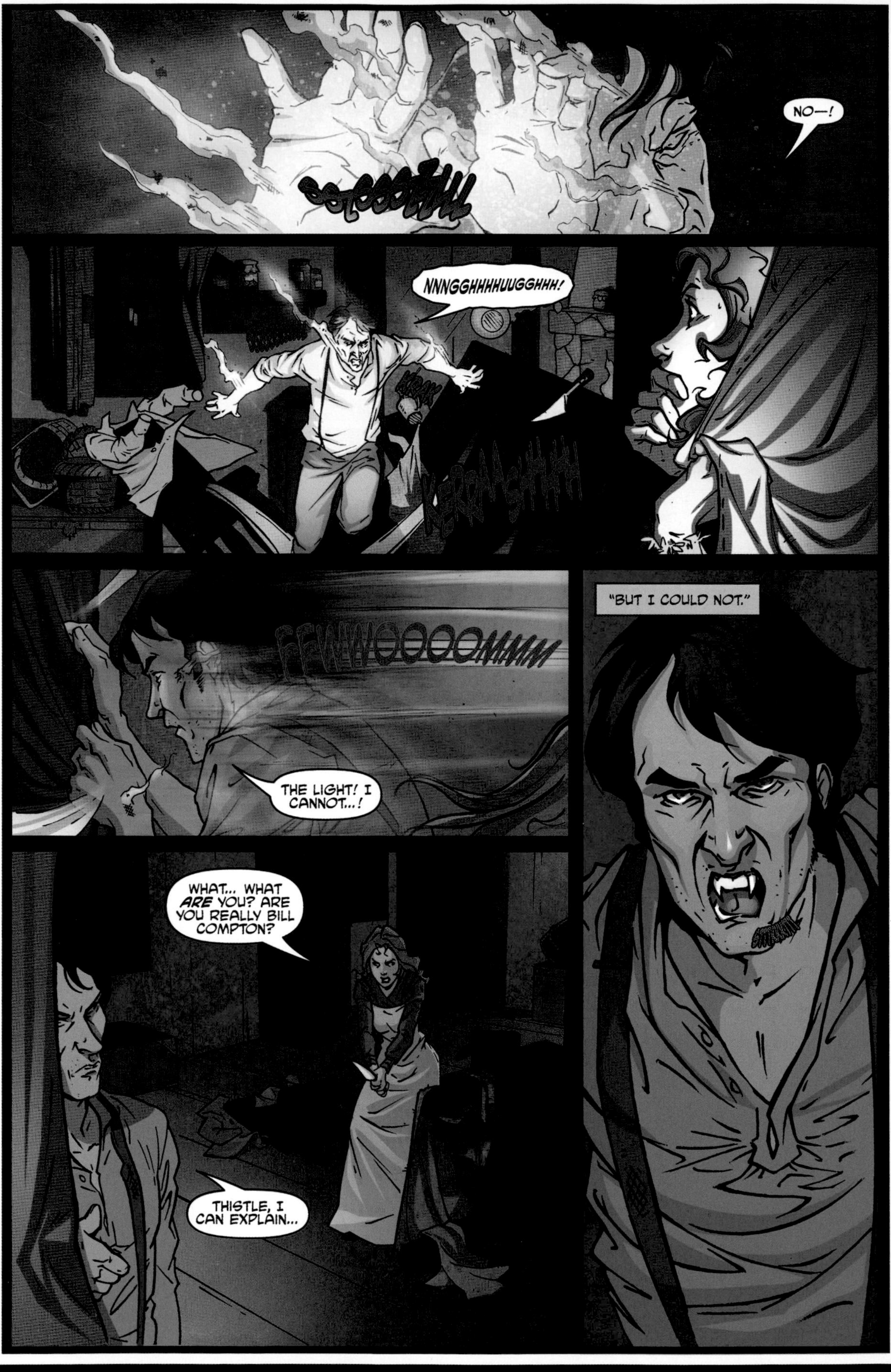
NO—!
SSSSSSSTHHH
NNNGGHHHHUUGGHHH!
KRAK
KERRAASHHHH
FFWWOOOOMMM
THE LIGHT! I CANNOT...!
"BUT I COULD NOT."
WHAT... WHAT *ARE* YOU? ARE YOU REALLY BILL COMPTON?
THISTLE, I CAN EXPLAIN...

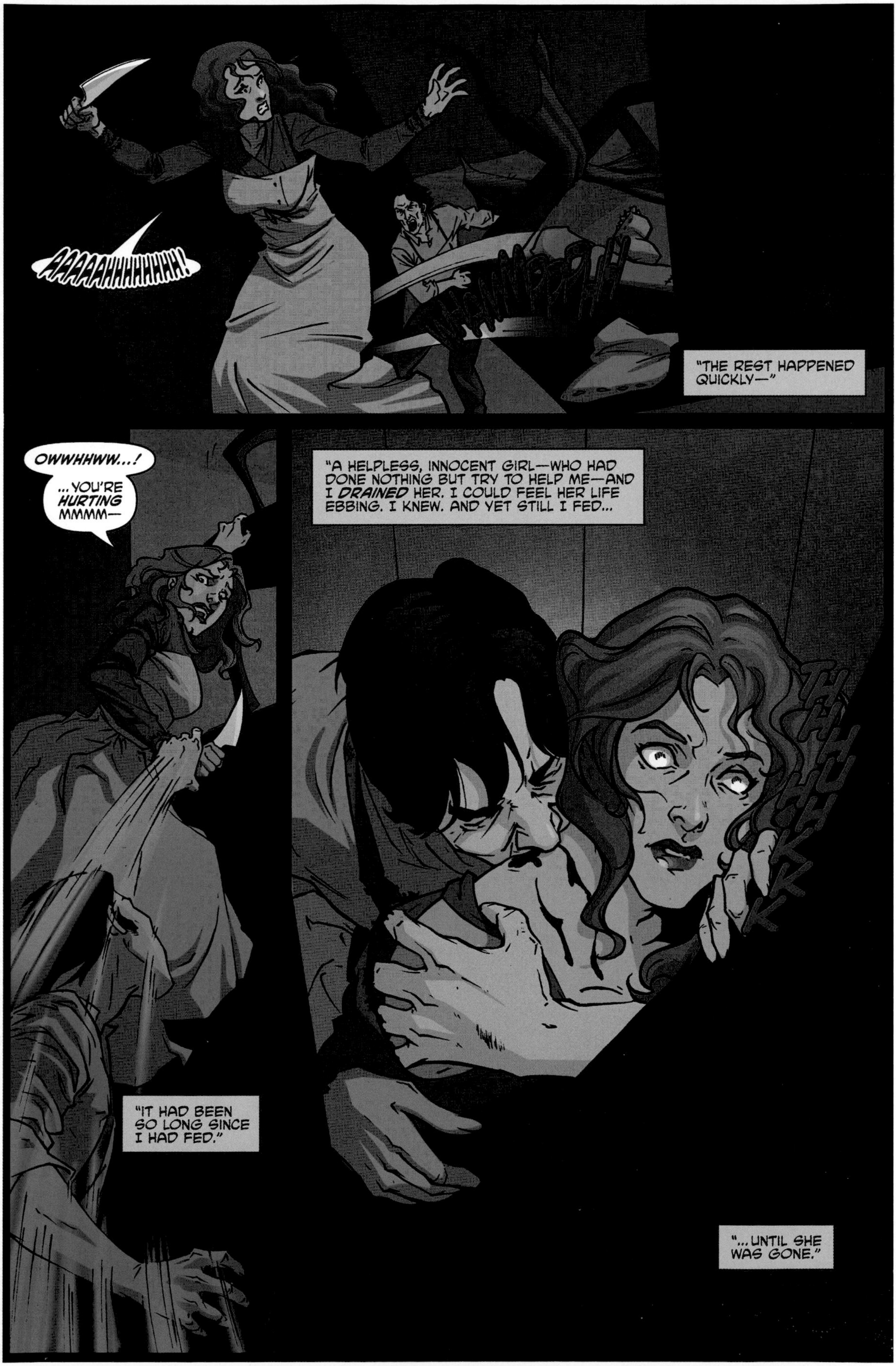
AAAAAHHHHHHHH!
"THE REST HAPPENED QUICKLY—"
OWWHHWW...!
...YOU'RE HURTING MMMM—
"A HELPLESS, INNOCENT GIRL—WHO HAD DONE NOTHING BUT TRY TO HELP ME—AND I DRAINED HER. I COULD FEEL HER LIFE EBBING. I KNEW. AND YET STILL I FED...
"IT HAD BEEN SO LONG SINCE I HAD FED."
"...UNTIL SHE WAS GONE."

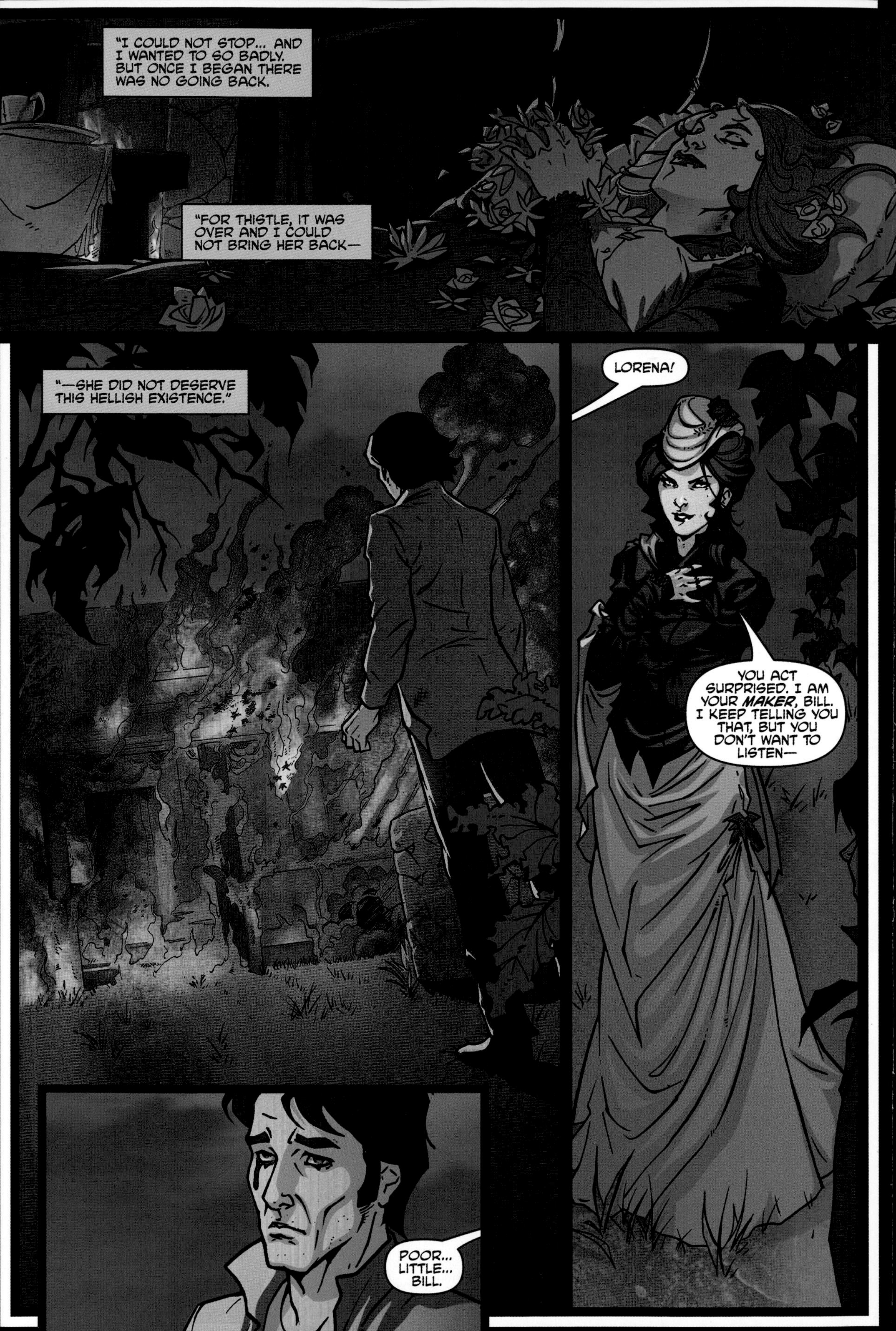
"I COULD NOT STOP... AND I WANTED TO SO BADLY. BUT ONCE I BEGAN THERE WAS NO GOING BACK.
"FOR THISTLE, IT WAS OVER AND I COULD NOT BRING HER BACK—
"—SHE DID NOT DESERVE THIS HELLISH EXISTENCE."
LORENA!
YOU ACT SURPRISED. I AM YOUR MAKER, BILL. I KEEP TELLING YOU THAT, BUT YOU DON'T WANT TO LISTEN—
POOR... LITTLE... BILL.

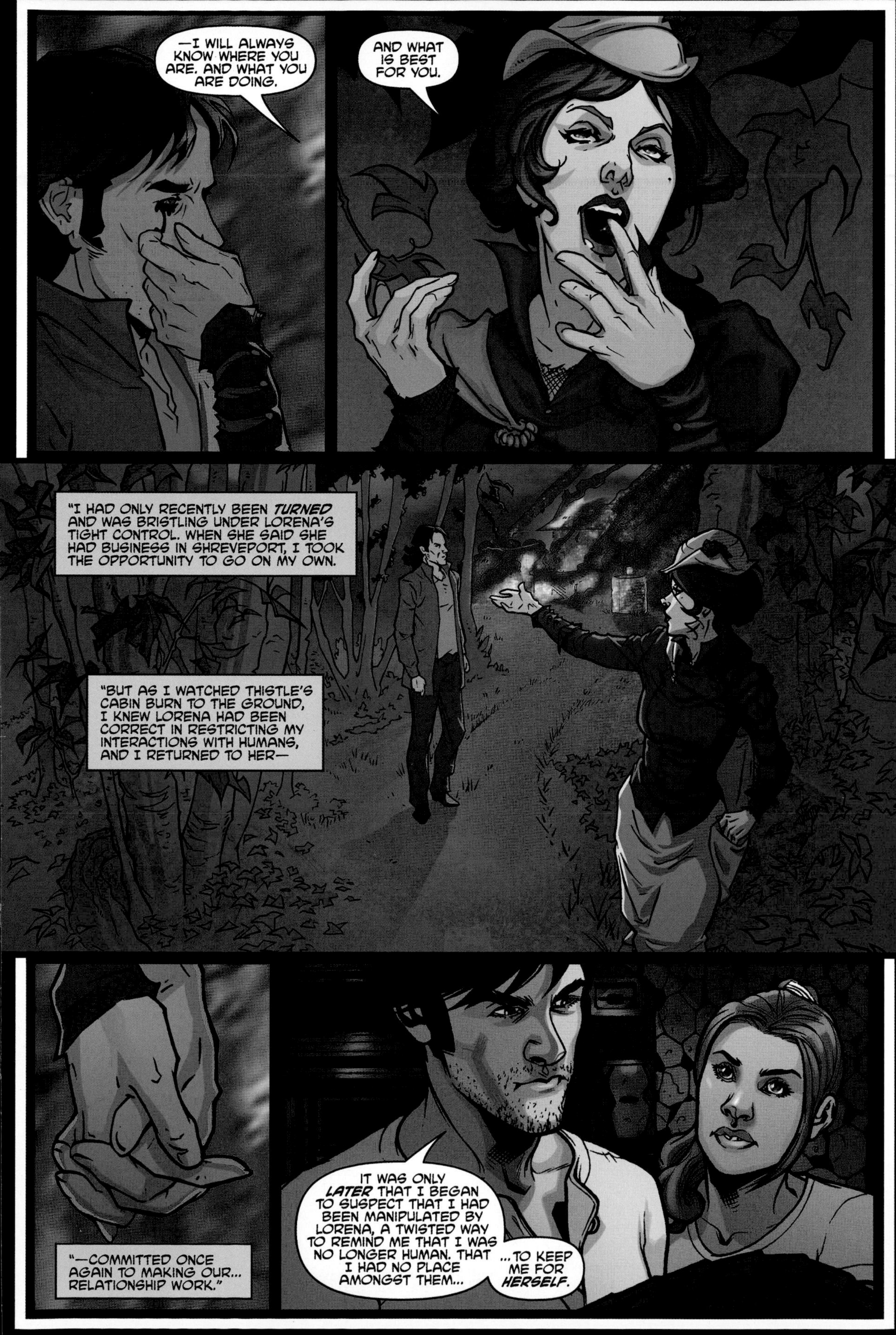
—I WILL ALWAYS KNOW WHERE YOU ARE. AND WHAT YOU ARE DOING.
AND WHAT IS BEST FOR YOU.
"I HAD ONLY RECENTLY BEEN *TURNED* AND WAS BRISTLING UNDER LORENA'S TIGHT CONTROL. WHEN SHE SAID SHE HAD BUSINESS IN SHREVEPORT, I TOOK THE OPPORTUNITY TO GO ON MY OWN.
"BUT AS I WATCHED THISTLE'S CABIN BURN TO THE GROUND, I KNEW LORENA HAD BEEN CORRECT IN RESTRICTING MY INTERACTIONS WITH HUMANS, AND I RETURNED TO HER—
"—COMMITTED ONCE AGAIN TO MAKING OUR... RELATIONSHIP WORK."
IT WAS ONLY *LATER* THAT I BEGAN TO SUSPECT THAT I HAD BEEN MANIPULATED BY LORENA, A TWISTED WAY TO REMIND ME THAT I WAS NO LONGER HUMAN. THAT I HAD NO PLACE AMONGST THEM...
...TO KEEP ME FOR *HERSELF*.

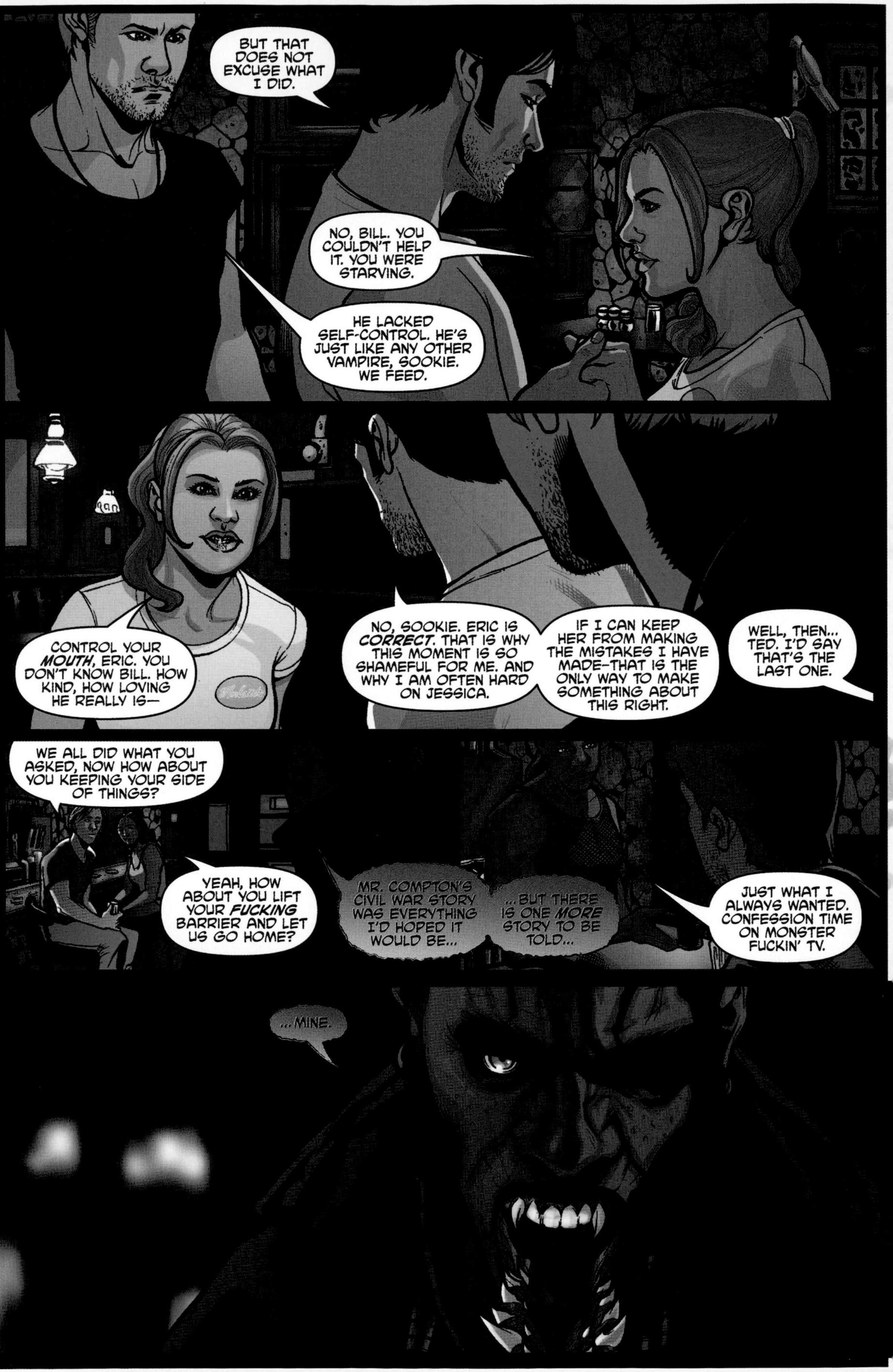
BUT THAT DOES NOT EXCUSE WHAT I DID.
NO, BILL. YOU COULDN'T HELP IT. YOU WERE STARVING.
HE LACKED SELF-CONTROL. HE'S JUST LIKE ANY OTHER VAMPIRE, SOOKIE. WE FEED.
CONTROL YOUR *MOUTH*, ERIC. YOU DON'T KNOW BILL. HOW KIND, HOW LOVING HE REALLY IS—
NO, SOOKIE. ERIC IS *CORRECT*. THAT IS WHY THIS MOMENT IS SO SHAMEFUL FOR ME. AND WHY I AM OFTEN HARD ON JESSICA.
IF I CAN KEEP HER FROM MAKING THE MISTAKES I HAVE MADE—THAT IS THE ONLY WAY TO MAKE SOMETHING ABOUT THIS RIGHT.
WELL, THEN... TED. I'D SAY THAT'S THE LAST ONE.
WE ALL DID WHAT YOU ASKED, NOW HOW ABOUT YOU KEEPING YOUR SIDE OF THINGS?
YEAH, HOW ABOUT YOU LIFT YOUR *FUCKING* BARRIER AND LET US GO HOME?
MR. COMPTON'S CIVIL WAR STORY WAS EVERYTHING I'D HOPED IT WOULD BE...
...BUT THERE IS ONE *MORE* STORY TO BE TOLD...
JUST WHAT I ALWAYS WANTED. CONFESSION TIME ON MONSTER FUCKIN' TV.
...MINE.

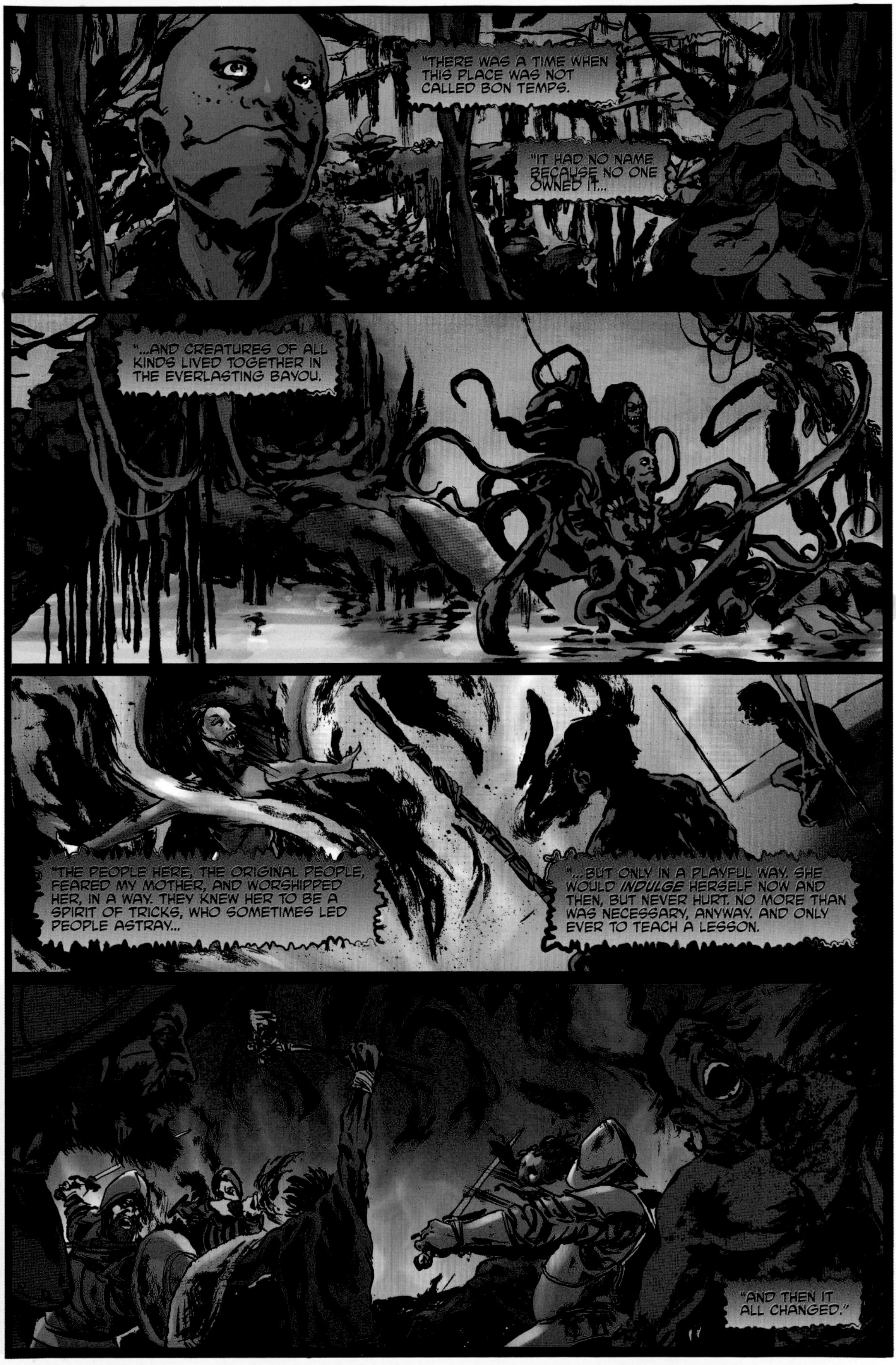
"THERE WAS A TIME WHEN THIS PLACE WAS NOT CALLED BON TEMPS.
"IT HAD NO NAME BECAUSE NO ONE OWNED IT...
"...AND CREATURES OF ALL KINDS LIVED TOGETHER IN THE EVERLASTING BAYOU.
"THE PEOPLE HERE, THE ORIGINAL PEOPLE, FEARED MY MOTHER, AND WORSHIPPED HER, IN A WAY. THEY KNEW HER TO BE A SPIRIT OF TRICKS, WHO SOMETIMES LED PEOPLE ASTRAY...
"...BUT ONLY IN A PLAYFUL WAY. SHE WOULD *INDULGE* HERSELF NOW AND THEN, BUT NEVER HURT. NO MORE THAN WAS NECESSARY, ANYWAY. AND ONLY EVER TO TEACH A LESSON.
"AND THEN IT ALL CHANGED."

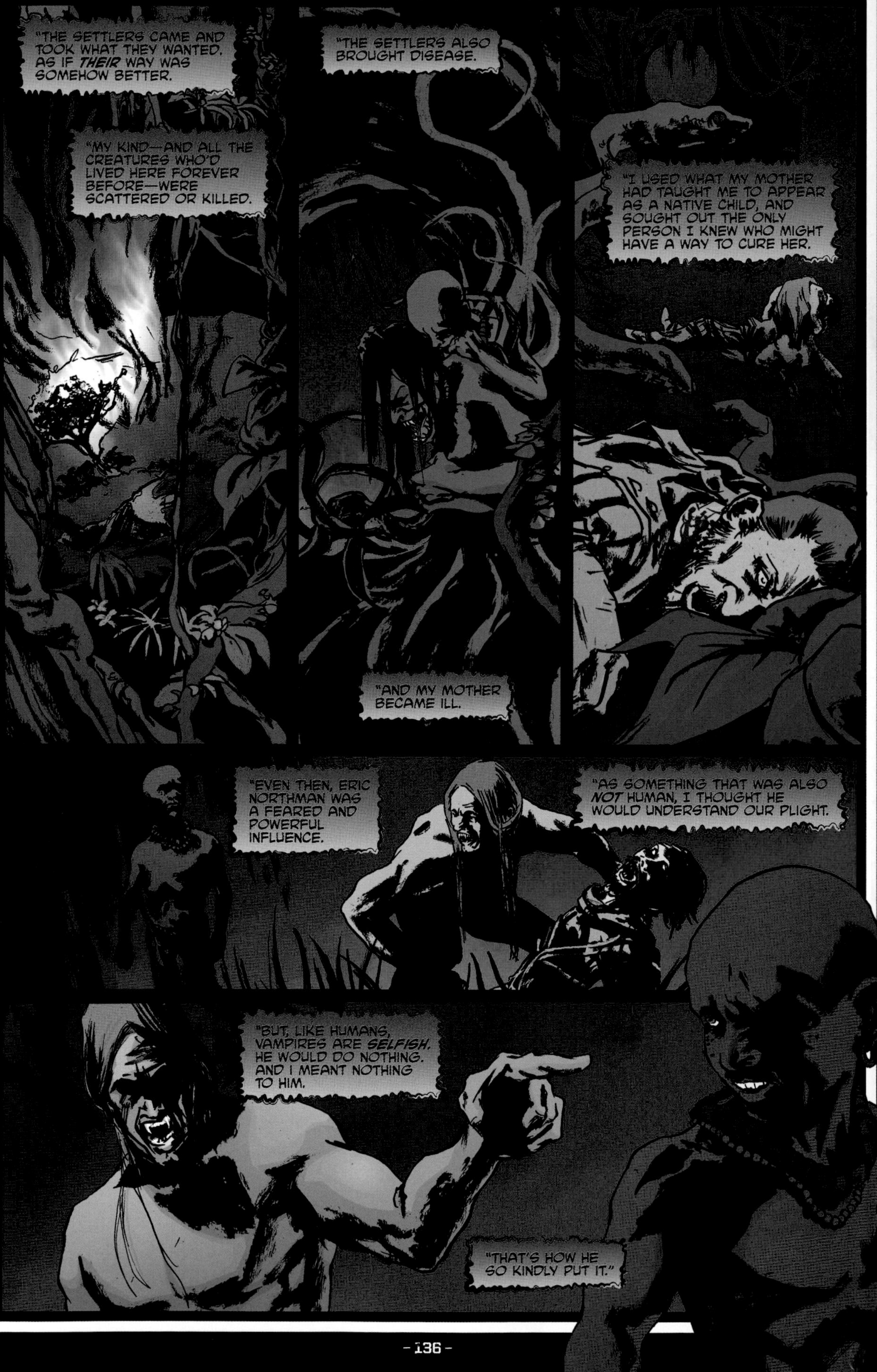
"THE SETTLERS CAME AND TOOK WHAT THEY WANTED, AS IF *THEIR* WAY WAS SOMEHOW BETTER.
"MY KIND—AND ALL THE CREATURES WHO'D LIVED HERE FOREVER BEFORE—WERE SCATTERED OR KILLED.
"THE SETTLERS ALSO BROUGHT DISEASE.
"AND MY MOTHER BECAME ILL.
"I USED WHAT MY MOTHER HAD TAUGHT ME TO APPEAR AS A NATIVE CHILD, AND SOUGHT OUT THE ONLY PERSON I KNEW WHO MIGHT HAVE A WAY TO CURE HER.
"EVEN THEN, ERIC NORTHMAN WAS A FEARED AND POWERFUL INFLUENCE.
"AS SOMETHING THAT WAS ALSO *NOT* HUMAN, I THOUGHT HE WOULD UNDERSTAND OUR PLIGHT.
"BUT, LIKE HUMANS, VAMPIRES ARE *SELFISH.* HE WOULD DO NOTHING. AND I MEANT NOTHING TO HIM.
"THAT'S HOW HE SO KINDLY PUT IT."

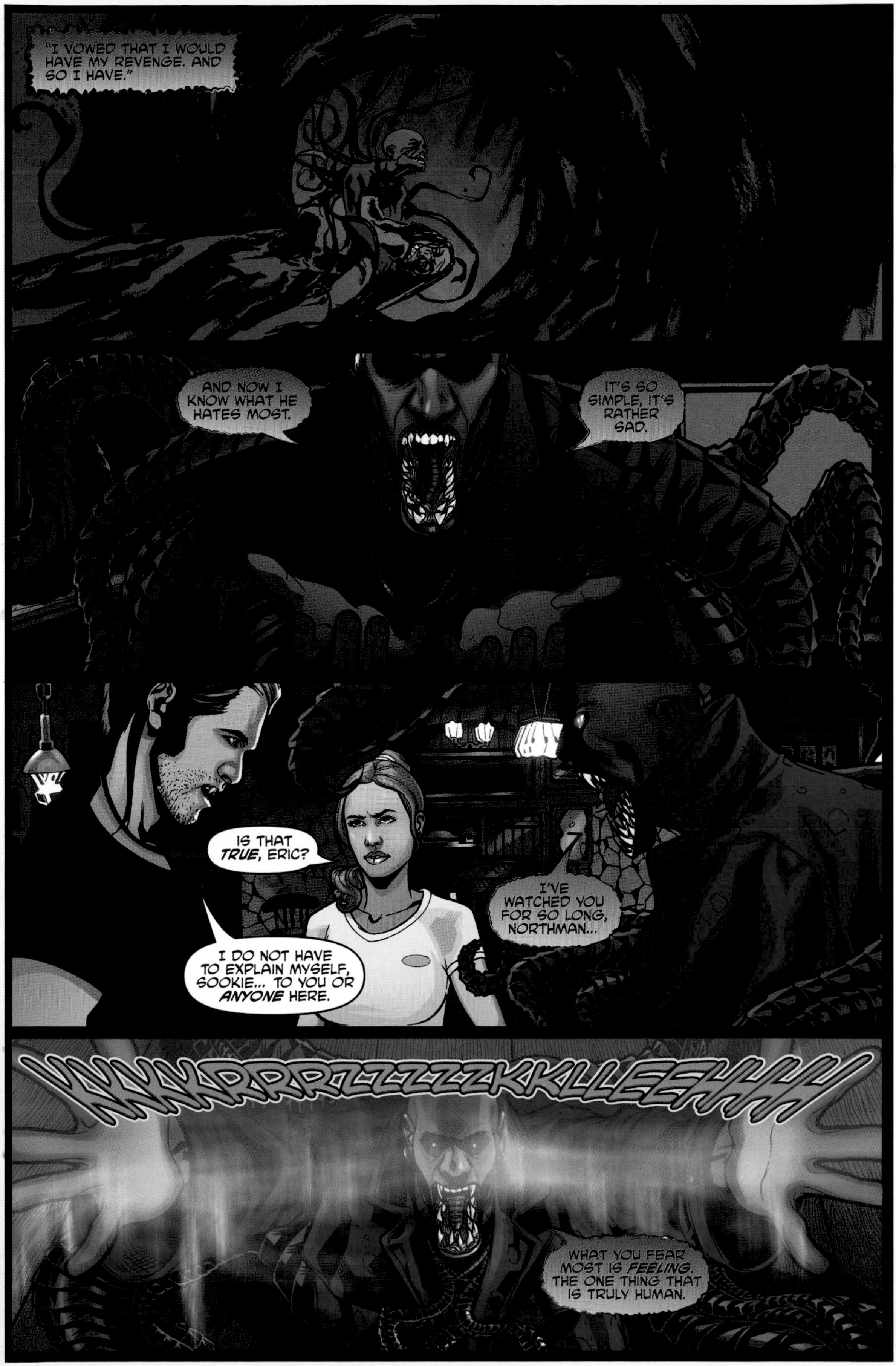
"I VOWED THAT I WOULD HAVE MY REVENGE. AND SO I HAVE."
AND NOW I KNOW WHAT HE HATES MOST.
IT'S SO SIMPLE, IT'S RATHER SAD.
IS THAT *TRUE*, ERIC?
I DO NOT HAVE TO EXPLAIN MYSELF, SOOKIE... TO YOU OR *ANYONE* HERE.
I'VE WATCHED YOU FOR SO LONG, NORTHMAN...
KKKKRRRRZZZZZZKKLLEEHHH
WHAT YOU FEAR MOST IS *FEELING*. THE ONE THING THAT IS TRULY HUMAN.

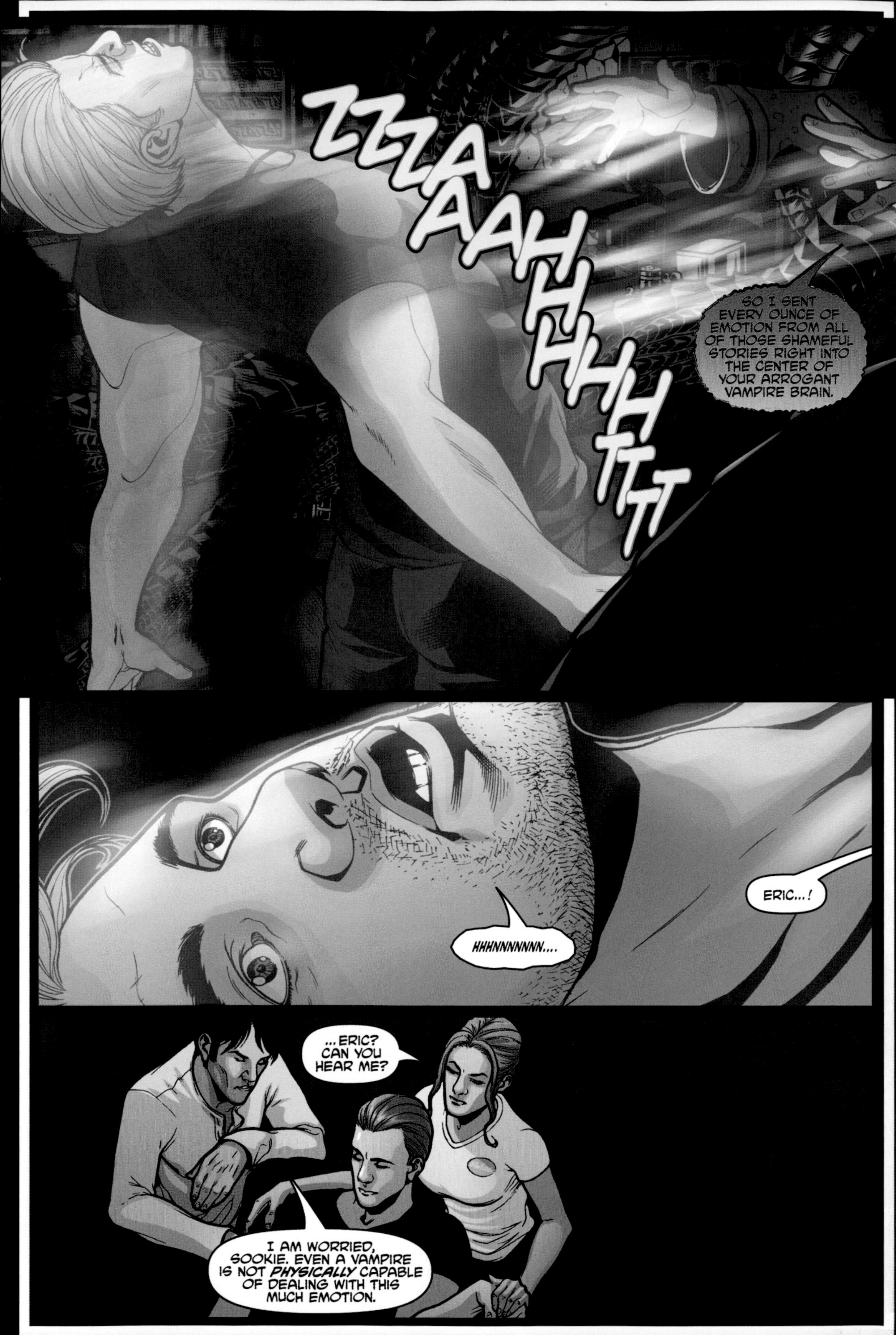
ZZZAAAHHHHHTTTT
SO I SENT EVERY OUNCE OF EMOTION FROM ALL OF THOSE SHAMEFUL STORIES RIGHT INTO THE CENTER OF YOUR ARROGANT VAMPIRE BRAIN.
ERIC...!
HHHNNNNNNN....
...ERIC? CAN YOU HEAR ME?
I AM WORRIED, SOOKIE. EVEN A VAMPIRE IS NOT *PHYSICALLY* CAPABLE OF DEALING WITH THIS MUCH EMOTION.

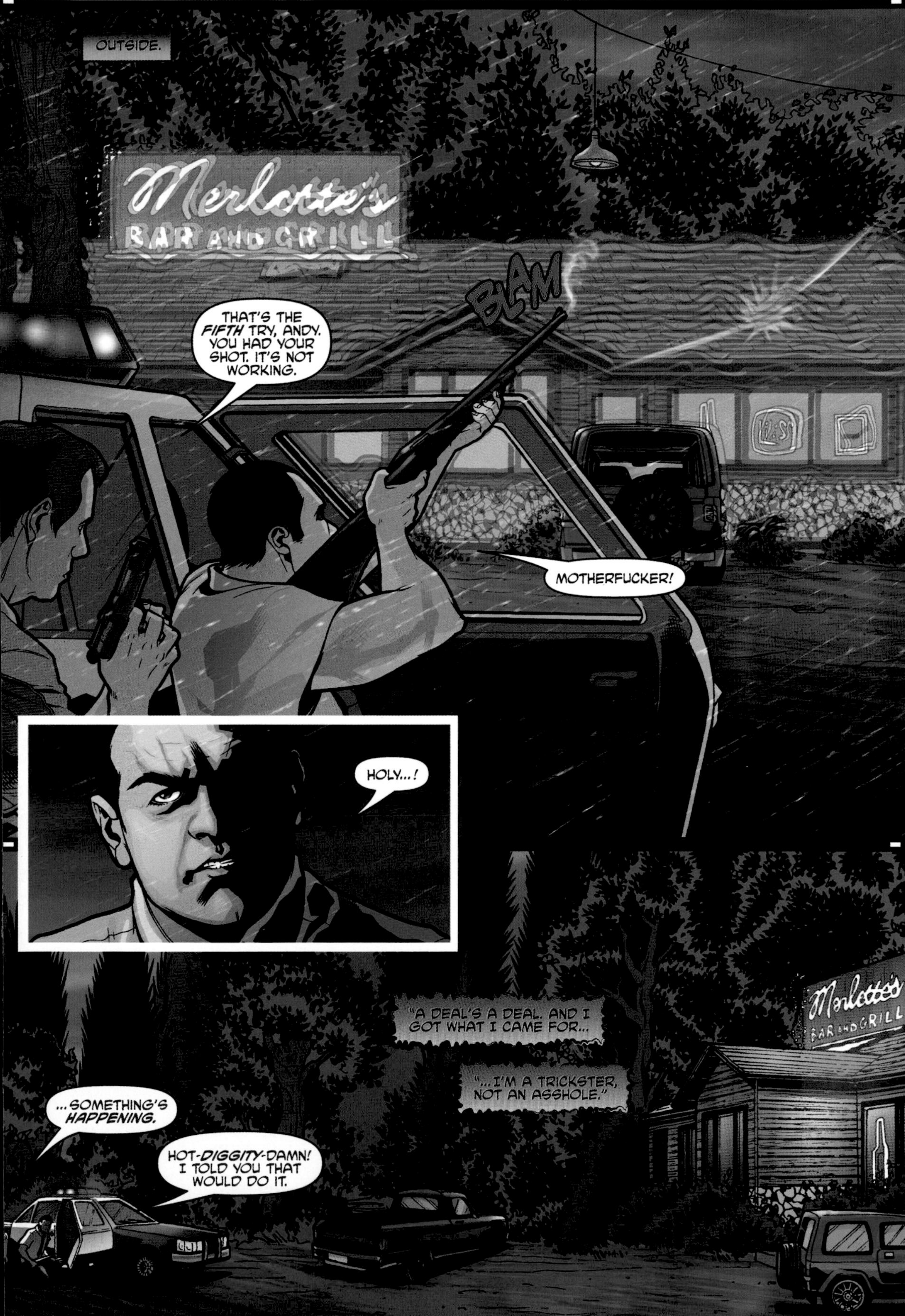
OUTSIDE.
Merlotte's BAR AND GRILL
BLAM
THAT'S THE FIFTH TRY, ANDY. YOU HAD YOUR SHOT. IT'S NOT WORKING.
MOTHERFUCKER!
HOLY...!
"A DEAL'S A DEAL. AND I GOT WHAT I CAME FOR...
"...I'M A TRICKSTER, NOT AN ASSHOLE."
...SOMETHING'S HAPPENING.
HOT-DIGGITY-DAMN! I TOLD YOU THAT WOULD DO IT.
Merlotte's BAR AND GRILL

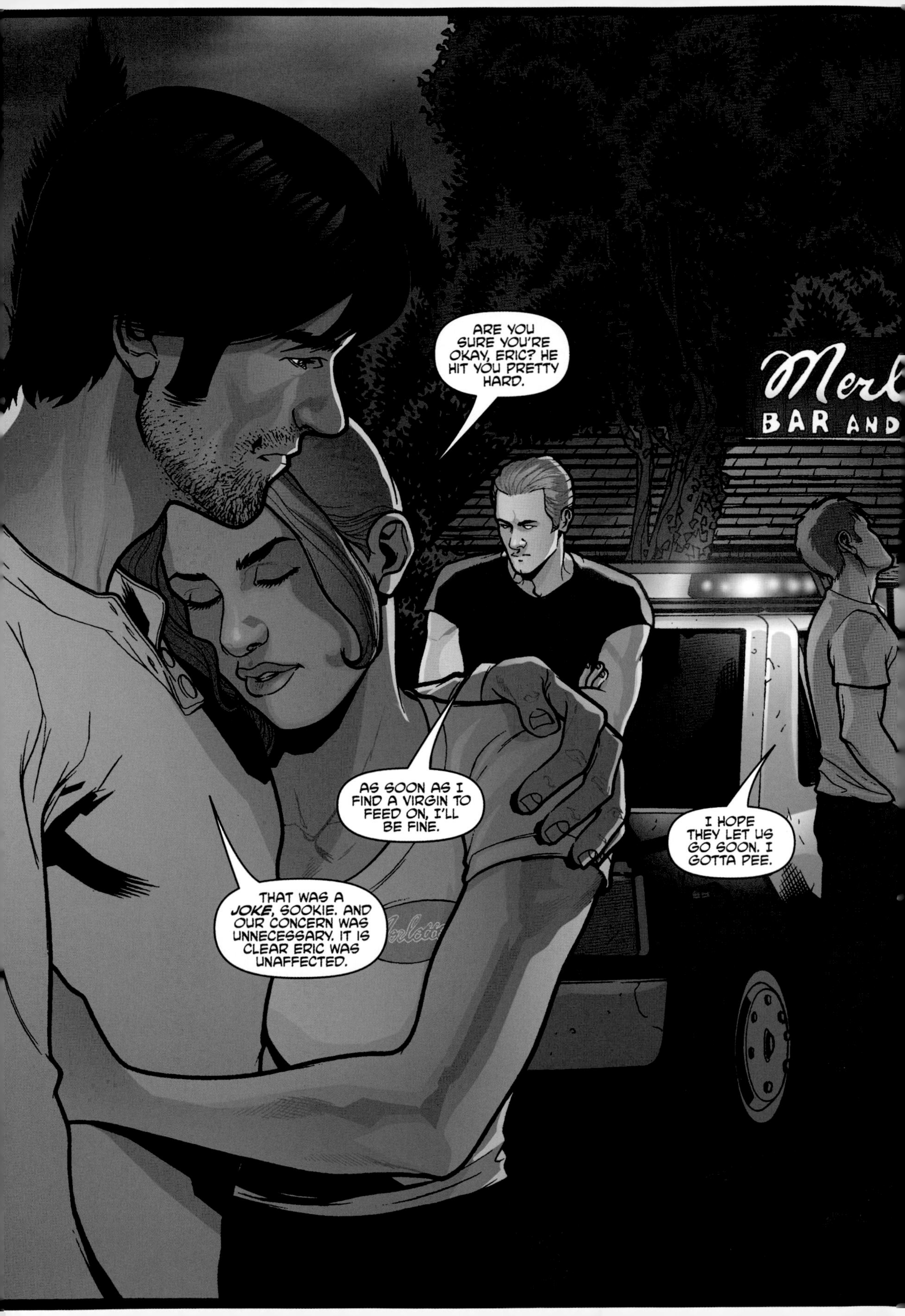
ARE YOU SURE YOU'RE OKAY, ERIC? HE HIT YOU PRETTY HARD.
AS SOON AS I FIND A VIRGIN TO FEED ON, I'LL BE FINE.
THAT WAS A *JOKE*, SOOKIE. AND OUR CONCERN WAS UNNECESSARY. IT IS CLEAR ERIC WAS UNAFFECTED.
I HOPE THEY LET US GO SOON. I GOTTA PEE.
BAR AND

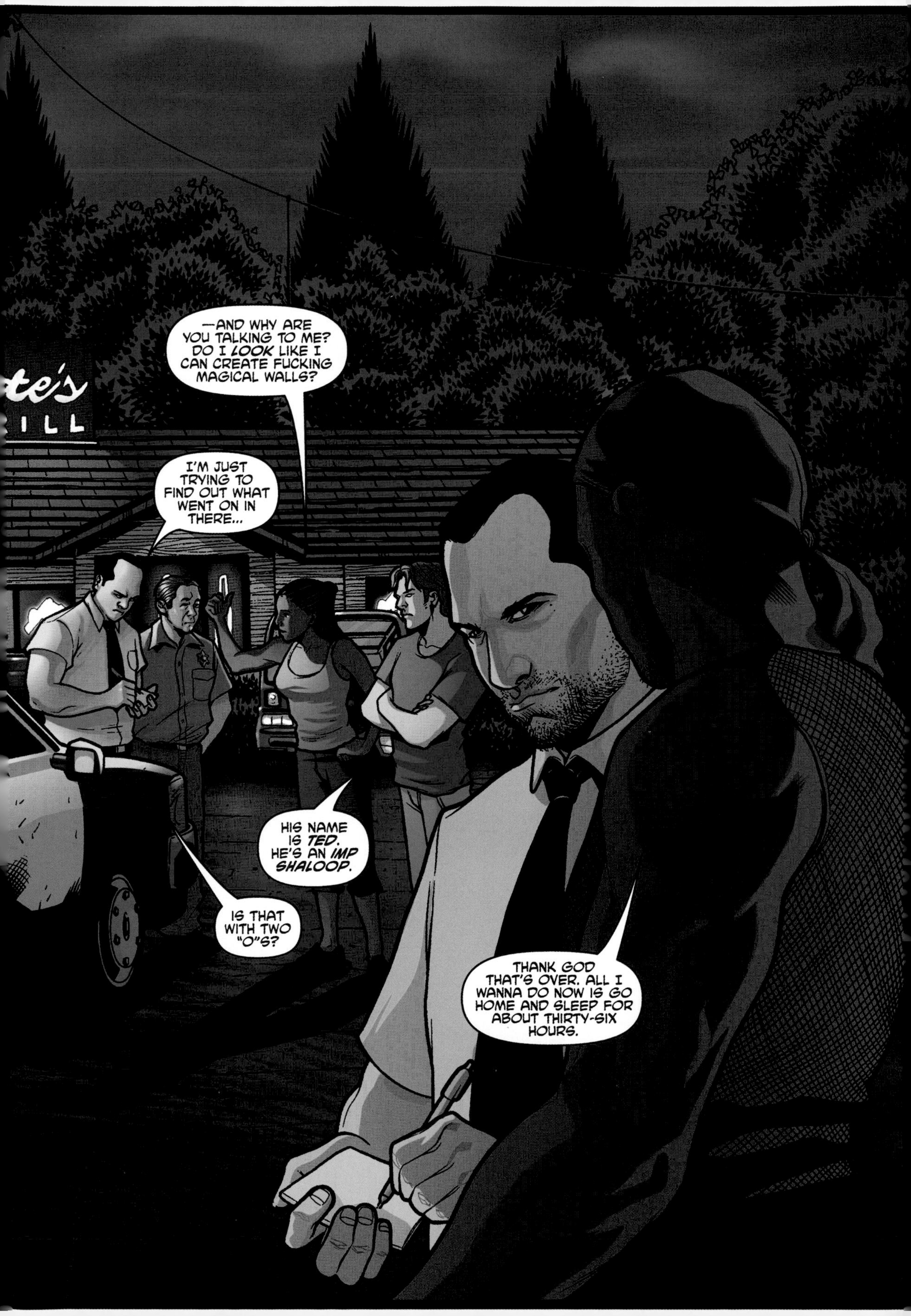

...TE'S
...ILL
—AND WHY ARE YOU TALKING TO ME? DO I *LOOK* LIKE I CAN CREATE FUCKING MAGICAL WALLS?
I'M JUST TRYING TO FIND OUT WHAT WENT ON IN THERE...
HIS NAME IS *TED*. HE'S AN *IMP SHALOOP*.
IS THAT WITH TWO "O"S?
THANK GOD THAT'S OVER. ALL I WANNA DO NOW IS GO HOME AND SLEEP FOR ABOUT THIRTY-SIX HOURS.

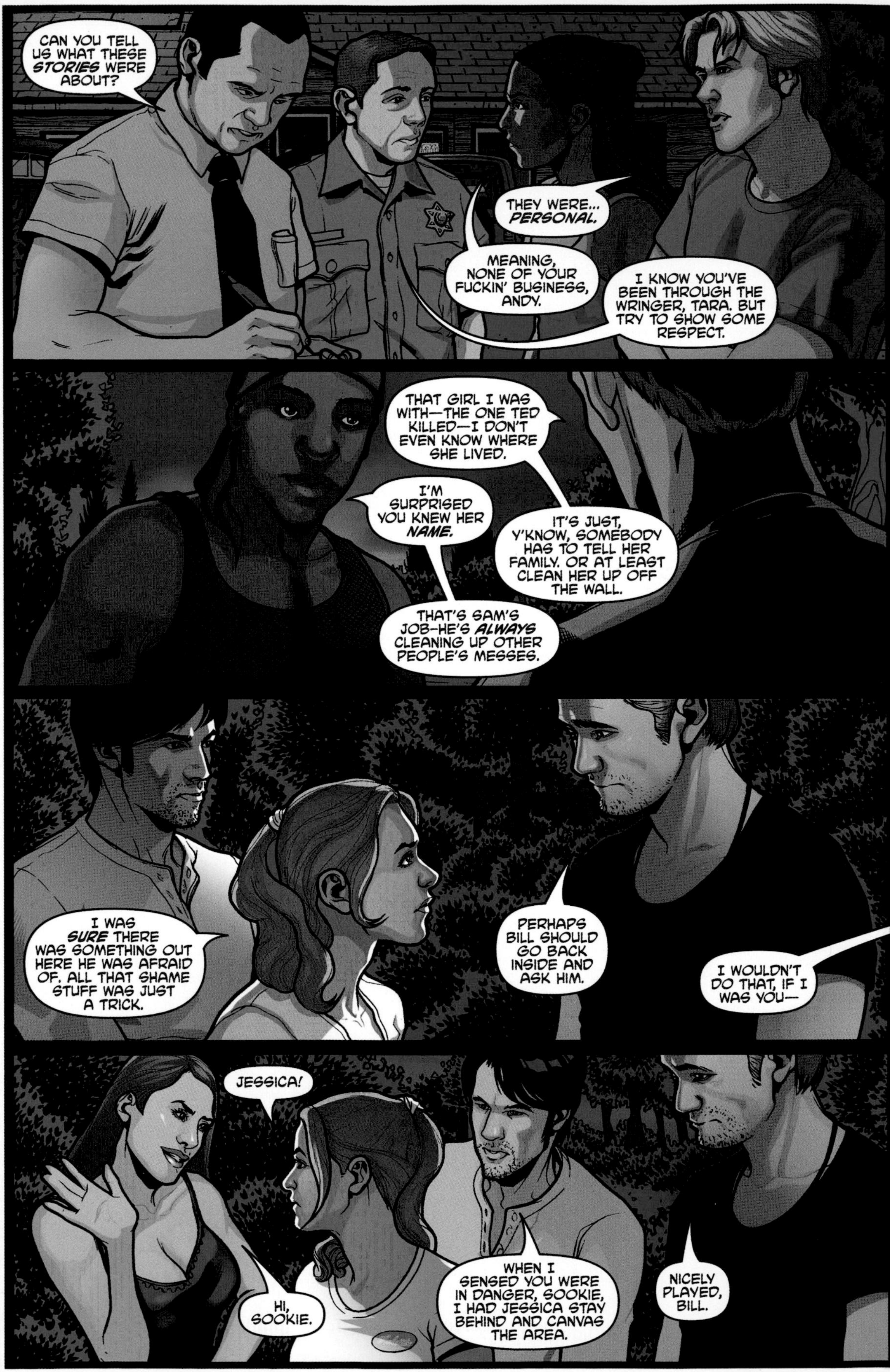
CAN YOU TELL US WHAT THESE *STORIES* WERE ABOUT?
THEY WERE... *PERSONAL.*
MEANING, NONE OF YOUR FUCKIN' BUSINESS, ANDY.
I KNOW YOU'VE BEEN THROUGH THE WRINGER, TARA. BUT TRY TO SHOW SOME RESPECT.
THAT GIRL I WAS WITH—THE ONE TED KILLED—I DON'T EVEN KNOW WHERE SHE LIVED.
I'M SURPRISED YOU KNEW HER *NAME.*
IT'S JUST, Y'KNOW, SOMEBODY HAS TO TELL HER FAMILY. OR AT LEAST CLEAN HER UP OFF THE WALL.
THAT'S SAM'S JOB-HE'S *ALWAYS* CLEANING UP OTHER PEOPLE'S MESSES.
I WAS *SURE* THERE WAS SOMETHING OUT HERE HE WAS AFRAID OF. ALL THAT SHAME STUFF WAS JUST A TRICK.
PERHAPS BILL SHOULD GO BACK INSIDE AND ASK HIM.
I WOULDN'T DO THAT, IF I WAS YOU—
JESSICA!
HI, SOOKIE.
WHEN I SENSED YOU WERE IN DANGER, SOOKIE, I HAD JESSICA STAY BEHIND AND CANVAS THE AREA.
NICELY PLAYED, BILL.

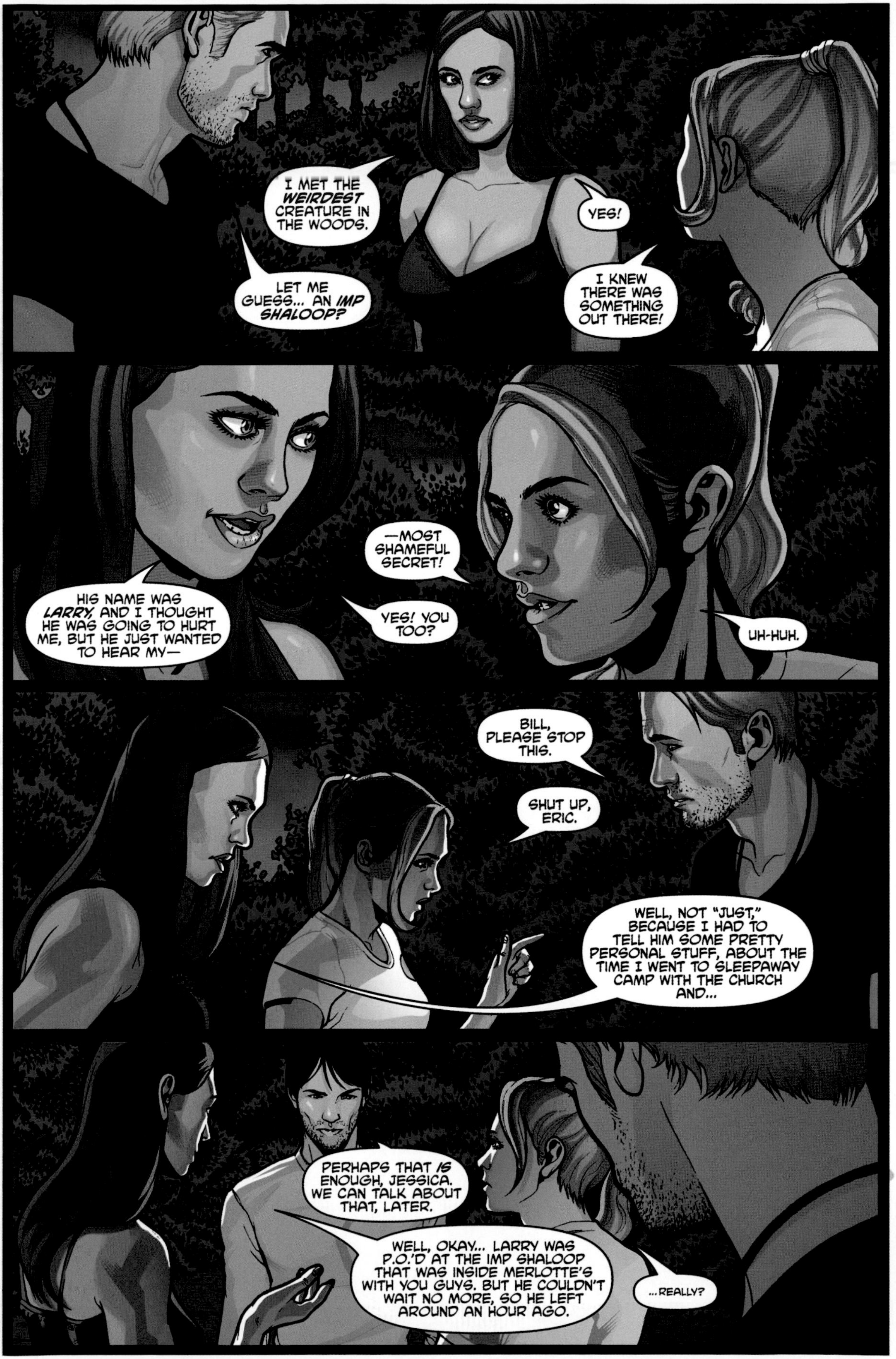
I MET THE *WEIRDEST* CREATURE IN THE WOODS.
LET ME GUESS... AN *IMP SHALOOP?*
YES!
I KNEW THERE WAS SOMETHING OUT THERE!
HIS NAME WAS *LARRY,* AND I THOUGHT HE WAS GOING TO HURT ME, BUT HE JUST WANTED TO HEAR MY—
YES! YOU TOO?
—MOST SHAMEFUL SECRET!
UH-HUH.
BILL, PLEASE STOP THIS.
SHUT UP, ERIC.
WELL, NOT "JUST," BECAUSE I HAD TO TELL HIM SOME PRETTY PERSONAL STUFF, ABOUT THE TIME I WENT TO SLEEPAWAY CAMP WITH THE CHURCH AND...
PERHAPS THAT *IS* ENOUGH, JESSICA. WE CAN TALK ABOUT THAT, LATER.
WELL, OKAY... LARRY WAS P.O.'D AT THE IMP SHALOOP THAT WAS INSIDE MERLOTTE'S WITH YOU GUYS. BUT HE COULDN'T WAIT NO MORE, SO HE LEFT AROUND AN HOUR AGO.
...REALLY?

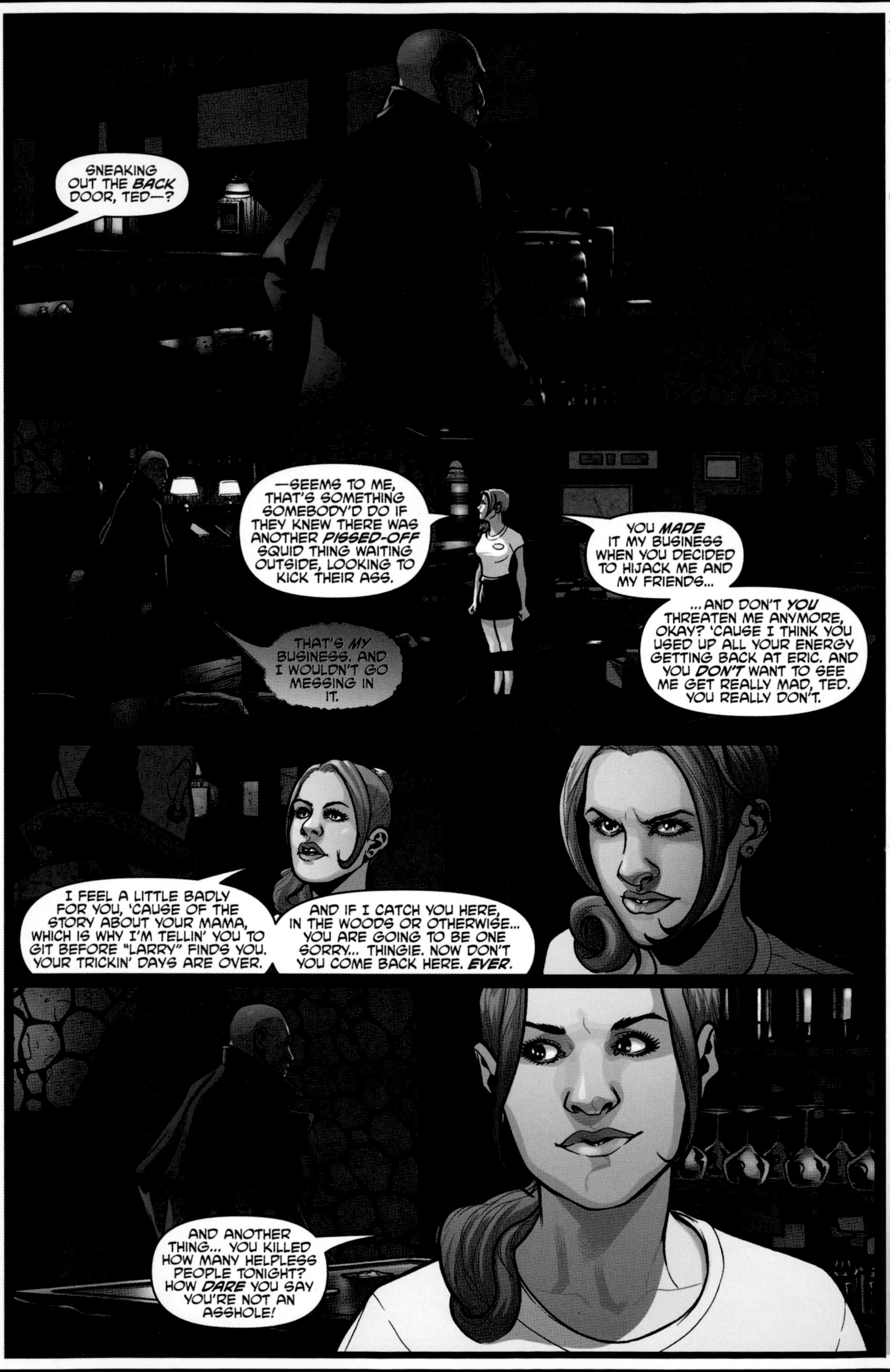

SNEAKING OUT THE *BACK* DOOR, TED—?
—SEEMS TO ME, THAT'S SOMETHING SOMEBODY'D DO IF THEY KNEW THERE WAS ANOTHER *PISSED-OFF* SQUID THING WAITING OUTSIDE, LOOKING TO KICK THEIR ASS.
THAT'S *MY* BUSINESS. AND I WOULDN'T GO MESSING IN IT.
YOU *MADE* IT MY BUSINESS WHEN YOU DECIDED TO HIJACK ME AND MY FRIENDS...
...AND DON'T *YOU* THREATEN ME ANYMORE, OKAY? 'CAUSE I THINK YOU USED UP ALL YOUR ENERGY GETTING BACK AT ERIC. AND YOU *DON'T* WANT TO SEE ME GET REALLY MAD, TED. YOU REALLY DON'T.
I FEEL A LITTLE BADLY FOR YOU, 'CAUSE OF THE STORY ABOUT YOUR MAMA, WHICH IS WHY I'M TELLIN' YOU TO GIT BEFORE "LARRY" FINDS YOU. YOUR TRICKIN' DAYS ARE OVER.
AND IF I CATCH YOU HERE, IN THE WOODS OR OTHERWISE... YOU ARE GOING TO BE ONE SORRY... THINGIE. NOW DON'T YOU COME BACK HERE. *EVER*.
AND ANOTHER THING... YOU KILLED HOW MANY HELPLESS PEOPLE TONIGHT? HOW *DARE* YOU SAY YOU'RE NOT AN ASSHOLE!

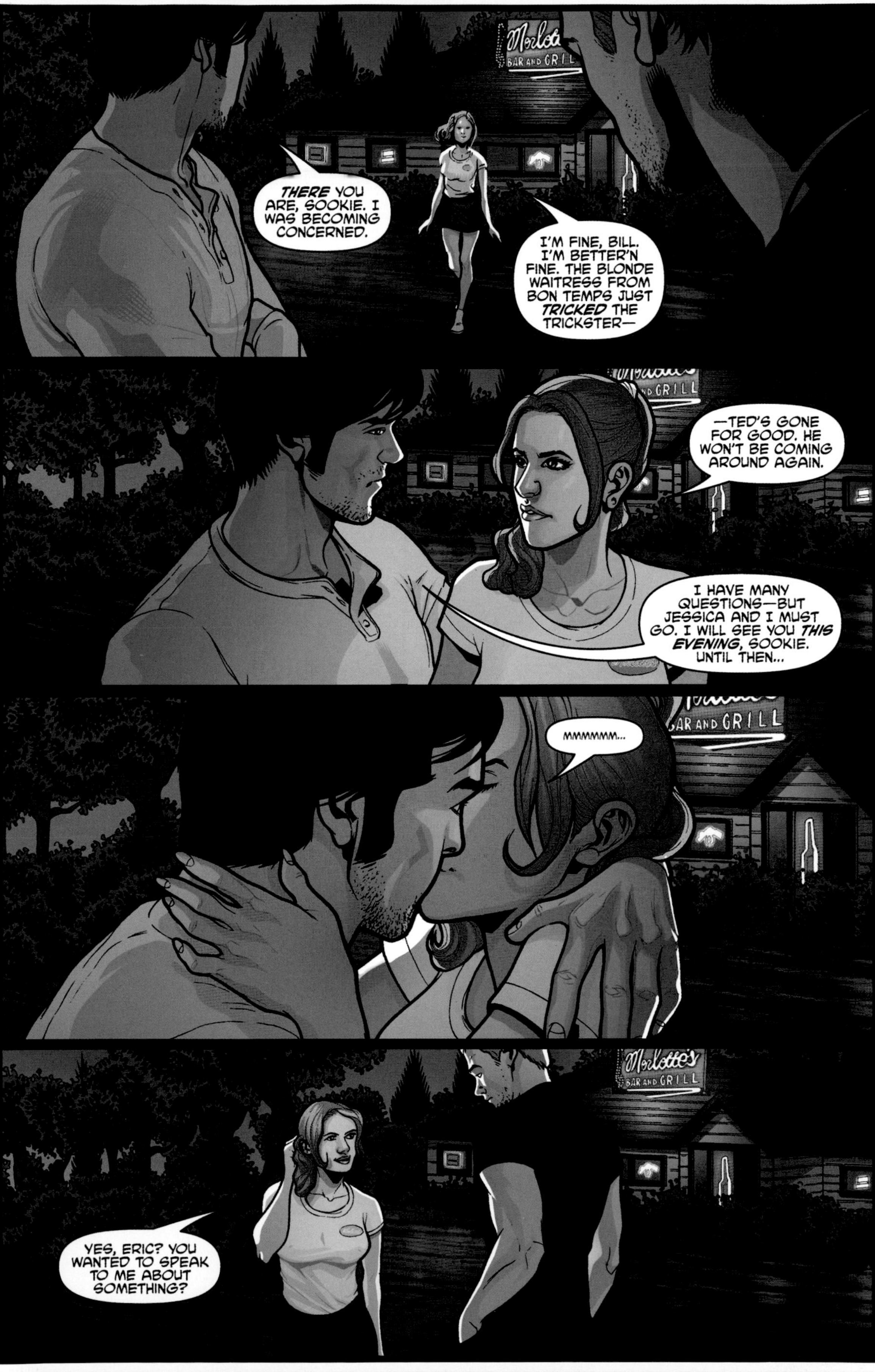
Merlotte's BAR AND GRILL
THERE YOU ARE, SOOKIE. I WAS BECOMING CONCERNED.
I'M FINE, BILL. I'M BETTER'N FINE. THE BLONDE WAITRESS FROM BON TEMPS JUST TRICKED THE TRICKSTER—
—TED'S GONE FOR GOOD. HE WON'T BE COMING AROUND AGAIN.
I HAVE MANY QUESTIONS—BUT JESSICA AND I MUST GO. I WILL SEE YOU THIS EVENING, SOOKIE. UNTIL THEN...
MMMMMMM...
YES, ERIC? YOU WANTED TO SPEAK TO ME ABOUT SOMETHING?

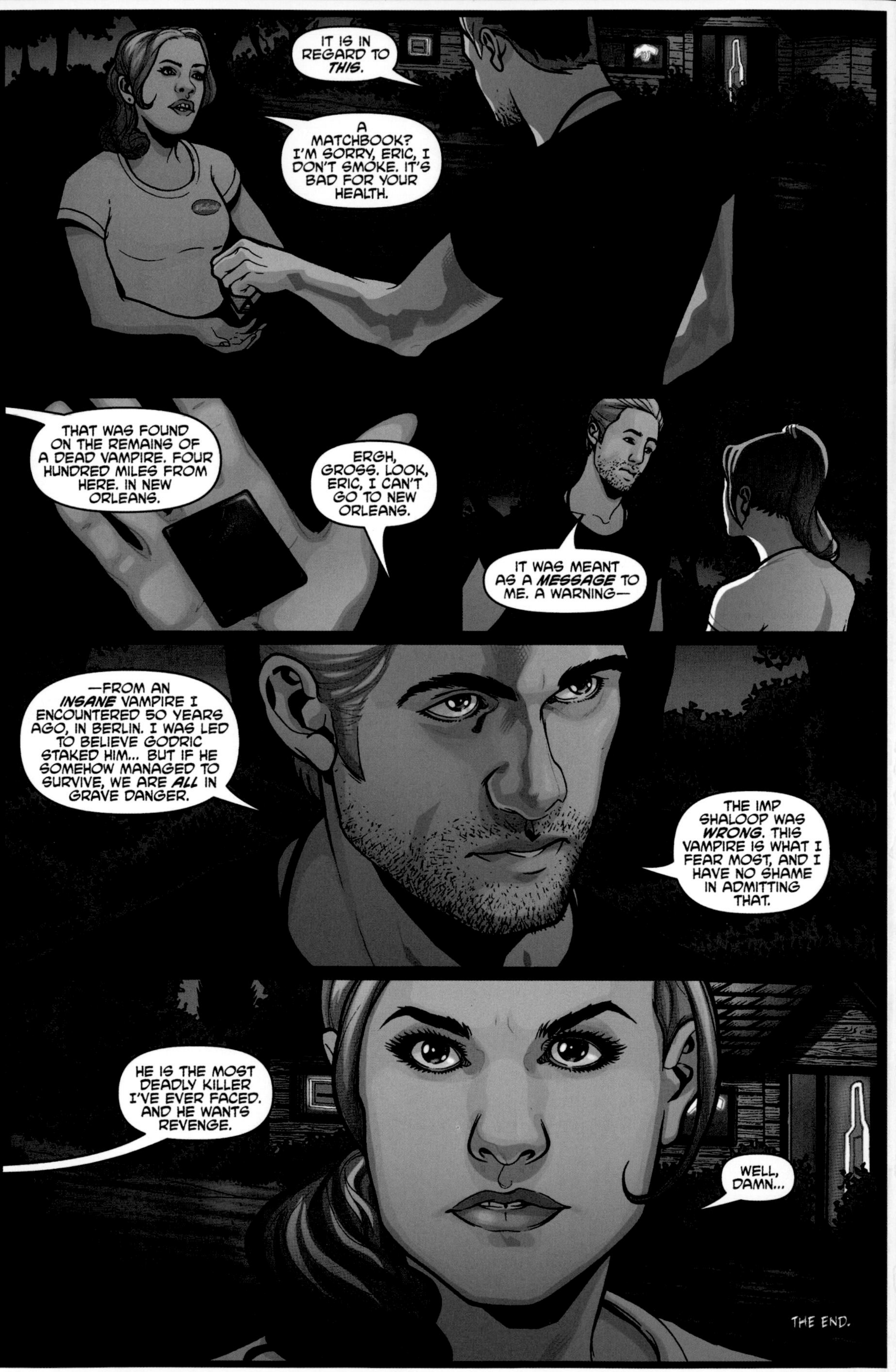
IT IS IN REGARD TO *THIS*.
A MATCHBOOK? I'M SORRY, ERIC, I DON'T SMOKE. IT'S BAD FOR YOUR HEALTH.
THAT WAS FOUND ON THE REMAINS OF A DEAD VAMPIRE. FOUR HUNDRED MILES FROM HERE. IN NEW ORLEANS.
ERGH, GROSS. LOOK, ERIC, I CAN'T GO TO NEW ORLEANS.
IT WAS MEANT AS A *MESSAGE* TO ME. A WARNING—
—FROM AN *INSANE* VAMPIRE I ENCOUNTERED 50 YEARS AGO, IN BERLIN. I WAS LED TO BELIEVE GODRIC STAKED HIM... BUT IF HE SOMEHOW MANAGED TO SURVIVE, WE ARE *ALL* IN GRAVE DANGER.
THE IMP SHALOOP WAS *WRONG*. THIS VAMPIRE IS WHAT I FEAR MOST, AND I HAVE NO SHAME IN ADMITTING THAT.
HE IS THE MOST DEADLY KILLER I'VE EVER FACED. AND HE WANTS REVENGE.
WELL, DAMN...
THE END.

art by J. SCOTT CAMPBELL
colors by NEI RUFFINO

ART GALLERY

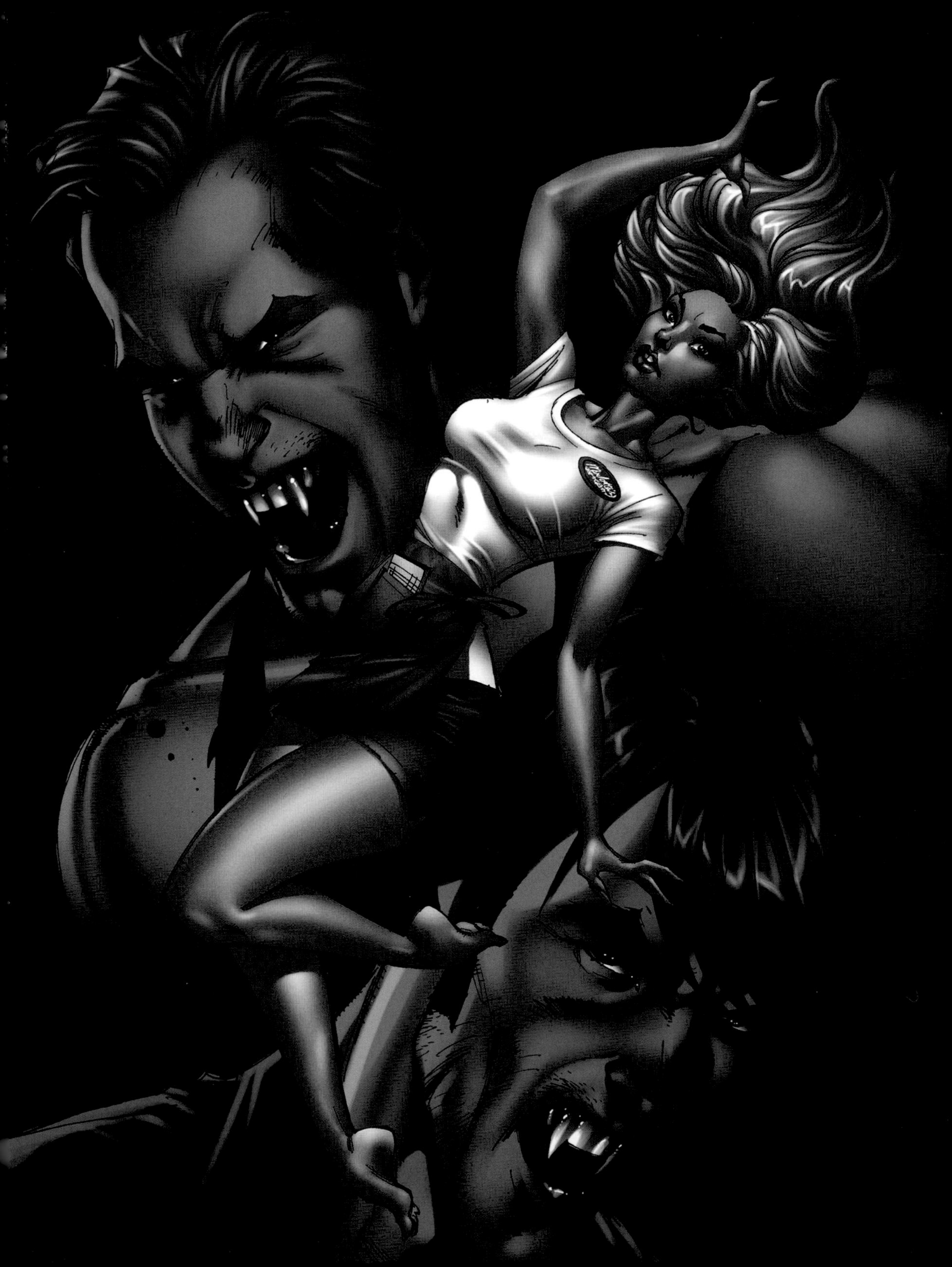

art by J. SCOTT CAMPBELL
colors by EDGAR DELGADO

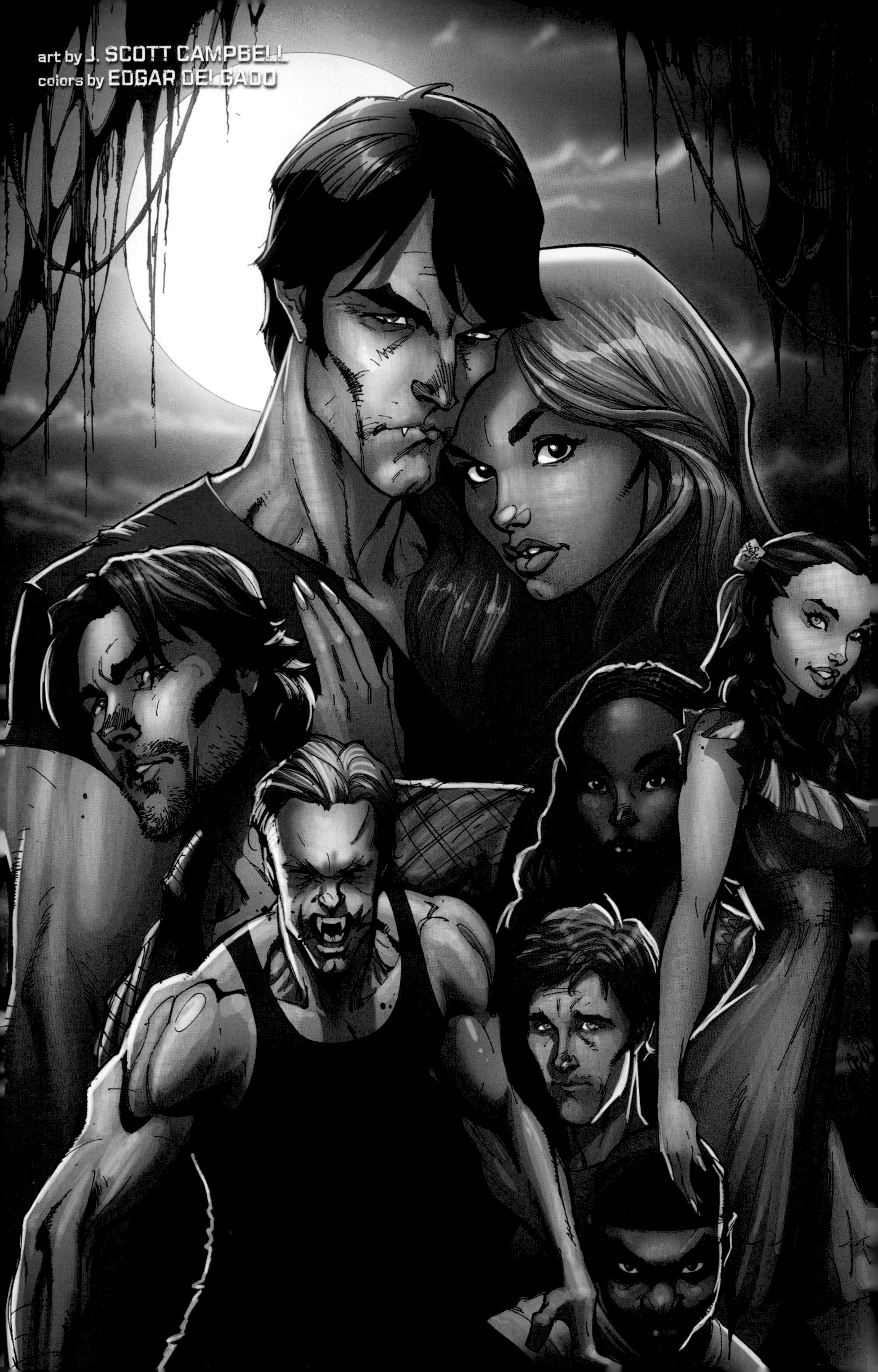

art by JOE CORRONEY

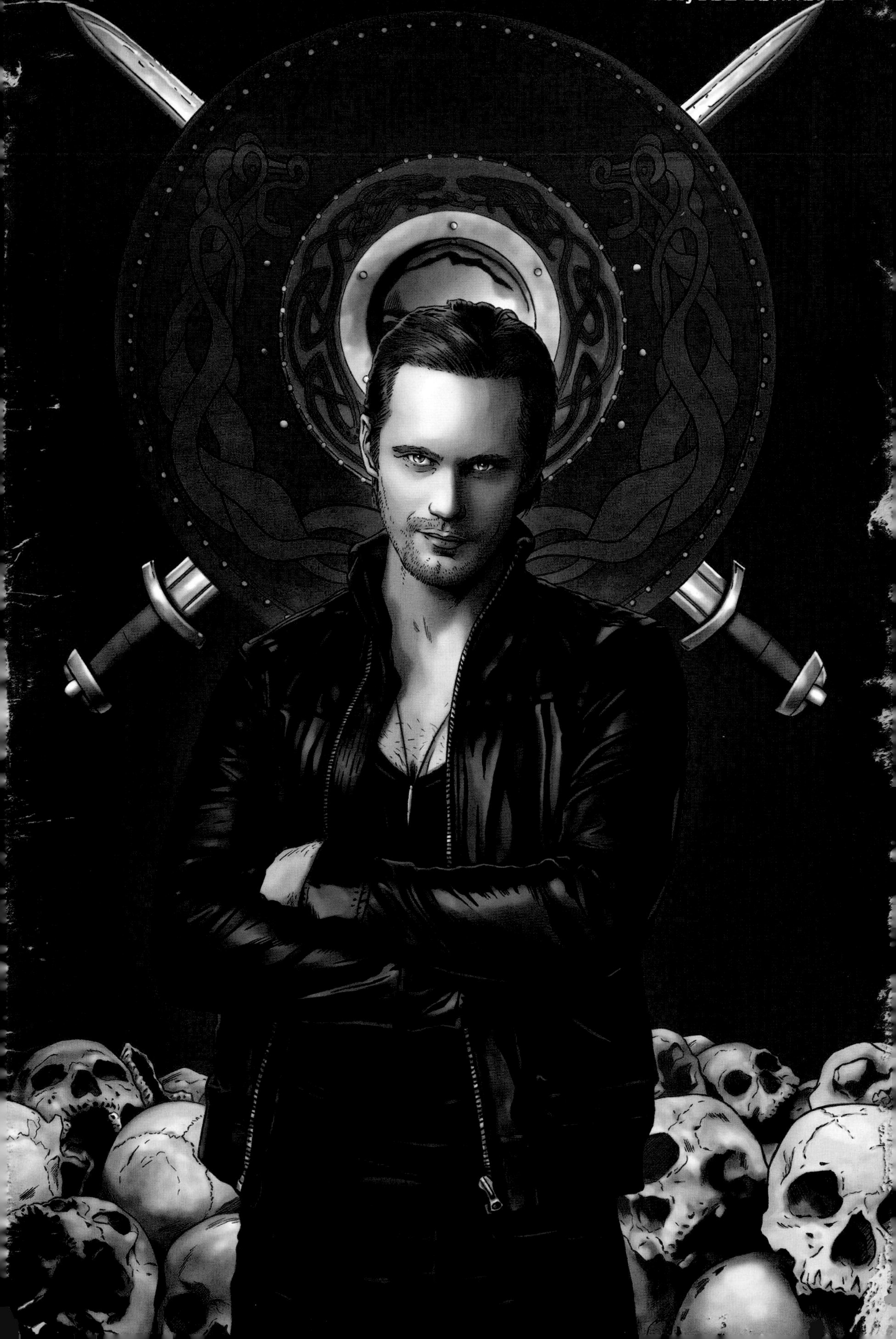

art by **JOE CORRONEY**

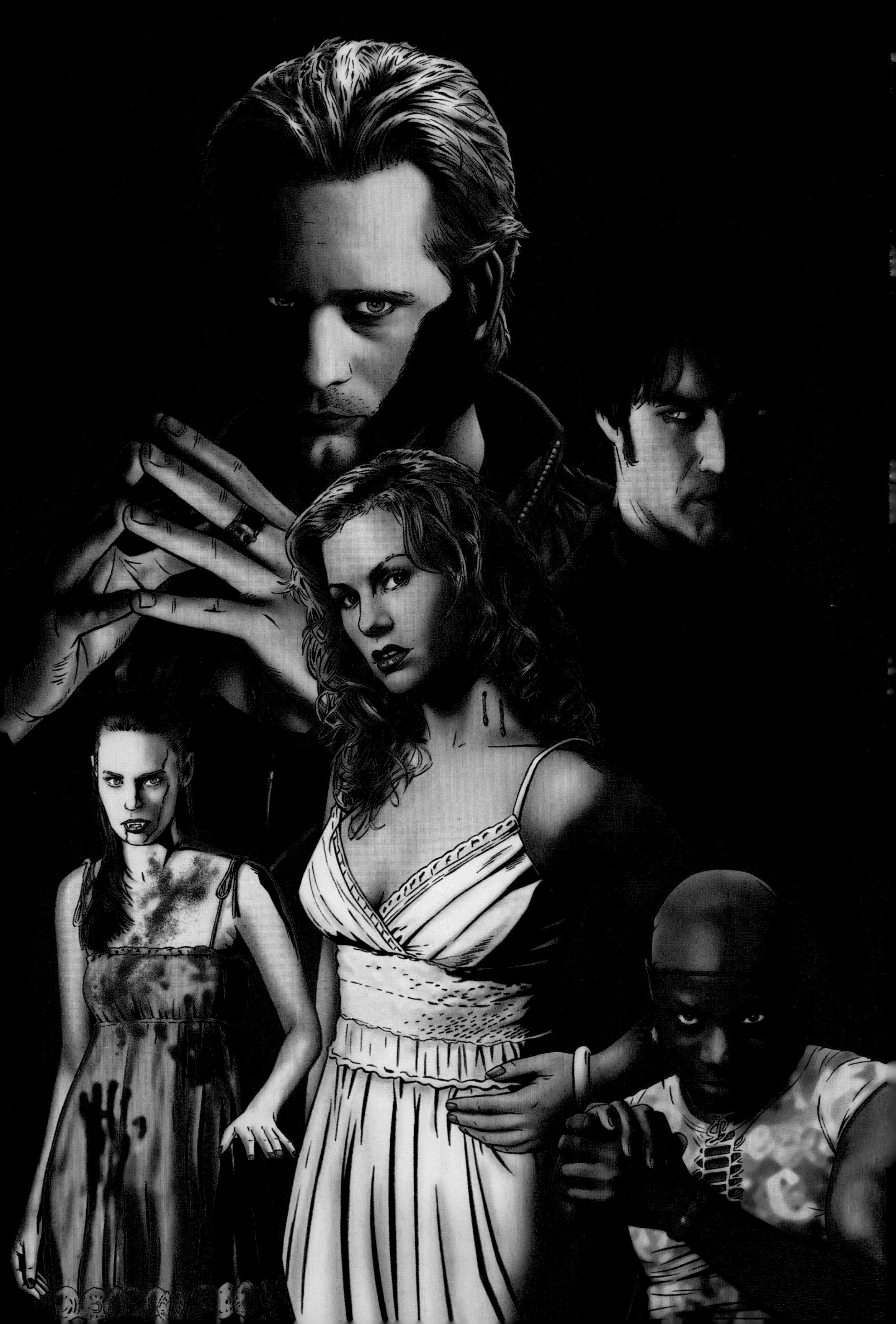

art by JOE CORRONEY

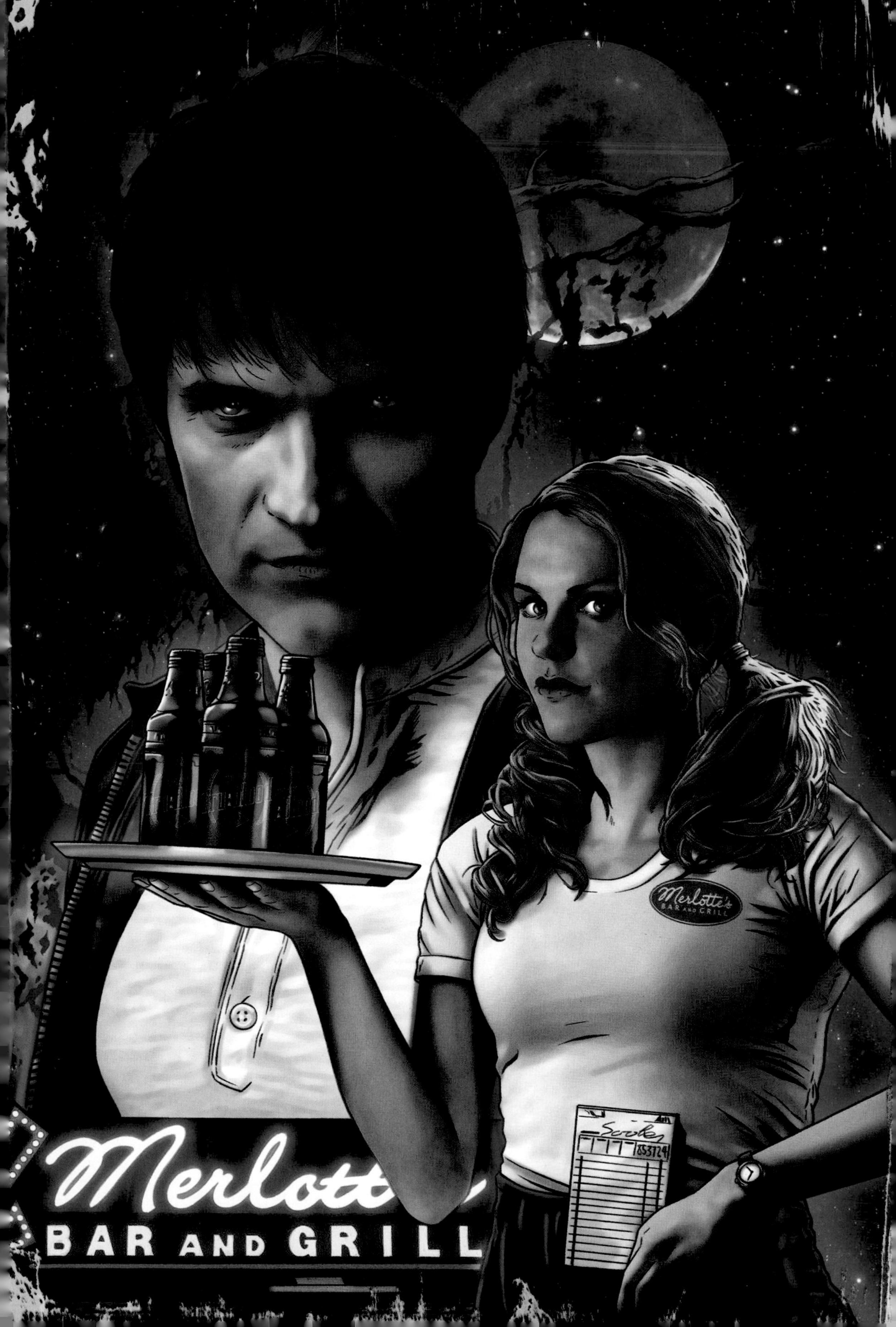
Merlotte's
BAR AND GRILL
BAR AND GRILL

art by JOE CORRONEY

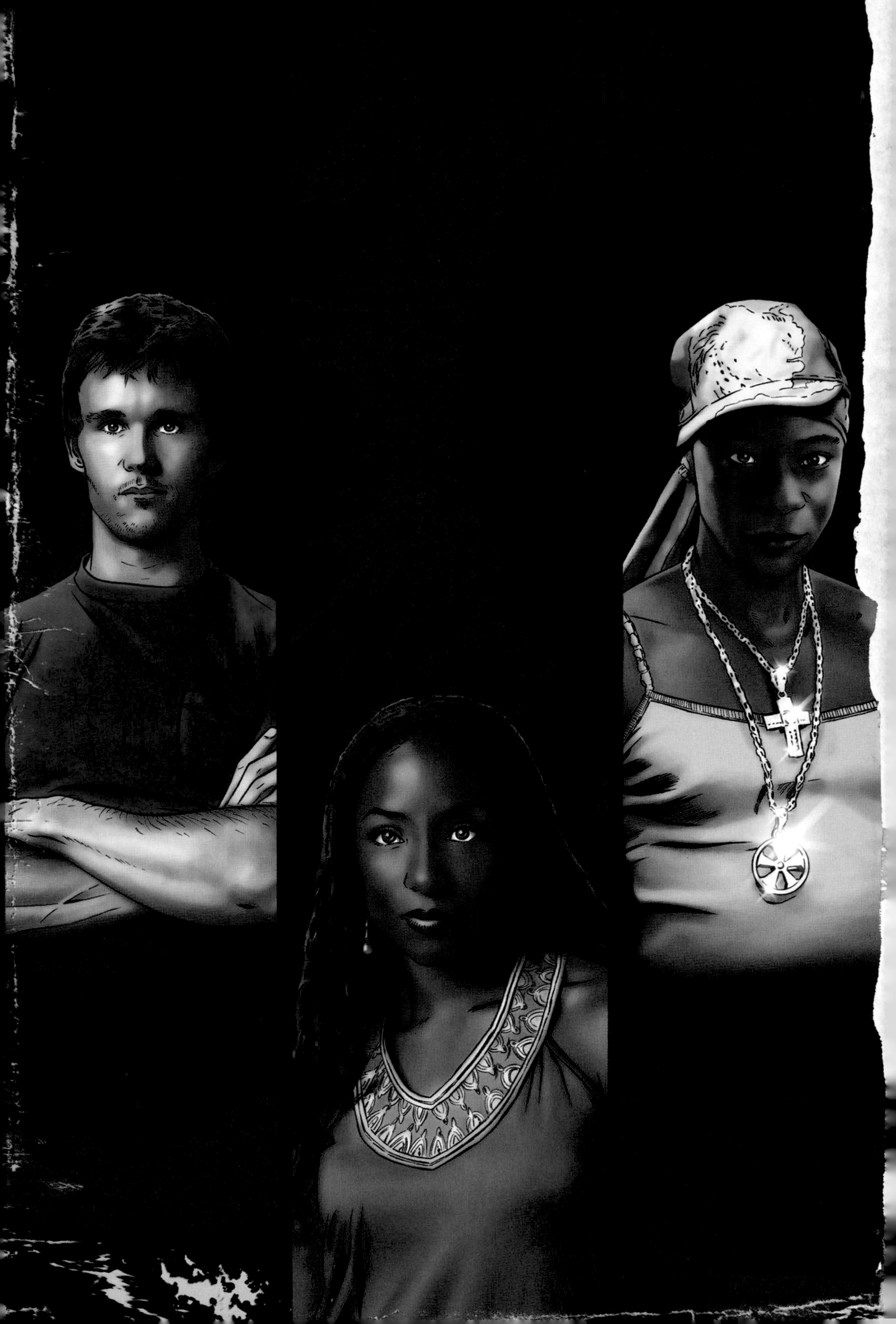

art by **ANDREW CURRIE**
colors by **LEN O'GRADY**

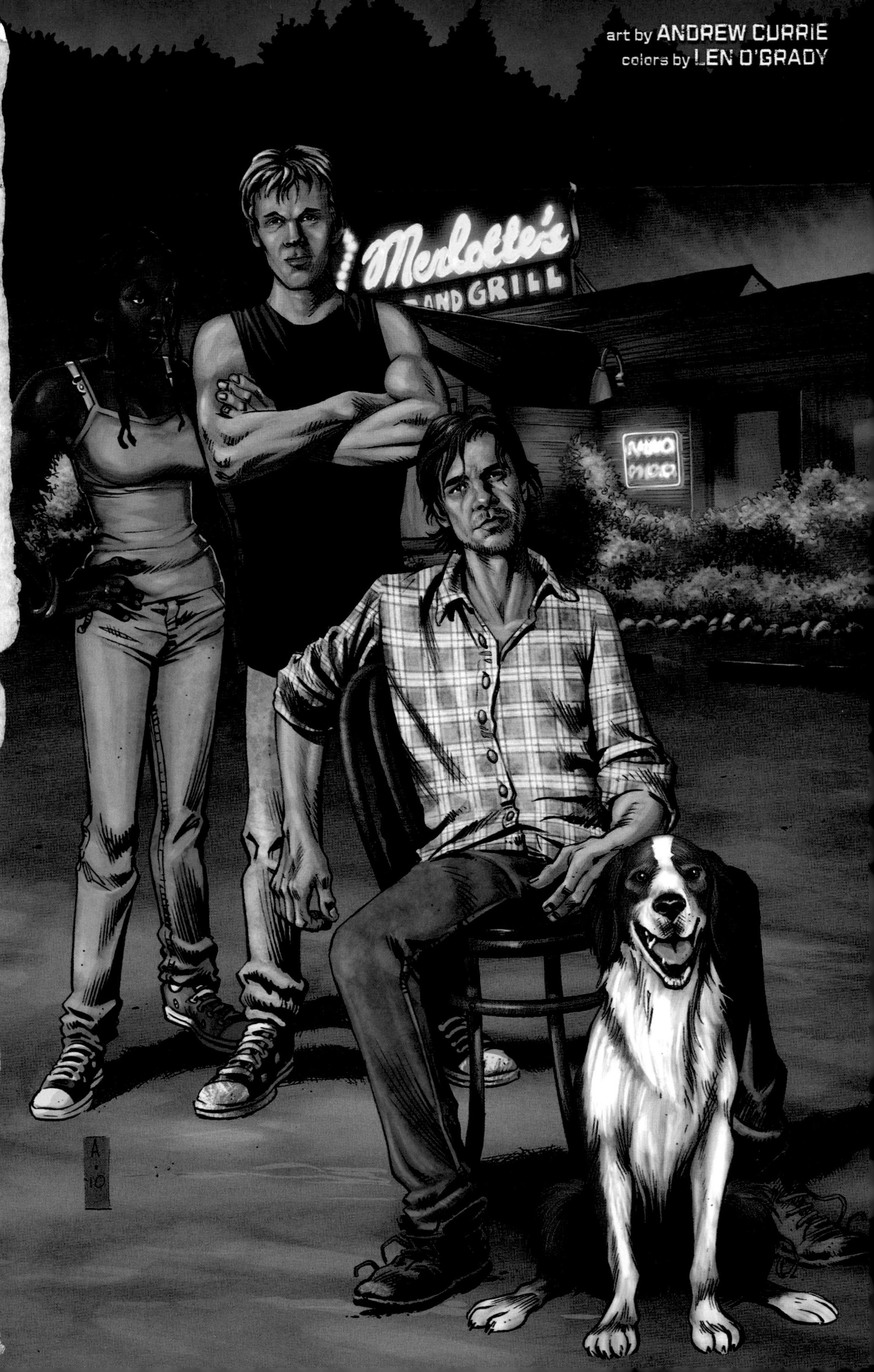
Merlotte's
AND GRILL

CREATOR BIOGRAPHIES

Photo by Jeff Kravitz

ALAN BALL

Academy and Emmy® Award-winning writer/director/producer Alan Ball is among our generation's most important creative voices. He is also one of the most daring, continually laying bare the often dark and occasionally humorous underbelly of the American experience while exploring complicated themes that inform our modern society.

Born in Atlanta, Ball studied Theatre Arts at Florida State University. After college, he moved to New York and established himself as a noted playwright. One of his early plays, *Five Women Wearing the Same Dress*, premiered in 1993 at the Manhattan Class Company. The play featured Allison Janney, who would later star in Ball's seminal work, *American Beauty*.

After moving to Hollywood, Ball caught his first big break writing for the sitcom *Grace Under Fire*. After one season on the show, Ball left to become a writer and eventually a co-producer on the sitcom *Cybill*, starring Cybill Shepherd. At the same time, Ball began to focus on screenwriting, and one of his first screenplays, *American Beauty*, an exploration of a dysfunctional American family, was bought by the newly formed DreamWorks SKG studio. The film— and Ball's screenplay—received overwhelming critical acclaim. In March 2000, *American Beauty* won five Academy Awards®, including Best Picture, with Best Original Screenplay honors going to Ball.

Staying close to his roots in television, Ball followed up *American Beauty* by creating and executive producing the groundbreaking HBO® drama *Six Feet Under*®, which followed the trials and tribulations of the Fisher family, set against the backdrop of the family-run funeral home. The series ran for five seasons and was one of the most watched series in HBO history. It was also one of the most honored, snaring two Golden Globes® and six Emmys®, among numerous awards. It also netted Ball an Emmy® and DGA Award for his direction of the series pilot, his directorial debut.

In 2007, Ball also made his feature film directorial debut on *Towelhead*, a coming-of-age drama that he adapted for the screen from the acclaimed Alicia Erian novel of the same name. The film, starring Aaron Eckhart, Maria Bello, and Toni Collette, premiered at the Toronto Film Festival and was distributed theatrically in 2008 by Warner Independent Pictures.

In 2008, Ball continued his successful collaboration with HBO by creating and executive producing the series *True Blood*®. Based on the Sookie Stackhouse novels by Charlaine Harris, *True Blood* garnered early critical and popular acclaim, and in its first season received a Golden Globe® nomination for Best Television Drama Series. The series finished its debut season with a record increase in viewers. Its second season earned another Golden Globe® nomination for Best Television Drama Series, as well as a Producer's Guild nomination and a Grammy® soundtrack nomination for Ball.

Alan Ball lives in Los Angeles.

CREATOR BIOGRAPHIES

DAVID MESSINA

Like all artists, David Messina is just a child who refuses to put down his crayons. He works for several publishers in Europe and the USA, but IDW remains his favorite. In his copious spare time (ha!), he teaches a new generation of artists at the Scuola Internazionale di Comics in Rome, and has since 2002. He maintains that many of his pupils, past and current, are trying to KILL him.

MARIAH HUEHNER

Mariah is an eccentric old lady who enjoys painting tentacles, making creatures, and throwing old-fashioned tea parties. Her favorite word is "aardvark." She also likes writing. A lot. It's the most fun you can have while lying, and no one can get mad at you for doing it. She thinks stories are the bee's knees. Also, cupcakes.

DAVID TISCHMAN

David Tischman has been a puppet, a pauper, a pirate, a poet, a pawn, and a king. But he prefers to write comic books. He still sees himself in the 20th century, which is why this young picture is so very old. He loves nice restaurants, reality television, and dirty jokes. He believes a good idea should take you (much) farther than it does.

ELISABETH R. FINCH

Elisabeth R. Finch earned her MFA from USC's School of Cinema Television and BA from Carnegie Mellon University, and has worked on such shows as *Star Trek: Enterprise*, *True Blood*, and *No Ordinary Family*. Her essays are published in *Fresh Yarn* and *Women in Film*'s *Traction* and she is a recent recipient of the Jerome Fellowship in Playwriting.

KATE BARNOW

Kate Barnow grew up in New York and Los Angeles. She attended Brown University. She has worked on shows such as *Will & Grace* and *Studio 60 on the Sunset Strip*. She currently writes for HBO's *True Blood* and the ABC series *No Ordinary Family*.

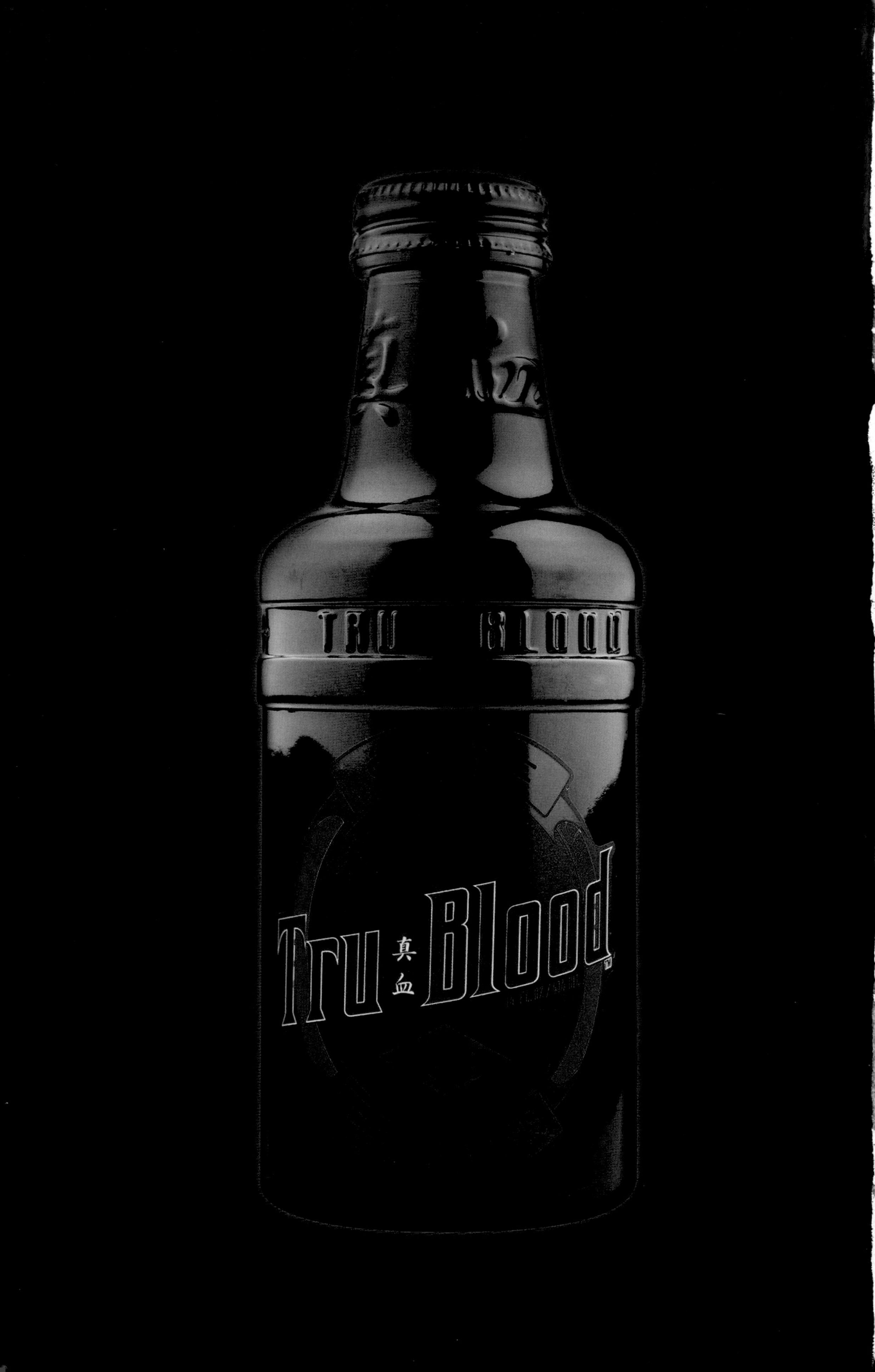
TRU BLOOD
Tru 真血 Blood